Accounting and Finance for Insurance Professionals

Accounting and Finance for Insurance Professionals

David H. Marshall, MBA, CPA, CMA
Professor of Accounting Emeritus
Millikin University

Wayne W. McManus, JD, MS, MBA, CPA, CMA, CIA
Senior Lecturer of Accounting
Community College of the Cayman Islands

Paul M. Kazenski, Ph.D.
Associate Professor of Accounting
University of Hawaii—Manoa

Kenneth N. Scoles Jr., Ph.D., AIAF
Director of Curriculum
American Institute for CPCU

First Edition • 1997

American Institute for CPCU
720 Providence Road, Malvern, Pennsylvania 19355-0770

Foreword

The American Institute for Chartered Property Casualty Underwriters, the Insurance Institute of America, and the Insurance Institute for Applied Ethics are independent, nonprofit, educational organizations serving the needs of the property and liability insurance business. The Institutes develop a wide range of programs—curricula, study materials, and examinations—in response to the educational requirements of various elements of the business.

The American Institute confers the Chartered Property Casualty Underwriter (CPCU®) professional designation on those who meet the Institute's experience, ethics, and examination requirements.

The Insurance Institute of America offers associate designations and certificate programs in the following technical and managerial disciplines:

Accredited Adviser in Insurance (AAI®)
Associate in Claims (AIC)
Associate in Underwriting (AU)
Associate in Risk Management (ARM)
Associate in Loss Control Management (ALCM®)
Associate in Premium Auditing (APA®)
Associate in Management (AIM)
Associate in Research and Planning (ARP®)
Associate in Insurance Accounting and Finance (AIAF)
Associate in Automation Management (AAM®)
Associate in Marine Insurance Management (AMIM®)
Associate in Reinsurance (ARe)
Associate in Fidelity and Surety Bonding (AFSB)
Associate in Insurance Services (AIS)
Associate in Surplus Lines Insurance (ASLI)
Associate in Personal Insurance (API)
Certificate in General Insurance
Certificate in Insurance Regulation
Certificate in Supervisory Management

Certificate in Introduction to Underwriting
Certificate in Introduction to Claims
Certificate in Introduction to Property and Liability Insurance
Certificate in Business Writing

The Insurance Institute for Applied Ethics was established in 1995 to heighten awareness of the pervasiveness of ethical decision making in insurance and to explore ways to raise the level of ethical behavior among parties to the insurance contract. The Ethics Institute sponsors seminars and workshops on the role of ethics in the insurance transaction. It also identifies and funds practical research projects on ethics-related topics and publishes the findings. In addition, it produces booklets, newsletters, and videotapes on ethics issues.

The Institutes began publishing textbooks in 1976 to help students meet the national examination standards. Since that time, we have produced more than ninety individual textbook volumes. Despite the vast differences in the subjects and purposes of these volumes, they all have much in common. First, each book is specifically designed to increase knowledge and develop skills that can improve job performance and help students achieve the educational objectives of the course for which it is assigned. Second, all of the manuscripts of our texts are widely reviewed before publication, by both insurance business practitioners and members of the academic community. In addition, all of our texts and course guides also reflect the work of Institute staff members. These writing or editing duties are seen as an integral part of their professional responsibilities, and no one earns a royalty based on the sale of our texts. We have proceeded in this way to avoid even the appearance of any conflict of interests. Finally, the revisions of our texts often incorporate improvements suggested by students and course leaders.

We welcome criticisms of and suggestions for improving our publications. It is only with such constructive comments that we can hope to improve the quality of our study materials. Please direct any comments you may have on this text to the Curriculum Department of the Institutes.

Lawrence G. Brandon, CPCU, AIM, ARM
President and Chief Operating Officer

Preface

This text, coupled with the course workbook and study guide, represents a new approach to the study of accounting and finance in the CPCU curriculum. It covers material that had heretofore been covered by three separate CPCU 8 texts, and it places that information into a context that should enable property-casualty insurance professionals to learn the material more easily. Students are not presumed to have had prior exposure to the topics. Accounting and finance are complex topics, and we at the American Institute for CPCU are continually striving to improve our presentation of those topics.

The Introduction that follows describes the contents of this text in detail, but this text is divided into three sections. Part I, "The Accounting Process," introduces basic accounting principles and financial statements for both noninsurance and insurance entities. Part II, "Applied Accounting and Finance," reinforces the principles presented in Part I by investigating the accounting and presentation of common items reported in financial statements. Finally, Part III, "Analytical Tools for Financial Decision Making," introduces financial analysis, which, when coupled with the concepts presented in Parts I and II, provides the basic tools needed for making informed business decisions.

This text is composed of material adapted from *Accounting: What the Numbers Mean*, by David H. Marshall and Wayne W. McManus, published by Richard D. Irwin, Inc. (third edition), and original material developed by the American Institute for CPCU. In addition to the authors named on the front cover, many experts have contributed ideas or written brief passages for, or have given detailed written critiques of, one or more chapters, and have thus enhanced the accuracy, clarity, and relevance of this text. These experts include:

Carolyn J. Dorsey, CPA
Consultant—Tax Accounting

William R. Feldhaus, Ph.D., CPCU, CLU
Associate Professor
Department of Risk Management and Insurance
College of Business Administration
Georgia State University

Christine L. Lewis, Ph.D., CPCU, CLU, ChFC, ARP
Senior Vice President and Chief Academic Officer
American Institute for CPCU

James J. Markham, J.D., CPCU, AIC, AIAF
Senior Vice President and General Counsel
American Institute for CPCU

Tom Mellor, CPCU
Claim Superintendent—Special Investigation Unit
State Farm Insurance Companies

Philip E. Nolt, CPCU, AIAF, AIM, ARP
Vice President—Information Services
Goodville Mutual Casualty

S. Wesley Porter, Jr., CPCU, AIM, AFSB
Director of Training and Director of Fidelity Surety Education
American Institute for CPCU

James A. Sherlock, MBA, CPCU, CLU, ARM
Consultant
CIGNA Property and Casualty Companies

Christine M. Singer, CPCU, AIAF, ARP
Consultant—Insurance Accounting

Leonard J. Watson, CPCU, CIC
Director of Curriculum
American Institute for CPCU

Lowell S. Young, CPCU, CLU
Director of Curriculum
American Institute for CPCU

Several people worked diligently on the editing, proofreading, and production of this text. Special thanks go to Michael J. Betz, AIM, for his valuable contribution as editor, Laurie C. Higgins for her contribution as typesetter and graphics designer, and Jacqueline M. Chestnut and Estelle L. Collette for their assistance in transcribing and formatting original manuscripts. Because accounting and finance are dynamic disciplines, changes inevitably will be needed in the text. Perhaps the greatest resource for ideas to improve our texts is our students. Constructive comments and suggestions are always welcome and should be addressed to my attention at the American Institute for CPCU so that this study material remains useful.

Kenneth N. Scoles Jr., Ph.D., AIAF

Contributing Authors

The American Institute for CPCU acknowledges with deep appreciation the help of the following contributing authors:

James J. Clarke, Ph.D.
Associate Professor of Finance
Villanova University

Michael W. Elliott, CPCU, AIAF
Assistant Vice President and Senior Director of Curriculum Design
American Institute for CPCU

Contents

Introduction

Beginning CPCU students, first encountering the word *accounting*, might envision many pages of tedious figures, the repetitive work of recording transactions, or headaches from irreconcilable account balances. Experienced business professionals, however, recognize accounting as the *language of business*. Accounting conveys important financial information that is used in the management decision-making processes integral to achieving organizational objectives. Therefore, some command of this language is necessary for those wishing to participate in these processes.

In no other business is a general understanding of accounting more important than it is in insurance. Representing a significant part of the financial services industry, insurance is predicated on the analysis of financial information to determine the amount of premium insurers need in order to assume loss exposures from insureds and make a reasonable profit. Insurance professionals regularly use financial information to make decisions about accepting and pricing risks, settling losses, and managing an insurer's operations.

Although accounting has for centuries been guided by standards of accepted practice, not until this century has deliberate effort been expended to establish and gain acceptance of uniform standards of accounting practice and professionalism.

In 1989, the American Accounting Association formed the Accounting Education Change Commission (AECC) "to foster changes in the academic preparation of accountants consistent with the goal of improving their capabilities for successful professional careers." To define the content of a first formal course in accounting, the AECC's Position Statement No. Two, "The First Course in Accounting" (June 1992), stated:

> The primary objective of the first course in accounting is for students to learn about accounting as an information development and communication function that supports economic decision-making. The knowledge and skills provided by the first course in accounting should facilitate subsequent learning **even if the student takes no additional academic work in**

accounting or directly related disciplines [emphasis added]. For example, the course should help students perform financial analysis; derive information for personal or organizational decisions; and understand business, governmental, and other organizational entities.[1]

This text and the course for which it was designed will help students achieve those objectives. The principal objective of this text is to help insurance professionals become informed users of accounting information. The text is not intended as a resource to prepare you to become an accountant, but to varying degrees all insurance professionals need to understand the principles of accounting. As an insurance professional, you need accounting information to evaluate the financial stability and management effectiveness of insured accounts and to qualify the financial strength of prospective brokers and agents, marketers, underwriters, and administrators. Agents and brokers analyze accounting information. Claim specialists use accounting information to qualify losses and to evaluate loss payments. Insurer managers require financial statistics about their own company to achieve corporate objectives and monitor asset and liability trends.

Coupled with the course workbook and study guide, this text will improve your familiarity with the most commonly used financial statements and show you how the information on those statements can provide tremendous insight into a business's financial condition and the effectiveness of its management. The text and workbook will help you use accounting in your activities as an insurance professional and evaluate your own financial condition or review information that businesses report to owners, regulators, and potential investors.

The text and workbook emphasize the *application* of accounting and finance principles in an insurance context. Topics in accounting and finance are presented at three progressively more challenging educational levels:

- Part I—The Accounting Process
- Part II—Applied Accounting and Finance
- Part III—Analytical Tools for Financial Decision Making

After mastering basic principles in Part I, you will reinforce your understanding of those principles by examining financial statement accounts in Part II. In Part III, you will integrate the concepts you learned in Parts I and II with techniques of financial analysis and apply them to evaluate the financial condition of business entities, both insurance and noninsurance, using financial statements and other information sources.

The workbook provides exercises and problems to gauge your understanding of important concepts presented in the text. You are encouraged to attempt *all* problems and exercises provided in the workbook. Those problems and exercises will be of greatest benefit to you if you consult the answers *only* after you have made a diligent effort to solve the problem unassisted. As with any course involving mathematics and analytical skills, the problem-solving process *is not* learned by watching someone else do the work or by looking up the answer to determine how to solve the problem. The text should be the first resource consulted if assistance is needed. If you cannot dedicate the time needed to complete the workbook exercises, you will substantially reduce your learning experience with the text. Although completing the problems and exercises is not a guarantee that you will pass an examination on the material, not completing the problems and exercises significantly decreases your chance of being successful. To provide an opportunity for you to gauge your understanding and comprehension of the material, the workbook provides sample 100-point examinations for Parts I, II, and III. Answers and solutions are provided following each examination.

Consisting of fifteen chapters divided into three parts, the text is organized as follows:

Part I: The Accounting Process
1. What Is Accounting, and Why Is It Important?
2. Understanding the Accounting Process and Financial Statements
3. Interpreting Basic Financial Statements
4. How Economic Transactions Affect Financial Statements
5. An Introduction to Insurer Financial Statements

Part II: Applied Accounting and Finance
6. Accounting for and Presentation of Current Assets
7. Accounting for and Presentation of Noncurrent Assets
8. Accounting for and Presentation of Liabilities
9. Accounting for and Presentation of Owners' Equity
10. Accounting for Revenues and Expenses
11. How to Interpret Property-Liability Insurer Financial Statements

Part III: Analytical Tools for Financial Decision Making
12. Reading Financial Statements in Context: What's Behind the Numbers?
13. Capital Budgeting
14. A Systematic Approach to Financial Statement Analysis
15. Fundamentals of Insurance Company Finance and Investments

Note

1. Accounting Education Change Commission, Position Statement No. Two, "The First Course in Accounting" (Torrence, CA: Accounting Education Change Commission, 1992), p. 2.

Part I

The Accounting Process

Chapter 1

What Is Accounting, and Why Is It Important?

The objective of this text is to present enough of the fundamentals of accounting to permit the nonaccountants of the insurance profession to understand the financial statements of a business and to understand how financial information can be used in the management planning, control, and decision-making processes. Although usually expressed in the context of profit-seeking businesses, most of the material is equally applicable to not-for-profit social service and governmental organizations.

Accounting is sometimes called the *language of business*, and it is appropriate for people who are involved in the economic activities of our society—that is, just about everyone—to know at least enough of this language to be able to make informed decisions and judgments about those economic activities. Insurance professionals, whether producers, underwriters, or claim adjusters, regularly use financial information to make decisions about insureds and new business applicants. Only with an understanding of the origin and development of that financial information can they make *informed* decisions about those risks.

This chapter describes accounting as a process of identifying, measuring, and communicating financial and economic information about an entity. The term **entity** is used to describe the subject of the financial information because that subject could be an individual or any one of several organization forms, such as a sole proprietorship, a partnership, or a corporation. The chapter compares some of the uses made of financial statements by the entity's management, its investors, its employees, and government agencies. The chapter also highlights some of the distinctions between major classifications in the specialized field of accounting. It describes the development of accounting in the United States, and it examines the benefits of standardized accounting practices. The chapter establishes this text's approach to account-

7

ing information as a collection of tools for the basic analysis of an entity's financial condition.

As you read this and the subsequent chapters, gaining familiarity with the accounting concepts presented, occasionally pause and think about how accounting is applied in the insurance environment with which you are familiar. The companion course workbook and study guide to this text will assist you by providing questions challenging you to apply the accounting tools presented in the text to realistic problems directly related to the field of insurance.

Educational Objectives

After studying this chapter, you should be able to:

1. Define accounting.
2. Explain who uses accounting information, and give examples of how they find accounting information useful, suggesting possible insurance applications.
3. Identify the categories of accounting, and provide examples of the kinds of work that professional accountants in each category perform.
4. Summarize the development of accounting.
5. Explain why financial statements do not evolve from a codified set of rules.
6. Provide examples of how alternative methods can account for similarly reported economic activities.
7. Describe the role of the Financial Accounting Standards Board (FASB) in setting generally accepted accounting principles (GAAP).
8. Explain the key elements of ethical behavior for a professional accountant, and compare them to the Code of Professional Ethics of the American Institute for Chartered Property Casualty Underwriters.
9. Explain the reasons for the FASB's Conceptual Framework project.
10. Summarize the objectives of financial reporting for business enterprises, and give examples of how financial reporting is used in insurance sales, underwriting, and claim adjusting.
11. Define or describe each of the Key Words and Phrases introduced in this chapter.

What Is Accounting?

In a broad sense, **accounting** is the process of identifying, measuring, and communicating economic information about an organization for the purpose of making decisions and informed judgments. (Accountants frequently use the term *entity* instead of *organization* because it is more inclusive.) This definition of accounting can be expressed schematically as follows:

Accounting is the process of

| Identifying Measuring Communicating | } | Economic information about an entity | } | For decisions and informed judgments |

Who makes these decisions and informed judgments? Users of accounting information include the management of the entity or organization, the owners of the organization (who are frequently not involved in the management process), potential investors in and creditors of the organization, employees, and various federal, state, and local governmental agencies that are concerned with regulatory and tax matters. Exhibit 1-1 illustrates some of the uses of accounting information. Try to think of at least one other decision or informed judgment that each of these users might make from the economic information that could be communicated about an entity.

Exhibit 1-1
Users and Uses of Accounting Information

User	Decision/Informed Judgment Made
Management	When performing its functions of planning, directing, and controlling, management makes many decisions and informed judgments. For example, when management considers the expansion of a product line, planning involves identifying and measuring costs and benefits; directing involves communicating the strategies selected; and controlling involves identifying, measuring, and communicating the results of the product line expansion during and after its implementation.
Investors	When considering whether to invest in the common stock of a company, **investors** use accounting information to help assess the amounts, timing, and uncertainty of future cash returns on their investment.
Creditors	When determining how much merchandise to ship to a customer before receiving payment, **creditors** assess the probability of collection and the risks of late payment or nonpayment.

Continued on next page.

Employees	When planning for retirement, employees assess the company's ability to offer long-term job prospects and an attractive retirement benefits package.
Securities and Exchange Commission (SEC)	When performing regulatory oversight, the SEC determines whether an entity's financial statements issued to investors fully disclose all required information.

Accounting information must be provided for just about every kind of organization. Although most people recognize that accounting is used by business firms, not-for-profit social service organizations, governmental units, educational institutions, social clubs, political committees, and other groups also require accounting for their economic activities.

Many perceive accounting as something that others do, not realizing how much it affects their lives on a daily basis. Accounting is a process of providing information that supports decisions and informed judgments that to varying degrees affect everyone. Almost everyone uses accounting information. The principal objective of this text is to help you become an informed user of accounting information, rather than to prepare you to become an accountant. This user orientation should be helpful to anyone who works in the financial services industry and provide a solid foundation for insurance professionals who choose to work in the accounting area.

The following sections introduce the major areas of practice within the accounting discipline and describe the types of work done by professional accountants within each of these broad categories. Knowing what is done in each of these areas will help insurance professionals to communicate with accountants and understand the accounting information they provide.

Financial Accounting

Financial accounting refers to the process of preparing and reporting these financial statements for an entity. As Chapter 2 will explain in more detail, financial statements present the financial position of an entity at a point in time, the results of the entity's operations for some period of time, the **cash flow** activities (cash receipts and disbursements) for the same period of time, and other information about the entity's financial resources, obligations, owners, interests, and operations.

Financial accounting is primarily externally oriented. Financial statements are directed to individuals who are not in a position to be aware of the entity's day-to-day financial and operating activities. Financial accounting is also primarily concerned with the historical results of an entity's performance. Financial statements reflect what has happened in the past, and although readers of financial statements may want to project past activities and their results into future performance, financial statements are not valid predictors of future performance.

Bookkeeping procedures are used to accumulate the results of many of an entity's activities, and these procedures are part of the financial accounting process. Bookkeeping procedures have been thoroughly systematized using manual, mechanical, and computer techniques, and although these procedures support the financial accounting process, they are only a part of the process.

Financial accounting is done by accounting professionals who have generally earned a bachelor of science degree in accounting. Entities employ financial accountants to use their expertise, analytical skills, and judgment in the many activities that are necessary for the preparation of financial statements. The title **controller** is used to designate the chief accounting officer of a corporation. The controller is usually responsible for both the financial and managerial accounting functions (see below) of the organization. Sometimes the title *comptroller* (the Old English spelling) is used for this position.

An individual earns the **Certified Public Accountant (CPA)** professional designation by passing a comprehensive four-part examination taken over two days. A uniform CPA exam is given nationally in May and November of each year, although it is administered by individual states. Some states require that candidates have accounting work experience before sitting for the exam. More than 30 states have enacted legislation requiring CPA candidates to complete a minimum of 150 semester hours of college study before becoming eligible to sit for the exam. This national trend to increase the educational requirements for CPA candidates reflects the increasing demands placed on accounting professionals to be both broadly educated and technically competent. Practicing CPAs work in all types of organizations, but as explained later, a CPA who expresses an auditor's opinion about an entity's financial statements must be licensed by the state in which he or she performs the auditing service.

Managerial Accounting/Cost Accounting

Managerial accounting uses economic and financial information to plan and control many of the entity's activities, and to support the management decision-making process. **Cost accounting** is a subset of managerial accounting that relates to the determination and accumulation of product, process, or service costs. Managerial accounting and cost accounting have primarily an internal orientation, as opposed to the primarily external orientation of financial accounting. Much of the same data used in or generated by the financial accounting process is used in managerial and cost accounting, but the data are more likely to be used in a future-oriented way, such as in the preparation of budgets.

Managerial accountants and cost accountants are professionals who have usually earned a bachelor of science degree in accounting. Their work frequently involves close coordination with the production, marketing, and finance functions of the entity. The **Certified Management Accountant (CMA)** professional designation is earned by management accountants/cost accountants who pass a broad four-part examination administered over two days, and who meet certain experience requirements.

Auditing-Public Accounting

Auditing occurs when an entity has its financial statements examined by an independent third party. This external review is a formal examination and verification of accounting records and procedures by a professionally and/or legally recognized authority. In most cases, securities laws require an audit if investors own an entity's stocks and bonds and trade them publicly. **Public accounting** firms and individual CPAs provide this auditing service, which constitutes an important part of the accounting profession.

The result of an audit is an **independent auditor's report**. The report usually has three relatively brief paragraphs. The first paragraph identifies the financial statements that were audited, explains that the statements are the responsibility of the company's management, and states that the auditor's responsibility is to express an opinion about the financial statements. The second paragraph explains that the audit was conducted "in accordance with **generally accepted auditing standards**," or the standards against which auditors evaluate an entity's accounting procedures, and describes briefly what those standards require and what work is involved in performing an audit. The third paragraph contains the auditor's opinion, which is usually that the named statements "present fairly in all material respects" the financial position of the entity and the results of its operations and cash flows for the identified periods "in conformity with **generally accepted accounting principles**," or the rules of accounting. This is an unqualified, or "clean," opinion. Occasionally the opinion will be qualified with respect to fair presentation, departure from generally accepted accounting principles, the auditor's inability to perform certain auditing procedures, or the firm's ability to continue as a going concern (that is, as a viable economic entity). An unqualified opinion is not a guarantee of either the entity's current financial condition or its future prospects. Readers must reach their own judgments about these and other matters after studying the **annual report**, which includes the financial statements and the explanatory notes to the financial statements.

Auditors who work in public accounting are professional accountants who have usually earned at least a bachelor of science degree in accounting. An auditor may work for a public accounting firm (a few firms have several thousand partners and professional staff) or as an individual practitioner. Most auditors seek and earn the CPA designation; a firm partner or an individual practitioner who signs an audit opinion must be a licensed CPA in the state in which he or she practices. To be licensed, the CPA must satisfy the character, education, and experience requirements of the state.

To see an example of the independent auditors' report, refer to page 43 of the 1994 annual report of Armstrong World Industries, Inc., which is reproduced in the Appendix to the companion course workbook and study guide.

Internal Auditing

Organizations with many locations or activities involving many financial transactions employ professional accountants to do **internal auditing**. In many cases, the internal auditor performs functions much like those of the external auditor/public accountant, but perhaps on a smaller scale. For example, internal auditors may be responsible for reviewing the financial statements of a single location, or for analyzing the operating efficiency of an entity's activities. The qualifications of an internal auditor are similar to those of any other professional accountant. In addition to having the CPA and/or the CMA designation, an internal auditor often will also have passed the examination to become a Certified Internal Auditor (CIA). Internal audits do not generally supplant required external audits.

Governmental and Not-for-Profit Accounting

Governmental units at the municipal, state, and federal levels and not-for-profit entities such as colleges and universities, hospitals, and voluntary health and welfare organizations require the same accounting functions to be performed as do other accounting entities. Religious organizations, labor unions, trade associations, performing arts organizations, political parties, libraries, museums, country clubs, and many other not-for-profit organizations employ accountants with similar educational qualifications as those employed in business and public accounting.

Income Tax Accounting

The growing complexity of federal, state, municipal, and foreign income tax laws has led to a demand for professional accountants who specialize in various aspects of taxation. Tax practitioners often develop specialties in the taxation of individuals, partnerships, corporations, trusts, and estates, or in international tax law. These accountants work for corporations, public accounting firms, governmental units, and other entities. Many tax accountants have bachelor's degrees and are CPAs; some are attorneys as well.

How Has Accounting Developed?

Accounting has developed in response to the needs of users of financial statements for financial information to support decisions and informed judgments like those mentioned in Exhibit 1-1 and others. Even though the numbers in financial statements convey an aura of exactness, a great deal of judgment and approximation is involved in determining the numbers to be reported. Accountants have no "code of accounting rules" to follow indiscriminately. Even though broad generally accepted accounting principles (GAAP) exist, different accountants may reach different but often equally legitimate conclusions about how to account for a particular transaction or event. A brief review of the history of the development of accounting principles may make this often confusing state of affairs a little easier to understand.

Early History

Not surprisingly, evidence of record-keeping of economic events has been found in earliest civilizations. Dating back to the clay tablets used by Mesopotamians of about 3000 B.C. to record tax receipts, accounting has responded to the information needs of users. In 1494, Luca Pacioli, a Franciscan monk and mathematics professor, published the first known text to describe a comprehensive double-entry bookkeeping system. Modern book-keeping systems (as discussed in Chapter 4) have evolved directly from Pacioli's "method of Venice" system, which was developed in response to the needs of the Italian mercantile trading practices in that period.

The Industrial Revolution generated the need for large amounts of capital to finance the enterprises that supplanted individual craftsmen. This need resulted in the corporate form of organization, marked by absentee owners, or investors, who entrusted their money to managers. Investors required reports from the corporation managers showing financial position and results of operations. In mid-19th century England, the independent (external) audit function added credence to financial reports. As British capital was invested in a growing U.S. economy in the late 19th century, British chartered accountants and accounting methods came to the United States. However, no group was legally authorized to establish financial reporting standards. This led to alternative methods of reporting financial condition and results of operations, which resulted in confusion and, in some cases, outright fraud.

The Accounting Profession in the United States

Accounting professionals in this country organized themselves in the early 1900s and established certification laws, standardized audit procedures, and other attributes of a profession. However, not until the end of 1934 did the American Institute of Accountants (predecessor of today's American Institute of Certified Public Accountants—AICPA) and the New York Stock Exchange agree after two years on five broad principles of accounting. This was the first formal accounting standard-setting activity. The accounting, financial reporting, and auditing weaknesses related to the 1929 stock market crash prompted this effort.

The Securities Act of 1933 and the Securities Exchange Act of 1934 apply to securities offered for sale in interstate commerce. These laws had a significant effect on the standard-setting process, because they gave the **Securities and Exchange Commission (SEC)** authority to establish accounting principles to be followed by companies whose securities must be registered with the SEC. The SEC still has this authority, but the standard-setting process has been delegated to other organizations over the years. Between 1939 and 1959, the Committee on Accounting Procedure of the American Institute of Accountants issued fifty-one *Accounting Research Bulletins* that dealt with accounting principles. This work was done without a common conceptual framework or set of rules for financial reporting. Each bulletin dealt with a specific issue in a relatively narrow context, and alternative methods of reporting the results of similar transactions remained.

In 1959, the Accounting Principles Board (APB) replaced the Committee on Accounting Procedure as the standard-setting body. Organized and funded by the AICPA, the APB was directed to engage in more research than its predecessor to resolve differing opinions of how specific problems in accounting should be addressed. Although the APB issued a number of opinions on serious accounting issues and the AICPA required that departure from those opinions be disclosed in footnotes to financial statements, the board failed to gain widespread acceptance of its opinions because of inadequate support from accounting theory or practice.

Financial Accounting Standard Setting Today

In 1973, as a result of congressional and other criticism of the accounting standard-setting process being performed by a board composed exclusively of members of the AICPA, the **Financial Accounting Foundation** was created as a more independent entity. The Foundation established the **Financial Accounting Standards Board (FASB)** as the authoritative standard-setting body within the accounting profession FASB embarked on a project called the Conceptual Framework of Financial Accounting and Reporting and issued six *Statements of Financial Accounting Concepts* through July 1995.

Concurrently with its conceptual framework project, the FASB has issued *Statements of Financial Accounting Standards* that have established standards of accounting and reporting for particular issues, much like the FASB's predecessors did. Alternative ways of accounting for and reporting the effects of similar transactions still exist. In many aspects of financial reporting, the accountant still must use judgment in selecting between equally acceptable alternatives. In order to make sense of financial statements, one must understand the effect of the accounting methods used by a firm, relative to alternative methods that were not selected. Subsequent chapters will describe many of these alternatives and the effect that various accounting choices have on financial statements.

The FASB does not set standards haphazardly. It follows an open, due process procedure. The FASB invites input from any individual or organization who cares to provide ideas and viewpoints about the particular standard under consideration. Among the many professional accounting and financial organizations that regularly present suggestions to the FASB, in addition to the AICPA and the SEC, are the American Accounting Association, the Institute of Management Accountants, the Financial Executives Institute, and the Institute of Chartered Financial Analysts.

As was mentioned earlier, financial accounting and reporting practices are not codified in a set of rules to be mastered and blindly followed. Financial accounting and reporting have evolved over time in response to changing needs, and they are still evolving.

Standards for Other Types of Accounting

Because managerial accounting/cost accounting is primarily oriented to internal use, internal users will presumably know about the accounting practices that their firms follow. As a result, the accounting profession has not regarded the development of internal reporting standards for use by management as an important issue. Instead, individual companies are generally allowed to self-regulate with respect to internal reporting matters. One significant exception is accounting for the cost of work done under government contracts. Various governmental agencies have issued directives prescribing the accounting procedures for government contractors to follow. Between 1970 and 1980, the **Cost Accounting Standards Board (CASB)** operated as a governmental body to establish standards applicable to government contracts. Congress abolished the CASB in 1981, although its standards remained in effect. In 1988, Congress reestablished the CASB as an independent body within the Office of Federal Procurement Policy and gave it authority to establish cost accounting standards for government contracts in excess of $500,000.

The Auditing Standards Board, a technical committee of the AICPA, establishes standards for auditing and public accounting. The SEC has had input into this process, and several auditing standards and procedures have been issued. One of the most important of these standards requires the auditor to be independent of the client whose financial statements are being audited. Auditors' judgment is still very important in the auditing process. Because of this, critics of the accounting profession often raise questions concerning the independence of CPA firms in the auditing process.

Congressional committees have held hearings about the role of a company's auditing firm when the company has been involved in a major fraud or has gone bankrupt shortly after receiving an unqualified opinion. In 1987, the National Commission on Fraudulent Financial Reporting, a private-sector initiative sponsored by several professional associations, including the AICPA, issued recommendations designed to reduce further the already low incidence of fraudulent financial reporting. An unqualified auditor's opinion, as discussed earlier, does not constitute a guarantee of either the entity's current financial condition or future prospects. The readers of the financial statements must reach their own judgments about these and other matters after studying the firm's annual report, which includes the financial statements and explanatory footnotes.

In 1984 the **Governmental Accounting Standards Board (GASB)** was established to develop guidelines for financial accounting and reporting by state and local governmental units. The GASB operates under the auspices of the Financial Accounting Foundation, which is also the parent organization of the FASB. The GASB is trying to unify the practices of the many state and municipal entities, thus providing investors with a better means of comparing financial data of the issuers of state and municipal securities. In the absence of a GASB standard for a particular activity or transaction occurring in both the public and private sectors, governmental entities will continue to use FASB standards for guidance. The GASB had issued several standards by the end of 1994.

In income tax matters, accountants use their judgment and expertise to design transactions so that the entity's overall income tax liability is minimized. In addition, accountants prepare or help prepare tax returns and may represent clients whose returns are being reviewed or challenged by tax authorities. The United States Internal Revenue Code and related regulations and the various state and local tax laws specify the rules to be followed in determining an entity's income tax liability. Although specific and complicated, the code and regulations provide rules of law to be followed.

International Accounting Standards

Accounting standards in other countries have evolved in response to the unique user needs and cultural attributes of each country. Thus, despite the development of a global marketplace, accounting standards in one country may differ significantly from those in another country. In 1973, the International Accounting Standards Committee (IASC) was formed to create and promote worldwide acceptance and observation of accounting and financial reporting standards. Although now supported by more than seventy-five nations, the development of uniform standards has been an almost impossible objective to achieve. One of the major challenges relates to a country's interest in protecting its local markets, where participants' interests frequently differ significantly from those of entities involved in a global financial network.

The IASC is now seeking methods of providing comparability between financial statements prepared according to one country's accounting standards and those prepared in accordance with the accounting standards of another country. The development of a single set of international accounting standards to be applied by all countries is a long way off and may never be achieved. The international diversity of accounting standards makes it important to understand the standards of one's own country so that appropriate consideration can be given to financial statements prepared according to another country's standards.

Ethics and the Accounting Profession

One of the characteristics frequently associated with professions is that those practicing the profession acknowledge the importance of an ethical code. This is especially important in the accounting profession because so much of an accountant's work involves providing information to support the informed judgments and decisions made by users of accounting information.

The AICPA and the Institute of Management Accountants (IMA) have both published ethics codes. The membership of the AICPA adopted the *Code of*

Professional Conduct, most recently revised in 1988. The organization's bylaws state that members shall conform to the rules of the Code or be subject to disciplinary action by the AICPA. Although it does not have the same enforcement mechanism, the IMA's *Standards of Ethical Conduct for Management Accountants* requires management accountants to maintain the highest standards of ethical conduct as they fulfill their obligations to the organizations they serve, their profession, the public, and themselves.

Both codes of conduct identify integrity and objectivity as two of the key elements of ethical behavior for a professional accountant. Having **integrity** means being honest and forthright in dealings and communications with others; **objectivity** means impartiality and freedom from conflict of interest. An accountant who lacks integrity or objectivity cannot be relied upon to produce complete and relevant information with which to make an informed judgment or decision.

Other elements of ethical behavior include independence, competence, and acceptance of an obligation to serve the best interests of the employer, the client, and the public. **Independence** is related to objectivity and is especially important to the auditor who must be independent both in appearance and in fact. Having competence means having the knowledge and professional skills to adequately perform the work assigned. Accountants should recognize that their work requires an understanding of the obligation to serve those who will use the information they communicated.

In the recent past, some highly publicized incidents have involved allegations that accountants have violated their ethical codes by being dishonest, biased, and/or incompetent. That some of these allegations have been proved true should not be used to condemn all accountants. The profession has used these rare circumstances to reaffirm that the public and the profession expect accountants to exhibit a very high level of ethical behavior.

The Conceptual Framework

Various accounting standards have existed for many years, but not until the mid-1970s did the FASB begin the process of identifying a structure or framework of financial accounting concepts. New users of financial statements can benefit from an overview of these concepts, because they provide the foundation for understanding financial accounting reports. The *Statements of Financial Accounting Concepts* that have been issued by the FASB through 1994 are as follows:

Number	Title	Issue Date
1.	*Objectives of Financial Reporting by Business Enterprises*	November 1978
2.	*Qualitative Characteristics of Accounting Information* (Amended by Statement 6)	May 1980
3.	*Elements of Financial Statements of Business Enterprises* (Replaced by Statement 6)	December 1980
4.	*Objectives of Financial Reporting by Nonbusiness Organizations*	December 1980
5	*Recognition and Measurement in Financial Statements of Business Enterprises*	December 1984
6.	*Elements of Financial Statements*	December 1985

These statements represent a great deal of effort by the FASB, and the progress made on this project has not come easily. The project has been controversial because of the concern that trying to define the underlying concepts of accounting may have a significant effect on current generally accepted accounting principles and may result in major changes to financial reporting practices. Critics believe that, at best, defining the underlying concepts would cause financial statement readers to become confused (or more confused than they are now) and, at worst, could disrupt financial markets and contractual obligations that are based on present financial reporting practices. The FASB has recognized this concern and has made the following assertions about the concepts statements:[1]

> Statements of Financial Accounting Concepts do not establish standards prescribing accounting procedures or disclosure practices for particular items or events, which are issued by the Board as Statements of Financial Accounting Standards. Rather, Statements in this series describe concepts and relations that will underlie future financial accounting standards and practices and in due course serve as a basis for evaluating existing standards and practices.

> Establishment of objectives and identification of fundamental concepts will not directly solve accounting and reporting problems. Rather, objectives give direction, and concepts are tools for solving problems.

> The Board itself is likely to be the most direct beneficiary of the guidance provided by the Statements in this series. They will guide the Board in developing accounting and reporting standards by providing the Board

with a common foundation and basic reasoning on which to consider merits of alternatives.

"Highlights" of Concepts Statement No. 1—Objectives of Financial Reporting by Business Enterprises

To set the stage more completely for the study of financial accounting, it is appropriate to study the "Highlights" of *Concepts Statement No. 1*, as contained in the full statement. The FASB does caution that these highlights are best understood in the context of the full statement.[2] The comments in brackets are not part of the statement:

- Financial reporting is not an end in itself but is intended to provide information that is useful in making business and economic decisions. [Financial reporting must meet the needs of users by providing information that is relevant to decisions and informed judgments.]

- The objectives of financial reporting are not immutable—they are affected by the economic, legal, political, and social environment in which financial reporting takes place. [Financial accounting standards are still evolving; in June 1993, the FASB issued Standard No. 117, which dealt with financial statements of not-for-profit organizations.]

- The objectives are also affected by the characteristics and limitations of the kind of information that financial reporting can provide.

  The information pertains to business enterprises rather than to industries or to the economy as a whole. [Accounting is done for individual firms, or entities.]

  The information often results from approximate, rather than exact, measures. [Some costs applicable to one year's results of operations may have to be estimated; for example, product warranty costs applicable to 1995 may not be finally determined until 1998.]

  The information largely reflects the financial effects of transactions and events that have already happened. [Financial accounting is historical record keeping; it is not future-oriented.]

  The information is but one source of information needed by those who make decisions about business enterprises. [For example, a potential employee might want to know about employee turnover rates.]

  The information is provided and used at a cost. [The benefit of the information to the user should exceed the cost of providing it.]

- The objectives in this Statement are those of general purpose external financial reporting by business enterprises. [Reporting for *internal* planning, control, and decision making need not be constrained by financial reporting requirements.]

The objectives stem primarily from the needs of external users who lack the authority to prescribe the information they want and must rely on the information management communicates to them. [Most users are external. For its own uses, management can prescribe the information it wants.]

The objectives are directed toward the common interests of many users and the ability of an enterprise to generate favorable cash flows but are phrased using investment and credit decisions as a reference to give them a focus. The objectives are intended to be broad, rather than narrow. [Many users of financial statements want to make a judgment about whether they are likely to receive payment of amounts due them from the company.]

The objectives pertain to financial reporting and are not restricted to financial statements. [Financial reporting includes footnotes and other disclosures.]

- The objectives state that:

Financial reporting should provide information that is useful to present and potential investors [stockholders] and creditors [lenders] and other users in making rational investment, credit, and similar decisions. The information should be comprehensible to those who have a reasonable understanding of business and economic activities and are willing to study the information with reasonable diligence. [The user asks, "Will I be paid the amounts due me if I provide goods or services to the firm or if I invest in the firm?" To answer this question, the user has the responsibility of understanding business practices and financial reporting.]

Financial reporting should provide information to help present and potential investors and creditors and other users in assessing the amounts, timing, and uncertainty of prospective cash receipts from dividends or interest and the proceeds from the sale, redemption, or maturity of securities or loans. Since investors' and creditors' cash flows are related to enterprise cash flows, financial reporting should provide information to help investors, creditors, and others assess the amounts, timing, and uncertainty of prospective net cash inflows to the related enterprise. [The company must receive cash from somewhere before it can be paid out to creditors for principal and interest obligations or to investors as dividend payments.]

Financial reporting should provide information about the economic resources of an enterprise, the claims to those resources (obligations of the enterprise to transfer resources to other entities and owners' equity), and the effects of transactions, events, and circumstances that change its resources and claims to those resources. [What economic resources does the firm own, how much does it owe, and what caused these amounts to change over time?]

- "Investors" and "creditors" are used broadly and include not only those who have or contemplate having a claim to enterprise resources but also those who advise or represent them. [For example, financial advisors and consultants base their recommendations on financial reports.]

- Although investment and credit decisions reflect investors and creditors' expectations about future enterprise performance, those expectations are commonly based at least partly on evaluations of past enterprise performance. [The future is unknown, but it is likely to be influenced by the past.]

- The primary focus of financial reporting is information about earnings and its components. [The user asks, "How much profit did the firm earn?"]

- Information about enterprise earnings based on accrual accounting generally provides a better indication of an enterprise's present and continuing ability to generate favorable cash flows than information limited to the financial effects of cash receipts and payments. [Accrual accounting—to be explained in more detail in Chapter 2—involves accounting for the effect of an economic activity, or transaction, on an entity when the activity has occurred, rather than when a cash receipt or payment related to the transaction takes place. Thus, the company for which you work reports a cost for your wages in the month in which you do the work, even though you may not be paid until next month.]

- Financial reporting is expected to provide information about an enterprise's financial performance during a period and about how management of an enterprise has discharged its stewardship responsibility to owners. [The user asks, "How much was the firm's profit for the year ending December 31, 1995?"]

- Financial accounting is not designed to measure directly the value of a business enterprise, but the information it provides may be helpful to those who wish to estimate its value. [The financial statements of a company do not change just because the market price of its stock changes.]

- Investors, creditors, and others may use reported earnings and information about the elements of financial statements in various ways to assess the prospects for cash flows. They may wish, for example, to evaluate management's performance, estimate "earning power," predict future earnings, assess risk, or to confirm, change, or reject earlier predictions or assessments. Although financial reporting should provide basic information to aid them, they do their own evaluating, estimating, predicting, assessing, confirming, changing, or rejecting. [Each user reads the financial statements of a firm with his or her own judgment and biases.]

- Management knows more about the enterprise and its affairs than investors, creditors, or other "outsiders" and accordingly can often increase the usefulness of financial information by identifying certain events and circumstances and explaining their financial effects on the enterprise. [Footnotes and other disclosures are just as important as the financial statements themselves.]

Objectives of Financial Reporting by Nonbusiness Organizations

Earlier, this chapter stated that the material to be presented, although usually to be expressed in the context of profitseeking business enterprises, would also apply to not-for-profit social service and governmental organizations. The FASB's "Highlights" of *Concepts Statement No. 4*, "Objectives of Financial Reporting by Nonbusiness Organizations," states, "Based on its study, the Board believes that the objectives of general purpose external financial reporting for government sponsored entities (for example, hospitals, universities, or utilities) engaged in activities that are not unique to government should be similar to those of business enterprises or other nonbusiness organizations engaged in similar activities."[3] *Statement 6* amended *Statement 2* by affirming that the qualitative characteristics described in *Statement 2* apply to the information about both business enterprises and not-for-profit organizations.

The objectives of financial reporting for nonbusiness organizations focus on providing information for resource providers (for example, taxpayers and donors to charitable organizations) rather than investors. Information is provided about the economic resources, obligations, net resources, and performance of an organization during a period of time. Thus, even though nonbusiness organizations have unique characteristics that distinguish them from profit-oriented businesses, the information characteristics of the financial reporting objectives for each type of organization are similar.

Plan of the Book

Part I of the text, "The Accounting Process," includes Chapters 1 through 5. This chapter described the accounting process and uses of accounting information. Chapter 2 describes financial statements, presents a model of how they are interrelated, and briefly summarizes key accounting concepts and principles. Later chapters elaborate on most of the material introduced in Chapter 1. Chapter 2 also includes the first four "Business Procedure Capsules." These capsules are brief explanations of business practices that make some of the accounting and reporting issues covered in the text easier to understand.

Chapter 3 describes some of the basic interpretations of financial statement data that financial statement users make. Although subsequent chapters present a more complete explanation of financial statement elements, understanding the basic relationships presented in Chapter 3 permits better comprehension of the effect of alternative accounting methods discussed later. You might want to consult Chapter 3 periodically when studying the in-depth discussion of financial analysis for insurance professionals presented in Chapter 14.

Chapter 4 describes the process of recording economic transactions, otherwise referred to as "bookkeeping," and presents a powerful transaction analysis model. Using this model, a financial statement user can understand the effect of any transaction on the statements and many of the judgments based on the statements. You will not be asked to learn bookkeeping in Chapter 4, nor is the purpose of this text to teach that subject.

Chapter 5 introduces insurer financial statements and explains how they differ from the financial statements of noninsurers because of the unique characteristics of the insurance business. That chapter also introduces statutory accounting principles imposed by insurance regulators and explains how the financial statements prepared in accordance with those principles differ from statements prepared in accordance with generally accepted accounting principles.

The companion course workbook and study guide to this text contains examinations covering each part of the text. Answers are provided in the workbook to enable you to evaluate your performance on these exams. If you are unable to complete the exam for Part I with a score of 75 percent or better, we recommend that you go back to the first chapter and study Part I again. It is very difficult for most students to comprehend the subjects presented in Chapters 6 through 15 without first understanding the basic concepts presented in Chapters 1 through 5.

Part II of the text, "Applied Accounting and Finance," consists of six chapters. Chapters 6 through 10 examine specific financial statement elements of noninsurance entities, and Chapter 11 examines those elements for insurer financial statements prepared on a statutory basis. Current and noncurrent assets are addressed in Chapters 6 and 7, respectively. Chapter 8 discusses liabilities, and Chapter 9 discusses owners' equity. Chapter 10 describes accounting for revenues and expenses.

Part III, "Analytical Tools for Financial Decision Making," consists of four chapters that present applications of the principles and concepts discussed in Parts I and II of the text. Chapter 12 examines the notes to financial statements, management discussion and analysis reports, and comparative standards for financial analysis that are available from commercial rating services such as Standard & Poor's, Dun & Bradstreet, A.M. Best, and other providers of business and industrial financial ratios. Chapter 13 provides an introduction to capital budgeting techniques and illustrates how those techniques can be applied in management decision making regarding investment alternatives. Chapter 14 presents a structured approach to financial analysis and explains how that approach can be used to analyze financial statements of both noninsurance and insurance entities. Chapter 15 presents the fundamentals of insurance company finance and investments, describes various risk measures, and explores portfolio management techniques applicable to both investment and underwriting portfolios.

Summary

Accounting is the process of identifying, measuring, and communicating economic information about an entity for the purpose of making decisions and informed judgments.

Users of financial statements include management, investors, creditors, employees, and government agencies. Decisions made by users relate, among other things, to entity operations, investment, credit, employment, and compliance with laws. Financial statements support these decisions because they communicate important financial information about the entity.

The major classifications of accounting include financial accounting, managerial accounting/cost accounting, auditing/public accounting, internal auditing, governmental and not-for-profit accounting, and income tax accounting.

Accounting has developed in response to the needs of users of financial statements for financial information. Different organizations have developed financial accounting standards. These standards are not a codified set of rules to be blindly followed; different entities use alternative methods of accounting for different activities. The Financial Accounting Standards Board is the standard-setting body for financial accounting. Other organizations are involved in establishing standards for cost accounting, auditing, governmental accounting, and income tax accounting.

Integrity, objectivity, independence, and competence are several characteristics of ethical behavior for a professional accountant. High standards of ethical conduct are appropriate for all persons, but professional accountants have a special responsibility because so many people make decisions and informed judgments using information provided by the accounting process.

The Financial Accounting Standards Board has issued several *Statements of Financial Accounting Concepts* resulting from the conceptual framework project that has been underway in recent years. These statements describe concepts and relations that will underlie future financial accounting standards and practices, and will in due course serve as a basis for evaluating existing standards and practices.

"Highlights" of the concepts statement dealing with the objectives of financial reporting stipulate that financial information provided should be useful to resolve investor and creditor concerns about the cash flows of the enterprise, the resources and obligations of the enterprise, and the profit of the enterprise. Financial accounting is not designed to measure directly the value of a business enterprise.

The objectives of financial reporting for nonbusiness enterprises are not significantly different from those for business enterprises, except that resource providers, rather than investors, are concerned about performance results, rather than profit.

Key Words and Phrases

accounting (p. 8) The process of identifying, measuring, and communicating economic information about an organization for the purpose of making decisions and informed judgments.

annual report (p. 13) A document distributed to shareholders that contains the financial statements for the fiscal year of the reporting firm, together with the report of the external auditor's examination of the financial statements.

auditing (p. 12) The process of reviewing the financial statements of an entity by an independent third party with the objective of expressing an opinion about the fairness of the presentation of the entity's financial position, results of operations, and changes in financial position. The practice of auditing is less precisely referred to as *public accounting*.

bookkeeping (p. 11) Procedures that are used to keep track of financial transactions and accumulate the results of an entity's financial activities.

cash flow (p. 10) Cash receipts or disbursements of an entity.

Certified Management Accountant (p. 12) A professional designation earned by passing a broad, four-part examination administered over a two-day period and meeting certain experience requirements. Examination topics include economics and business finance; organization and behavior (including ethical considerations); public reporting standards, auditing, and taxes; internal reporting and analysis; and decision analysis, including modeling and information systems.

Certified Public Accountant (p. 11) A professional designation earned by passing a comprehensive four-part examination taken over a two-day period. Examination topics include accounting theory and practice, income tax accounting, auditing, and business law.

controller (p. 11) The job title of the person who is the chief accounting officer of an organization. The controller is usually responsible for both the financial and managerial accounting functions. Sometimes referred to as *comptroller*.

cost accounting (p. 12) A subset of managerial accounting that relates to the determination and accumulation of product, process, or service costs.

Cost Accounting Standards Board (p. 17) A group authorized by the U.S. Congress to establish cost accounting standards for government contractors.

creditor (p. 9) An organization or individual who lends to the entity. Examples include suppliers who ship merchandise to the entity before receiving payment for their goods and banks who lend cash to the entity.

entity (p. 7) An organization or individual, or a group of organizations or individuals, for which accounting is done.

financial accounting (p. 10) Accounting that focuses on reporting financial position at a point in time and/or results of operations for a period of time.

Financial Accounting Foundation (p. 16) An organization composed of people from the public accounting profession, businesses, and the public that is responsible for the funding of and appointing members to the Financial Accounting Standards Board.

Financial Accounting Standards Board (p. 16) The body responsible for establishing generally accepted accounting principles.

generally accepted accounting principles (p. 12) Pronouncements of the Financial Accounting Standards Board (FASB) and its predecessors that constitute appropriate accounting for various transactions used for reporting financial position and results of operations to investors and creditors.

generally accepted auditing standards (p. 12) Standards for auditing that are established by the Auditing Standards Board of the American Institute of Certified Public Accountants.

Governmental Accounting Standards Board (p. 17) Established by the Financial Accounting Foundation to develop guidelines for financial accounting and reporting by state and local governmental units.

independence (p. 19) The personal characteristic of an accountant, especially an auditor, that refers to both appearing and being objective and impartial.

independent auditor's report (p. 12) The report accompanying audited financial statements that explains briefly the auditor's responsibility and the extent of work performed. The report includes an opinion about whether the information contained in the financial statements is presented fairly in accordance with generally accepted accounting principles.

integrity (p. 19) The personal characteristic of honesty, including being forthright in dealings and communications with others.

internal auditing (p. 13) The practice of auditing within a company by employees of the company.

investor (p. 9) An organization or individual who has an ownership interest in the firm. For corporations, referred to as *stockholder* or *shareholder*.

managerial accounting (p. 11) Accounting that is concerned with the use of economic and financial information to plan and control many of the activities of an entity and to support the management decision-making process.

objectivity (p. 19) The personal characteristic of impartiality, including freedom from conflict of interest.

public accounting (p. 12) The segment of the accounting profession that provides auditing, income tax accounting, and management consulting services to clients.

Securities and Exchange Commission (p. 15) A unit of the federal government that is responsible for establishing regulations and assuring full disclosure to investors about companies and their securities that are traded in interstate commerce.

Statements of Financial Accounting Standards (p. 16) Pronouncements of
the Financial Accounting Standards Board that constitute generally accepted accounting principles.

Chapter Notes

1. Preface, FASB *Statement of Financial Accounting Concepts No. 6* (Stamford, CT,
1985). Copyright © the Financial Accounting Standards Board, High Ridge
Park, Stamford, CT 06905, U.S.A. Excerpted with permission. Copies of the
complete document are available from the FASB.
2. "Highlights," FASB *Statement of Financial Accounting Concepts No. 1* (Stamford,
CT, 1978). Copyright © the Financial Accounting Standards Board, High Ridge
Park, Stamford, CT 06905, U.S.A. Excerpted with permission. Copies of the
complete document are available from the FASB.
3. FASB *Statement of Financial Accounting Concepts No. 4* (Stamford, CT, 1980).
Copyright © the Financial Accounting Standards Board, High Ridge Park,
Stamford, CT 06905, U.S.A. Excerpted with permission. Copies of the complete
document are available from the FASB.

Chapter 2

Understanding the Accounting Process and Financial Statements

Financial statements are the product of the financial accounting process. They are the means of communicating economic information about the entity to individuals who want to make decisions and informed judgments about the entity. Each of the four principal financial statements (the balance sheet, the income statement, the statement of cash flows, and the statement of changes in owners' equity) has a unique purpose. These four statements are interrelated, and they must be considered together to assess the financial strength of the reporting entity.

Insurance professionals must frequently use financial statements when evaluating an application for insurance, a renewal of coverage, or a claim for loss payment. Commercial lines underwriters, when evaluating a prospective risk, are concerned about the risk's financial stability. The determination of risk acceptability and pricing, including experience modification and price credits, can be affected by the underwriter's opinion about the entity's ability to grow, meet its business obligations, and make timely premium payments. A financially distressed commercial risk might present a moral hazard to the insurer, influencing both the chance of a loss occurring and the severity of loss once it does occur.

Financial analysis is crucial for determining a firm's capacity to cover its financial obligations. An example of a situation in which an increased chance of loss results from a business's financial condition would be a contractor with insufficient financial capacity. Insufficient capacity could occur from under-bidding a project, past debts, or overdue accounts receivable. Insufficient capacity might present an increased exposure to arson, mysterious disappearance, on-the-job injuries resulting from carelessness, or failure to complete the job in the time allotted or as stipulated by the contract. Even a brief review of a business's financial statements by a producer or underwriter might reveal conditions indicating an increased chance of loss.

A producer's development of the client contract should include inspection of the business premises or job site. Characteristics of the business practice, job site hazards, safety procedures, and values exposed all might suggest a need to examine the firm's financial statements. Financial statements can identify assets exposed to loss and sources of financial liability. They can also reveal trends in the client's financial performance signaling potential future problems or growth opportunities.

All insurance professionals are potential users of financial statements. Users cannot make meaningful interpretations of financial statement data without understanding the concepts and principles that relate to the entire financial accounting process. Users must also understand that these concepts and principles are broad; they do not constitute a fixed set of rules, but instead serve as guidelines for the development of sound financial reporting practices. Producers, underwriters, and claim adjusters all need to understand the concepts and principles underlying an entity's financial statements. Insurance professionals who lack that understanding are likely to make poor underwriting or claim decisions because they are likely to misinterpret the financial information upon which the decisions are based.

The previous chapter described the general process of accounting and how it has developed. This chapter introduces the four basic financial statements and describes the information they contain. Chapters 3 and 4 will explain how financial statements can be used to gain information about the reporting entity and how that entity's economic transactions affect its financial statements.

Educational Objectives

After studying this chapter, you should be able to:

1. Provide examples of economic activity that constitutes transactions.

2. Describe the basic accounting equation, and explain how it is useful for describing transactions.

3. Describe what kind of information is reported on each of the financial statements illustrated in this chapter and how those statements are related to each other.

4. Explain the meaning of each of the captions on the financial statements illustrated in this chapter.

5. Describe the broad, generally accepted concepts and principles that apply to the accounting process.

6. Describe the limitations of financial statements.

7. Explain what a corporation's annual report is and why it is issued.

8. Describe business procedures related to organizing a business, fiscal year, par value, and parent-subsidiary corporations.

9. Define or describe each of the Key Words and Phrases introduced in this chapter.

Financial Statements

This section explains how transactions are recorded in financial statements and gives illustrations of the four principal financial statements.

From Transactions to Financial Statements

An entity's financial statements are the product of a process that starts with transactions between the entity and other organizations and individuals. **Transactions** are economic interchanges between entities, for example, a sale/purchase or a receipt of cash by a borrower and the payment of cash by a lender. The flow from transactions to financial statements can be illustrated as follows:

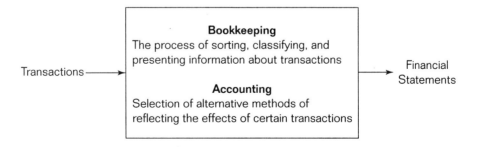

Current generally accepted accounting principles and auditing standards require that the financial statements of an entity show the following for the reporting period:

- Financial position at the end of the period
- Earnings for the period
- Cash flows during the period
- Investments by and distributions to owners during the period

The financial statements that satisfy these requirements are, respectively, as follows:

- Balance sheet (or statement of financial position)
- Income statement (or statement of earnings, profit and loss statement, or statement of operations)
- Statement of cash flows
- Statement of changes in owners' equity (or statement of changes in capital stock and/or statement of changes in retained earnings)

In addition to the financial statements themselves, the annual report will probably include several accompanying footnotes or explanations of the accounting policies and detailed information about many of the amounts and **captions** (explanatory or identifying comments) shown on the financial statements. These notes are designed to assist the reader of the financial statements by disclosing as much relevant supplementary information as the company and its auditors deem necessary and appropriate. For Armstrong World Industries, Inc., the notes to the 1994 financial statements are shown in the financial review section on pages 28-42 of the annual report in the companion workbook to this text. Chapter 12 will describe the explanatory notes to the financial statements in detail.

Financial Statements Illustrated

Main Street Store, Inc., was organized as a corporation and began business during September 1995 (see Business Procedure Capsule 1). The company buys clothing and accessories from distributors and manufacturers and sells these items from a rented building. The financial statements of Main Street Store, Inc., at August 31, 1996, and for the fiscal year (see Business Procedure Capsule 2) ending on that date are presented in Exhibits 2-1 through 2-4.

As you look at these financial statements, you will probably have several questions concerning specific accounts and how the numbers are computed. For now, concentrate on the explanations and definitions that are appropriate and necessary for understanding the purpose of financial statements. Notice especially the characteristic differences among the four financial statements. Many of your questions about specific accounts will be answered in subsequent chapters that explain the individual statements and their components in detail.

Explanations and Definitions

As each of the four principal financial statements is introduced, many of the terms relating to the statements will be clarified.

Balance Sheet

The **balance sheet** is a listing of the organization's assets, liabilities, and owners' equity *at a point in time*. In this sense, the balance sheet is like a snapshot of the organization's financial position, frozen at a specific point in time. The balance sheet is sometimes called the **statement of financial position**, because it summarizes the entity's resources (assets), obligations (liabilities), and owners' claims (owners' equity). Exhibit 2-1 illustrates the balance sheet for Main Street Store, Inc., at August 31, 1996, the end of the firm's first year of operations. Notice the two principal sections of the balance sheet which are shown side by side: (1) assets and (2) liabilities and owners' equity.

• **BUSINESS PROCEDURE CAPSULE 1**
  Organizing a Business

There are three principal forms of business organization: proprietorship, partnership, and corporation. In the United States, there are about 16 million proprietorships, 1.5 million partnerships, and 4 million corporations.[1]

A **proprietorship** is a business activity conducted by an individual. Operating as a proprietorship is the easiest way to get started in a business activity. Other than the possibility of needing a local license, no formal prerequisites are necessary for beginning a proprietorship. Besides being easy to start, a proprietorship has the advantage, according to many people, that the owner is his or her own boss. A principal disadvantage of the proprietorship is that the owner's liability for business debts is not limited by the assets of the business. That is, if the business fails, and if, after all available business assets are used to pay business debts, the business creditors are still owed money, the business creditors can claim the owner's personal assets. Another disadvantage is that the proprietor may have difficulty raising the money needed to provide the capital base that will be required if the business is to grow substantially. Because of the ease of getting started, most business activities begin as proprietorships.

Continued on next page.

A **partnership** is essentially two or more proprietors who have banded together. The unlimited liability characteristic of the proprietorship still exists, but with several partners the ability of the firm to raise capital may be improved. Income earned from partnership activities is taxed at the individual partner level; the partnership itself is not a tax-paying entity. Accountants, attorneys, and other professionals frequently operate their firms as partnerships.

Most large businesses, and many new businesses, use the corporate form of organization. The owners of the corporation are called **stockholders**. They have invested funds in the corporation and received shares of **stock** as evidence of their ownership. Stockholders' liability is limited to the amount invested; creditors cannot seek recovery of losses from the personal assets of stockholders. Large amounts of capital can frequently be raised by selling shares of stock to many individuals. One person may also own all the stock of a corporation. A stockholder can usually sell his or her shares to other investors, or buy more shares from other stockholders if a change in ownership interest is desired. A **corporation** is formed by having a charter and bylaws prepared and registered with the appropriate office in one of the fifty states. The cost of forming a corporation is usually greater than the cost of starting a proprietorship or forming a partnership.

A major disadvantage of the corporate form of business is that corporations are tax-paying entities. Thus, any income distributed to shareholders is taxed first as income of the corporation, and then a second time as income of the individual shareholders.

A form of organization that many states have approved is the *limited liability company*. For accounting and legal purposes, this type of organization is treated as a corporation even though some of the formalities of business structure that must be maintained, meetings that must be held, and reports that must be filed with the corporate form of organization are not present. Shareholders of small corporations may find that banks and major creditors usually require the personal guarantees of the principal shareholders as a condition to granting credit to the corporation. Therefore, the limited liability of the corporate form may be, in the case of small corporations, more theoretical than real.

- **BUSINESS PROCEDURE CAPSULE 2**
  Fiscal Year

A firm's **fiscal year** is the annual period used for reporting to owners, the government, and others. Many firms select the calendar year as their fiscal year, but other twelve-month periods can also be selected. Some firms select a reporting period ending on a date when inventories will be relatively low or business activity will be slow, because that time of the year facilitates the process of preparing financial statements.

Many firms select fiscal periods that relate to the pace of their business activity. Food retailers, for example, have a weekly operating cycle, and many of these firms select a fifty-two-week fiscal year (with a fifty-three-week fiscal year every five or six years so that their year end remains near the same date every year).

For internal reporting purposes, many firms use periods other than the month (for example, thirteen four-week periods). Those firms want the same number of operating days in each period so that comparisons between the same period of different years can be made without having to consider differences in the number of operating days in the respective periods.

Exhibit 2-1
Balance Sheet

MAIN STREET STORE, INC.
Balance Sheet
August 31, 1996

Assets		Liabilities and Owners' Equity	
Current assets:		Current liabilities:	
Cash	$ 34,000	Short-term debt	$ 20,000
Accounts receivable	80,000	Accounts payable	35,000
Merchandise inventory	170,000	Other accrued liabilities	12,000
Total current assets	$284,000	Total current liabilities	$ 67,000
Equipment	40,000	Long-term debt	50,000
Less: Accumulated		Total liabilities	$117,000
depreciation	(4,000)	Owners' equity	203,000
		Total liabilities and	
Total assets	$320,000	owners' equity	$320,000

The dollar total of $320,000 is the same for each side. This equality is sometimes referred to as the **accounting equation** or the **balance sheet equation**. The term *balance sheet is* derived from the equality, or balance, of those two amounts.

$$Assets = Liabilities + Owners' equity$$

From Exhibit 2-1, the accounting equation for Main Street is as follows:

$$\$320,000 = \$117,000 + \$203,000$$

FASB defines **assets** as "probable future economic benefits obtained or controlled by a particular entity as a result of past transactions or events."[2] In brief, assets represent the amount of resources *owned* by the entity. Assets are frequently tangible; they can be seen and handled (such as, cash, merchandise inventory, or equipment), or evidence of their existence can be observed (for example, a customer's acknowledgment of receipt of merchandise and the implied promise to pay the amount due when agreed upon—an account receivable).

FASB defines **liabilities** as "probable future sacrifices of economic benefits arising from present obligations of a particular entity to transfer assets or provide services to other entities in the future as a result of past transactions or events."[3] In brief, liabilities are amounts *owed* to other entities. For example, the accounts payable arose because suppliers shipped merchandise to Main Street Store, Inc., which will pay for this merchandise at some point in the future. In other words, the supplier has an "ownership right" in the merchandise until it is paid for and thus has become a creditor to the firm by supplying merchandise on account.

Owners' equity is the ownership right of the owner or owners of the entity in the assets that remain after the liabilities are deducted. (A car or house owner uses this term when referring to his or her **equity** as the market value of the car or house less the loan or mortgage balance.) Owners' equity is sometimes referred to as **net assets**. Owners' equity can be calculated by rearranging the basic accounting equation:

$$\text{Assets} - \text{Liabilities} = \text{Owners' equity}$$
$$\text{Net assets} = \text{Owners' equity}$$

Another term sometimes used when referring to owners' equity is **net worth**. However, this term is misleading because it implies that the net assets are "worth" the amount reported on the balance as owners' equity. *Financial statements prepared according to generally accepted accounting principles (GAAP) do not purport to show the current market value of the entity's assets, except in a few restricted cases.*

Each of the individual assets and liabilities reported by Main Street Stores, Inc., warrants a brief explanation. Each **account** (caption in the financial statements) will be discussed in more detail in later definitions and chapters.

Cash represents money on hand and in the bank or banks used by Main Street Store, Inc. If the firm had made any temporary cash investments in order to earn interest, these marketable securities would probably be shown as a separate asset because those funds are not as readily available as money on hand.

Accounts receivable represent amounts due from customers who have purchased merchandise on credit and who have agreed to pay within a specified period or when billed by Main Street Store, Inc.

Merchandise inventory represents the cost to Main Street Store, Inc., of the merchandise that it has acquired but not yet sold.

Equipment represents the cost to Main Street Store, Inc., of the display cases, racks, shelving, and other store equipment purchased and installed in the rented building in which it operates. The building is not shown as an asset because Main Street Store, Inc., does not own it.

Accumulated depreciation represents the portion of the cost of the equipment that is estimated to have been used up in the process of operating the business. In Exhibit 2-1, one-tenth ($4,000 / $40,000) of the equipment has been depreciated. From this relationship, one might assume that the equipment is estimated to have a useful life of ten years because the amounts are reported on the balance sheet at the end of the firm's first year of operations. However, **depreciation** *in accounting is the process of spreading the cost of an asset over its useful life to the entity. It is not an attempt to recognize the economic loss in value or the actual change in value of an asset because of its age or use. Such loss, or change in value, cannot be determined until the asset is sold.*

Short-term debt represents amounts borrowed, probably from banks, that will be repaid within one year of the balance sheet date.

Accounts payable represents amounts owed to suppliers of merchandise inventory that was purchased on credit and will be paid within a specific period of time.

Other **accrued liabilities** represents amounts owed to creditors, including any wages owed to employees for services provided to Main Street Store, Inc., through August 31, 1996, the balance sheet date.

Long-term debt represents amounts borrowed from banks or others that will not be repaid within one year from the balance sheet date.

Owners' equity, shown as a single amount in Exhibit 2-1, is explained in more detail later in this chapter in the discussion of the statement of changes in owners' equity.

In Exhibit 2-1, some assets and liabilities are classified as "current." **Current assets** are cash and other assets that are likely to be converted into cash or used to benefit the entity within one year, and **current liabilities** are liabilities that are likely to be paid with cash within one year of the balance sheet date. In this example, the accounts receivable from the customers of Main Street Store, Inc., are expected to be collected within a year, and the merchandise inventory is expected to be sold within a year of the balance sheet date. This time-frame classification is important and, as will be explained later, is used in assessing the entity's ability to pay its obligations when they come due.

To summarize, the balance sheet is a listing of the entity's assets, liabilities, and owners' equity. A balance sheet can be prepared as of any date but is most frequently prepared as of the end of a fiscal reporting period (for example, month end or year end). The balance sheet as of the end of one period is the balance sheet as of the beginning of the next period. This balance sheet time line can be illustrated as follows:

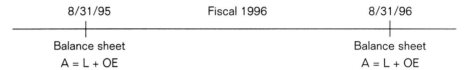

8/31/95	Fiscal 1996	8/31/96
Balance sheet A = L + OE		Balance sheet A = L + OE

On the time line, Fiscal 1996 refers to the twelve months during which the entity carried out its economic activities.

Income Statement

The principal purpose of the **income statement**, or **statement of earnings**, **profit and loss statement**, or **statement of operations**, is to answer the question, "Did the entity operate at a profit for the period of time under consideration?" **Profit** is defined as the net of revenues over expenses. The question is answered by first reporting **revenues** from the entity's operating activities (for example, selling merchandise, services, or production), and then subtracting the costs and **expenses** incurred in generating those revenues and operating the entity. **Gains** and **losses** are also reported on the income statement. Gains and losses result from nonoperating activities rather than from the day-to-day operating activities that generate revenues and expenses. The income statement reports results *for a period of time*, in contrast to the balance sheet focus on a single date. In this sense, the income statement is more like a movie than a snapshot; it depicts the results of activities that have occurred over a specific period of time.

The income statement for Main Street Store, Inc., for the year ending August 31, 1996, is presented in Exhibit 2-2. The statement starts with **net sales** (which are revenues), and the various costs and expenses are subtracted to arrive at net income in total and per share of common stock outstanding. **Net income** is the profit for the period; if costs and expenses exceed net sales, a net loss results. Chapter 9 will explain the reasons for reporting net income or net loss per share of common stock outstanding and the calculation of this amount.

Now look at the individual captions on the income statement. This section will explain each caption briefly, and subsequent chapters will provide more detail.

Exhibit 2-2
Income Statement

MAIN STREET STORE, INC.
Income Statement
For the Year Ended August 31, 1996

Net sales	$1,200,000
Cost of goods sold	850,000
Gross profit	$ 350,000
Selling, general, and administrative expenses	311,000
Earnings from operations	$ 39,000
Interest expense	9,000
Earnings before taxes	$ 30,000
Income taxes	12,000
Net income	$ 18,000
Net income per share of common stock outstanding	$ 1.80

Net sales represents the amount of sales of merchandise to customers, less the amount of sales originally recorded but that were canceled because customers subsequently returned the merchandise. The sales amount is frequently called *sales revenue*, or just *revenue*. Revenue results from selling a product or service to a customer.

Cost of goods sold represents the total cost of merchandise removed from inventory and delivered to customers as a result of sales. This is shown as a separate expense because of its significance and because of the desire to show gross profit as a separate item.

Gross profit is the difference between net sales and cost of goods sold and represents the seller's maximum amount of margin from which all other expenses of operating the business must be met before it is possible to have net income. Gross profit (sometimes referred to as *gross margin*) is shown as a separate item because it is significant to both management and nonmanagement readers of the income statement. The uses made of this amount will be explained in subsequent chapters.

Selling, general, and administrative expenses represents the entity's operating expenses. In some income statements, these expenses are not combined as they are in Exhibit 2-2, but they are reported separately for each of several operating expense categories.

Earnings from operations (or operating income) represents one of the most important measures of the firm's activities. Earnings from operations can be related to the assets available to the firm to obtain a useful measure of management's performance. Chapter 3 will describe a method for doing that.

Interest expense represents the cost of using borrowed funds. This item is reported separately because it is a function of how assets are financed, not of how assets are used.

Income taxes is shown after all of the other income statement items have been reported because income taxes are a function of the firm's earnings before taxes.

Net income per share of common stock outstanding is reported as a separate item at the bottom of the income statement because of its significance in evaluating the market value of a share of common stock. Chapter 9 will explain this measure in more detail.

To review, the income statement summarizes the entity's income- or loss-producing activities *for a period of time*. Transactions that affect the income statement will also affect the balance sheet. For example, a sale made for cash increases sales revenue on the income statement and increases cash, an asset on the balance sheet. Likewise, wages earned by employees during the last week of the current year to be paid early in the next year are an expense of the current year. These wages will be deducted from revenues in the income statement and are considered a liability reported on the balance sheet at the end of the year. Thus, the income statement is a link between the balance sheets at the beginning and end of the year. How the link is made is explained in the next section, which describes the statement of changes in owners' equity. The time line presented earlier can be expanded as follows:

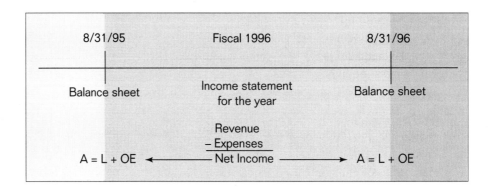

Statement of Changes in Owners' Equity

The **statement of changes in owners' equity**, or **statement of changes in capital stock** or **statement of changes in retained earnings**, like the income statement, involves a stated *period of time*. This statement shows the detail of owners' equity and explains the changes that occurred in the components of owners' equity during the year.

Exhibit 2-3 illustrates this statement for Main Street Store, Inc., for the year ended August 31, 1996. These are the results of Main Street Store's first year of operations, so the beginning-of-the-year balances are zero. On subsequent years' statements, the beginning-of-the-year amount is the ending balance from the prior year.

In Exhibit 2-3, owners' equity is made up of two principal components: **paid-in capital** and **retained earnings**. These items are briefly explained here and are discussed in more detail in Chapter 8.

Exhibit 2-3
Statement of Changes in Owners' Equity

MAIN STREET STORE, INC. Statement of Changes in Owners' Equity For the Year Ended August 31, 1996	
Paid-in capital:	
Beginning balance	$ -0-
Common stock, par value, $10; 50,000 shares authorized,	
10,000 shares issued and outstanding	100,000
Additional paid-in capital	90,000
Balance, August 31, 1996	$190,000
Retained earnings:	
Beginning balance	$ -0-
Net income for the year	18,000
Less: Cash dividends of $.50 per share	(5,000)
Balance August 31, 1996	$ 13,000
Total owners' equity	$203,000

Paid-in capital represents the total amount invested in the entity by the owners—in this case, the stockholders. When the stock issued to the owners has a **par value** (see Business Procedure Capsule 3), there will usually be two categories of paid-in capital: common stock and additional paid-in capital.

Common stock reflects the number of shares authorized by the corporation's charter, the number of shares that have been issued to stockholders, and the number of shares that the stockholders still hold. When the common stock has a par value or stated value, the amount shown for common stock in the financial statements will always be the par value or stated value multiplied by the number of shares issued. If the common stock does not have a par value or stated value, the amount shown for common stock in the financial statements will be the total amount invested by the owners. **Additional paid-in capital** is the difference between the total amount invested by the owners and the par value or stated value of the stock. (If no-par-value stock without a stated value is issued to the owners, there will be no additional paid-in capital because the total amount paid in, or invested, by the owners will be shown as common stock.)

Retained earnings is the second principal category of owners' equity and represents the cumulative net income of the entity that has been retained for use in the business. **Dividends** are distributions of earnings that have been made to the owners, so they reduce retained earnings. If retained earnings have a negative balance because cumulative losses and dividends have exceeded cumulative net income, this part of owners' equity is referred to as *deficit*.

- **BUSINESS PROCEDURE CAPSULE 3**
  Par Value

  Par value is a relic from the past that has, for all practical purposes, lost its significance. The par value of common stock is an arbitrary value assigned when the corporation is organized. Par value bears no relationship to the fair market value of a share of stock (except that a corporation may not issue its stock for less than par value). Because of investor confusion about the significance of par value, most states now permit corporations to issue no-par-value stock. Some state laws permit a firm to assign a stated value to its no-par-value stock, in which case the stated value operates as a par value.

In Exhibit 2-3, the net income for the year of $18,000 added to retained earnings is the amount of net income reported in Exhibit 2-2. The retained earnings section of the statement of changes in owners' equity is where the link between the balance sheet and income statement is made. The expanded and modified time-line model appears on the following page.

The total owners' equity reported in Exhibit 2-3 equals the owners' equity shown on the balance sheet in Exhibit 2-1. Most balance sheets include the amount of common stock, additional paid-in capital, and retained earnings within the owners' equity section. Changes that occur in these owners' equity components are likely to be shown in a separate statement so that users of the financial statements can learn what caused these important balance sheet elements to change.

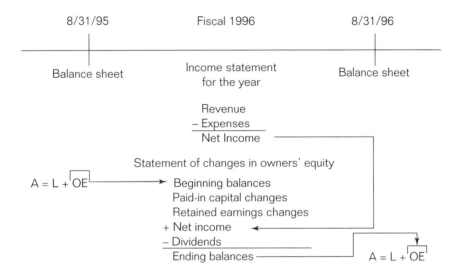

Statement of Cash Flows

The purpose of the **statement of cash flows** is to identify the sources and uses of cash during the year. This objective is accomplished by reporting the changes in all of the other balance sheet items. Because assets and liabilities plus owners' equity are equal, the total of the changes in every other asset and each liability and element of owners' equity will equal the change in cash. Chapter 10 will describe the statement of cash flows in detail. For now, understand the three principal activity groups that cause cash to change, and see how the amounts on this statement relate to the balance sheet in Exhibit 2-1.

Exhibit 2-4 illustrates the statement of cash flows for Main Street Store, Inc., for the year ending August 31, 1996. Notice that this statement, like the income statement and statement of changes in owners' equity, is *for a period of time*. Notice also the three activity categories: operating activities, investing activities, and financing activities.

Exhibit 2-4
Statement of Cash Flows

MAIN STREET STORE, INC.
Statement of Cash Flows
For the Year Ended August 31, 1996

Cash flows from operating activities:	
Net income	$ 18,000
Add (deduct) items not affecting cash:	
Depreciation expense	4,000
Increase in accounts receivable	(80,000)
Increase in merchandise inventory	(170,000)
Increase in current liabilities	67,000
Net cash used by operating activities	$(161,000)
Cash flows from investing activities:	
Cash paid for equipment	$ (40,000)
Cash flows from financing activities:	
Cash received from issue of long-term debt	$ 50,000
Cash received from sale of common stock	190,000
Payment of cash dividend on common stock	(5,000)
Net cash provided by financing activities	$ 235,000
Net increase in cash for the year	$ 34,000

Cash flows from operating activities are shown first, and net income is the starting point for this measure of cash generation. Using net income also directly relates the income statement (see Exhibit 2-2) to the statement of cash flows. Next, items that affected net income but that did not affect cash are considered.

Depreciation expense is added back to net income because even though it was deducted as an expense in determining net income, *depreciation expense did not require the use of cash*. As was mentioned earlier, depreciation in accounting is the process of spreading the cost of an asset over its estimated useful life.

The increase in accounts receivable is deducted because this increase reflects sales revenues, included in net income, that have not yet been collected in cash.

The increase in merchandise inventory is deducted because cash was spent to acquire the increase in inventory.

The increase in current liabilities is added because cash has not yet been paid for the products and services that have been received during the current fiscal period.

Cash flows from investing activities shows the cash used to purchase long-lived assets. The increase in equipment appears in the balance sheet (Exhibit 2-1), which shows the cost of the equipment owned on August 31, 1996. Since this is the first year of the firm's operations, the equipment purchase required the use of $40,000 during the year.

Cash flows from financing activities includes amounts raised from the sale of long-term debt and common stock, and dividends paid on common stock. Locate each of these financing amounts in the balance sheet (Exhibit 2-1) or the statement of changes in owners' equity (Exhibit 2-3). For example, the $190,000 received from the sale of stock is shown on the statement of changes in owners' equity (Exhibit 2-3) as the increase in paid-in capital during the year.

The net increase in cash for the year of $34,000 is the amount of cash in the August 31, 1996, balance sheet. The firm started in business during September 1995, so it had no cash to begin with.

The statement of cash flows results in a further expansion of the time-line model that can be seen in the diagram that follows:

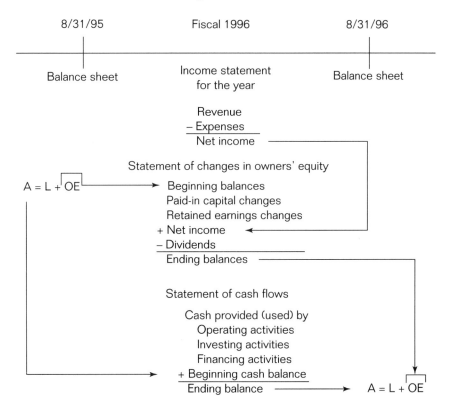

Comparative Statements in Subsequent Years

The financial statements presented for Main Street Store, Inc., show data as of August 31, 1996 and for the fiscal year that ended then. Because this was the first year of the firm's operations, comparative financial statements are not possible. In subsequent years, however, comparative statements for the current and prior year should be presented so that users of the data can more easily spot changes in the firm's financial position and in its results of operations. Some companies present data for two prior years in their financial statements. Most companies include selected data from their balance sheets and income statements for at least five years, and sometimes for up to twenty-five years, as supplementary information in their annual report to stockholders.

Illustration of Financial Statement Relationships

Exhibit 2-5 uses the financial statements of Main Street Store, Inc., to illustrate the financial statement relationships just discussed. Note that in Exhibit 2-5 amounts are shown in thousands of dollars, and that the August 31, 1995, balance sheet has no amounts. That is because Main Street Store, Inc., started business in September 1995. Net income for the year was an increase in retained earnings and is one of the reasons retained earnings changed during the year.

In subsequent chapters, the relationship between the balance sheet and income statement will be presented using the following diagram:

Balance sheet	Income statement
Assets = Liabilities + Owners' equity ←	Net income = Revenues – Expenses

The arrow from net income in the income statement to owners' equity in the balance sheet is to indicate that net income affects retained earnings, which is a component of owners' equity.

The following examples also illustrate the relationships within and between the principal financial statements. Using the August 31, 1996, Main Street Store, Inc., data for assets and liabilities in the balance sheet equation of A = L + OE, owners' equity at August 31, 1996, can be calculated as follows:

$$
\begin{aligned}
A &= L + OE \\
\$320 &= \$117 + OE \\
\$203 &= OE
\end{aligned}
$$

Another term for owners' equity is *net assets*. Owners' equity is shown clearly in the above calculation as the difference between assets and liabilities.

Exhibit 2-5
Financial Statement Relationships

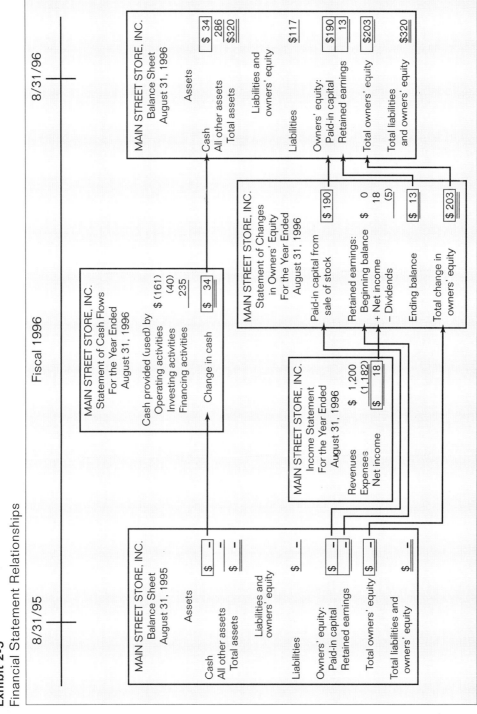

8/31/95   Fiscal 1996   8/31/96

MAIN STREET STORE, INC.
Balance Sheet
August 31, 1995

Assets

Cash	$ —
All other assets	—
Total assets	$ —

Liabilities and owners' equity

Liabilities	$ —

Owners' equity:

Paid-in capital	$ —
Retained earnings	—
Total owners' equity	$ —
Total liabilities and owners' equity	$ —

MAIN STREET STORE, INC.
Income Statement
For the Year Ended
August 31, 1996

Revenues	$ 1,200
Expenses	(1,182)
Net income	$ 18

MAIN STREET STORE, INC.
Statement of Cash Flows
For the Year Ended
August 31, 1996

Cash provided (used) by

Operating activities	$ (161)
Investing activities	(40)
Financing activities	235
Change in cash	$ 34

MAIN STREET STORE, INC.
Statement of Changes
in Owners' Equity
For the Year Ended
August 31, 1996

Paid-in capital from sale of stock	$ 190

Retained earnings:

Beginning balance	$ 0
+ Net income	18
– Dividends	(5)
Ending balance	$ 13
Total change in owners' equity	$ 203

MAIN STREET STORE, INC.
Balance Sheet
August 31, 1996

Assets

Cash	$ 34
All other assets	286
Total assets	$320

Liabilities and owners' equity

Liabilities	$117

Owners' equity:

Paid-in capital	$190
Retained earnings	13
Total owners' equity	$203
Total liabilities and owners' equity	$320

Now suppose that during the year ending August 31, 1997, total assets increase $10, and total liabilities decrease $3. What was owners' equity at the end of the year? There are two ways of solving the problem. First, focus on the changes in the elements of the balance sheet equation:

$$A = L + OE$$

Change: $+10 = -3 + ?$

For the equation to stay in balance, owners' equity must have increased $13. Since owners' equity was $203 at the beginning of the year, it must have been $216 at the end of the year.

The second approach to solving the problem is to calculate the amount of assets and liabilities at the end of the year and then to solve for owners' equity at the end of the year, as follows:

	A	=	L	+ OE
Beginning:	320	=	117	+ 203
Change:	+ 10	=	− 3	+ ?
Ending:	330	=	114	+ ?

The ending owners' equity or net assets is $330 − $114 = $216. And since ending owners' equity is $216, it increased $13 from August 31, 1996, to August 31, 1997.

Assume that during the year ending August 31, 1997, the owners invested an additional $8 in the firm and that dividends (payments to the owners of the business for the risk that they have taken by investing money, also referred to as paid-in capital, in Main Street) of $6 were declared. How much net income did the firm have for the year ending August 31, 1997? Recall that net income is one of the items that affects the retained earnings component of owners' equity. Dividends also affect retained earnings. Since owners' equity increased from $203 to $216 during the year, and since the items causing that change were net income, dividends, and the additional investment by the owners, the amount of net income can be calculated as follows:

Owners' equity, beginning of year	$203
Increase in paid-in capital from additional investment by owners	8
Net income	?
Dividends	− 6
Owners' equity, end of year	$216

Solving for the unknown, net income is equal to $11.

An alternative solution to determine net income for the year involves focusing on just the *changes* in owners' equity during the year, as follows:

Increase in paid-in capital from additional investment by owners	$ 8
Net income	?
Dividends	– 6
Change in owners' equity for the year	$13

Again, solving for the unknown, net income is equal to $11.

The important points to remember are the following:

1. The balance sheet shows the amount of assets, liabilities, and owners' equity at a point in time.
2. The balance sheet equation must always be in balance.
3. The income statement shows net income for a period of time.
4. The retained earnings component of owners' equity changes over time as a result of the firm's net income (or loss) and dividends for that period of time.

Accounting Concepts and Principles

In order to understand the kinds of decisions and informed judgments that can be made from the financial statements, you need to understand some of the broad concepts and principles of accounting that have become generally accepted for financial accounting and reporting purposes. Some of these ideas relate directly to the financial accounting concepts introduced in Chapter 1, and others relate to the broader notion of generally accepted accounting principles. Again, you should recognize that these concepts and principles are more like practices that have been generally agreed upon over a period of time than rules or laws such as those encountered in the physical sciences.

These concepts and principles can be related to the basic model of the flow of data from transactions to financial statements illustrated earlier, as shown in the accounting entity illustration in the next section.

Concepts and Principles Related to the Entire Model

The basic accounting equation described earlier in this chapter is the mechanical key to the entire financial accounting process because the equation must be in balance after every transaction has been recorded in the accounting records. Chapter 4 will describe the method for recording transactions and maintaining this balance.

Accounting entity refers to the entity for which the financial statements are being prepared. The entity can be a proprietorship, a partnership, a corporation, or even a group of corporations (see Business Procedure Capsule 4—Parent and Subsidiary Corporations). The accountant defines the entity for which the accounting is being done, and even though the entities may be related (for example, an individual and the business he or she owns), the accounting is done for the defined entity.

- **BUSINESS PROCEDURE CAPSULE 4**
  Parent and Subsidiary Corporations

New corporations that want to expand their operations can form a separate corporation to carry out their plans. In such a case, the original corporation owns all of the stock of the new corporation; it has become the "parent" of a "**subsidiary**." One parent may have several subsidiaries, and the subsidiaries themselves may be parents of subsidiaries. The parent does not need to own 100 percent of the stock of another corporation for the parent-subsidiary relationship to exist. If one corporation owns more than half of the stock of another, the majority owner can presumably exercise enough control to create a parent-subsidiary relationship. When a subsidiary is not wholly owned, the other stockholders of the subsidiary are referred to as *minority* stockholders.

In most instances, the financial statements issued by the parent corporation include the assets, liabilities, owners' equity, revenues, expenses, and gains and losses of the subsidiaries. Financial statements that reflect the financial position, results of operations, and cash flows of a parent and one or more subsidiaries are called *consolidated financial statements*.

The **going concern concept** refers to the assumption that the entity will continue to operate in the future—or that future liquidation will not be necessary. This continuity assumption is necessary because the amounts shown on the balance sheet for various assets do not reflect the liquidation value of those assets.

The diagram on the next page expands on the diagram provided earlier in the chapter by identifying those accounting principles that apply to transactions, bookkeeping, or financial statements in the following sections.

Concepts and Principles Related to Transactions

In the United States, the dollar is the *unit of measurement* for all transactions. No adjustment is made for changes in the purchasing power of the dollar. No attempt is made to reflect qualitative economic factors in the measurement of transactions.

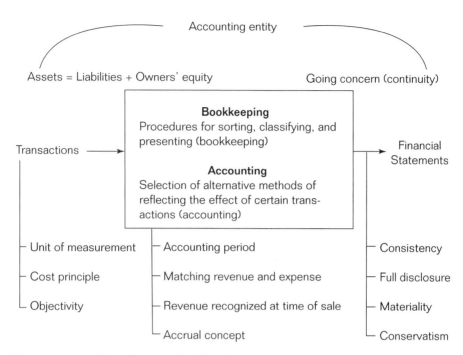

The *cost principle* refers to the fact that transactions are recorded at their original cost to the entity as measured in dollars. For example, if a parcel of land were purchased by a firm for $8,600 even though an appraisal showed the land to be worth $10,000, the purchase transaction would be reflected in the accounting records, and the financial statements would report the land at its cost of $8,600. If the land is still owned and being used fifteen years later, it would continue to be reported in the balance sheet at its original cost of $8,600, even if it had increased in value to $80,000.

Objectivity refers to accountants' desire to have a given transaction recorded in the same way in all situations. This objective is facilitated by using the dollar as the unit of measurement and by applying the cost principle. However, as previously stressed, for some transactions, the exercise of professional judgment could result in alternative recording results. Subsequent chapters will describe these alternatives.

Concepts and Principles Related to Bookkeeping Procedures and the Accounting Process

These concepts and principles relate to the *accounting period*, that is, the period of time selected for reporting results of operations and changes in financial position. Financial position will be reported at the end of this period of time (and the balance sheet at the beginning of the period will probably be included with the financial statements). For most entities, the accounting period is one year.

Matching revenue and expense is necessary if the results of the firm's operations are to reflect accurately its economic activities during the period. The **matching concept** does not mean that revenues and expenses for a period are equal. Revenue is not earned without effort, and expenses are the measure of the economic efforts exerted to generate revenues. A fair presentation of the results of a firm's operations during a period of time requires that all expenses incurred in generating that period's revenues be deducted from the revenues earned. This results in an accurate measure of the net income or net loss for the period. This seems like common sense, but there are alternative methods of determining some of the expenses to be recognized in any given period. This concept of matching revenue and expense is very important and will be referred to repeatedly as accounting practices are discussed in the following chapters.

Revenue is recognized at the time of sale, which is when title to the product being sold passes from the seller to the buyer, or when the services involved in the transaction have been performed. Passing of legal ownership (title) is the crucial event for accounting purposes, not the cash payment from buyer to seller.

Accrual accounting recognizes revenue at the point of sale and recognizes expenses as they are incurred, even though the cash receipt or payment occurs at another time or in another accounting period. Thus, many activities of the firm involve two transactions: one that recognizes the revenue or expense, and another that reflects the receipt or payment of cash. The use of accrual procedures accomplishes much of the matching of revenues and expenses because most transactions between business firms (and between many firms and individuals) involve purchase/sale at one point in time and cash payment/receipt at some other time.

Financial statement users rely on the concepts and principles related to the accounting period when making judgments and informed decisions about an entity's financial position and results of operations.

Concepts and Principles Related to Financial Statements

Consistency in financial reporting is essential if meaningful trend comparisons are to be made using an entity's financial statements for several years. Thus, an entity should not change from one generally accepted accounting alternative for a particular type of transaction to another generally accepted method, unless both (1) that the change has been made and (2) the effect of the change on the financial statements are explicitly described in the financial statements or the accompanying notes and explanations.

Full disclosure means that the financial statements and notes or explanations should include all necessary information to prevent a reasonably astute user of the financial statements from being misled. The Securities and Exchange Commission has helped to define this standard over the years. This requirement for full disclosure is one reason that the notes and explanations are usually considered to be an integral part of the financial statements.

Materiality means that absolute exactness, even if that idea could be defined, is not necessary in the amounts shown in the financial statements. Because of the numerous estimates involved in accounting, amounts reported in financial statements may be approximate, but they will not be "wrong" enough to be misleading. The financial statements of publicly owned corporations usually show amounts rounded to the nearest thousand, hundred thousand, or even million dollars. This rounding does not impair the information content of the financial statements and probably makes them easier to read. A management concept related to materiality is the cost-benefit relationship. Just as a manager would not spend $500 to get $300 worth of information, the incremental benefit of increased accuracy in accounting estimates is frequently not worth the cost of achieving the increased accuracy.

Conservatism in accounting relates to making judgments and estimates that result in lower profits and asset valuation estimates rather than higher profits and asset valuation estimates. Accountants try to avoid wishful thinking or unrealistic estimates that could result in overstating profits for a current period. They seek to be realistic, but are conservative when in doubt.

Limitations of Financial Statements

Financial statements report quantitative economic data; they do not reflect qualitative economic variables. For example, the value to the firm of its management team or of workforce morale is not included as a balance sheet asset because it cannot be objectively measured. Such qualitative attributes of the firm are frequently relevant to the decisions and informed judgments that the financial statement user is making, but they are not communicated in the financial statements.

As already emphasized, the cost principle requires assets to be recorded at their original cost. The balance sheet does not show the current market value or the replacement cost of the assets. Some assets are reported at the lower of their cost or market value, and in some cases market value may be reported parenthetically, but asset values are not increased to reflect current value. For example, the trademark of a firm has virtually no cost; its value has developed over the years as the firm has met customers' needs. Thus, trademarks are usually excluded from the balance sheet listing of assets.

Estimates are used in many areas of accounting, and when the estimate is made, about the only fact known is that the estimate is probably not equal to the "true" amount. Nevertheless, the estimate usually is near the "true" amount (the concept of materiality). For example, recognizing depreciation expense involves estimating both the useful life to the entity of the asset being depreciated and the probable salvage value of the asset to the entity when it is disposed of. The original cost minus the salvage value is the amount to be depreciated or recognized as expense over the asset's life. Estimates must also be made to determine pension expense, warranty costs, and numerous other expense and revenue items to be reflected in the current year's income statement because they reflect the economic activity of the current year. These estimates also affect balance sheet accounts. Even though the balance sheet balances to the penny, do not be misled by this aura of exactness. Accountants do their best to make their estimates as accurate as possible, but estimates are still estimates.

The principle of consistency suggests that an entity should not change from one generally accepted method of accounting for a particular item to another generally accepted method of accounting for the same item. However, two firms operating in the same industry may follow different methods. This means that *comparability* between firms may not be appropriate, or if comparisons are made, that the effects of any differences between the accounting methods followed by the firms must be understood.

Related to the use of the original cost principle is the fact that financial statements are not adjusted to show the effect of inflation. Land acquired by a firm fifty years ago is still reported at its original cost, even though it may have a significantly higher current value because of inflation. Likewise, depreciation expense and the cost of goods sold, both significant expense elements of the income statement of many firms, reflect original cost, not replacement cost. This weakness is not significant when the rate of inflation is low, but the usefulness of financial statements is seriously impaired when the inflation rate rises to double digits. In 1980, the FASB began to require that large, publicly owned companies report certain data to show some of the effects of changing prices as supplementary information in the footnotes to the financial statements. In 1986, the FASB discontinued the requirement that this information be presented, but it encouraged further supplementary disclosures of the effects of inflation and changes in specific prices. This is a very controversial issue that will become more important if the rate of inflation rises significantly in the future.

Financial statements do not reflect **opportunity cost**, which is an economic concept relating to income not earned because an opportunity to earn income was not pursued. For example, if an individual or organization maintains a checking account balance that is $300 more than that required to avoid any service charges, the opportunity cost associated with that $300 is the interest that could otherwise be earned on the money if it had been invested. Financial accounting does not give formal recognition to opportunity cost; however, financial managers should be aware of the concept as they plan the use of the firm's resources.

The Corporation's Annual Report

The annual report is the document distributed to shareholders that contains the reporting firm's financial statements for the fiscal year, together with the report of the external auditor's examination of the financial statements. The annual report document can be as simple as a transmittal letter from the president or chairman of the board of directors along with the financial statements, or as fancy as a glossy, 100-page booklet that showcases the firm's products, services, and personnel, as well as its financial results.

In addition to the financial statements described above and the explanatory comments (or footnotes or financial review) described more fully in Chapter 12, some other financial data are usually included in the annual report. Highlights for the year, including total revenues and net income, net income per share of common stock outstanding, and dividends paid during the year, appear inside the front cover or on the first page of the report. Most firms also include a historical summary of certain financial data for at least the past five years. This summary is usually located near the back of the annual report.

In the Appendix at the back of the companion workbook to this text is a copy of the financial information from the 1994 Annual Report of Armstrong World Industries, Inc. These financial statements are the product of the financial reporting process. Subsequent chapters will examine many of the specific elements of these financial statements.

Summary

Financial statements are used to communicate economic information for decisions and informed judgments.

The bookkeeping and accounting processes result in an entity's numerous transactions with other entities being reflected in the financial statements. The financial statements presented by an entity are the balance sheet, income statement, statement of changes in owners' equity, and statement of cash flows.

The balance sheet is a listing of the entity's assets, liabilities, and owners' equity at a point in time. Assets are probable future economic benefits (things or claims against others) controlled by the entity. Liabilities are amounts owed by the entity. An entity's owners' equity is the difference between its assets and liabilities. This relationship is known as the accounting equation. Current assets are cash and assets likely to be converted to cash or used to benefit the entity within one year of the balance sheet date, such as accounts receivable and inventories. Current liabilities are expected to be paid within one year of the balance sheet date. The balance sheet as of the end of a fiscal period is also the balance sheet as of the beginning of the next fiscal period.

The income statement reports the results of the entity's operating activities for a period of time. Revenues are reported first, and costs and expenses are subtracted to arrive at net income or net loss for the period.

The statement of changes in owners' equity describes changes in paid-in capital and retained earnings during the period. Retained earnings are increased by the amount of net income and decreased by dividends paid to stockholders (and by any net loss for the period). Through retained earnings, the income statement is linked to the balance sheet.

The statement of cash flows summarizes the effect on cash of the entity's operating activities, investing activities, and financing activities during the period. The bottom line of this financial statement is the change in cash from the amount shown in the balance sheet at the beginning of the period to that shown in the balance sheet at the end of the period.

Financial statements are usually presented on a comparative basis so that users can easily spot significant changes in an entity's financial position (balance sheet) and results of operations (income statement).

The financial statements are interrelated. Net income for the period (from the income statement) is added to retained earnings, a part of owners' equity (in the balance sheet). The statement of changes in owners' equity explains the difference between the amounts of owners' equity at the beginning and the end of the fiscal period. The statement of cash flows explains the change in the amount of cash from the beginning to the end of the fiscal period.

Accounting concepts and principles reflect generally accepted practices that have evolved over time. They can be related to a schematic model of the flow of data from transactions to the financial statements. Pertaining to the entire model are the accounting entity concept, the accounting equation, and the going concern concept.

Transactions are recorded in currency units without regard to purchasing power change. Thus, transactions are recorded at an objectively determinable original cost amount.

The concepts and principles for the accounting period involve recognizing revenue when a sale of a product or service is made and then relating to that revenue all of the costs and expenses incurred in generating the revenue of the period. This matching of revenues and expenses is a fundamental concept to understand if accounting itself is to be understood. The accrual concept is used to implement the matching concept by recognizing revenues when earned and expenses when incurred, regardless of whether cash is received or paid in the same fiscal period.

The concepts of consistency, full disclosure, materiality, and conservatism relate primarily to financial statement presentation.

The information presented in financial statements is limited. These limitations are related to the concepts and principles that have become generally accepted. Thus, subjective qualitative factors, current values, the effect of inflation, and opportunity cost are not usually reflected in financial statements. In addition, many financial statement amounts involve estimates. Permissible alternative accounting practices may mean that interfirm comparisons are not appropriate.

Corporations and other organizations include financial statements in an annual report made available to stockholders, employees, potential investors, and others interested in the entity. Refer to the financial statements on pages 25 to 27 of the Armstrong World Industries, Inc., annual report in the Appendix of the workbook and to the financial statements of other annual reports you have to see how the material discussed in this chapter is applied to real companies.

Key Words and Phrases

account (p. 38) A record in which transactions affecting individual assets, liabilities, owners' equities, revenues, and expenses are recorded.

account payable (p. 39) A liability representing an amount payable to another entity, usually because of the purchase of merchandise or service on credit.

account receivable (p. 38) An asset representing a claim against another entity, usually arising from selling goods or services on credit.

accounting equation (p. 37) Assets = Liabilities + Owners' equity (A = L + OE). The fundamental relationship represented by the balance sheet, and the foundation of the bookkeeping process.

accrual accounting (p. 54) Accounting that recognizes revenues and expenses as they occur, even though the cash receipt from the revenue or the cash disbursement related to the expense may occur before or after the event that causes revenue or expense recognition.

accrued liabilities (p. 39) Amounts that are owed by an entity on the balance sheet date.

accumulated depreciation (p. 39) The sum of the depreciation expense that has been recognized over time. Accumulated depreciation is a contra asset that is subtracted from the cost of the related asset on the balance sheet. (Contra assets are defined in Chapter 6.)

additional paid-in capital (p. 44) The excess of the amount received from the sale of stock over the par value of the shares sold.

assets (p. 37) Probable future economic benefits obtained or controlled by an entity as a result of past transactions or events.

balance sheet (p. 35) The financial statement that is a listing of the entity's assets, liabilities, and owners' equity at a point in time. Sometimes this statement is called the *statement of financial position*.

balance sheet equation (p. 37) Another term for the *accounting equation*.

captions (p. 34) Explanatory or identifying comments describing accounting items reported in a financial statement.

cash (p. 38) An asset on the balance sheet that represents the amount of cash on hand and balances in bank accounts maintained by the entity.

common stock (p. 44) The class of stock that represents residual ownership of the corporation.

corporation (p. 36) A form of organization in which ownership is evidenced by shares of stock owned by stockholders; its features (for example, limited liability) make this the principal form of organization for most business activity.

cost of goods sold (p. 41) Cost of merchandise sold during the period; an expense deducted from net sales to arrive at gross profit.

current assets (p. 39) Cash and assets that are likely to be converted to cash or used to benefit the entity within one year of the balance sheet date.

current liabilities (p. 39) Liabilities due to be paid within one year of the balance sheet date.

depreciation (p. 39) The accounting process of recognizing that the cost of an asset is used up over its useful life to the entity.

depreciation expense (p. 46) The expense recognized in a fiscal period for the depreciation of an asset.

dividend (p. 44) A distribution of earnings to the owners of a corporation.

earnings from operations (p. 42) The difference between gross profit and operating expenses. Also referred to as *operating income*.

equity (p. 38) The ownership right associated with an asset. See *owners' equity*.

expenses (p. 40) Outflows or other using up of assets or incurrences of liabilities during a period from delivering or producing goods, rendering services, or carrying out other activities that constitute the entity's major operations.

fiscal year (p. 36) The annual period used for reporting financial results to owners and other interested parties.

gains (p. 40) Increases in net assets from incidental transactions and other events affecting an entity during a period, except those that result from revenues or investments by owners.

going concern concept (p. 52) A presumption that the entity will continue in existence for the indefinite future.

gross profit (p. 41) The difference between net sales and cost of goods sold. Sometimes called *gross margin*.

income statement (p. 40) The financial statement that summarizes the entity's revenues, expenses, gains, and losses for a period of time and reports the entity's results of operations for that period of time.

liabilities (p. 38) Probable future sacrifices of economic benefits arising from present obligations of a particular entity to transfer assets or provide services to other entities in the future as a result of past transactions or events.

losses (p. 40) Decreases in net assets from incidental transactions and other events affecting an entity during a period, except those that result from expenses or distributions to owners.

matching concept (p. 54) Results in a fair presentation of the results of a firm's operations during a period by requiring the deduction of all expenses incurred in generating that period's revenues from the revenues earned in the period.

merchandise inventory (p. 39) Items held by an entity for sale to potential customers in the normal course of business.

net assets (p. 39) The difference between assets and liabilities; also referred to as *owners' equity*.

net income (p. 40) The excess of revenues and gains over expenses and losses for a fiscal period.

net income per share of common stock outstanding (p. 42) Net income available to the common stockholders divided by the average number of shares of common stock outstanding during the period. Usually referred to as *earnings per share*.

net sales (p. 40) Gross sales less sales discounts and sales returns and allowances.

net worth (p. 38) Another term for *net assets* or *owners' equity*, but not as appropriate because the term *worth* may be misleading.

opportunity cost (p. 57) An economic concept relating to income forgone because an opportunity to earn income was not pursued.

owners' equity (p. 38) The equity of the entity's owners in the assets of the entity. Sometimes called *net assets*; the difference between assets and liabilities.

paid-in capital (p. 43) The amount invested in the entity by the owners.

par value (p. 43) An arbitrary value assigned to a share of stock when the corporation is organized. This term is sometimes used to describe the stated value or face amount of a share of stock.

partnership (p. 36) A form of organization indicating ownership by two or more individuals or corporations without the limited liability and other features of a corporation.

profit (p. 40) The excess of revenues and gains over expenses and losses for a fiscal period; another term for *net income*.

profit and loss statement (p. 40) Another term for the *income statement*.

proprietorship (p. 35) A form of organization indicating individual ownership without the limited liability and other features of a corporation.

retained earnings (p. 43) Cumulative net income that has not been distributed to the owners of a corporation as dividends.

revenues (p. 40) Inflows of cash or increases in other assets, or settlement of liabilities during a period, as a result of delivering or producing goods, rendering services, or performing other activities that constitute the entity's major operations.

statement of cash flows (p. 45) The financial statement that explains why cash changed during a fiscal period. Cash flows from operating, investing, and financing activities are shown in the statement.

statement of changes in capital stock (p. 43) The financial statement that summarizes changes during a fiscal period in capital stock and additional paid-in capital. This information may be included in the statement of changes in owners' equity.

statement of changes in owners' equity (p. 43) The financial statement that summarizes the changes during a fiscal period in capital stock, additional paid-in capital, retained earnings, and other elements of owners' equity.

statement of changes in retained earnings (p. 43) The financial statement that summarizes the changes during a fiscal period in retained earnings. This information may be included in the statement of changes in owners' equity.

statement of earnings (p. 40) Another term for the *income statement*; it shows the revenues, expenses, gains, and losses for a period of time and the entity's results of operations for that period of time.

statement of financial position (p. 35) Another term for the *balance sheet*; a listing of the entity's assets, liabilities, and owners' equity at a point in time.

statement of operations (p. 40) Another term for the *income statement.*

stock (p. 36) The evidence of ownership of a corporation.

stockholders (p. 36) The owners of a corporation's stock; sometimes called *shareholders.*

subsidiary (p. 52) A corporation whose stock is more than 50 percent owned by another corporation.

transactions (p. 33) Economic interchanges between entities that are accounted for and reflected in financial statements.

Chapter Notes

1. U.S. Department of Commerce, Bureau of Census, *Statistical Abstract of the United States*, 1996, Table No. 827.

2. FASB, *Statement of Financial Accounting Concepts No. 6*, "Elements of Financial Statements," para. 25.

3. FASB, para. 35.

Chapter 3

Interpreting Basic Financial Statements

Chapter 2 presented an overview of the financial statements that result from the financial accounting process. This chapter previews some of the interpretations made by financial statement users to support their decisions and informed judgments. Understanding the uses of accounting information will make its development more meaningful. Current and potential stockholders want to make their own assessments about management's stewardship of the resources made available by the owners. For example, judgments about profitability affect investment decisions. Creditors assess the entity's ability to repay loans and pay for products and services. Insurance producers and underwriters are similarly concerned about the entity's ability to cover its financial obligations. An entity experiencing liquidity or cash flow problems might later look for quick cash relief as it seeks recovery for a building loss caused by arson or theft of nonexistent business property.

Assessments by creditors and insurance professionals about the profitability and debt-paying ability of an entity involve interpreting the relationships among amounts reported in the entity's financial statements. Subsequent chapters will examine most of these relationships. They are introduced here to illustrate how management's financial objectives for the firm are quantified so that you may begin to understand what the numbers mean. Likewise, these concepts will prepare you to understand the effects of alternative accounting methods on financial statements when those accounting alternatives are explained in subsequent chapters.

This chapter introduces some basic financial statement analysis concepts. Chapter 14 provides a comprehensive explanation of how to use financial statement data to analyze an entity's financial condition and results of operations. You will better understand topics in that chapter after you have studied the financial accounting material in Chapters 6 through 10 for noninsurance entities and in Chapter 11 for insurance entities.

Educational Objectives

After studying this chapter, you should be able to:

1. Explain why financial statement ratios are important.
2. Explain how ratio trends can be used most effectively.
3. Explain the significance of the return on investment, and show how it is calculated.
4. Show how the DuPont Model is an expansion of the basic return on investment calculation, and explain the terms *margin* and *turnover*.
5. Explain the significance of the return on equity, and show how it is calculated.
6. Define liquidity, and explain why it is so important.
7. Explain the significance of and calculate the three measures of liquidity: working capital, current ratio, and acid-test ratio.
8. Explain why an entity's liquidity and profitability are important to an insurance professional who is assessing the entity's desirability as a potential insured.
9. Define or describe each of the Key Words and Phrases introduced in this chapter.

Financial Ratios and Trend Analysis

The large dollar amounts reported on the financial statements of many companies and the varying size of companies make ratio analysis the only sensible method of evaluating various financial characteristics of a company. Students are frequently awed by the number of ratio measurements commonly used in financial management and are sometimes intimidated by the prospect of calculating a ratio. But a ratio is simply the relationship between two numbers. In addition, the name of virtually every financial ratio describes the numbers to be related and usually how the ratio is calculated. As you study this material, concentrate on understanding why the ratio is considered to be important, and try to understand the meaning of the ratio. If you do these things, you should avoid much of the stress associated with understanding financial ratios.

In most cases, a single ratio does not describe very much about the company whose statements are being studied. **Trend analysis** can provide much more meaningful information by examining the *trend* of a particular ratio over several time periods. Of course, consistency in financial reporting and in defining the ratio components is crucial if the trend is to be meaningful.

Most industry and trade associations publish industry average ratios based on aggregated data compiled by the association from reports submitted by association members. Comparison of an individual company's ratio with the comparable industry ratio is frequently made as a means of assessing a company's relative standing in its industry. However, comparison of a single observation for a company with that of the industry may not be very meaningful because that company may use a financial accounting alternative that is different from that used by the rest of the industry. Trend analysis results in a much more meaningful comparison because even though the data used in the ratio may have been developed under different financial accounting alternatives, internal consistency within each of the trends will permit useful trend comparisons.

Trend analysis is described later in this chapter, but a brief example now will illustrate the process. Suppose that a student's grade point average for last semester was 2.8 on a 4.0 scale. That GPA by itself says little about the student's work. However, suppose you learn that this student's GPA was 1.9 four semesters ago, 2.3 three semesters ago, and 2.6 two semesters ago. The upward trend of grades suggests that the student's overall performance is improving. This conclusion would be reinforced if you knew that the average GPA for all students in this student's class was 2.6 for each of the four semesters. You still do not know everything about the individual student's academic performance, but the comparative trend data allow you to make a more informed judgment than was possible with just the grades from one semester.

Return on Investment

Imagine that you are presented with two investment alternatives. Each investment will be made for a period of one year, and each investment is equally risky. At the end of the year you will get your original investment back, plus income of $75 from investment A and $90 from investment B. Which investment alternative would you choose? The answer seems so obvious that you believe the question might be misleading, so you hesitate to answer. But why is this a trick question? A little thought should make you think of a question to which you need an answer before you can select between investment A and investment B: "How much money would I have to invest in either alternative?" If the amount to be invested is the same, for example, $1,000, then clearly you would select investment B because your income would be greater than that earned on investment A for the same amount invested. If the amount to be invested in investment B is more than that required for investment A, you would have to calculate the rate of return on each investment in order to choose the more profitable alternative.

Rate of return is calculated by dividing the amount of return (the income of $75 or $90 in the above example) by the amount of the investment. For example, using an investment of $1,000 for each alternative yields the following rates of return:

Investment A:

$$\text{Rate of return} = \frac{\text{Amount of return}}{\text{Amount invested}} = \frac{\$75}{\$1,000} = 7.5\%$$

Investment B:

$$\text{Rate of return} = \frac{\text{Amount of return}}{\text{Amount invested}} = \frac{\$90}{\$1,000} = 9\%$$

Investment B is the better investment because its rate of return is higher than that of investment A.

This example assumed the investments would be made for one year. Unless otherwise specified, rate of return calculations assume that the time period of the investment and return is one year.

The rate of return calculation is derived from the following equation:

$$\text{Interest} = \text{Principal} \times \text{Rate} \times \text{Time}$$

Interest is the income or expense from investing or borrowing money. **Principal** is the amount invested or borrowed. Rate is the **interest rate** per year expressed as a percentage. Time is the length of time the funds are invested or borrowed, expressed in years.

When time is assumed to be one year, that term of the equation using years becomes 1/1, or 1, and it disappears. Thus, the rate of return calculation is simply a rearranged interest calculation that solves for the annual interest rate.

Assume that the amounts required to be invested are $500 for investment A and $600 for investment B. The following calculations indicate that with differing amounts of investment, the rate of return for the two investments might be the same:

Investment A:

$$\text{Rate of return} = \frac{\text{Amount of return}}{\text{Amount invested}} = \frac{\$75}{\$500} = 15\%$$

Investment B:

$$\text{Rate of return} = \frac{\text{Amount of return}}{\text{Amount invested}} = \frac{\$90}{\$600} = 15\%$$

All other things being equal (and they seldom are except in textbook illustrations), you would be indifferent with respect to the alternatives available to you, because each has a rate of return of 15 percent (per year).

The expected rate of return and risk related to an investment are directly related. **Risk** relates to the range of possible outcomes from an activity. The wider the range of possible outcomes is, the greater the risk. An investment in a bank savings account is less risky than an investment in the stock of a corporation because investors are virtually assured of receiving their principal and interest from the savings account, but the market value of stock may fluctuate widely even over a short period of time. Thus, investors anticipate a higher rate of return from the stock investment than from the savings account as compensation for taking on additional risk. Yet the greater risk of the stock investment means that the actual rate of return earned could be considerably less (even negative) or much greater than the interest earned on the savings account. Market prices for products and commodities, as well as stock prices, reflect this basic risk/reward relationship. The higher the rate of return of one investment is relative to another, the greater the risk associated with the higher return investment.

Rate of return is a universally accepted measure of profitability. Because rate of return is a ratio, unequal investments can be compared, and risk/reward relationships can be evaluated. Bank advertisements for certificates of deposit feature the interest rate, or rate of return, that depositors will earn. Investors evaluate the profitability of an investment by making a rate of return calculation.

Return on investment (ROI), or return on assets (ROA), is the label usually assigned to the rate of return calculation made using data from financial statements. There are many ways of defining both the amount of return and the amount invested. For now, this text will use net income as the amount of return and average total assets during the year as the amount invested. Using total assets as reported on a single year-end balance sheet is not appropriate because that is the total at one point in time—the balance sheet date. Net income was earned during the entire fiscal year, so it should be related to the assets that were used during the entire year. Average assets used during the year are usually estimated by averaging the assets reported at the beginning of the year (the prior year-end balance sheet total) and assets reported at the end of the year. Recall from Chapter 2 that the income statement for the year is the link between the beginning and ending balance sheets. If seasonal fluctuations in total assets are significant (the materiality concept) and if quarter-end or month-end balance sheets are available, a more refined average asset calculation may be made.

The ROI of a firm is significant to most financial statement readers because it describes the rate of return management earned on the assets that it had available to use during the year. Investors make decisions and informed judgments about the quality of management and the relative profitability of a company based on its ROI. Many financial analysts believe that ROI is the most meaningful measure of a company's profitability. Knowing net income alone is not enough to adequately measure profitability. *An informed judgment about the firm's profitability requires relating net income to the assets used to generate that net income.*

Calculation of ROI is illustrated below, using data from the condensed balance sheets and income statement of Cruisers, Inc. (a hypothetical company), which are presented in Exhibit 3-1:

From the firm's balance sheets:

Total assets, September 30, 1995	$364,720
Total assets, September 30, 1996	$402,654

From the firm's income statement:
for the year ended September 30, 1996

Net income	$32,936

$$\text{Return on investment} = \frac{\text{Net income}}{\text{Average total assets}}$$

$$= \frac{\$32,936}{\dfrac{(\$364,720 + \$402,654)}{2}} = 8.6\%$$

Some financial analysts prefer to use operating income (or earnings before interest and income taxes) and average operating assets in the ROI calculation. They believe that excluding interest expense, income taxes, and assets not used in operations provides a better measure of the operating results of the firm. Other analysts make similar adjustments to arrive at the amounts used in the ROI calculation. Consistency in the definition of terms is more important than the definition itself because the trend of ROI will be more significant for decision making than the absolute result of any one year. However, you should understand the definitions used in any ROI results that you see.

Exhibit 3-1
Condensed Balance Sheets and Income Statement of Cruisers, Inc.

	CRUISERS, INC. Comparative Condensed Balance Sheets September 30, 1996 and 1995			CRUISERS, INC. Condensed Income Statement For the Year Ended September 30, 1996
	1996	*1995*		*1996*
Current assets:			Net sales	$611,873
Cash and marketable			Cost of goods sold	428,354
securities	$ 22,286	$ 16,996	Gross margin	$183,519
Accounts receivable	42,317	39,620	Operating expenses	122,183
Inventories	53,716	48,201	Earnings before interest	
Total current			and taxes	$ 61,336
assets	$118,319	$104,817	Interest expense	6,400
Other assets	284,335	259,903	Earnings before taxes	$ 54,936
Total assets	$402,654	$364,720	Income taxes	22,000
			Net income	$ 32,936
Current liabilities	$ 57,424	$ 51,400	Earnings per share	$ 1.21
Other liabilities	80,000	83,000		
Total liabilities	$137,424	$134,400		
Owners' equity	265,230	230,320		
Total liabilities and				
owners' equity	$402,654	$364,720		

The DuPont Model, an Expansion of the ROI Calculation

Financial analysts at E. I. DuPont de Nemours & Co. are credited with developing the **DuPont Model,** an expansion of the basic ROI calculation, in the late 1930s. They reasoned that profitability from sales and the use of assets to generate sales revenue were both important factors to be considered when evaluating a company's overall profitability. One popular adaptation of their model introduces total sales revenue into the ROI calculation as follows:

$$\text{Return on investment} = \frac{\text{Net income}}{\text{Sales}} \times \frac{\text{Sales}}{\text{Average total assets}}$$

The first term, net income/sales, is **margin.** The second term, sales/average total assets, is **asset turnover,** or simply **turnover.** Of course, the sales quantities cancel out algebraically, but they are introduced to this version of the ROI model because of their significance. *Margin* emphasizes that from every dollar of sales revenue, some amount must work its way to the bottom line, net income, if the company is to be profitable. *Turnover* relates to the efficiency with which the firm's assets are used in the revenue-generating process.

The following example illustrates the significance of turnover. Most of us look forward to working forty hours per week, generally thought of as five eight-hour days. Imagine if a company's factory were to operate on such a schedule—one shift per day, five days per week. For what percentage of the available time is that factory operating? You may have answered 33 percent or one-third of the time, because eight hours make up one-third of a day. But what about Saturday and Sunday? In fact, there are twenty-one shifts available in a week (7 days × 3 shifts per day), so a factory operating five shifts per week is only being used 5/21 of the time—less than 25 percent. The factory is idle more than 75 percent of the time. Many of the occupancy costs (such as real estate taxes, utilities, and insurance) are incurred whether or not the plant is in use. This problem of covering occupancy costs explains why many firms operate their plant on a two-shift, three-shift, or even seven-day basis rather than build additional plants. The higher costs associated with multiple-shift operations (for example, late-shift premiums for workers and additional shipping costs relative to shipping from multiple locations closer to customers) increase the company's operating expenses, thereby lowering net income and decreasing margin. However, the multiple-shift company's overall ROI will be higher if turnover (for this example, sales compared to investment in the factory) is increased proportionately more than margin is reduced.

Calculation of ROI using the DuPont Model is illustrated below, using data from the financial statements of Cruisers, Inc., in Exhibit 3-1:

From the firm's balance sheets:

Total assets, September 30, 1995	$364,720
Total assets, September 30, 1996	$402,654

From the firm's income statement:
for the year ended September 30, 1996

Net sales	$611,873
Net income	$ 32,936

$$\text{Return on investment} = \text{Margin} \times \text{Turnover}$$

$$= \frac{\text{Net income}}{\text{Sales}} \times \frac{\text{Sales}}{\text{Average total assets}}$$

$$= \frac{\$32,936}{\$611,873} \times \frac{\$611,873}{\dfrac{(\$364,720 + \$402,654)}{2}}$$

$$= .054 \times 1.6$$

$$= .086, \text{ or } 8.6\%$$

The significance of the DuPont Model is that it has led many managers to consider use of assets, including keeping investment in assets as low as feasible, to be just as important to overall performance as generating profit from sales.

A rule of thumb useful for putting ROI in perspective is that average ROI, based on net income, for most American merchandising and manufacturing companies is between 5 percent and 8 percent. Average ROI based on operating income (earnings before interest and taxes) for the same set of firms is between 10 percent and 15 percent. Average margin, based on *net income*, ranges from about 5 percent to 8 percent. Using *operating income*, average margin ranges from 10 percent to 15 percent. Asset turnover is usually about 1.0.

Return on Equity

Recall that the balance sheet equation is as follows:

Assets = Liabilities + Owners' equity

The return on investment calculation relates net income (perhaps as adjusted for interest, income taxes, or other items) to assets. Assets (perhaps adjusted to exclude nonoperating assets or other items) represent the amount invested to generate earnings. The balance sheet equation indicates that the investment in assets can result from either amounts borrowed from creditors (liabilities) or amounts invested by the owners. Owners and others are interested in expressing the profits of the firm as a rate of return on the amount of owners' equity; this is called **return on equity (ROE)**, and it is calculated as follows:

$$\text{Return on equity} = \frac{\text{Net income}}{\text{Average owners' equity}}$$

Return on equity is calculated using average owners' equity during the period for which the net income was earned for the same reason that average assets is used in the ROI calculation; net income is earned over a period of time, so it should be related to the owners' equity over the same period of time.

Calculation of ROE is illustrated below using data from the financial statements of Cruisers, Inc., in Exhibit 3-1:

From the firm's balance sheets:

Total owners' equity, September 30, 1995	$230,320
Total owners' equity, September 30, 1996	$265,230

From the firm's income statement:

for the year ended September 30, 1996

Net income	$32,936

$$\text{Return on equity} = \frac{\text{Net income}}{\text{Average owners' equity}}$$

$$= \frac{\$32,936}{\dfrac{(\$230,320 + \$265,230)}{2}}$$

$$= \frac{\$32,936}{\$247,775}$$

$$= 13.3\%$$

A rule of thumb useful for putting ROE in perspective is that average ROE for most American merchandising and manufacturing companies is between 10 percent and 15 percent.

Adjustments to both net income and average owners' equity may be appropriate, and some of these will be explained later in the text. For now, understand that both return on investment and return on equity are fundamental measures of the profitability of a firm and that the data for making these calculations come from the firm's financial statements.

Return on equity is a special case application of the rate of return concept. ROE is important to current stockholders and prospective investors because it relates earnings to the owners' investment, that is, the owners' equity in the assets of the entity.

Working Capital and Measures of Liquidity

Liquidity refers to a firm's ability to meet its current obligations and is measured by relating its current assets and current liabilities as reported on the balance sheet. **Working capital** is the excess of a firm's current assets over its current liabilities. Current assets are cash and other assets that are likely to be converted to cash within a year (principally accounts receivable and merchandise inventories). Current liabilities are obligations that are expected to be paid within a year, including loans, accounts payable, and other accrued liabilities (such as wages payable, interest payable, and rent payable). Most financially healthy firms have positive working capital. Even though firms are not likely to have cash on hand at any point in time equal to their current liabilities, they expect to collect accounts receivable or to sell merchandise inventory and then collect the resulting accounts receivable in time to pay the liabilities when they are scheduled for payment. Of course, in the process of converting inventories to cash, a firm will be purchasing additional merchandise for its inventory, and the suppliers will want to be assured of collecting the amounts due according to the previously agreed provisions for when payment is due.

Liquidity can be measured using working capital, the current ratio, or the acid-test ratio:

1. Working capital = Current assets – Current liabilities

2. $$\text{Current ratio} = \frac{\text{Current assets}}{\text{Current liabilities}}$$

3. $$\text{Acid-test ratio} = \frac{\text{Cash} + \text{Marketable securities} + \text{Accounts receivable}}{\text{Current liabilities}}$$

The dollar amount of a firm's working capital is not as significant as the ratio of its current assets to current liabilities, which is the **current ratio**, because the amount can be misleading unless it is related to another quantity (that is, how large is large?). Therefore, the *trend* of a company's current ratio is most useful in judging its current bill-paying ability. The **acid-test ratio**, also known as the *quick ratio*, is a more conservative short-term measure of liquidity because merchandise inventories are excluded from the computation. This ratio provides information about an almost worst-case situation—the firm's ability to meet its current obligations even if none of the inventory can be sold.

Liquidity measure calculations are illustrated below using September 30, 1996, data from the financial statements of Cruisers, Inc., in Exhibit 3-1:

$$\text{Working capital} = \text{Current assets} - \text{Current liabilities}$$

$$= \$118,319 - \$57,424$$

$$= \$60,895$$

$$\text{Current ratio} = \frac{\text{Current assets}}{\text{Current liabilities}} = \frac{\$118,319}{\$57,472} = 2.1$$

$$\text{Acid-test ratio} = \frac{\text{Cash} + \text{Marketable securities} + \text{Accounts receivable}}{\text{Current liabilities}}$$

$$= \frac{\$22,286 + \$42,317}{\$57,424}$$

$$= 1.1$$

As a general rule, a current ratio of 2.0 and an acid-test ratio of 1.0 are considered indicative of adequate liquidity. From these data it can be concluded that Cruisers, Inc., has a high degree of liquidity; it should not have any trouble meeting its current obligations as they become due.

In terms of debt-paying ability, the higher the current ratio is, the better. Yet an overly high current ratio can sometimes be a sign that the company has not made the most productive use of its assets. In recent years, many large, well-managed corporations have tried to streamline operations by reducing their current ratios to the 1.4-1.6 range, with corresponding reductions in their acid-test ratios. Investments in cash, accounts receivable, and inventories are being minimized because these current assets tend to be the least productive assets employed by the company. For example, very little, if any, ROI is earned on accounts receivable or inventory. Money freed up by reducing the investment in working capital items can be used to purchase new production equipment or to expand marketing efforts for existing product lines.

Remember, however, that judgments based on the results of any of these calculations using data from a single balance sheet are not as meaningful as the trend of the results over several periods. Noting the composition of working capital and understanding the effect on the ratios of equal changes in current assets and current liabilities are also important. As the following illustration shows, if a short-term bank loan were repaid just before the balance sheet date, working capital would not change (because current assets and current liabilities would each decrease by the same amount), but the current ratio (and the acid-test ratio) would change:

	Before Loan Repayment	After $20,000 Loan Repaid
Current assets	$200,000	$180,000
Current liabilities	100,000	80,000
Working capital	$100,000	$100,000
Current ratio	2.0	2.25

If a new loan were taken out just after the balance sheet date, the level of the firm's liquidity at the balance sheet date as expressed by the current ratio would have been overstated. Thus, liquidity measures should be viewed with skepticism since the timing of short-term borrowings and repayments is within management's control.

Measures of liquidity are used primarily by potential creditors who want to make a judgment about their prospects of being paid promptly if they enter into a creditor relationship with the firm whose liquidity is being analyzed (see Business Procedure Capsule 5—Establishing a Credit Relationship).

The statement of cash flows is also useful in assessing the reasons for a firm's liquidity or illiquidity. Recall that this financial statement identifies the reasons for the change in a firm's cash during the period (usually a year) by reporting the changes during the period in noncash balance sheet items.

Illustration of Trend Analysis

Trend analysis of return on investment, return on equity, and working capital and liquidity measures is illustrated in the following tables and exhibits. The data in these illustrations come primarily from the financial statements in the 1994 annual report of Armstrong World Industries, Inc., reproduced in the companion course workbook and study guide.

- **BUSINESS PROCEDURE CAPSULE 5**
  Establishing a Credit Relationship

Most transactions between businesses and many transactions between individuals and businesses are credit transactions. That is, the sale of the product or provision of the service is completed sometime before the purchaser pays for it. Usually, before delivering the product or service, the seller wants to have some assurance that the bill will be paid when due. This involves determining that the buyer is a good **credit risk**.

Individuals usually establish credit by submitting to the potential creditor a completed credit application, which includes information about employment, salary, bank accounts, liabilities, and other credit relationships (such as charge accounts) already established. Most credit grantors are looking for a good record of timely payments on existing credit accounts, so an individual's first credit account is usually the most difficult to obtain. Potential credit grantors may also check an individual's credit record as maintained by the credit bureau in the city in which the applicant lives or has lived.

Businesses seeking credit may follow a procedure similar to that used by individuals. Alternatively, they may provide financial statements and names of firms with which they have established a credit relationship. A newly organized firm may have to pay for its purchases in advance or with **cash on delivery (COD)** until it has been in operation for several months. Then the seller may set a relatively low credit limit for sales on credit. Once a record is established of having paid bills when due, the credit limit will be raised. After a firm has been in operation for a year or more, its credit history may be reported by the Dun & Bradstreet credit reporting service—a national credit bureau to which many companies subscribe. Even after a credit relationship has been established, firms commonly continue providing financial statements to their principal creditors.

Most of the data in Table 3-1 come from the "nine-year summary" of financial information on page 52 of Armstrong's 1994 annual report. The data in Table 3-1 are then presented graphically in Exhibits 3-2 through 3-4. The sequence of the years in the table is opposite from that of the years in the graphs. Tabular data are frequently presented so that the most recent year is closest to the captions of the table. Graphs of time series data usually flow from left to right. In any event, you should notice and understand the captions of both tables and graphs.

The graph in Exhibit 3-2 illustrates that both ROI and ROE fell from 1990 to 1991, became negative in 1992, recovered in 1993, and continued to move upward in 1994. The negative results in 1992 were caused by three principal factors: severe competition that resulted in a sharply lower margin, as illustrated in Exhibit 3-3; a large restructuring charge related to plant closings and a reduction in the number of employees; and the cumulative effect of changes in accounting for postretirement and postemployment benefits. The changes in accounting resulted from pronouncements of the Financial Accounting Standards Board that Armstrong World Industries, Inc., elected to recognize immediately.

Table 3-1
Armstrong World Industries, Inc. (Profitability and Liquidity Data, 1990-1994)

	1994	1993	1992	1991	1990
Earnings (loss) from continuing business as a percentage of:					
Sales (margin)	7.6%	2.5%	−2.3%	2.5%	5.8%
Average monthly assets (ROI)	10.5%	3.2%	−2.8%	2.9%	7.1%
Earnings (loss) as a percentage of average shareholders' equity (ROE)	31.3%	9.0%	−33.9%	3.3%	13.0%
Asset turnover*	1.4	1.3	1.2	1.2	1.2
Year-end position (in millions)					
Current assets†	$691.0	$640.4	$712.7	$718.8	$726.6
Current liabilities†	387.3	436.3	545.6	479.9	544.8
Working capital	$303.7	$204.1	$167.1	$238.9	$181.8
Current ratio††	1.8	1.5	1.3	1.5	1.3

* Not included in the Nine-Year Summary. Calculated using margin and ROI (ROI = Margin × Turnover; Turnover = ROI/Margin).

† Not included in the Nine-Year Summary. These amounts are from the balance sheets of this and prior annual reports. (Amounts at year-end 1994 and 1993 can be found on page 26 of the annual report in the course workbook and study guide.)

†† Not included in the Nine-Year Summary; calculated using current assets and current liabilities (Current ratio = Current assets/Current liabilities).

Source: Armstrong World Industries, Inc., 1994 Annual Report, pp. 26, 52.

Exhibit 3-3 illustrates that margin declined in 1991 and 1992. The improvement in 1993 and 1994 suggests that the restructuring recognized in 1992 was effective. Although turnover has not changed very much, the slight upward trend is desirable.

Both working capital and the current ratio, plotted in Exhibit 3-4, remained stable from 1990 to 1993 despite the significant fluctuations in profitability. One reason for this stability is that the cumulative effect of changes in accounting for postretirement and postemployment benefits did not affect either current assets or current liabilities.

Exhibit 3-2
Armstrong World Industries, Inc., Return on Investment (ROI) and Return on Equity (ROE), 1990-1994

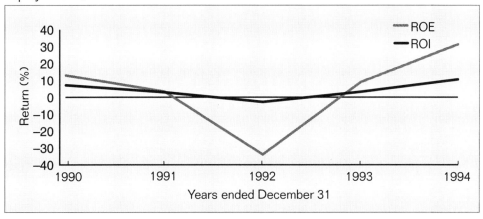

Exhibit 3-3
Armstrong World Industries, Inc., Margin and Turnover, 1990-1994

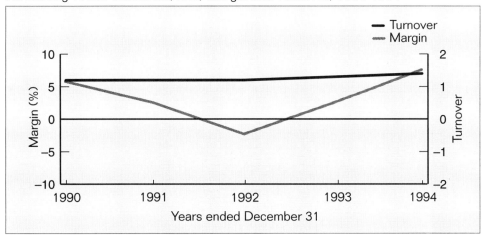

Exhibit 3-4
Armstrong World Industries, Inc., Working Capital and Current Ratio, 1990-1994

The improvement in working capital and the current ratio in 1994 reflects a significant reduction in short-term debt at the end of 1994. Armstrong World Industries, Inc., has maintained its liquidity over this four-year period.

A potential investor in the common stock of Armstrong World Industries, Inc., would probably be interested in the company's profitability compared to the industry within which it operates. Table 3-2 summarizes data taken from the Value Line Investment Survey, an investment advisory service. These data are graphed in Exhibit 3-5.

Table 3-2
Value Line Investment Survey (Percentage Earned on Net Worth, 1990-1994)

Armstrong World Industries, Inc., and the Building Materials Industry					
	For the Year				
	1994	*1993*	*1992*	*1991*	*1990*
Armstrong World Industries, Inc.*	26.2	21.7	11.1	6.8	12.9
Building materials industry	14.0	14.1	12.0	NMF†	14.7

*Nonrecurring items excluded.
†Not a meaningful figure.

Value Line Investment Survey, Part III, vol. L, no. 32 (April 21, 1995), pp. 851, 854.
Copyright © 1995 by Value Line Publishing, Inc. Reprinted by permission. All rights reserved.

Value Line classifies Armstrong World Industries, Inc., in the building materials industry. The Value Line calculations are based on net worth, a synonym for total owners' equity, and the amounts are different from the return on common stockholders' equity reported in the nine-year summary of the Armstrong World Industries, Inc., annual report and in Table 3-1. This definitional distinction will be clarified in a later chapter. Value Line does not report an industry value for 1991, perhaps because the industry value was negative. Value Line's calculations for Armstrong World Industries, Inc., exclude nonrecurring income statement items such as the restructuring charges and the cumulative effect of the changes in accounting. The graph in Exhibit 3-5 shows that the percentage earned on net worth of Armstrong World Industries, Inc., has been improving at a greater rate than that of the industry since 1992.

Exhibits 3-2 and 3-5 illustrate a subtle point about graphical presentations. The vertical axis scale of Exhibit 3-5 is about two times greater than that of Exhibit 3-2. That is, the vertical distance equal to 10 percentage points in Exhibit 3-5 is about equal to the vertical distance of 20 percentage points in Exhibit 3-2. Thus, the slopes of the lines in Exhibit 3-5 are steeper than if the graph had been constructed using the same scale as Exhibit 3-2. The visual message conveyed by a graph can be influenced by the scale selected. Remember to note the scale before determining the significance of the changes suggested by the slope of the lines on a graph.

Exhibit 3-5
Armstrong World Industries, Inc., and Building Materials Industry (Percentage Earned on Net Worth, 1990-1994)

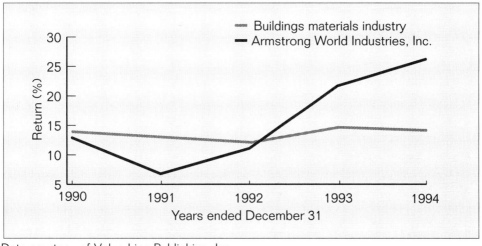

Data courtesy of Value Line Publishing, Inc.

All of the graphs presented in this chapter use an arithmetic vertical scale. This means that the distance between values shown on the vertical axis is the same. So if the data being plotted increase at a constant rate over the period of time shown on the horizontal scale, the plot will be a line that curves upward more and more steeply. Many analysts prefer to plot data that will change significantly over time (a company's sales, for example) on a graph that has a logarithmic vertical scale, where intervals between values are proportional to the logarithm of the quantities to which they correspond. This is called a **semilogarithmic graph** because only the vertical scale is logarithmic. The horizontal scale is still arithmetic. The intervals between years, for example, will be equal. The advantage of a semilogarithmic presentation is that a constant rate of growth results in a straight-line plot. Exhibit 3-6 illustrates this point.

Exhibit 3-6
Arithmetic Versus Semilogarithmic Graphing Scale

Situation: Cruisers, Inc., has experienced growth in sales over the past several years, as follows:

Year	Sales ($millions)	% change
1991	$15.0	—
1992	19.5	30.0
1993	25.4	30.2
1994	32.9	29.5
1995	42.8	30.1
1996	55.6	29.9

Notice the difference in the visual images being portrayed when these data are plotted using graph paper having an arithmetic scale compared to graph paper having a semilogarithmic scale.

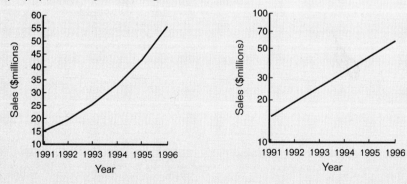

In the first graph, the rate of growth in sales for Cruisers seems to have increased each year. In the semilogarithmic graph, however, sales seem to have grown at a *steady* rate over the five years. The actual growth rate has been between 29.5 percent and 30.2 percent during the five years.

Summary

Financial statement users express financial statement data in ratio format to facilitate making informed judgments and decisions. Users are especially interested in the trend of a company's ratios over time and the comparison of the company's ratio trends with those of its industry as a whole.

The rate of return on investment is a universally accepted measure of profitability. Rate of return is calculated by dividing the amount of return, or profit, by the amount invested. Rate of return is expressed as an annual percentage rate.

Return on investment (ROI) is one of the most important measures of profitability because it relates the income earned during a period to the assets that were invested to generate those earnings. The DuPont Model for calculating ROI expands the basic model by introducing sales to calculate margin (net income/sales) and asset turnover (sales/average assets); ROI equals margin × turnover. Margin describes the profit from each dollar of sales, and turnover expresses the sales-generating capacity (efficiency) of the firm's assets.

Return on equity (ROE) relates net income earned for the year to the average owners' equity for the year. This rate of return measure is important to current and prospective owners because it relates earnings to the owners' investment.

Creditors are interested in an entity's liquidity, that is, its ability to pay its liabilities when due. The amount of working capital, the current ratio, and the acid-test ratio are measures of liquidity. These calculations are made using the amounts of current assets and current liabilities reported on the balance sheet.

When ratio trend data are plotted graphically, determining the significance of ratio changes, and evaluating a firm's performance are easy. However, pay attention to how graphs are constructed, because the visual image presented can be influenced by the scales used.

Key Words and Phrases

acid-test ratio (p. 75) The ratio of the sum of cash, marketable securities, and accounts receivable to current liabilities. A primary measure of a firm's liquidity.

asset turnover (p. 71) The quotient of sales divided by average assets for the year or other fiscal period.

COD (p. 77) Cash on delivery, or collect on delivery.

credit risk (p. 77) Refers to the uncertainty about a debtor's (issuer's) ability to make the required principal and interest payments as they come due.

current ratio (p. 75) The ratio of current assets to current liabilities. A primary measure of a firm's liquidity.

DuPont Model (p. 71) An expansion of the return on investment calculation to margin × turnover.

interest (p. 68) The income or expense from investing or borrowing money.

interest rate (p. 68) The percentage amount used, together with principal and time, to calculate interest.

liquidity (p. 74) Refers to a firm's ability to meet its current financia obligations.

margin (p. 71) The percentage of net income to net sales. Sometimes margin is calculated using operating income or other intermediate subtotals of the income statement. The term can also refer to the *amount* of gross profit, operating income, or net income.

principal (p. 68) The amount of money invested or borrowed.

rate of return (p. 68) A percentage calculated by dividing the amount of return on an investment for a period of time by the average amount invested for the period. A primary measure of profitability.

return on equity (ROE) (p. 73) The percentage of net income divided by average owners' equity for the fiscal period in which the net income was earned; frequently referred to as *ROE*. A primary measure of a firm's profitability.

return on investment (ROI) (p. 69) The rate of return on an investment; frequently referred to as *ROI*. This measure may also be referred to as *return on assets*. A primary measure of a firm's profitability.

risk (p. 69) A concept that describes the range of possible outcomes from an action. The greater the range of possible outcomes, the greater the risk.

semilogarithmic graph (p. 82) A graph format in which the vertical axis is a logarithmic scale.

trend analysis (p. 67) Evaluation of the trend of data over time.

turnover (p. 71) The quotient of sales divided by the average assets for the year, or some other fiscal period. A descriptor, such as total assets, inventory, or plant and equipment, that usually precedes the turnover term. A measure of the efficiency with which assets are used to generate sales.

working capital (p. 74) The difference between current assets and current liabilities. A measure of a firm's liquidity.

Chapter 4

How Economic Transactions Affect Financial Statements

Chapters 2 and 3 presented a *static* approach to interpreting basic financial statements—looking only at the ending account balances reported in the financial statements. In contrast, this assignment presents a *dynamic* approach to interpreting financial statements, called *transaction analysis*, that looks at how economic transactions affect the account balances reported in the financial statements. A component of the bookkeeping process, transaction analysis provides a means of analyzing the effect of economic transactions on an entity's financial statements. Economic transactions can be reduced to their individual components by using the basic and extended accounting equations. Those components can be assigned to existing account balances represented in the accounting equation. Isolating these incremental changes to account balances helps the users of financial statements identify changes in the relationship among key financial variables used to measure an entity's financial position (at different points in time or over time).

Although this text is not intended to teach you to become a bookkeeper or CPA, a basic understanding of the bookkeeping process should help you identify underlying causes of financial statement changes. Before one can interpret what is reported in an entity's financial statements, whether that information indicates a problem, and, if so, what to do to correct the problem, one must understand how the reported information was developed.

An insurance producer, underwriter, or claim adjuster frequently needs to evaluate the financial condition of a customer. To assess the ability of an insurer to pay future claims, producers might need to review the financial statements of an insurer with whom they place business. Underwriting or premium collection departments might need to audit agent and broker records to determine whether those producers should retain their premium collection authority.

Performing even the most basic of financial analyses requires that the analyst use financial statements. For insurance professionals to more fully understand the information contained in financial statements, they should understand how that information was developed through the bookkeeping process. The bookkeeping process provides for the transformation of detailed information about transactions to meaningful financial statements reporting summaries of account balances. The broader your understanding of that process, the better able you will be to interpret financial statements.

Educational Objectives

After studying this chapter, you should be able to:

1. Show how the income statement is linked to the balance sheet through owners' equity, and explain why this connection might be important in evaluating the owners' equity or net worth of a prospective insured.

2. Explain how the expanded basic accounting equation includes revenues and expenses, and give examples of the types of revenues and expenses that might concern an insurance agent or broker.

3. Show how the expanded accounting equation stays in balance after every transaction.

4. Explain how the bookkeeping system is a mechanical adaptation of the extended accounting equation.

5. Explain the meaning of the terms *journal, ledger, T-account, account balance, debit, credit,* and *closing the books.*

6. List and explain the five questions of transaction analysis.

7. Explain and give examples of the processes of analyzing a transaction, preparing a journal entry, and determining the effect of a transaction on working capital.

8. Define or describe each of the Key Words and Phrases introduced in this chapter.

The Bookkeeping/Accounting Process

The bookkeeping/accounting process starts with **transactions** (economic interchanges between entities that are accounted for and reflected in financial statements) and culminates in the financial statements. This flow was illustrated in Chapter 2 as follows:

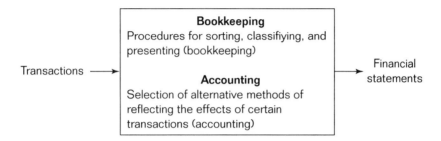

This chapter presents an overview of bookkeeping procedures so that you will be able to determine the effects of any transaction on the financial statements. This ability is crucial to the process of making informed judgments and decisions from the financial statements. Bookkeepers (and accountants) use special terms to describe the bookkeeping process, and you will have to learn those terms. The bookkeeping process itself is a mechanical process, however, and once you understand the language of bookkeeping, you will see that the process is straightforward.

The Balance Sheet Equation—A Mechanical Key

The balance sheet equation expresses the equality between an entity's assets and the claims to those assets:

$$Assets = Liabilities + Owners' equity$$

For present illustration purposes, consider a firm without liabilities. What happens to the amounts in the equation if the entity operates at a profit? Assets (perhaps cash) increase, and, if the equation is to balance (as it must), then clearly owners' equity must also increase. Profits increase owners' equity, and to keep the equation in balance, assets will increase and/or liabilities will decrease. Every financial transaction that is accounted for will cause a change somewhere in the balance sheet equation, and the equation will remain in balance after every transaction.

Remember that a firm's net income (profit) or loss is the difference between the revenues and expenses reported on its income statement (Exhibit 2-2). Also, remember that net income from the income statement is reported as one of the factors causing a change in the retained earnings part of the statement of changes in owners' equity (Exhibit 2-3). The other principal element of owners' equity is the amount of capital invested by the owners, that is, the paid-in capital shown Exhibit 2-3. Given these components of owners' equity, the basic balance sheet equation can be modified as follows:

Assets = Liabilities + Owners' equity

Assets = Liabilities + Paid-in capital + Retained earnings

Assets = Liabilities + Paid-in + Retained earnings + Revenues − Expenses
capital (beginning of period)

To understand the operation of this equation and the effect of several transactions, study how the following transactions are reflected in Exhibit 4-1. In the exhibit, specific assets and liabilities have been identified within those general categories, and columns have been established for each.

Transactions

The following are the transactions of a hypothetical firm:

1. Investors organized the firm and invested $30. (In this example the broad category *paid-in capital* is used rather than *common stock* and, possibly, *additional paid-in capital*. There is no beginning balance in retained earnings because the firm is just getting started.)
2. Equipment costing $25 was purchased for cash.
3. The firm borrowed $15 from a bank.
4. Merchandise costing $20 was purchased for inventory; $10 was paid in cash, and $10 was charged on account.
5. Equipment that cost $7 was sold for $7; $2 was received in cash, and $5 will be received later.
6. The $5 account receivable from the sale of equipment was collected.

Each column of the exhibit is totaled after transaction 6. The total of all the asset columns equals the total of all the liability and owners' equity columns.

The firm has had no revenue or expense transactions yet, so the transactions continue:

7. Merchandise inventory was sold that had a cost of $12 for a selling price of $20; the sale was made **on account** (that is, on credit), and the customer

Exhibit 4-1
Transaction Summary

	Assets				=	Liabilities		+	Owners' equity			
Transaction	Cash	Accounts Receivable	Merchandise Inventory	Equipment	=	Notes Payable	Accounts Payable	+	Paid-In Capital	Retained Earnings	+ Revenue	− Expenses
1.	+30								+30			
2.	−25			+25								
3.	+15					+15						
4.	−10		+20				+10					
5.	+2	+5		−7								
6.	+5	−5										
Total	17	0	20	18		15	10		30	—	—	—
7. Revenues		+20									+20	
7. Expenses			−12									−12
8.							+3					−3
Total	17	20	8	18		15	13		30	+5	20	−15

will pay later. In Exhibit 4-1, this transaction is shown on two lines; one reflects the revenue of $20, and the other reflects the expense, or cost of the merchandise sold, of $12.

8. Wages of $3 earned by the firm's employees are accrued. This means that the expense is recorded even though it has not yet been paid. Employees have earned the wages (the expense has been incurred), and the wages are owed, but have not yet been paid; they will be paid in the next accounting period. The accrual is made in this period so that revenues and expenses of the current period will be matched (the matching concept was discussed in Chapter 2), and net income will reflect the economic results of this period's activities.

Again, each column of the exhibit is totaled, and the total of all the asset columns equals the total of all the liability and owners' equity columns. If the accounting period were to end after transaction 8, the income statement would report net income of $5, and the balance sheet would show total owners' equity of $35. Simplified financial statements for Exhibit 4-1 data after transaction 8 are presented in Exhibit 4-2.

Notice especially in Exhibit 4-2 how net income on the income statement is accounted for in the balance sheet via the retained earnings section of owners' equity. In the equation of Exhibit 4-1, revenues and expenses were treated as a part of owners' equity to keep the equation in balance. For financial reporting purposes, however, revenues and expenses are shown in the income statement. In order to have the balance sheet balance, net income must be reflected in the balance sheet, and this is done in retained earnings. If any retained earnings are distributed to the owners as a dividend, the dividend does not show on the income statement but is a deduction from retained earnings, shown in the statement of changes in retained earnings. This is because a dividend is not an expense (it is not incurred in the process of generating revenue). A dividend is a distribution of earnings to the owners of the firm.

The steps just described are the essence of the bookkeeping process. Transactions are analyzed to determine which asset, liability, or owners' equity category is affected and how each is affected. The amount of the effect is recorded, the amounts are totaled, and financial statements are prepared.

Bookkeeping Procedures and Jargon

Because of the complexity of most business operations and the frequent need to refer to past transactions, a bookkeeping system has evolved to facilitate the record-keeping process. The system may be manual or computerized, but the general features are virtually the same.

Exhibit 4-2
Financial Statements for Exhibit 4-1 Data

	Exhibit 4-1 Data *Income Statement for* *Transactions 1 through 8*	

Exhibit 4-1 Data *Income Statement for* *Transactions 1 through 8*		*Exhibit 4-1* *Statement of Change in* *Retained Earnings*	
Revenues	$ 20	Beginning balance	$ 0
Expenses	(15)	Net income	5
		Dividends	(0)
Net income	$ 5	Ending balance	$ 5

Exhibit 4-1 Data
Balance Sheet after Transaction 8

Assets		**Liabilities & Owners' Equity**	
Cash	$17	Note payable	$15
Accounts receivable	20	Accounts payable	13
Merchandise inventory	8	Current liabilities	$28
Current assets	$45	Owners' equity:	
Equipment	18	Paid-in capital	$30
		Retained earnings	5
		Total owners' equity	$35
		Total liabilities &	
Total assets	$63	owners' equity	$63

Transactions are initially recorded in a **journal**. A journal (derived from the French word *jour*, meaning *day*) is a day-by-day, or chronological, record of transactions. Transactions are then recorded in—**posted** to—a **ledger**. The ledger serves the purpose of the worksheet shown in Exhibit 4-1, but rather than having a large sheet with a column for each asset, liability, and owners' equity category, there is an account for each category. In a manual bookkeeping system, each account is a separate page in a book much like a loose-leaf binder. Accounts are arranged in a sequence to facilitate the posting process. Usually the sequence is assets, liabilities, owners' equity, revenues, and expenses. A **chart of accounts** serves as an index to the ledger, and each account is numbered to facilitate the frequent written references that are made to it.

The account format that has been used for several hundred years looks like a "T." (In the diagram that follows, notice the T under the captions for assets, liabilities, and owners' equity.) On one side of the T, additions to the account are recorded, and on the other side of the T, subtractions are recorded. The **account balance** at any point in time is the arithmetic difference between the prior balance and the additions and subtractions. Exhibit 4-1 illustrates that the account balances after transactions 6 and 8 are the sum of the prior balance, plus the additions, minus the subtractions.

To facilitate referring to account entries and balances, the left-hand side of a **T-account** is called the *debit* side, and the right-hand side of a T-account is called the *credit* side. In bookkeeping and accounting, **debit** and **credit** mean left and right, respectively, and nothing more (see Business Procedure Capsule 6—Bookkeeping Language in Everyday English). A record of a transaction involving a posting to the left-hand side of an account is called a *debit entry*. An account that has a balance on its right-hand side is said to have a *credit balance*.

In the bookkeeping system, debit and credit entries to accounts and account balances are set up so that if debits equal credits, the balance sheet equation will be in balance. The key to balance is that asset accounts will normally have a debit balance: increases in assets are recorded as debit entries to these accounts, and decreases in assets are recorded as credit entries to these accounts. For liabilities and owners' equity accounts, the opposite will be true. The following diagram illustrates how the equation balances:

Assets		=	Liabilities		+	Owners' Equity	
Debit	*Credit*		*Debit*	*Credit*		*Debit*	*Credit*
Increases	Decreases		Decreases	Increases		Decreases	Increases
+	−		−	+		−	+
Normal				Normal			Normal
balance				balance			balance

Not coincidentally, the debit and credit system of normal balances coincides with the balance sheet presentation illustrated earlier. In fact, the balance sheets illustrated so far have been presented in what is known as the *account format*. An alternative approach is to use the *report format*, in which assets are shown above liabilities and owners' equity.

Entries to revenue and expense accounts follow a pattern that is consistent with entries to other owners' equity accounts. Revenues are increases in owners' equity, so revenue accounts will normally have a credit balance and will increase with credit entries. Expenses are decreases in owners' equity, so expense accounts will normally have a debit balance and will increase with debit entries. Gains and losses are recorded like revenues and expenses, respectively.

The debit or credit behavior of accounts for assets, liabilities, owners' equity, revenues, and expenses is summarized in the following illustration:

Account Name *Account Number*

Debit side	*Credit* side
Normal balance for: Assets Expenses	Normal balance for: Liabilities Owners' equity Revenues
Debit entries increase: Assets Expenses	Credit entries increase: Liabilities Owners' equity Revenues
Debit entries decrease: Liabilities Owners' equity Revenues	Credit entries decrease: Assets Expenses

Referring to the transactions that were illustrated in Exhibit 4-1, a bookkeeper would say that in transaction 1, which was the investment of $30 in the firm by the owners, cash was debited—it increased—and paid-in capital was credited, each for $30. Transaction 2, the purchase of equipment for $25 cash, would be described as a $25 debit to equipment and a $25 credit to cash. How would a bookkeeper describe the remaining transactions of that illustration?

• BUSINESS PROCEDURE CAPSULE 6
Bookkeeping Language in Everyday English

Many bookkeeping and accounting terms have found their way into everyday language, especially in the business context. Debit and credit have become common terms, and some brief examples may explain the left-right orientation. Banks use the terms *debit* and *credit* to describe additions to or subtractions from an individual's checking account. For example, your account is credited for interest earned and is debited for a service charge or for the cost of checks that are furnished to you. From the bank's perspective, your account is a liability; that is, the bank owes you the balance in your account. Interest earned by your account increases that liability of the bank; hence, the interest is credited. Service charges reduce your claim on the bank—its liability to you—so those are debits. Perhaps because of these effects on a checking or savings account balance, many people think that debit is a synonym for bad, and that credit means good. In certain contexts, these synonyms may be appropriate, but they do not apply in accounting.

A synonym for debit that is used in accounting is *charge*. To **charge** an account is to make a debit entry to the account. This terminology is used when merchandise or services are purchased on credit; that is, they are received now and will be paid for later. This credit arrangement is frequently called a *charge account* because from the seller's perspective, an asset (accounts receivable) is increasing as a result of the transaction, and assets increase with a debit entry. When a credit card is used, the *credit transaction* increases the purchaser's liability.

An alternative to the credit card that merchants and banks have developed is the "debit card." From the bank's perspective, when a debit card is used at an electronic point-of-sale terminal, the purchaser's bank account balance will be immediately reduced by the amount of the purchase, and the seller's bank account balance will be increased. Consumers have been reluctant to switch from credit cards to debit cards because they would rather pay later than sooner for several reasons, not the least of which is that they may not have the cash until later.

The bookkeeper would say, after transaction 8 has been recorded, that the Cash account has a debit balance of $17, that the Note Payable account has a credit balance of $15, and that the Expense account has a debit balance of $15. (The example had only one expense account; usually there will be a separate account for each category of expense and each category of revenue.) What kind of balance do the other accounts have after transaction 8?

The journal was identified earlier as the chronological record of the firm's transactions. The journal is also the place where transactions are first recorded, and it is sometimes referred to as the *book of original entry*. The **journal entry** format is a convenient way of describing the effect of a transaction on the accounts involved and will be used in subsequent chapters of this text.

The general format of the journal entry is as follows:

Date   Dr.   Account name .... Amount
       Cr.   Account name .... Amount

The date is recorded to provide a cross-reference to the transaction. In many of the examples discussed in this text, a transaction reference number will be used instead of a date to provide a cross-reference.

The name of the account to be debited and the debit amount are to the left (remember, debit means *left* and credit means *right*) of the name of the account to be credited and the credit amount.

The abbreviations *Dr.* and *Cr.* are used for *debit* and *credit*, respectively. These identifiers are frequently omitted from the journal entry to reduce writing time and because the practice of indenting debits and credits is universally followed and understood.

A journal entry can have more than one debit account and amount, and/or more than one credit account and amount. The only requirement of a journal entry is that the total of the debit amounts equal the total of the credit amounts. A brief explanation of the transaction frequently appears beneath the journal entry, especially if the **entry** is not self-explanatory.

The journal entry for transaction (1) of Exhibit 4-1 would appear as follows:

(1) Dr.   Cash   30
        Cr.   Paid-in capital   30
            To record investment in the firm by the owners

Technically, the journal entry procedure illustrated here is for a *general journal entry*. Most bookkeeping systems also use specialized journals, but they are still books of original entry, recording transactions chronologically, involving various accounts, and resulting in entries in which debits equal credits. If you understand the basic general journal entry illustrated above, you will be able to understand a specialized journal.

Transactions generate **source documents**, such as an invoice from a supplier, a copy of a credit purchase made by a customer, a check stub, or a tape printout of the totals from a cash register's activity for a period. These source documents are the raw materials used in the bookkeeping process and support the journal entry.

The following flowchart illustrates the bookkeeping process that this chapter has explored thus far:

Understanding the Effects of Transactions on the Financial Statements

T-accounts and journal entries are models used by accountants to explain and understand the effects of transactions on the financial statements. These models are frequently difficult for nonaccountants to use because one must know what kind of account (asset, liability, owners' equity, revenue, or expense) is involved, where in the financial statements (balance sheet or income statement) the account is found, and how the account is affected by the debit or credit characteristic of the transaction.

An alternative to the T-account and journal entry models that should be useful to you is the following horizontal financial statement relationship model first introduced in Chapter 2. The **horizontal model** is as follows:

Balance sheet	Income statement
Assets = Liabilities + Owners' equity ←	Net income = Revenues − Expenses

The key to using this model is to keep the balance sheet in balance. The arrow from net income in the income statement to owners' equity in the balance sheet indicates that net income affects retained earnings, which is a component of owners' equity. For a transaction affecting both the balance sheet and income statement, the balance sheet will balance when the income statement effect on owners' equity is considered. In this model, the account name is entered under the appropriate financial statement category, and the dollar effect of the transaction on that account is entered with a plus or minus sign below the account name. For example, the journal entry shown earlier, which records the investment of $30 in the firm by the owners, would be shown in this horizontal model as follows:

Balance sheet	Income statement
Assets = Liabilities + Owners' equity ←	Net income = Revenues − Expenses
Cash Paid-in capital	
+30 +30	

To further illustrate the model's use, assume a transaction in which the firm paid $12 for advertising. The effect on the financial statements is as follows:

Balance sheet	Income statement
Assets = Liabilities + Owners' equity ←	Net income = Revenues − Expenses
Cash	Advertising
−12	expense
	−12

The entry would be as follows:

Dr.	Advertising expense	12	
	Cr.	Cash	12

In the horizontal model, the amount of advertising expense is shown with a minus sign because the expense reduces net income, which reduces owners' equity. A plus or minus sign is used in the context of each financial statement equation (A = L + OE, and NI = R − E). Thus, a minus sign for expenses means that net income is reduced (expenses are greater), not that expenses are lower.

A transaction can affect two accounts in a single balance sheet or income statement category. For example, assume a transaction in which a firm receives $40 that a customer owed it for services performed in a prior period. The effect of this transaction is shown as follows:

Balance sheet	Income statement
Assets = Liabilities + Owners' equity ⟵	Net income = Revenues – Expenses
Cash +40	
Accounts receivable –40	

The entry would be as follows:

Dr.	Cash	40
Cr.	Accounts receivable	40

A transaction can also affect more than two accounts. For example, assume a transaction in which a firm provided $60 worth of services to a client, $45 of which was collected when the services were provided and $15 of which will be collected later. The effect on the financial statements is shown below:

Balance sheet	Income statement
Assets = Liabilities + Owners' equity ⟵	Net income = Revenues – Expenses
Cash +45	Fee revenues +60
Accounts receivable +15	

The entry would be as follows:

Dr.	Cash	45
Dr.	Accounts receivable	15
Cr.	Fee revenues	60

Recall that revenues and expenses from the income statement are increases and decreases, respectively, to owners' equity. Thus, the horizontal model and its two financial statement equations can be combined into a single equation:

$$\text{Assets} = \text{Liabilities} + \text{Owners' equity} + \text{Revenues} - \text{Expenses}$$

The equal sign in the horizontal model is between assets and liabilities. You can check that a transaction recorded in the horizontal model keeps the balance sheet in balance by mentally (or actually) checking that the total of the entries on the left side of the equation equals the total of the entries on the right side of the equation.

Become familiar with the horizontal model (by solving problems in the accompanying course workbook and study guide) so that it will be easier for you to understand the effects on the financial statements of transactions that you will encounter later in this book and on the job. As a financial statement user (as opposed to a financial statement preparer), you will find that the horizontal model is an easily used tool. With practice you will also become proficient at understanding how an amount on either the balance sheet or income statement probably affected other parts of the financial statements.

Adjustments/Adjusting Entries

After the end of the accounting period, the bookkeeper will probably have to record some **adjusting journal entries**. These entries are made to reflect accrual accounting in the financial statements. As discussed in Chapters 1 and 2, **accrual** accounting recognizes revenues and expenses as they occur, even though the cash receipt from the revenue or the cash disbursement related to the expense may occur before or after the event that causes revenue or expense recognition. Although prepared after the end of the accounting period, adjustments are dated and recorded as of the end of the period.

Adjustments result in revenues and expenses being reported in the appropriate fiscal period. For example, a firm may *earn* revenue in fiscal 1996 from selling a product or providing a service, and the customer/client may not pay until fiscal 1997. (Most firms pay for products purchased or services received within a week to a month after receiving the product or service.) Some expenses *incurred* in fiscal 1996 will probably not be paid for until fiscal 1997. (Utility costs and employee wages are examples.) Alternatively, an entity might receive cash from a customer/client for a product or service in fiscal 1995 and not sell the product or provide the service until fiscal 1996. (Subscription fees and insurance premiums are usually received before economic value is re-ceived.) Likewise, the entity may pay for an item in fiscal 1995, but the expense applies to fiscal 1996. (Insurance premiums and rent are usually paid in advance.) These alternative activities are illustrated on the following time line:

Fiscal 1995	12/31/95	Fiscal 1996	12/31/96	Fiscal 1997
Cash received		Product sold or service provided and revenue earned		Cash received
Cash paid		Expense incurred		Cash paid

There are two categories of adjusting entries:

1. **Accruals**—Recording transactions for which cash has not yet been received or paid, but the effect of which must be reflected in the accounts in order to accomplish a matching of revenues and expenses and accurate financial statements.

2. **Reclassifications**—The initial recording of a transaction, although a true reflection of the transaction at the time does not result in assigning revenues to the period in which they were earned or expenses to the period in which they were incurred, so an amount must be reclassified from one account to another.

The first type of adjustment is illustrated by the accrual of wages expense and wages payable. For example, work performed by employees during March, for which they will be paid in April, results in wages expense to be included in the March income statement and a wages payable liability to be included in the March 31 balance sheet. To illustrate this accrual, assume that employees earned $60 in March that will be paid to them in April. Using the horizontal model, the **accrued** wages adjustment has the following effect on the financial statements:

Balance sheet	Income statement
Assets = Liabilities + Owners' equity ←	Net income = Revenues – Expenses
Wages payable +60	Wages expense –60

The entry would be as follows:

Dr.	Wages expense..	60
Cr.	Wages payable...	60

Thus, the March 31 balance sheet will reflect the wages payable liability, and the income statement for March will include all of the wages expense incurred in March. Again, the recognition of the expense of $60 is shown with a minus sign because as expenses increase, net income and owners' equity (retained earnings) decrease. The balance sheet remains in balance after this adjustment because the $60 increase in liabilities is offset by the $60 decrease in owners' equity. When the wages are paid in April, both the cash and wages payable accounts will be decreased; wages expense is not affected.

Similar adjustments are made to accrue revenues (for example, for services performed but not yet billed, or for interest earned but not yet received) and other expenses, including various operating expenses, interest expense, and income tax expense.

The effect on the financial statements, using the horizontal model, of accruing $50 of interest income that has been earned but not yet received is shown as follows:

Balance sheet	Income statement
Assets = Liabilities + Owners' equity ⟵	Net income = Revenues – Expenses
Interest receivable +50	Interest income +50

The entry would be as follows:

```
Dr.      Interest receivable ......................................        50
    Cr.      Interest income .................................              50
```

An example of the second kind of adjustment is the reclassification for supplies. If the purchase of supplies at a cost of $100 during February was initially recorded as an increase in the supplies (asset) account (and a decrease in cash), the cost of supplies used during February must be removed from the asset and recorded as supplies expense for February. Assuming that supplies costing $35 were used during February, the reclassification adjustment would be reflected in the horizontal model as follows:

Balance sheet	Income statement
Assets = Liabilities + Owners' equity ⟵	Net income = Revenues – Expenses
Supplies –35	Supplies expense –35

The entry would be as follows:

```
Dr.      Supplies expense ......................................        35
    Cr.      Supplies ...........................................          35
```

Conversely, if the purchase of supplies during February at a cost of $100 was originally recorded as an increase in supplies expense for February, the cost of supplies still on hand at the end of February ($65, if supplies costing $35 were used during February) must be removed from the supplies expense account for February and recorded as an asset at the end of February. The reclassification adjustment for the $65 of supplies still on hand at the end of February would be reflected in the horizontal model as follows:

Balance sheet	Income statement
Assets = Liabilities + Owners' equity ⟵	Net income = Revenues – Expenses
Supplies +65	Supplies expense +65

The entry would be as follows:

Dr.	Supplies	65	
	Cr.	Supplies expense	65

Supplies costing $100 were originally recorded as an expense (a minus 100 in the expense column offset by a minus 100 of cash in the asset column). The expense should be only $35 because $65 of the supplies are still on hand at the end of February, so supplies expense is reduced to $35 by showing a plus $65 in the expense column. The model is kept in balance by increasing supplies in the asset column by $65.

Adjustments for prepaid insurance (insurance premiums paid in a fiscal period before the insurance expense has been incurred) and revenues received in advance (cash received from customers before the service has been performed or the product has been sold) are also reclassification adjustments.

Generally speaking, every adjusting entry affects both the balance sheet and the income statement. That is, if one part of the entry—either the debit or the credit— affects the balance sheet, the other part affects the income statement. The result of adjusting entries is to make both the balance sheet at the end of the accounting period and the income statement for the accounting period more accurate. That is, asset and liability account balances are appropriately stated, all revenues earned during the period are reported, and all expenses incurred in generating those revenues are subtracted to arrive at net income. If the matching concept is properly applied, the entity's return on investment (ROI), return on equity (ROE) and liquidity calculations will be valid measures of results of operations and financial position.

After the adjustments have been posted to the ledger accounts, account balances are determined. The financial statements are prepared using the account balance amounts, which are usually summarized to a certain extent. For example, if the company has only one ledger account for cash, the balance in that account is shown on the balance sheet as cash. If the company has several separate selling expense accounts (for example, advertising expense, sales force travel expense, and sales force commissions), these account balances are added together to get the selling expense amount shown on the income statement.

This entire procedure of summarizing the account balances is called **closing the books** and usually takes at least several working days to complete. At the end of the fiscal year for a large, publicly owned company, four to ten weeks may be required for this process because of the complexities involved, including the annual audit by the firm's public accountants.

The bookkeeping process itself is procedural, and the same kinds and sequence of activities are repeated in each fiscal period. These procedures and the sequence make mechanization and computerization feasible. Mechanical bookkeeping system aids were developed many years ago. Today many computer programs use transaction data as input and, with minimum operator intervention, complete the bookkeeping procedures and prepare financial statements. Accounting knowledge and judgment are as necessary as ever, however, to ensure that transactions are initially recorded in an appropriate manner, that required adjustments are made, and that the output of the computer processing makes sense.

Transaction Analysis Methodology

The key to understanding the effect of any transaction on the financial statements is being able to analyze the transaction. **Transaction analysis methodology** involves answering five questions:

1. What kind of economic transactions occur?
2. What accounts are affected?
3. How are the accounts affected?
4. Does the balance sheet balance? (Do the debits equal the credits?)
5. Does my analysis make sense?

What kind of economic transactions occur? To analyze any transaction, understanding the transaction is necessary—that is, understanding the activity that is taking place between the entity for which the accounting is being done and the other entity involved in the transaction. Most elementary accounting texts, including this one, explain many business transactions. Understanding the effect of a transaction on the financial statements is impossible if the basic activity being accounted for is not understood.

What accounts are affected? This question is frequently answered by the answer to "What kind of economic transactions occur?" because the specific account name is often included in that explanation. This question may also be answered by a process of elimination. First, consider whether one of the accounts is an asset, a liability, owners' equity, revenue, or an expense. From the broad category, identifying a specific account is usually possible.

How are the accounts affected? First, answer this question with the word *increasing* or *decreasing*; then, if you are using the journal entry or T-account model, translate the first answer to a *debit* or *credit*. Accountants learn to think directly in debit and credit terms after much more practice than you will probably have. When you use the horizontal model, the debit/credit issue is avoided.

Does the balance sheet balance? If the horizontal model is being used, determining that the balance sheet equation is in balance can be done by observing the arithmetic sign and amounts of the transaction. Remember that the operational equal sign in the model is between assets and liabilities. Alternatively, the journal entry for the transaction can be written, or T-accounts can be sketched, and the equality of the debits and credits can be verified. If the balance sheet equation is not in balance or if the debits do not equal the credits, your analysis of the transaction is wrong.

Does my analysis make sense? This is the most important question. You must determine whether the horizontal model effects or the journal entry that results from your analysis causes changes in account balances and the financial statements that are consistent with your understanding of the economic transaction that is occurring. If the analysis does not make sense to you, then go back to question number 1 and start again.

Exhibit 4-3 illustrates the application of this five-question transaction analysis routine. The exhibit also illustrates the determination of the effect of a transaction on a firm's working capital. You are learning transaction analysis to help you better understand how the amounts reported on financial statements got there, which in turn will improve your ability to make decisions and informed judgments from those statements.

Exhibit 4-3
Transaction Analysis

Situation:
On September 1, Cruisers, Inc., borrowed $2,500 from its bank; a note was signed that provided that the loan, plus interest, was to be repaid in 10 months.

Required:

a. Analyze the transaction and prepare a journal entry or use the horizontal model to record the transaction.

b. Describe the effect of the loan transaction on working capital and the current ratio of Cruisers, Inc.

Solution:

a. *Analysis of transaction:*

- What kind of economic transaction occurs? The firm signed a note at the bank and is receiving cash from the bank.

- What accounts are affected? Notes payable (a liability) and cash (an asset).

Continued on next page.

- How are they affected? Notes payable is increasing, and cash is increasing. Does the balance sheet balance? If the horizontal model is used, the effect of the loan transaction on the financial statements is as follows:

Balance sheet		Income statement
Assets = Liabilities + Owners' equity	←	Net income = Revenues − Expenses
Cash Note payable		
+2,500 +2,500		

- Does the balance sheet balance? Yes, assets and liabilities each increased by $2,500. The journal entry for this transaction, in which debits equal credits, is as follows:

Sept. 1   Dr.   Cash   2,500

                 Cr.   Note payable   2,500
         Bank loan received

- Does this accounting make sense? Yes, because a balance sheet prepared immediately after this transaction will show an increased amount of cash and the liability to the bank. The interest associated with the loan is not reflected in this entry because at this point Cruisers, Inc., has not incurred any interest expense, nor does the firm owe any interest; if the loan were to be immediately repaid, no interest would be due the bank. Interest expense and the liability for the interest payable will be recorded as adjustments over the life of the loan.

Let's get a preview of future entries by looking at how the interest would be accrued each month (the expense and liability have been incurred, but the liability has not yet been paid) and by looking at the ultimate repayment of the loan and accrued interest. Assume that the interest rate on the note is 12% (remember, an interest rate is an annual rate, unless otherwise specified). Interest expense for one month would be calculated as follows:

Annual interest = Principal × Annual rate × Time (in years)

Monthly interest = Principal × Annual rate × Time /12 (months)

$$= \$2,500 \times .12 \times 1/12$$

$$= \$25$$

The monthly financial statements of Cruisers, Inc., accurately reflect the firm's interest expense for the month and its interest payable liability at the end of the month. To achieve this accuracy, the following adjusting entry would be made at the end of every month of the 10-month life of the note:

Each   Dr.   Interest expense 25
month-end   Cr.   Interest payable 25
To accrue monthly interest on bank loan

If the horizontal model is used, the effect of this interest adjustment on the financial statements is as follows

Balance sheet	Income statement
Assets = Liabilities + Owners' equity ⟵	Net income = Revenues − Expenses
Interest payable +25	Interest expense −25

(A reduction in net income,
an increase in expenses.)

Remember, a minus sign for expenses means that net income is reduced, not that expenses are reduced. As explained earlier, if the two financial statement equations are combined into the single equation

Assets = Liabilities + Owners' equity + Revenues − Expenses

the equation's balance will be preserved after each transaction or adjustment.

At the end of the tenth month, when the loan and accrued interest are paid, the following entry would be made:

June 30   Dr.   Interest expense 2,500
Dr.   Interest payable 250
Cr.   Cash 2,750
Payment of bank loan and accrued interest

If the horizontal model is used, the effect of this transaction on the financial statements is as follows:

Balance sheet		Income statement
Assets = Liabilities + Owners' equity ⟵		Net income = Revenues − Expenses
Cash −2,750	Note payable −2,500	
	Interest payable −250	

Apply the five questions of transaction analysis to both the monthly interest expense/interest payable accrual and to the payment. Also consider the effect of each of these entries on the financials statements. What is happening to net income each month? What has

Continued on next page.

happened to net income for the 10 months? What has happened to working capital each month? What happened to working capital when the loan and accrued interest were paid?

b. *Effect of the loan transaction on working capital and the current ratio:* Remember from the discussion in Chapter 3 that working capital is the difference between current assets and current liabilities. Cash is a current asset. The note payable is a current liability because it is to be paid within a year. Because both current assets and current liabilities are increasing by the same amount, working capital will not be affected. The current ratio is the ratio of current assets to current liabilities. Assuming that before this transaction the firm had positive working capital, its current ratio would have been greater than 1. Because both current assets and current liabilities have increased by the same amount, the proportionate increase in current assets is less than the proportionate increase in current liabilities. Therefore, the current ratio has decreased. This can be shown by calculating the current ratio using assumed amounts for current assets and current liabilities.

Before: $\text{Current ratio} = \dfrac{\text{Current assets}}{\text{Current liabilities}} = \dfrac{\$10,000}{\$5,000} = 2.0$

After: $\text{Current ratio} = \dfrac{\text{Current assets}}{\text{Current liabilities}} = \dfrac{\$12,500}{\$7,500} = 1.7$

You can test this conclusion by using other assumed amounts for current assets and current liabilities before the transaction, and then increasing each by the borrowed $2,500. If working capital had been negative before the transaction (an unusual situation because it reflects very low liquidity), the transaction would have increased the current ratio but still would not have affected the amount of working capital.

Transaction analysis methodology and knowledge about the arithmetic operation of a T-account can also be used to understand the activity that is recorded in an account. For example, assume that the interest receivable account shows the following activity for a month:

Interest Receivable

Beginning balance	2,400		
		Transactions	1,700
Month-end adjustment	1,300		
Ending balance	2,000		

What transactions caused the credit to this account? Since the credit to this asset account represents a reduction in the account balance, the question can be rephrased, "What transaction would cause interest receivable to decrease?" The answer is receipt of cash from entities that owed this firm interest. The journal entry summarizing these transactions is as follows:

Dr.	Cash	1,700	
	Cr.	Interest receivable	1,700

What is the month-end adjustment that caused the debit to the account? The rephrased question is, "What causes interest receivable to increase?" The answer is accrual of interest income that was earned this month. The adjusting journal entry to record this accrual is as follows:

Dr.	Interest receivable	1,300	
	Cr.	Interest income	1,300

The horizontal model is used to measure the effect of the transaction and of the adjustment on the financial statements as follows:

Balance sheet	Income statement
Assets = Liabilities + Owners' equity ← Net income = Revenues – Expenses	

Transaction:
Cash
+1,700

Interest
receivable
–1,700

Adjustment:
Interest	Interest
receivable	income
+1,300	+1,300

The T-account format is a useful way of visualizing the effect of transactions and adjustments on the account balance. In addition, because of the arithmetic operation of the T-account (beginning balance +/– transactions and adjustments = ending balance), if all of the amounts except one are known, the unknown amount can be calculated.

You should invest practice and study time to learn to use transaction analysis procedures and understand the horizontal model, journal entries, and T-accounts because these are tools used in subsequent chapters to describe the effect of transactions on the financial statements. Although these models are part of the bookkeeper's tool kit, you are not learning them to become a bookkeeper—you are learning them to become an informed user of financial statements.

Summary

Financial statements result from the bookkeeping (procedures for sorting, classifying, and presenting the effects of a transaction) and accounting (the selection of alternative methods of reflecting the effects of certain transactions) processes. Bookkeeping procedures for recording transactions use the accounting equation (Assets = Liabilities + Owners' equity), which must be kept in balance.

The income statement is linked to the balance sheet through the retained earnings component of owners' equity. Revenues and expenses of the income statement are subparts of retained earnings that are reported separately as net income (or net loss). Net income (or net loss) for a fiscal period is added to (or subtracted from) retained earnings at the beginning of the fiscal period in the process of determining retained earnings at the end of the fiscal period.

Bookkeeping procedures involve establishing an account for each asset, liability, owners' equity element, revenue, and expense. Accounts can be represented by a "T"; the left side is the debit side and the right side is the credit side. Transactions are recorded in journal entry format, which is as follows:

Dr.   Account name .... Amount
     Cr.   Account name .... Amount

The journal entry is the source of amounts recorded in an account. The ending balance in an account is the positive difference between the debit and credit amounts recorded in the account, including the beginning balance. Asset and expense accounts normally have a debit balance; liability, owners' equity, and revenue accounts normally have a credit balance.

The horizontal model is an easy and meaningful way of understanding the effect of a transaction on the balance sheet and/or income statement. The representation of the horizontal model is as follows:

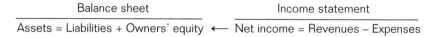

Balance sheet		Income statement
Assets = Liabilities + Owners' equity	←	Net income = Revenues − Expenses

The key to using this model is to keep the balance sheet in balance. The arrow from net income in the income statement to owners' equity in the balance sheet indicates that net income affects retained earnings, which is a component of owners' equity. For a transaction affecting both the balance sheet and income statement, the balance sheet will balance when the income statement effect on owners' equity is considered. In this model, the account name is entered under the appropriate financial statement category, and the dollar effect of the transaction on that account is entered with a plus or minus sign below the account name. The horizontal model can be shortened to the single equation:

$$\text{Assets} = \text{Liabilities} + \text{Owners' equity} + \text{Revenues} - \text{Expenses}$$

Adjusting journal entries describe accruals or reclassifications rather than transactions. Adjustments usually affect both a balance sheet account and an income statement account. Adjustments are part of accrual accounting, and they are required to achieve a matching of revenue and expense so that the financial statements reflect accurately the financial position and results of operations of the entity.

Transaction analysis is the process of determining how a transaction affects the financial statements. Transaction analysis involves asking and answering five questions:

1. What kind of economic transactions occur?
2. What accounts are affected?
3. How are the accounts affected?
4. Does the balance sheet balance? (Do the debits equal the credits?)
5. Does my analysis make sense?

Transactions can be initially recorded in virtually any way that makes sense. Before the preparation of period-end financial statements, a reclassification adjustment can be made to reflect the appropriate asset/liability and revenue/expense recognition with respect to the accounts affected by the transaction (for example, purchase of supplies) and subsequent activities (for example, use of supplies).

Key Words and Phrases

account balance (p. 92) The arithmetic sum of the additions and subtractions to an account through a given date.

accrual (pp. 98, 99) The process of recognizing revenue that has been earned but not collected, or an expense that has been incurred but not paid.

accrued (p. 99) Describes revenue that has been earned and a related asset that will be collected, or an expense that has been incurred and a related liability that will be paid.

adjusting journal entry (p. 98) A journal entry usually made during the process of closing the books that results in more accurate financial statements. Adjusting journal entries involve accruals and reclassifications.

charge (p. 94) In bookkeeping, a synonym for *debit*.

chart of accounts (p. 91) An index of the accounts contained in a ledger.

closing the books (p. 101) The process of posting transactions and adjustments to the ledger and preparing the financial statements.

credit (p. 92) The right side of an account. A decrease in asset and expense accounts; an increase in liability, owners' equity, and revenue accounts.

debit (p. 92) The left side of an account. An increase in asset and expense accounts; a decrease in liability, owners' equity, and revenue accounts.

entry (p. 95) A journal entry or a posting to an account.

horizontal model (p. 96) A representation of the balance sheet and income statement relationship that is useful for understanding the effects of transactions and adjustments on the financial statements.

Balance sheet	Income statement
Assets = Liabilities + Owners' equity ←	Net income = Revenues – Expenses

journal (p. 91) A chronological record of transactions.

journal entry (p. 94) A description of a transaction in a format that shows the debit accounts and amounts and credit accounts and amounts.

ledger (p. 91) A book or file of accounts.

on account (p. 88) Used to describe a purchase or sale transaction for which cash will be paid or received at a later date. A credit transaction.

post (p. 91) The process of recording a transaction in the ledger by using a journal as the source of the information recorded.

source document (p. 95) Evidence of a transaction that supports the journal entry recording the transaction.

T-account (p. 92) An account format with a debit (left) side and a credit (right) side.

transactions (p. 87) Economic interchanges between entities that are accounted for and reflected in financial statements.

transaction analysis methodology (p. 102) The process of answering five questions to ensure that a transaction is understood:

1. What kind of economic transactions occur?
2. What accounts are affected?

3. How are the accounts affected?
4. Does the balance sheet balance? (Do the debits equal the credits?)
5. Does my analysis make sense?

Chapter 5

An Introduction to Insurer Financial Statements

The first four chapters of this text introduced the development of accounting and its basic concepts and principles; described basic financial statements and the information they contain; and explained how the recording of economic transactions affects financial statements. Thus far, the scope of the discussion has been limited to accounting for noninsurance entities and the generally accepted accounting principles (GAAP) by which their financial statements are prepared.

Because of the specialized information needs of regulators and other financial statement users, entities in some industries must produce statements conforming to accounting principles other than GAAP. Insurance is one example of such an industry. In addition to the usual GAAP-based financial statements prepared by other entities subject to SEC reporting requirements, insurers prepare financial statements conforming to statutory accounting principles (SAP).

This chapter explains how statutory accounting evolved to help insurance regulators fulfill their oversight responsibilities such as monitoring insurer solvency. Catastrophic events and market failures, common in the early U.S. insurance markets, illustrate why regulatory intervention is needed. The fiscal conservatism of statutory accounting provides a margin of added protection for insurance consumers. The unique future financial promise of insurance transactions distinguishes insurance from other types of business, justifying SAP's more conservative valuation approach than that afforded by GAAP.

This chapter introduces both GAAP-based and SAP-based insurer financial statements and illustrates how they differ from financial statements prepared by noninsurance entities. Balance sheets and income statements illustrate how relating selected account balances to one another can reveal meaningful information about an insurer's operations and financial condition.

Besides regulators, investors, and insurance producers, insurance consumers benefit from understanding the information contained in SAP-based financial statements. Students interested in understanding insurer financial statements need a working knowledge of *both* GAAP and SAP. This chapter describes differences between GAAP and SAP and establishes a foundation for the more detailed investigation of statutory accounting contained in later chapters.

Educational Objectives

After studying this chapter, you should be able to:

1. Describe major events in the evolution of property-liability insurance in the United States that led to the regulatory intervention in insurance markets.

2. Explain the origin of statutory accounting principles and how they help insurance regulators accomplish their oversight responsibilities. You should be able to:
   - Identify the primary objectives of insurance regulation
   - Explain how accomplishing those objectives can help provide protection for insurance consumers
   - Explain how statutory accounting requirements help regulators meet those objectives

3. Explain how the composition of insurer financial statements differs from that of statements prepared for other business entities. You should be able to:
   - Identify accounts that are unique to insurer operations
   - Identify insurer accounts that, though labeled differently, are similar to accounts usually appearing in noninsurer financial statements

4. Distinguish between each of the following items:
   - Admitted assets and nonadmitted assets
   - Reserves as an allocation of equity and reserves as a liability

- Policyholders' surplus and owners' equity
- Losses and loss adjustment expenses incurred and reserved (unpaid)

5. Explain how statutory accounting principles (SAP) differ from generally accepted accounting principles (GAAP).

6. Given a case situation, describe an insurer's financial position using GAAP-based and SAP-based annual statements.

7. Explain how each of the following performance measures can be determined using accounting information from GAAP-based and SAP-based insurer financial statements:

- Return on owners' equity
- Pure loss ratio
- Net loss ratio
- Financial basis expense ratio
- Trade basis expense ratio
- Financial basis combined ratio
- Trade basis combined ratio

8. Define or describe each of the Key Words and Phrases introduced in this chapter.

Origin and Scope of Statutory Accounting

Information needs can vary widely among financial statement users. Accounting systems must therefore serve different purposes for different users. *Investors* and *security analysts*, for example, are primarily interested in financial accounting information providing income and cash flow measurements. *Lenders* and those responsible for making retail credit decisions are similarly interested in income and cash flow measurements to evaluate a customer's ability to pay, and also in net worth information and assets that could be attached should a customer's account become delinquent. *Managers* need budgets and pro forma financial statements (based on estimates of future operating results) to help them determine whether goals and objectives are being met. *Executives* need cost accounting information from which cost-volume-profit relationships can be identified.

Because an accounting system serves different purposes for different users, a single system would be required to provide various kinds of information simultaneously. For example, cost accounting systems classify, allocate, and assign production costs to the applicable divisions of production. Tax accounting systems provide information to evaluate the company's compliance with tax laws.[1]

Since it would be extremely difficult for one accounting system to meet the needs of all users, separate and distinctly different accounting systems are often used at the same time. Consequently, an entity has a legitimate reason to keep more than one set of books because different users of accounting information have different needs requiring that information be reported in a specified format and conform to prescribed accounting principles. The nature of an organization and the intended use of the financial information reported determine which accounting system is appropriate. Regardless of the accounting system adopted, however, financial statements should be prepared using standard accounting principles. If standard accounting principles were not used consistently, the financial statements of different companies would not be uniform in their presentation and could not be meaningfully compared.

Each of the accounting systems described thus far develops financial statements conforming to generally accepted accounting principles (GAAP). Occasionally, the information needs of a particular group of users are so different that those users require financial reports be prepared in accordance with accounting principles other than GAAP. The insurance industry is one example for which such requirements exist.

What Is Statutory Accounting?[2]

In the United States, property-liability insurers are regulated by the insurance departments of the states. Insurance commissioners and department staff need meaningful financial, statistical, marketing, and operating information to assist them in fulfilling their duties. The regulators' interests and concerns often vary from those of other financial statement users, and in recognition of these special concerns and responsibilities, statutory accounting principles have been established by statute, regulation, and practice.

Statutory accounting principles (SAP) are the accounting principles or practices prescribed or permitted by an insurer's domiciliary insurance department for completion of financial statements filed with that department. These statutory accounting principles have been interspersed in the insurance laws, regulations, and administrative rulings of the various states, the instructions and footnotes to the Annual Statement, the National Association of Insurance Commissioners (NAIC) *Examiners Handbook,* the *Valuations of Securities* manual, NAIC committee minutes, and accepted practices.

Statutory accounting principles are conservative in most respects, but they should be examined in light of the primary statutory responsibility to regulate for financial solvency. SAP tries to determine at the financial statement date the insurer's ability to satisfy its obligations to its policyholders and creditors.

How Statutory Accounting Has Evolved

A better understanding of why statutory accounting principles exist can be gained by reviewing the development of the industry in which they evolved. The history of insurance in the United States reveals key factors that led to regulation of the insurance industry and explains why accounting principles other than GAAP are deemed the appropriate basis for insurer financial statements prepared for use by insurance regulators and others responsible for reviewing insurer operations.

Today, the United States produces the world's largest volume of property-casualty insurance, writing direct premiums exceeding $273 billion, supported by policyholders' surplus exceeding $230 billion in 1995.[3] Although it is today a prominent role model for many developing insurance markets, the U.S. insurance industry experienced many troublesome periods during its early years of development.

During the colonial period, for example, American immigrants were generally poor and individually lacked the wealth necessary to capitalize insurance operations. Collectively, as well, colonists were not allowed to underwrite marine insurance, the most prevalent form of coverage at that time, because a law adopted by Parliament in 1719 (extended to the colonies in 1741) expressly "prohibited partnerships and corporations, except for two corporations designated by the king, from engaging in the marine insurance business."[4] The few individuals willing to underwrite coverage were required to secure risks of loss using their personal assets. As conveyed by the following advertisement, which in 1721 appeared in the *American Weekly Mercury*, the financial strength, character, and stability of the underwriter were, as they are today, of major importance to the prospective insurance buyer.

ADVERTISEMENTS.

Philadelphia, May 25, 1721.

ASSURANCES *from Loffes happening at Sea &c. being found to be very much for the Eafe and Benefit of the Merchants and Traders in general; and whereas the Merchants of this City of* Philadelphia *and other Parts, have been obliged to fend to* London *for fuch Affurance, which has not only been tedious and troublefome, but even very precarious, For remedying of which,* An Office of Publick Infurance on Veffels, Goods and Merchandizes, *will,* on Monday next, be Opened and Books kept by John Copfon *of this City, at his Houfe in the* High Street, *where all Perfons willing to be Infured may apply: And Care fhall be taken by the faid* J. Copfon. *That the Affurors or Under Writers be Perfons of un-doubted Worth and Reputation, and of confiderable Intereft in this City and Province.*

Although marine insurance was generally available at major seaports within the colonies, few individuals were willing to assume the loss exposures associated with fire insurance. Fire, when it did occur, often destroyed the entire structure and its contents: "Most homes and buildings of the period were of frame construction with wooden roofs, and fire protection ranged from inadequate to nonexistent."[5] Fires, a frequent occurrence in the second half of the eighteenth century, often destroyed entire communities or significant portions thereof. For example, a 1740 fire in Charleston, South Carolina, destroyed nearly two-thirds of the city.

Adoption of the Declaration of Independence on July 4, 1776, rendered inoperative the British law prohibiting partnerships and corporations in the colonies.[6] Although individual marine underwriters were still unwilling to assume exposure for fire insurance, other individuals of prominence began pooling their resources to capitalize fire insurance companies. Many of these early companies were undercapitalized and unable to pay their customers' claims when catastrophic losses occurred. When a local insurer became insolvent, the community was often left with little or no protection against future loss, and citizens incurred the financial burden of rebuilding structures for which insurance had already been purchased. Insurers from neighboring communities would often take advantage of the opportunity and rush to the stricken market, offering coverage at prices far less than amounts warranted by the loss exposure. These *foreign* (out-of-state) insurers were often more prone to insolvency than the insurer they replaced because they not only were inadequately capitalized, but were also selling coverage below cost. **Insolvency** occurs when an insurer's available resources are not adequate to cover its financial obligations.

Insolvencies resulting from undercapitalization or inadequate pricing, severe competition of foreign insurers, which often led to price inadequacy, and instances of fraud by principals capitalizing insurance companies caused state legislators to intervene. Attempting to provide protection for their citizens against abuses of unscrupulous or poorly managed insurers, state legislatures set out to devise ways of regulating the formation and licensing of insurers and to institute means by which insurer operations could be monitored and insolvencies prevented. Most business regulation in the nineteenth century was protectionistic. **Protectionist** regulation favors the development and growth of domestic business by discouraging foreign (nondomestic) entities from entering the market. Such competition might force the market price down to such a level that small domestic entities would be forced out of business. Many states instituted licensing and discriminatory tax provisions in the early 1800s in attempts to exclude or reduce the threat of nondomestic insurers.[7]

Many states also passed legislation requiring insurers to file financial statements regularly with the insurance commissioner's office. Massachusetts, in 1837, and New York, in 1853, required statements of such detail that insurers were required to provide estimates of reserves for losses and unearned premiums, respectively. Although the format of early financial reports bears little resemblance to today's Annual Statement, the form was designed to provide regulators with a quick overview of an insurer's liquidity. Exhibit 5-1 illustrates the content of the 1837 Massachusetts form.

By the end of the nineteenth century, most states had instituted formal insurance regulation. Early statutes generally granted authority to license, tax premiums, and require financial reporting. In the early 1900s, legislatures began to broaden regulators' authority to include the supervision of ratemaking and product distribution.

Exhibit 5-1
Annual Statement Form for Insurance Companies in Massachusetts, 1837

Location
Name
Capital
United States Stocks
Massachusetts Stocks
Loans on Bottomry and Respondentia   ***Fund How Invested***
Invested in Real Estate
Secured by Mortgage on Same
Loans on Collateral or Personal Security
Cash on Hand
Due as Book
Reserve Fund

***Names of the Banks and
Amounts owned in Each***

Debts owed
Losses as Ascertained and unpaid
Estimated Amt. of Losses Exclusive of Salvage
At Risk Fire
At Risk Marine
Average Annual Dividend   ***Amount Due***
Highest Rate of Interest Paid or Discount   ***from offices***
    received on Any One Loan
What Amount of Bank Stock returned as
    being owned by the Co. is pledged for
    money borrowed

Source: Claude Lilly, "A History of Insurance Regulation in the United States," *CPCU Annals*, vol. 29, no. 2, June 1976, p. 100, from *Laws of Massachusetts 1837*, Ch. 192, Sec. 2.

Protectionist regulation of the past has given way to a cooperative system of state regulation coordinated through the NAIC. Although regulation has advanced significantly in providing market stability and consumer protection, insolvencies still occur. The regulation of insurance must be responsive to an ever-changing industry and the needs of insurance consumers.

Objectives of Insurance Regulation

Most state insurance codes reflect the language of two Supreme Court decisions that have been instrumental in defining the responsibilities of insurance regulators. In a 1914 case involving the right of the state of Kansas to regulate rates, the Court declared that the business of insurance was "affected with a public interest" and therefore subject to governmental regulation.[8] In 1934, the Court implied that insurance company operations and regulation should fulfill certain public policy objectives.[9] Although statutes differ among individual states, the majority identify those objectives as follows:[10]

- Preserve and enhance solvency
- Promote adequate and fair premium rates
- Ensure fairness, equity, and reasonableness in insurance markets
- Fulfill certain social goals not necessarily pertinent to a successful insurance operation

Uniform statutory accounting principles and financial reporting requirements help provide the information needed by regulators to monitor insurer solvency and accomplish the above objectives. Statutory accounting directly addresses the first objective cited above. The conservative valuation methods emphasized in SAP, described in greater detail in later sections of this chapter and in Chapter 11, provide a conservative statement of an insurer's net worth, the estimated value that could be realized if the insurer were immediately forced to liquidate its assets. Less conservative valuation methods employed by GAAP are based on the going-concern assumption and report a net worth value that might not be realizable should the insurer be forced to liquidate its assets immediately.

To a lesser degree, statutory accounting addresses the remaining three objectives by providing a standard basis for reporting insurers' accounting information to those responsible for their regulatory oversight and solvency surveillance. Access to accounting information prepared on a standard basis allows regulators to readily compare one insurer's operating results to those of other insurers or industry benchmarks and determine whether the insurer's performance measures are within an acceptable range or whether its financial strength meets minimum statutory requirements.

Although statutory accounting has evolved to meet the unique information needs of insurance regulators, significant benefits accrue to others involved with the insurance industry because of SAP's standardized financial reporting. Insurers and their customers can make direct comparisons among companies to evaluate their operating performance and financial condition.

Unique Characteristics of Insurers and Their Financial Statements

The business of insurance differs from other types of business in many respects. Similarly, financial statements of insurers differ from those prepared by other business entities. The intangible nature of the insurance product, a guarantee of future financial performance, sets the industry apart from manufacturing or merchandising, in which outputs are generally physical products delivered at the point of sale. The capital structure, resource allocation, and business operation of insurance entities are also markedly different from a typical manufacturing or merchandising entity.

Because the insurance industry is a segment of the financial services economic sector, one might expect insurance entities to resemble other financial institutions in terms of their assets and liabilities. The opposite is true, however. The composition of a property-liability insurer's balance sheet is significantly different from the balance sheet of a commercial bank or a savings and loan. Understanding how the insurance mechanism works helps explain why many of these differences exist.

Insurance Defined

The following statement provides an operational definition of insurance that helps explain how insurance differs from other types of business:

> Insurance is a *social device* in which a *group* of individuals *transfer risk* in order to combine experience, which permits *mathematical prediction* of losses, and provides for payment of losses from *funds contributed* [pooled] by all members who transferred risk. Those who transfer risk are called insureds. Those who assume risk are called insurers.[11]

Key concepts in the above definition of insurance are the *transfer of risk* from insured to insurer and the pooling of funds from a group of insureds that collectively pay future losses of those insureds. **Risk** is present when the *actual* outcome of an event can vary from the *expected* outcome for that event. This is a slightly different perspective of risk than that used in Chapter 3, which stated that risk relates to the range of possible outcomes, and as that range increases, so does the risk. Every business, including insurance, incurs risk in its operations: risk resulting from external market influence such as changing demand and risk associated with generating sufficient revenues to cover its costs including costs of financing the business. An insurer, however, adds to the risks normally experienced by all businesses when it *assumes* risk associated with the loss exposures of insureds.

When risk exists, funds contributed to the pool must be sufficient to cover the unknown future loss amounts of the few members that experience an insured loss. Not only must the funds be *adequate* to pay those losses, but the funds must also be *readily available* for payment when those losses are reported. If either of these conditions is not met, the insurer cannot meet its contractual obligations and will likely be deemed insolvent. Solvency requires that an insurer have adequate resources to cover all insured losses regardless of risks associated with changing market conditions or its operating performance.

In most businesses, goods or services are delivered at the point of sale for a price that covers known production costs and a reasonable margin for profit. In insurance, however, the product is a contractual guarantee of future financial performance (at some unknown time) contingent on the occurrence of an insured event resulting in loss (for some unknown amount) but sold for a specific (known) premium amount.[12] The purpose of insurance regulators' emphasis on solvency is to ensure that insurers have sufficient net worth available to allow for a margin of safety should an insurer's estimate of future loss or required premium amount be inadequate.

Comparing Financial Statements of Insurers and Noninsurers

The output produced by a firm and the nature of its business operations have considerable influence on the composition of its financial statements. One might expect that the balance sheet for a manufacturing firm would report large amounts for fixed plant and equipment items and for inventories of raw materials or goods in process. Similarly, a merchandising firm's balance sheet would typically report large amounts for merchandise inventory and accounts receivable.

Both manufacturing and merchandising entities report the cost of goods produced or sold on their income statement. Insurers, however, neither manufacture goods (so they have no need for plant and equipment) nor sell physical merchandise to customers or distributors (so they have no need for merchandise inventory). Nor do insurers incur those costs associated with the manufacture or purchase of goods for sale. What, then, do insurers report on their financial statements, and how does the composition of those statements compare with noninsurance business entities?

Balance Sheet Comparison

Exhibit 5-2 provides abbreviated balance sheets and income statements for The Home Depot, Inc., and Argonaut Insurance Group for the operating year 1995. For Home Depot, inventories account for 29.6 percent of the entity's total assets, and property, plant, and equipment (net of depreciation) account for 60.7 percent. By contrast, Argonaut Insurance Group does not even include those items on its balance sheet.

Insurers typically report a high concentration of assets in marketable securities or other investments. The GAAP-based balance sheet for Argonaut shows that it has 52.9 percent of its total assets invested in bonds and 19.5 percent in stocks. Holding such a high proportion of assets in marketable securities is consistent with insurance being a part of the financial services economic sector.

Because insurance premiums generally must be paid before the policy period, insurers do not have customer accounts receivable balances to report. They do, however, report premiums receivable and reinsurance recoverable. **Premiums receivable** represent premium amounts due from agents or other insurers for exposures assumed by the reporting insurer. The **reinsurance recoverable** amount represents losses and loss adjustment expense amounts owed the reporting insurer under reinsurance agreements for losses paid. Argonaut reports a premiums receivable amount equal to 10 percent of its total assets and a reinsurance recoverable amount equal to 9.9 percent of its total assets.

Liabilities for Home Depot are primarily composed of accounts payable (11.2 percent of total assets) and long-term debt (9.8 percent of total assets). In contrast, Argonaut does not report *any* accounts labeled "payables." Instead, the insurer reports reserve accounts for losses and unearned premiums. For insurance entities, **reserves** are liabilities associated with the future performance of service that may be required under the insurance contract. For noninsurance entities, the term "reserves" is typically used to identify a restriction on retained earnings for a particular purpose, indicating that such an amount cannot be used to pay dividends. **Loss and loss adjustment expense reserves** (L&LAE reserves) represent the insurer's liability for unpaid losses and associated adjustment expenses. Similarly, **unearned premiums** represent the portion of insurance premiums written that has not yet been earned and is attributable to unexpired coverage (the insurer's remaining contractual obligation).

A significant distinction between Argonaut and Home Depot is the proportion of total liabilities and owners' equity represented by total liabilities: the amount is nearly twice as large for Argonaut (59.7 percent) as it is for Home Depot (32.2 percent). This is because the asset structure for an insurer is concentrated in highly liquid current assets (not in plant and equipment, generally financed with fixed debt) and because most claims against those assets are related to performance obligations under the insurance contract, many of which will not be fulfilled until some future period perhaps several years from now. The accumulated value of these future obligations results in total liabilities representing a greater proportion of the right side of the balance sheet for an insurer than for a noninsurer. Also, insurers rarely use long-term debt (bonds) to finance operations, relying instead on the investment returns from cash flows generated from insurance transactions.

Although the proportion of total liabilities and owners' equity (equal to total assets) represented by owners' equity is much greater for Home Depot (67.8 percent) than it is for Argonaut (40.3 percent), the proportion represented by retained earnings is roughly equivalent (35.1 percent for Home Depot and 29.8 percent for Argonaut).

Income Statement Comparison

The income statement for Home Depot shown in Exhibit 5-2 looks like the income statements shown in previous chapters. The most significant expense items are cost of goods sold (72.3 percent of net sales) and selling, general, and administrative expense (20.1 percent of net sales). The income statement for Argonaut Insurance Group, however, does not report these items. In fact, the statement barely resembles the income statements addressed so far. Argonaut's income statement is organized to reflect the dual operations of an insurer: insurance underwriting activities and investing activities. Related to each activity are revenues earned and expenses incurred for that activity.

Unlike the abbreviated statement in Exhibit 5-2, most statements for insurers actually divide the income statement into activity-related sections. Major items reported for underwriting activities are premiums earned, losses and loss adjustment expense incurred, and other underwriting expenses. **Premiums earned** represent the portion of insurance premiums written, including unearned amounts carried forward from prior periods, that has been earned during the period for insurance services provided. **Losses and loss adjustment expenses incurred** represent amounts paid for losses and loss adjustment plus changes in reserves for those items during the period reported. **Other underwriting expenses** represent expenses associated with underwriting the insured exposure including acquisition costs, engineering and inspection fees, and costs to maintain the underwriting department.

Major items reported for investing activities are net investment income and net realized capital gains. **Net investment income** includes such items as stock dividends, bond coupons, and rental income received. **Net realized capital gains** reflect amounts received, net of expenses, from the sale of invested assets.

Comparing GAAP-Based and SAP-Based Insurer Financial Statements

Several differences exist between an insurer's GAAP-based and SAP-based financial statements, most of which result from conventions adopted as

Exhibit 5-2

Comparison of Financial Statements—1995 Operations (All dollar amounts in millions)

Argonaut Insurance Group
Balance Sheet
as of December 31, 1995

Assets / Admitted assets	GAAP		SAP	
Cash	$ 23.3	1.2%	$ 22.9	1.3%
Bonds	1,063.8	52.9	1,016.5	58.8
Stocks	393.4	19.5	416.2	24.1
Short-term investments	34.9	1.7	27.6	1.6
Premiums receivable	201.3	10.0	175.4	10.1
Reinsurance recoverable	198.6	9.9	31.2	1.8
Accrued invest. income	23.9	1.2	23.9	1.4
Other assets	73.1	3.6	16.3	0.9
Total assets/Admitted assets	$2,012.3	100.0	$1,730.0	100.0

Liabilities & Owners' equity / Policyholders' surplus	GAAP		SAP	
Loss & LAE reserves	$1,060.9	52.7%	$ 892.9	51.6%
Unearned premiums	64.0	3.2	61.2	3.5
Excess statutory reserves	n.a.	n.a.	21.7	1.3
Other liabilities	76.6	3.8	123.4	7.1
Total liabilities	$1,201.5	59.7	$1,099.2	63.5
Common capital stock	2.4	0.1	4.5	0.3
Additional paid-in capital	97.7	4.9	59.0	3.4
Retained earnings/ Unassigned funds	598.9	29.8	534.3	30.9
Unrealized capital gains	111.8	5.6	33.0	1.9
Owners' equity/ Policyholders' surplus	$ 810.8	40.3	$ 630.8	36.5
Total liabilities & OE/Surplus	$2,012.3	100.0	$1,730.0	100.0

The Home Depot, Inc.
Balance Sheet
as of January 28, 1996

Assets	GAAP	
Cash	$ 53.3	0.7%
Marketable securities	54.8	0.7
Receivables	325.4	4.4
Inventories	2,180.3	29.6
Other current assets	58.2	0.8
Property, plant & equip. (net)	4,461.0	60.7
Intangibles	87.2	1.2
Other assets	133.8	1.8
Total assets	$7,354.0	100.0

Liabilities & Owners' equity	GAAP	
Accounts payable	$ 824.8	11.2%
Accrued expenses	554.1	7.5
Long-term debt	720.1	9.8
Other liabilities	267.2	3.6
Total liabilities	$2,366.2	32.2
Common capital stock	23.9	0.3
Additional paid-in capital	2,407.8	32.7
Retained earnings	2,579.1	35.1
Other equities (min. int. liab.)	(23.0)	(0.3)
Owners' equity	$4,987.8	67.8
Total liabilities & Owners' equity	$7,354.0	100.0

Argonaut Insurance Group
Income Statement
for the Year Ended December 31, 1995

	GAAP		SAP	
Premiums earned	$208.1	100.0%	$208.1	100.0%
Losses & LAE incurred	152.8	73.4	152.9	73.5
Other underwriting expenses	67.3	32.3	68.4	32.9
Net underwriting gain (loss)	$(12.0)	(5.8)	$(13.2)	(6.3)
Net investment income	102.0	49.0	100.0	48.1
Net realized capital gains	3.1	1.5	3.4	1.6
Net investment gain (loss)	$105.1	50.5	$103.4	49.7
Other income (expense)	(23.4)	(11.2)	(27.6)	(13.3)
Provision for income taxes	12.8	6.2	4.5	2.2
Net income	$ 56.9	27.3	$ 58.1	27.9

The Home Depot, Inc.
Income Statement
for the Year Ended January 28, 1996

	GAAP	
Net sales	$15,470.4	100.0%
Cost of goods sold	11,184.8	72.3
Gross profit	$ 4,285.6	27.7
Selling, general, admin. expenses	3,105.7	20.1
Nonoperating income	19.6	0.1
Earnings before int. & taxes	$ 1,199.5	7.8
Interest	4.2	0.0
Earnings before taxes	$ 1,195.3	7.7
Provision for income taxes	463.8	3.0
Net income	$ 731.5	4.7

Sources: Argonaut Group, Inc., GAAP-based financial information obtained from the group's 1995 Annual Report.

Argonaut Group, Inc., SAP-based financial information obtained from the 1995 Combined Annual Statement of the Argonaut Insurance Company and its Affiliated Property and Casualty Insurers reported to the NAIC.

Home Depot, Inc., financial statement information obtained from Disclosure, Inc., on America Online.

statutory accounting evolved or from valuation differences that exist between SAP and GAAP. This section will identify the major differences between the abbreviated SAP-based and GAAP-based financial statements for Argonaut Insurance Group shown in Exhibit 5-2. Later sections of this chapter and Chapter 11 will explain the specific differences in asset and liability valuation methods, revenue recognition, and application of the matching concept stemming from statutory accounting.

Balance Sheet Comparison

Perhaps the most readily apparent distinctions between the SAP-based and GAAP-based balance sheets are the labels for an insurer's assets and its net worth. As stated in Chapter 1, assets represent the value of resources the entity owns. Statutory accounting, however, restricts what assets can appear on the statutory balance sheet. Those allowable assets under SAP are referred to as "admitted assets." On a GAAP-based balance sheet, an entity's net worth is labeled "owners' equity." SAP labels the insurer's net worth as **policyholders' surplus**. This difference reflects the major focus of insurance regulation that sufficient resources be available to satisfy *policyholders'* claims at all times, recognizing that even when the best valuation methods are used, assets might be overvalued and unpaid loss liabilities (reserves) might be undervalued.

Other significant differences exist between an insurer's SAP-based and GAAP-based balance sheets in the amounts reported for admitted assets (total assets under GAAP) and for policyholders' surplus (owners' equity under GAAP). Amounts reported for many asset items under SAP are smaller than amounts reported for those same items under GAAP. This can be seen by comparing the amounts reported for premiums receivable and reinsurance recoverable on Argonaut Insurance Group's balance sheets in Exhibit 5-2. Amounts for both asset items are much smaller as reported under SAP than under GAAP. The reason for those differences will be explained later in this chapter and in Chapter 11.

Similarly, the net worth amount reported as policyholders' surplus under SAP is less than the net worth amount reported as owners' equity under GAAP. Those differences in asset and net worth amounts result from applying the conservative valuation rules under statutory accounting.

Income Statement Comparison

Negligible differences exist between an insurer's SAP-based and GAAP-based income statements in terms of amounts reported for various items. Differences in amounts reported under SAP and GAAP for two items, however, can be much larger than those shown for Argonaut Insurance Group in Exhibit 5-2.

First, if premium volume is growing, the amount reported for other underwriting expenses is typically larger on an insurer's SAP-based income statement than on its GAAP-based income statement. (The opposite would be true if the insurer's premium volume were declining.) This difference results because SAP requires immediate expense recognition instead of the GAAP method of *matching* expenses with the revenues they generate for the period. Second, the amounts reported under the label "provision for income taxes" will likely differ between an insurer's SAP-based and GAAP-based income statements because of the income effect of timing differences in expense recognition, which creates a *deferred federal income tax liability*.[13] These deferred federal income taxes will be paid in a later tax year.

Balance Sheet Differences Due to Organizational Form

For ease of comparison with noninsurance entities, this chapter limited the discussion of insurer financial statements to include only those of *stock* insurance companies. Not all insurance companies, however, are capitalized by selling shares of stock. A **mutual insurance company** is organized and owned by its *policyholders*. Mutual insurers do not issue stock and thus have no stockholders. The balance sheet effect as explained by the Insurance and Accounting Systems Association (IASA) is that "the original net worth of a mutual company consists *only* of surplus paid in by the original policyholders, or by an interested party who wishes to get the mutual company into operation."[14] Another difference between mutual and stock companies is that the surplus paid-in is entered on the line entitled *guaranty funds* in the policyholders' surplus section of the mutual insurer's balance sheet. As stockholders do in a stock insurance company, policyholders elect the directors, who in turn appoint officers to manage the mutual insurance company. With the exception that capital stock does not appear in the policyholders' surplus section of a mutual insurer's balance sheet and the label for surplus paid-in, discussion to this point has applied to both stock insurance companies and mutual insurance companies.

How Statutory Accounting Principles Differ From Generally Accepted Accounting Principles

The evolution of GAAP reflects the needs of a large and diverse group of users—primarily those concerned with making investment and credit decisions—for "general purpose" financial information. In contrast, statutory accounting principles have evolved in response to the specific information needs of insurance regulators. Consequently, differences between GAAP and SAP are directly linked to the objectives of regulation and to the information needed to assure that regulatory objectives are accomplished.

Going Concern Versus Solvency Perspective

Most investment and credit decisions involve business enterprises that are expected to continue operating into the future. Generally accepted accounting principles reflect this expectation, placing the focus of financial reporting on earnings rather than on trying to measure the value of an enterprise. The focus on earnings is considered appropriate because investors and creditors are concerned with an enterprise's ability to generate favorable future cash flows that will provide them with both a return *on* their investment as well as a return *of* their investment. The assumption of business continuity, also referred to as the going-concern assumption, is fundamental to financial accounting and reporting under GAAP: it supports the use of accrual accounting and the matching principle and provides a conceptual basis for classifying balance sheet items as either current or long term. However, when information suggests that an entity will not continue in business, conventional accounting is suspended in favor of liquidation accounting. The focus of financial reporting under **liquidation accounting** is on reporting assets and liabilities at their liquidation values.

Solvency regulation is one of the primary responsibilities of state insurance regulators. Although regulators still consider earnings important, regulators are more concerned with the ability of an insurer to discharge its financial obligations to policyholders and claimants at a given point in time. Statutory accounting principles reflect this concern, placing the focus of financial reporting on measuring financial condition instead of operating performance, specifically profitability. Consequently, SAP rules emphasize the measurement of policyholders' surplus (net assets), placing less emphasis on the matching of revenues and expenses. This balance sheet emphasis is further reinforced by requiring that certain items be measured using more conservative liquidation values than those allowed under GAAP. Use of liquidation values, in turn, is justified because SAP does not strictly adhere to the going-concern assumption.

Conservative Valuation of Policyholders' Surplus

Valuation is a measurement process that assigns dollar values to elements of an economic transaction or event. In this regard, the principle of conservatism plays an important role in both GAAP and SAP. The principle of conservatism holds that when two or more accounting methods are acceptable for a particular transaction or event, the method least likely to overstate owners' equity should be chosen. That is, preference is given to methods that are *least likely* to overstate income, revenues, or assets, and methods that are *least likely* to understate expenses or liabilities.

The specific valuation rules required by statutory accounting principles have been developed to support the objectives of solvency regulation. These rules are intended to assure that policyholders' surplus is conservatively measured. Conservative valuation of policyholders' surplus is made possible, in part, by favoring the use of liquidation rather than going-concern values for certain assets, applying specific valuation rules to certain liabilities included in an insurer's statutory balance sheet, and adopting rules that modify the recognition of expenses.

Asset Valuation

GAAP formally defines assets as items that represent "probable future economic benefits" to the business enterprise. With few exceptions, assets are recorded and maintained on the balance sheet at their original cost. Statutory accounting principles are much more restrictive. Assets must meet minimum standards of liquidity before they are recognized on the balance sheet for statutory reporting purposes. These liquidity standards require that an asset be quickly convertible into cash without risking a significant loss relative to market value.[15] Investments in securities, for example, can usually be sold immediately at a known price. Other assets (such as office furniture and supplies) might require a longer period to sell and may only be salable at a discounted price.

Consequently, some assets that would be included in a balance sheet prepared in accordance with GAAP are *excluded* from the balance sheet prepared in accordance with SAP. Assets included in the SAP balance sheet are collectively referred to as **admitted assets**. Assets excluded from the SAP balance sheet are referred to as **nonadmitted assets**. Excluding nonadmitted assets from the balance sheet is equivalent to assigning *no* value to these assets for statutory reporting purposes.

Nonadmitted assets include the following:[16]

- Furniture, fixtures, and equipment
- Supplies
- Automobiles
- Uncollected premiums (accounts receivable) over ninety days past due

Since SAP follow the basic accounting equation,

Assets = Liabilities + Policyholders' surplus, or
Policyholders' surplus = Assets – Liabilities,

assigning a zero value to any asset results in a dollar-for-dollar reduction in the value of policyholders' surplus. To the extent that an insurer holds nonadmitted assets, the amount of policyholders' surplus shown in its SAP balance sheet will be less than the amount of owners' equity shown on its GAAP balance sheet. The amount of the difference would be equal to the value of nonadmitted assets.

For illustration purposes in this and future chapters, the financial statements for a hypothetical company, Exemplar Insurance, will be used.

Assume that Exemplar's GAAP balance sheet shows total assets of $1,693,000 and $1,036,000 of liabilities. For statutory reporting purposes, $254,000 of furniture and fixtures is classified as nonadmitted assets. Exhibit 5-3 shows the balance sheet effects of nonadmitted assets.

Exhibit 5-3
Balance Sheet Effects of Nonadmitted Assets for Exemplar Insurance Co.

	Assets	=	Liabilities	+	Policyholders' Surplus (Owners' Equity)
GAAP	$1,693,000	=	$1,036,000	+	$ 657,000
Nonadmitted Assets	(254,000)	=	—	+	(254,000)
SAP	$1,439,000	=	$1,036,000	+	$ 403,000

The example in Exhibit 5-3 illustrates how effective the use of liquidation values for certain assets can be in supporting the regulatory objective of conservatively valuing policyholders' surplus. The effect of imposing the conservative asset valuation rules required by SAP is to reduce the reported value of policyholders' surplus by an amount equal to the value of nonadmitted assets. In this example, reducing Exemplar's total assets by $254,000 represents a 15 percent reduction in assets, but reducing policyholders' surplus by the same $254,000 represents a 39 percent reduction in policyholders' surplus.

Liability Valuation

Both GAAP and SAP define liabilities as future economic sacrifices that will require a future outflow of assets (such as the payment of cash) or the rendering of services (such as providing insurance coverage) to settle existing obligations to creditors. When more than one acceptable method for measuring a liability's value is available, the principle of conservatism gives preference to the method that yields the higher value. The concept of conservatism plays an important role in SAP because the major liabilities of property liability insurers—the reserves for losses and loss adjustment expenses—are based on estimates.

Reserves for losses and loss adjustment expenses represent the dollar amount that would be required to settle all of an insurer's unpaid claims. Precise valuation of this liability would require that the insurer know with certainty not only the costs associated with claims that have already been submitted to it, but also the number and dollar amounts of claims for losses that have occurred but not yet been presented to the insurer. Since these amounts are uncertain, part of the reserve for L&LAE must be estimated.

The sufficiency of these reserves is crucial to evaluating the financial health of an insurer. On average, the reserves for L&LAE account for about 70 percent of an insurer's total liabilities and are about twice the amount of policyholders' surplus. Consequently, errors in the valuation of the reserve for L&LAE can have significant effects on the value of policyholders' surplus and, therefore, on the financial strength of the insurer.

Several acceptable mathematical techniques can be used to establish the value of the L&LAE reserve for each line of insurance. These generally provide a range of estimates rather than a single "best" estimate for the value of the total L&LAE liability. Although conservatism gives preference to the method that yields the highest value for the liability, statutory accounting principles go one step further by requiring that the reserves for certain lines of insurance be subject to a minimum amount, determined by applying a specified formula. When this minimum amount is greater than the estimated value reported in the insurer's SAP balance sheet, the difference is recorded as an additional liability—**excess of statutory reserves over statement reserves**. Generally accepted accounting principles do not require the insurer to recognize this additional liability.

Five lines of insurance are now subject to this statutory minimum reserve requirement:

- Automobile liability (private passenger and commercial)
- Other liability and products liability
- Medical malpractice
- Workers compensation
- Credit accident and health

Each of these lines of business covers risks to which the general public is exposed and typically represent lines of insurance subject to extended periods of loss development. Setting minimum reserves for these lines is consistent with the regulatory objective of assuring protection of the public interest.

Exhibit 5-3 assumed that an insurer's GAAP balance sheet shows total assets of $1,693,000 and total liabilities of $1,036,000. For statutory reporting purposes, $254,000 of furniture and fixtures is classified as nonadmitted. Further assume that the insurer's liabilities consist of $710,000 of L&LAE reserves and $326,000 of other liabilities. Also assume that the insurer is required to report an additional $14,000 as excess of statutory reserves over statement reserves. Exhibit 5-4 shows the comparative GAAP and SAP balance sheets for Exemplar Insurance Company.

Exhibit 5-4
Comparative GAAP and SAP Balance Sheets for Exemplar Insurance Co.

	GAAP	GAAP-SAP Difference	SAP
Total assets	$1,693,000	Less $254,000 of nonadmitted assets	$1,439,000
Liabilities			
L&LAE reserves	$ 710,000	None	$ 710,000
Other liabilities	326,000	None	326,000
Excess of statutory reserves		Additional liability for SAP purposes only	$ 14,000
Total liabilities	$1,036,000		$1,050,000
Owners' equity (Surplus)	657,000	Decrease of 41%	389,000
Total liabilities & owners' equity (Surplus)	$1,693,000	Decrease of 15%	$1,439,000

Conservative Income Measurement

The year-end value of policyholders' surplus reported in an insurer's balance sheet includes the amount of net income reported in the income statement for the accounting period. Under GAAP, matching the amount of revenue and expense within an accounting period (as directed by the matching principle) is a primary concern.

Applying the concept of conservatism to income measurement gives preference to methods that show the smallest amounts of net income. This conservative measurement can be achieved by using methods that either result in *recognizing less revenue* or result in *recognizing more expense* within the accounting period.

Revenue Measurement

Determining the amount of net income begins with measuring the amount of revenue to be recognized in the accounting period. Property-liability insurer revenues are derived from the premiums paid or owed to the insurer by customers in return for the insurer's promise to provide them with financial protection for a given period of time (the policy term). Generally, insurance premiums are paid in advance, and the policy term will typically span two of the insurer's fiscal years. For example, a customer may pay the full $600 premium on a six-month automobile insurance policy that covers the period from November 1 through April 30 of the following year. Since the insurer prepares its financial statements on December 31, an important question is: How much of the premium received in October should be shown as revenue for the period ending December 31?

For income determination, both GAAP and SAP recognize the amount of revenue *earned* during an accounting period. In the example above, the insurer would have provided the customer with insurance coverage for the period from November 1 through December 31, one-third of the six-month policy term. Consequently, only one-third, $200, of the premium received would be included in the income statement as "premiums earned." At December 31, the remaining $400 of *unearned premium* is shown on the insurer's balance sheet as a liability because it represents an obligation of the insurer to provide coverage to its customer in the first four months of the next calendar year. Exhibit 5-5 shows the effects on an insurer's December 31 balance sheet and income statement.

Exhibit 5-5
Income Determination

	Balance Sheet	Income Statement
Cash received (asset)	$600①	
Written premiums (revenue)		$600 ①
Unearned premiums (liability)	$400②	–400 ②
Earned premiums		$200 ③

In Step 1, the insurer records receipt of the premium as a $600 increase in assets (cash) and a $600 increase in written premiums (premium revenue). At the end of the year, the insurer recognizes that two-thirds of the premium is still unearned. Step 2 shows that revenues are reduced by the amount that remains unearned ($400), and a corresponding liability—unearned premiums—is recorded. The remaining $200 shown in Step 3 is the amount of premium revenue earned during the period and used in determining the amount of the insurer's income for the period.

Expense Measurement

Insurers incur a number of expenses that are directly traceable to providing insurance coverage to their customers. These costs consist of such items as commissions paid to agents, the costs of printing and mailing the insurance policy, set-up costs to record the initial premium, and state premium taxes, among others. Collectively, these costs are referred to as **policy acquisition costs** because they are directly associated with the issuance of insurance coverage and occur at the inception of the policy term.

GAAP views these costs as benefiting the insurer over the policy term. Applying the matching principle, GAAP recognizes these costs as expenses on a pro rata basis to achieve a matching of revenues (earned premiums) and related expenses (in this case, policy acquisition costs) in the same accounting period. Policy acquisition costs that have not yet been charged to expense are shown as a prepaid asset (deferred policy acquisition costs) on the GAAP balance sheet. The appropriateness of this treatment depends on GAAP's maintaining the going-concern assumption: a cost incurred today can only provide benefits in future periods if the business enterprise continues to operate into the future.

SAP follows a more conservative approach—all policy acquisition costs are immediately charged to expense. Consequently, policy acquisition costs are not included in the SAP balance sheet as prepaid assets. Immediately expensing policy acquisition costs is justified because SAP does not strictly adhere to the going-concern assumption. It is a conservative approach in that it accelerates the recognition of an expense, thereby decreasing income during the period in which the costs (such as acquisition expense) are incurred. Consequently, in an environment of increasing written premium any increase in an insurer's policyholders' surplus attributable to net income will be less when the financial statements are prepared in accordance with SAP than when they are prepared in accordance with GAAP.

The information that was presented in Exhibit 5-4 can be used to construct a more complete version of Exemplar's income statement and balance sheet.

The balance sheet and income statement presented in Exhibit 5-8 include the effects of the conservative SAP valuation rules that have been discussed so far. In addition, some additional detail has been added, for example, an itemized list of the insurer's assets. The additional information will prove useful in the discussion about how to obtain information from insurer's financial statements in the next section.

To construct the income statement, assume that Exemplar has written premiums of $515,000 during 1997. At December 31, 1997, the balance of unearned premiums is $251,000. During 1997, Exemplar also incurred losses of $218,000 and loss adjustment expenses of $40,000 (as shown in Exhibit 5-8). Policy acquisition costs (underwriting expenses) of $84,000 were incurred and paid during 1997.

For GAAP purposes only, the insurer needs to report deferred policy acquisition costs. Assume Exemplar began the year with $31,000 of deferred policy acquisition costs and reports $49,000 of deferred policy acquisition costs in its year-end balance sheet.

To construct the income statement, the amount of the revenues for the period needs to be determined first. To do this, some additional information from the prior year's balance sheet is needed. Exemplar reported $56,000 of unearned premiums in its prior-year's balance sheet, and the amount of earned premiums used in calculating income can be found in Exhibit 5-6.

Exhibit 5-6
Determining the Amount of Premiums Earned for Exemplar (GAAP and SAP)

Unearned premiums	
beginning balance	$ 56,000
Add: Net premiums written	515,000
	$571,000
Less: Unearned premiums	
ending balance	251,000
Premiums earned, current year	$320,000

The amount of earned premiums calculated in Exhibit 5-6 is used in constructing both the GAAP and the SAP income statements.

Second, the amount of expense that will be deducted from revenues to determine underwriting income needs to be determined. The issue here is to recognize the difference between how GAAP and SAP treat policy acquisition costs. For SAP purposes, all policy acquisition costs are expensed when incurred. Consequently, the full $84,000 incurred and paid in the current year would be expensed for SAP purposes. For GAAP, an additional calculation is required. Exhibit 5-7 shows this calculation.

The $66,000 of expense calculated in Exhibit 5-7 is the amount recognized as expense on the GAAP income statement. Although other differences between GAAP and SAP can affect income, this text will only consider this difference.

Exhibit 5-7
Determining Current Period Expenses for Exemplar (GAAP only)

Deferred policy acquisition costs	
Beginning balance	$ 31,000
Plus: Current year costs incurred	84,000
	$115,000
Less: Ending balance	49,000
Current period expense	$ 66,000

Exhibit 5-8 shows the resulting GAAP and SAP balance sheets and income statements, incorporating the calculations from Exhibits 5-6 and 5-7, for Exemplar Insurance Company. Amounts reported in the GAAP and SAP balance sheets reflect the different treatments given to nonadmitted assets, deferred policy acquisition costs, and the recognition of excess of statutory reserves over statement reserves as an additional liability. As noted above, the income statements reflect only the difference in treatment given to policy acquisition costs.

Exhibit 5-8
Comparative GAAP/SAP Financial Statements for Exemplar Insurance Co.

Balance Sheet:	GAAP	SAP
Assets:		
Cash	$ 145,000	$ 145,000
Investments	1,150,000	1,150,000
Premiums receivable	95,000	95,000
Deferred policy acquisition costs	49,000	—
Furniture and fixture	254,000	—
Total assets	$1,693,000	$1,390,000

	GAAP	SAP
Liabilities:		
Loss reserves	$ 530,000	$ 530,000
Loss adjustment expense reserves	180,000	180,000
Excess of statutory over statement reserves	—	14,000
Unearned premiums	251,000	251,000
Other liabilities	75,000	75,000
Total liabilities	$1,036,000	$1,050,000
Owners' equity (Policyholders' surplus):		
Common stock	150,000	150,000
Additional paid-in capital	50,000	50,000
Retained earnings (Unassigned funds)	457,000	140,000
Total equity (Surplus)	$ 657,000	$ 340,000
Total liabilities and equity (Surplus):	$1,693,000	$1,390,000

	GAAP	SAP
Statement of Income:		
Premiums earned	$ 320,000	$ 320,000
Underwriting deductions:		
Losses	218,000	218,000
Loss adjustment expenses	40,000	40,000
Other underwriting expenses (policy acquisition costs)	66,000	84,000
Total underwriting deductions	$ 324,000	$ 342,000
Net underwriting gain or (loss)	$ (4,000)	$ (22,000)
Net investment income	77,000	77,000
Other income	3,000	3,000
Income before income taxes	$ 76,000	$ 58,000
Income taxes	22,000	22,000
Net income	$ 54,000	$ 36,000

Statement of Retained Earnings (GAAP):

	GAAP
Retained earnings, beginning of year	$ 403,000
Net income	54,000
Dividends to shareholders	0
Retained earnings, end of year	$ 457,000

Statement of Changes in Policyholders' Surplus (SAP):

	SAP
Policyholders' surplus, beginning of year	$ 298,000
Net income	36,000
Increase in nonadmitted assets	12,000
Decrease in excess statutory reserves	(6,000)
Dividends to shareholders	0
Change in surplus for the year	$ 42,000
Policyholders' surplus, end of year	$ 340,000

Obtaining Information From Insurer Financial Statements

Financial statements of a business enterprise convey summary information to users about the firm's financial position and the results of its operations. For some purposes, the amounts reported in the income statement and balance sheet may be used directly, that is, without any further analysis. In most cases, however, some additional analysis is necessary before meaningful conclusions can be drawn. This section will narrowly focus on additional analysis by looking at relationships among individual items appearing in the financial statements through the use of some basic but widely used ratios.

Drawing Information Directly From the Financial Statements

Exhibit 5-8 provides the balance sheet at December 31, 1997, and income statement for the year ended December 31, 1997, of the Exemplar Insurance Company on both a GAAP and SAP basis. Taking the reported amount for total assets directly from the GAAP balance sheet, or the amount of admitted assets from the SAP balance sheet provides the user with a basis for classifying Exemplar into one of several size categories. Such classifications are routinely made by reporting agencies such as Best's. For this purpose, the reported amount is significant by itself.

Focusing on the bottom line of Exemplar's GAAP and SAP income might cause a user to conclude that this insurer operated profitably during 1997. However, a user cannot determine whether Exemplar's earnings are improving or declining, nor can a user determine whether Exemplar's earnings are above average or below average. To draw these conclusions, additional information and analysis are required.

The financial statements can also convey information by what they do or do not contain. For example, Exemplar's SAP balance sheet shows that policy-holders' surplus reported at December 31, 1997, was reduced by $14,000 because of the recognition of excess statutory reserves over statement reserves. However, further analysis is required before a user can conclude that Exemplar's management is being overly optimistic in estimating its loss reserves.

These are but a few examples of information that can be drawn directly from the financial statements. In almost every case, however, the usefulness of such information can be enhanced when the user also makes comparisons over time, between companies, to industry averages or examines relationships among financial statement items. Chapter 3 introduced several ratios used in the evaluation of noninsurance companies. This section describes how ratios can be applied to insurance company financial statements. It begins by examining the effects of using information prepared on a GAAP and SAP basis to calculate one of these ratios.

The Effects of SAP Valuation on Ratio Measures of Profitability

One measure of an insurer's ability to use its resources to generate income is measured by the ratio of net income to average policyholders' surplus. **Return on net worth** is the insurance industry's equivalent of the return on equity ratio. Formally, these two ratios are defined as follows:

$$\frac{\text{Return on net worth}}{\text{(SAP basis)}} = \frac{\text{Net income}}{\text{Average policyholders' surplus}}$$

$$\frac{\text{Return on equity}}{\text{(GAAP basis)}} = \frac{\text{Net income}}{\text{Average owners' equity}}$$

The only apparent difference between return on net worth and return on equity is the use of policyholders' surplus in place of owners' equity in the denominator. Although this change may appear insignificant, the amounts shown in the statutory financial statements reflect the conservative valuation requirements of SAP. Consequently, the ratio values obtained using amounts reported in the GAAP financial statements are not directly comparable with the ratio values obtained using SAP based financial statement data. This difference can be seen more clearly when the calculated values of the ratios are compared.

$$\frac{\text{Return on net worth}}{\text{(SAP basis)}} = \frac{\text{Net income}}{\text{Average policyholders' surplus}}$$

$$= \frac{\$36,000}{\dfrac{(\$298,000 + \$340,000)}{2}}$$

$$= .113, \text{ or } 11.3\%$$

$$\frac{\text{Return on equity}}{\text{(GAAP basis)}} = \frac{\text{Net income}}{\text{Average owners' equity}}$$

$$= \frac{\$54,000}{\dfrac{(\$603,000 + \$657,000)}{2}}$$

$$= .086, \text{ or } 8.6\%$$

The difference between these calculated returns is substantial. In percentage terms, the difference (using the 8.6 percent GAAP return as a base) is about 31 percent. How can two closely related ratios calculated for the same company in the same year differ by so much? The answer lies in the financial statement effects of the SAP conservative valuation rules described previously.

Consider the numerator (top number) of the ratio. Net income in Exemplar's SAP financial statements is $18,000 less than that shown in its GAAP financial statements. This difference arises because Exemplar is required to expense the total amount of policy acquisition costs incurred during the year. For GAAP purposes, some of these policy acquisition costs are deferred and shown as an asset on the GAAP balance sheet. If this were the only difference, then the return on net worth should be less than the return on equity.

SAP valuation requirements also affect Exemplar's policyholders' surplus. First, $254,000 of furniture and fixtures that appeared on the GAAP balance sheet was excluded from the SAP balance sheet. Second, Exemplar's admitted assets do not include any deferred policy acquisition costs. Third, Exemplar was required to report an additional liability—excess of statutory over statement reserves. In each case, the result is a dollar-for-dollar reduction in policyholders' surplus.

Since SAP valuation rules can affect both the numerator and denominator of a given ratio, how the ratios calculated on a GAAP and SAP basis might differ is not always easy to see in advance. These examples should also reinforce that intelligent use of summary information, like that provided by ratios, requires knowing more than just how a given ratio is calculated. It also requires the user to understand the basis of accounting that was used to obtain the numbers themselves.

Insurance Industry Performance Measures

Perhaps the single most widely used number for summarizing the profitability of the insurance industry is the **combined ratio**. This ratio is used to summarize the overall underwriting performance of the industry in aggregate, individual insurers, and even individual lines of business. The combined ratio is actually made up of two components, a loss ratio and an expense ratio. Each of these ratios, as well as alternative methods to calculate them, is discussed below.

The Pure Loss Ratio

The relationship between losses and premiums is a matter of fundamental importance to users of insurer financial information. The loss ratio easily summarizes this relationship. In its simplest form, this ratio is called the **pure loss ratio**. It is calculated as follows:

$$\text{Pure loss ratio} = \frac{\text{Losses incurred}}{\text{Premiums earned}}$$

The name "pure loss" is used because only losses are considered; no account is taken of any loss adjustment or other expenses. In this ratio, losses incurred and premiums earned are properly matched in the same accounting period. This matching, in turn, provides a measure that is comparable among accounting periods regardless of whether premium volume is increasing or decreasing. Although the calculated value of this ratio will be the same whether GAAP- or SAP-based data are used, the amount reported as losses incurred is derived from estimates. Consequently, the value of this ratio can be distorted by either under- or over-estimation of incurred losses for a period.

The information needed to calculate the pure loss ratio for Exemplar Insurance Company is available in the SAP statement of income presented Exhibit 5-8, and Exemplar's pure loss ratio is calculated as follows:

$$\text{Pure loss ratio} = \frac{\text{Losses incurred}}{\text{Premiums earned}}$$

$$= \frac{\$218,000}{\$320,000}$$

$$= .68, \text{ or } 68\%$$

Exemplar's pure loss ratio indicates that for every dollar of premiums earned, Exemplar expects to pay 68 cents for losses. That leaves 32 cents of each premium dollar earned to cover loss adjustment and other underwriting expenses and perhaps make some contribution to profit.

The Net Loss Ratio

An expansion of the pure loss ratio considers both losses and loss adjustment expenses. In practice, this ratio is often referred to simply as "the loss ratio." The formula for the **net loss ratio** is as follows:

$$\text{Net loss ratio} = \frac{\text{Losses incurred + Loss adjustment expenses incurred}}{\text{Premium earned}}$$

The advantage of calculating the ratio in this way lies in the fact that it includes all costs associated with losses in one summary measure. Losses incurred, loss adjustment expenses incurred, and premiums earned are all properly matched in the same accounting period. Like the pure loss ratio, this matching provides a measure that is comparable between accounting periods. Again, the values of this ratio calculated from GAAP- and SAP-based data are the same. As with the pure loss ratio, the value of the loss ratio can be affected by inaccurate estimates of losses and loss adjustment expense reserves.

The information needed to calculate the net loss ratio for Exemplar Insurance Company is available from the SAP-based statement of income presented in Exhibit 5-8, and Exemplar's net loss ratio calculated as follows:

$$\text{Net loss ratio} = \frac{\text{Losses incurred} + \text{Loss adjustment expenses incurred}}{\text{Premiums earned}}$$

$$= \frac{\$218,000 + \$40,000}{\$320,000}$$

$$= .806, \text{ or } 80.6\%$$

Exemplar's net loss ratio indicates that for every dollar of premiums earned, Exemplar expects to pay 80.6 cents for losses and loss adjustment expenses. After these costs are covered, 19.4 cents of each premium dollar earned are available to cover other underwriting expenses and contribute to Exemplar's profits.

Expense Ratios

The second component of the combined ratio, the expense ratio, summarizes the relationship between underwriting expenses and premiums. This ratio can be calculated by using either premiums earned or premiums written. When premiums earned are used, the result is referred to as the **financial basis expense ratio**. Substituting premiums written into the ratio gives the **trade basis expense ratio**. These ratios are defined as follows:

$$\text{Financial basis expense ratio} = \frac{\text{Underwriting expenses incurred}}{\text{Premiums earned}}$$

$$\text{Trade basis expense ratio} = \frac{\text{Underwriting expenses incurred}}{\text{Premiums written}}$$

The financial basis expense ratio is most commonly used to make comparisons with companies outside the insurance industry, that is, between an insurer and a noninsurer. One limitation of calculating the expense ratio on a financial basis is that because it uses SAP figures for underwriting expenses, it fails to account for deferred policy acquisition costs. Consequently, premiums and costs are not perfectly matched within an accounting period.

By using premiums written, the trade basis expense ratio partially addresses this limitation. This form of the ratio takes into account that policy acquisition costs are more directly related to premiums written than premiums earned. The trade basis expense ratio is most commonly used to make comparisons within the insurance industry—comparing the performance of one insurer to another insurer or to the industry as a whole. Most financial reporting services report insurer expense ratios calculated on the trade basis.

All the information necessary to calculate the financial basis expense ratio for Exemplar Insurance Company can be found in the income statement presented in Exhibit 5-8. For this example, policy acquisition costs and underwriting expenses are taken to be the same. Premiums written, necessary to calculate the ratio on a trade basis, can be found in Exhibit 5-6. Following is the calculation of Exemplar's financial basis expense ratio:

$$\text{Financial basis expense ratio} = \frac{\text{Underwriting expenses incurred}}{\text{Premium earned}}$$

$$= \frac{\$84,000}{\$320,000}$$

$$= .263, \text{ or } 26.3\%$$

$$\text{Trade basis expense ratio} = \frac{\text{Underwriting expenses incurred}}{\text{Premiums written}}$$

$$= \frac{\$84,000}{\$515,000}$$

$$= .163, \text{ or } 16.3\%$$

When calculated on a financial basis, underwriting expenses consume 26.3 cents of each premium dollar earned. Calculated on a trade basis, underwriting expenses consume 16.3 cents of each dollar of premiums written.

Since all elements of underwriting income—premiums, losses, loss adjustment expenses, and underwriting expenses (policy acquisition costs)—have been accounted for, the loss and expense ratios can be used to construct a summary measure to show overall underwriting profitability. Indeed, this is how the combined ratio is formed.

The Combined Ratio

The combined ratio is simply a combination of the net loss ratio and the expense ratio. Of all the ratios that are used to evaluate insurance company performance, the combined ratio is particularly important because it can summarize, in a single number, the underwriting performance of an individual insurer or the industry as a whole. The industry combined ratio not only communicates information about the financial state of the industry as whole, but also serves as a benchmark for comparing a single company's performance to its competitors.

Since there are two bases for calculating the expense ratio, there are also two ways of calculating the combined ratio—on a financial basis and on a trade basis. With the net loss ratio and the expense ratio calculated above, the combined ratio for Exemplar Insurance Company can be computed as follows:

$$\text{Combined ratio} = \text{Net loss ratio} + \text{Expense ratio}$$
$$\text{Financial basis} = 80.6\% + 26.3\%$$
$$= 106.9\%$$
$$\text{Trade basis} = 80.6\% + 16.3\%$$
$$= 96.9\%$$

The financial basis combined ratio matches the results shown in Exemplar's SAP-based income statement (Exhibit 5-8). Under SAP, Exemplar experienced an underwriting loss of $22,000 in 1997. This loss is equal to 6.9 percent (106.9% − 100%) of its $320,000 of earned premiums. A combined ratio greater than 100 indicates an underwriting loss for the period. A combined ratio of less than 100 indicates an underwriting profit (gain) for the period. If Exemplar had operated at break even (with revenues exactly matching expenses), the combined ratio would be equal to 100.

In contrast to the results obtained using the financial basis combined ratio, Exemplar's underwriting experience for 1997 appears to have been profitable when the trade basis combined ratio is used. Remember, this ratio matches underwriting expenses with premiums written, rather than with premiums earned, to achieve a better matching of revenues and expenses for the period. Using the trade basis combined ratio, a user can conclude that each dollar of earned premium contributed 3.1 cents to profit (100 − 96.9 = 3.1). Insurance industry reporting agencies such as A.M. Best report the combined ratio calculated on a trade basis. Not since 1979 has the property-liability insurance industry's overall combined ratio (on a financial basis) been less than 100 percent.

Summary

Information needs vary widely among financial statement users. Catastrophes and market failures in the early development of insurance in the U.S. caused legislators great concern over the interests of insurance consumers. Viability of the insurance mechanism depends on the solvency and long-range stability of the insurers providing coverage. Insurance regulation has evolved from a need to protect consumers by monitoring the financial condition and operations of insurers in the market. Statutory accounting principles have been developed to help provide the unique accounting information needed by regulators to accomplish their objectives. The objectives of insurance regulation are as follows:

- To preserve and enhance solvency
- To promote adequate and fair premium rates
- To ensure fairness, equity, and reasonableness in insurance markets
- To fulfill certain social goals not necessarily pertinent to a successful insurance operation

Insurer financial statements reveal many of the unique characteristics of insurance compared to other business operations. As providers of financial services, insurers maintain a large proportion of their assets in financial securities rather than as inventories or plant and equipment, and their operations are primarily capitalized by investment returns from cash flows generated from insurance sales.

Statutory accounting adopts a liquidation perspective rather than the going-concern perspective used in GAAP. Consistent with that perspective, conservative valuation rules are applied to both assets and liabilities, which yield a conservative estimate of policyholders' surplus, the statutory equivalent of owners' equity (net worth). Certain asset items (nonadmitted assets) are excluded from the statutory balance sheet, and others (admitted assets) are reported at the least of several available values. Conversely, liabilities are reported at the greatest of available values, as illustrated by the statutory accounting item "excess of statutory reserves over statement reserves," which reports the difference between an insurer's reserve estimate for losses and the minimum required by SAP for certain lines of insurance. Also consistent with the solvency perspective, SAP recognizes policy acquisition costs and other underwriting expenses *immediately* rather than using the matching concept employed by GAAP.

Several measures of profitability and financial performance can be used to evaluate an insurer's operations. Overall profitability can be measured by computing the return on net worth (SAP basis) or the return on equity (GAAP basis). Performance measures frequently used within the insurance industry are the pure loss ratio, the net loss ratio, the financial basis expense ratio, trade basis expense ratio, the financial basis combined ratio, and the trade basis combined ratio. These measures can be used to measure the performance of individual companies or the insurance industry in aggregate.

Key Words and Phrases

admitted assets (p. 131) Assets meeting minimum standards of liquidity that are allowed to be reported on an insurer's balance sheet prepared in accordance with statutory accounting principles.

combined ratio (p. 142) A widely used measure of underwriting profitability for the insurance industry or for individual insurers, calculated by adding the net loss ratio and an expense ratio (either the financial basis expense ratio or the trade basis expense ratio).

excess of statutory reserves over statement reserves (p. 133) A liability item reported on an insurer's statutory balance sheet representing the difference between the statutory minimum loss reserve (for certain lines) and the insurer's reported loss reserve, when the statutory minimum exceeds the insurer's reported reserve amount.

financial basis expense ratio (p. 144) A ratio relating underwriting expenses to premiums earned, most commonly used to make comparisons with companies outside the insurance industry.

insolvency (p. 119) Occurs when an insurer's available resources are not adequate to cover its financial obligations. Formally, insolvency occurs when an insurer's net admitted assets (deducting all liabilities and reserves) do not exceed the amount required by its state of domicile. That required amount is determined by the NAIC's risk-based capital model or by statute.

liquidation accounting (p. 130) A financial reporting perspective in which assets and liabilities are reported at their liquidation values.

loss and loss adjustment expense reserves (p. 124) The insurer's liability for unpaid losses and associated adjustment expenses.

losses and loss adjustment expenses incurred (p. 125) Amounts paid for losses and loss adjustment plus changes in reserves for those items during the period reported.

mutual insurance company (p. 129) An insurance company organized and owned by its policyholders. Mutual insurers do not issue stock and thus have no stockholders.

net investment income (p. 125) Includes such items as stock dividends, bond coupons, and rental income received.

net loss ratio (p. 143) A ratio relating the sum of losses and loss adjustment expense to premiums earned, providing a summary measure of the proportion of earned premium revenues used to cover loss costs.

net realized capital gains (p. 125) Amounts received, net of expenses, from the sale of invested assets.

nonadmitted assets (p. 131) Assets excluded from an insurer's statutory balance sheet because of their relative illiquidity.

other underwriting expenses (p. 125) Represent expenses associated with underwriting the insured exposure including acquisition costs, engineering and inspection fees, and costs to maintain the underwriting department.

policy acquisition costs (p. 136) Collectively, costs attributed to agents' commissions, policy printing and mailing, state premium taxes, and other costs associated with placing and business on the books.

policyholders' surplus (p. 128) Under statutory accounting, represents the insurer's net worth. Represents the net of admitted assets after deducting all liabilities.

premiums earned (p. 125) The portion of insurance premiums written, including unearned amounts carried forward from periods, that has been earned during the period for insurance services provided.

premiums receivable (p. 124) Premium amounts due from agents or other insurers for insurance assumed by the reporting company.

protectionist (form of regulation) (p. 119) Regulation designed to favor the formation and development of domestic business by restricting market entry or competing influence of nondomestic entities.

pure loss ratio (p. 143) A ratio relating losses incurred to premiums earned. The pure loss ratio does not recognize loss adjustment expenses.

reinsurance recoverable (p. 124) Amounts for losses and loss adjustment expense owed the reporting insurer under reinsurance agreements covering paid losses.

reserves (p. 124) Under statutory accounting, liabilities associated with the performance of service under the insurance contract. Under GAAP, used to refer to a restriction on retained earnings for a particular purpose, indicating that such an amount cannot be used to pay dividends.

return on net worth (p. 141) A profitability measure relating net income (SAP basis) to average policyholders' surplus that provides the insurance industry's equivalent of the return on equity measure usually applied to noninsurance entities.

risk (p. 122) Occurs when the actual outcome of an event can vary from the expected outcome for that event. Risk increases as the amount of variation increases.

statutory accounting principles (p. 116) Accounting principles or practices prescribed or permitted by an insurer's domiciliary insurance department for completion of financial statements it files with that department.

trade basis expense ratio (p. 144) A ratio relating underwriting expenses to premiums written, preferred by insurers as a measure of underwriting efficiency because it better matches underwriting expenses (recognized immediately under SAP) with the revenues they generate (written premiums).

unearned premiums (p. 124) The portion of insurance premiums written that has not yet been earned or that is attributable to unexpired coverage. The portion of an insurer's written premium that has not yet been earned, for which service under the policies is yet to be provided.

valuation (p. 130) A measurement process that assigns dollar values to elements of an economic transaction or event.

Chapter Notes

1. Terrie E. Troxel and George E. Bouchie, *Property-Liability Insurance Accounting and Finance*, 4th ed. (Malvern, PA: American Institute for CPCU, 1995), p. 2.

2. This section adapted from NAIC's *Accounting Practices and Procedures Manual for Property/Casualty Insurance Companies* (Kansas City, MO: National Association of Insurance Commissioners, 1990), p. ii.

3. *Best's Aggregates & Averages: Property-Casualty, 1996 Edition* (Oldwick, NJ: A.M. Best Company, 1996), pp. 95, 100.

4. Bernard L. Webb, "Notes on the Early History of American Insurance," *CPCU Annals*, vol. 29, no. 2, June 1976, p. 89.

5. Webb, p. 90.

6. Webb, p. 92.

7. Claude C. Lilly, "A History of Insurance Regulation in the United States," *CPCU Annals*, vol. 29, no. 2, June 1976, pp. 99-101.

8. German Alliance Insurance Company v. Lewis, 233 U.S. 389 (1914).

9. Nebbis v. New York, 291 U.S. 502 (1934).

10. Troxel and Bouchie, p. 4.

11. James L. Athearn, S. Travis Pritchett, and Joan T. Schmit, *Risk and Insurance*, 6th ed. (St. Paul, MN: West Publishing Company, 1989), p. 50.

12. Kathleen Heald Ettlinger, Karen L. Hamilton, and Gregory Krohm, *State Insurance Regulation* (Malvern, PA: Insurance Institute of America, 1995), p. 130.

13. Troxel and Bouchie, pp. 20-23.

14. D. Keith Bell, "Other Labilities, Capital and Surplus," in *Property-Casualty Insurance Accounting*, 6th ed. (Durham, NC: Insurance Accounting and Systems Association, 1994), pp. 6-11.

15. This definition of liquidity differs from the definition presented earlier in this text. There, liquidity is defined in terms of a firm's ability to generate sufficient cash to meet its current obligations *in the normal course of business*. Here, the going-concern assumption is dropped. SAP assumes that the insurer ceases operation and attempts to convert *all* of its assets to cash as quickly as possible.

16. This is only a partial list. Other nonadmitted assets will be discussed later in the text.

Part II

Applied Accounting and Finance

Chapter 6

Accounting for and Presentation of Current Assets

Chapters 1 through 5 provided a basic foundation for understanding accounting systems by examining financial statements of both insurance and noninsurance entities, determining how economic transactions affect financial statements, and demonstrating how financial statements can be used to gain useful information about the business entities for which they were created. Chapters 6 through 11 examine in detail the accounts reported on financial statements to identify their unique characteristics, their reporting requirements, and their method of valuation. Chapters 6 through 10 discuss accounts typically captioned in the financial statements of noninsurance entities. Chapter 11 will discuss accounts typically captioned in the financial statements of insurance entities.

This chapter concentrates on current assets, a major component of any business entity's balance sheet. Current assets represent a group of accounts that is of particular interest to insurance professionals who might be called on to assess the liquidity of a firm's assets or its solvency. Current assets include cash and assets that are expected to be converted to cash or used up within one year or within an operating cycle, whichever is longer. An entity's **operating cycle** is the average time necessary to convert an investment in inventory back to cash. The following diagram illustrates the operating cycle:

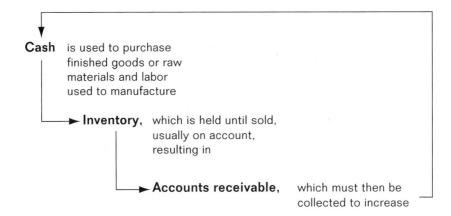

Cash is used to purchase finished goods or raw materials and labor used to manufacture

Inventory, which is held until sold, usually on account, resulting in

Accounts receivable, which must then be collected to increase

For most firms, the normal operating cycle is less than one year. A shorter operating cycle permits a lower investment in current assets. A lower investment in current assets results in an increase in turnover, which in turn increases return on investment (ROI). Many firms try to reduce their operating cycle and increase profitability by trying to sell inventory and collect accounts receivable as quickly as possible.

Because they represent the liquid resources used to cover a business entity's current financial obligations, the quality and availability of current assets are major concerns for financial statement users trying to assess the entity's financial condition. In insurance, investors, creditors, underwriters, and claim adjusters analyze current assets and net worth to assess a firm's liquidity and bill-paying capacity. Marginal liquidity might be a warning of perilous financial conditions leading to eventual insolvency or conditions that would motivate an unscrupulous insured to submit a fraudulent claim to generate much-needed cash resources.

Current asset captions usually seen in a balance sheet are as follows:

- Cash
- Marketable (or Short-term) securities
- Accounts and Notes receivable
- Inventories
- Prepaid expenses or Other current assets

Before beginning their study of this chapter, students should refer to the Armstrong World Industries, Inc., Consolidated Balance Sheets on page 26 of the Appendix to the course workbook and study guide. The balance sheet reference will help establish an association between the account items as they are discussed and their placement on the balance sheet. Armstrong's current assets at December 31, 1994, total $691.0 million and account for about 31 percent of the company's total assets. The largest current asset amounts are for accounts and notes receivable, and inventories. Now refer to the balance sheets in other annual reports that you have, and examine the composition of current assets. Do they differ significantly from Armstrong's balance sheet? The objective of this chapter is to permit you to understand the current asset presentation of any balance sheet.

Educational Objectives

After studying this chapter, you should be able to:

1. Explain what is included in the cash amount reported on the balance sheet.
2. Describe the bank reconciliation procedure.
3. Explain how short-term marketable securities are reported on the balance sheet.
4. Explain how accounts receivable are reported on the balance sheet, including the valuation allowances for estimated uncollectible accounts and estimated cash discounts.
5. Describe the features of a system of internal control and why internal controls are important.
6. Explain how notes receivable and related accrued interest are reported on the balance sheet.
7. Explain how inventories are reported on the balance sheet.
8. Compare the alternative inventory cost-flow assumptions and their respective effects on the income statement and balance sheet when price levels are changing.
9. Define prepaid expenses, and explain how they are reported on the balance sheet.
10. Define or describe each of the Key Words and Phrases introduced in this chapter.

Cash

The amount of cash reported on the balance sheet represents the cash that is available to the entity as of the close of business on the balance sheet date.

This amount includes cash on hand in change funds, undeposited cash receipts (including checks, money orders, and bank drafts), the amount of cash available to the firm in its various bank accounts and **petty cash** funds (see Business Procedure Capsule 7—Petty Cash Funds).

Cash equivalents included with cash on the balance sheets of Armstrong World Industries, Inc., are short-term investments. Since cash on hand or in bank accounts earns little if any interest, management of just about every organization will develop a cash management system to permit investment of cash balances not currently required for the entity's operation. In addition, management develops policies to minimize the chances for customer theft and employee embezzlement. These are part of the **internal control system** (see Business Procedure Capsule 8—The Internal Control System).

The Bank Reconciliation

To determine the amount of cash available in the bank, the cash account balance as shown in the general ledger should be reconciled with the balance reported by the bank. The **bank reconciliation** process, which you do (or should do) for your own checking account, involves bringing into agreement the account balance reported by the bank on the bank statement with the account balance in the ledger. The balances might differ for two reasons: timing differences and errors.

Timing differences arise because the firm knows about some transactions affecting the cash balance about which the bank is not yet aware, or the bank has recorded some transactions about which the firm is not yet aware. The most common timing differences involve the following:

Deposits in transit, which have been recorded in the entity's cash account, but which have not yet been added to the entity's balance on the bank's records. From the entity's point of view, a deposit in transit represents cash on hand because it has been received.

Outstanding checks, which have been recorded as credits (reductions) to the entity's cash balance, but which have not yet been presented to the bank for payment. From the entity's point of view, outstanding checks should not be included in its cash balance because it intended to disburse cash when it issued the checks.

Bank service charges against the entity's account and interest income added to the entity's balance during the period by the bank. The entity should recognize the bank service charge and interest income in the period incurred or earned since both of these items affect the cash balance at the end of the period.

Not sufficient funds (NSF) checks, which are checks that have "bounced" from the maker's bank because the account did not have enough funds to cover the check. Because the entity that received the check recorded it as a cash receipt and added the check amount to the balance of its cash account, an account receivable must be established for the amount due from the maker of the NSF check.

•   **BUSINESS PROCEDURE CAPSULE 7**
    Petty Cash Funds

Although most of the cash disbursements of a firm should be and are made by check for security and record-keeping purposes, many firms have one or more petty cash funds for small payments for which writing a check is inconvenient. For example, postage due or **collect on delivery (COD)** charges, or the cost of an office supply item that is needed immediately and is not in the storeroom, could be paid from the petty cash fund.

The petty cash fund is an **imprest account**; that term means that the sum of the cash on hand in the petty cash box and the receipts (called *petty cash vouchers*) that support disbursements should equal the amount initially put into the petty cash fund.

Periodically (usually at the end of the accounting period), the petty cash fund is reimbursed; that is, the cash in the fund is brought back to the original amount. At this time, the expenses paid through the fund are recognized in the accounts.

The amount of the petty cash fund is included in the cash amount reported on the firm's balance sheet.

Errors, which either the firm or the bank can make, are detected in what may be a trial-and-error process if the book balance and bank balance do not reconcile after timing differences have been recognized. Finding errors is a tedious process involving verifing the timing difference amounts (for example, double-checking the composition and total of the list of outstanding checks), verifying the debits and credits to the firm's ledger account, and verifying the arithmetic and amounts included on the bank statement. If the error is in the recording of cash transactions on the firm's books, then an appropriate journal entry must be made to correct the error. If the bank made the error, the bank is notified, but no change is made to the cash account balance.

There are a number of ways of performing the bank reconciliation. The reverse side of the bank statement usually has a reconciliation format printed on it. Exhibit 6-1 illustrates a simple and clear technique for setting up the reconciliation.

Exhibit 6-1
The Bank Reconciliation

Assumptions:

The balance in the Cash account of Cruisers, Inc., at September 30 was $4,614.58.

The bank statement showed a balance of $5,233.21 as of September 30.

Included with the bank statement were notices that the bank had deducted a service charge of $42.76 and had credited the account with interest of $28.91 earned on the average daily balance.

An NSF check for $35.00 from a customer was returned with the bank statement.

A comparison of deposits recorded in the cash account with those shown on the bank statement showed that the September 30 deposit of $859.10 was not on the bank statement. This is not surprising because the September 30 deposit was put in the bank's night depository on the evening of September 30.

A comparison of the record of checks issued with the checks returned in the bank statement showed that the amount of outstanding checks was $1,526.58.

Reconciliation as of September 30:

From Bank Records		*From Company Books*	
Indicated balance	$ 5,233.21	Indicated balance	$4,614.58
Add: Deposit in transit	859.10	Add: Interest earned	28.91
Less: Outstanding		Less: Service charge	(42.76)
checks	(1,526.58)	NSF check...................	(35.00)
Reconciled balance	$ 4,565.73	Reconciled balance	$4,565.73

The following adjusting journal entry would be made to adjust the balance in the company's general ledger account before reconciliation (the "indicated balance") to the correct amount after reconciliation.

Dr.	Service charge expense	42.76	
Dr.	Accounts receivable	35.00	
	Cr. Interest income		28.91
	Cr. Cash		48.85

Using the horizontal model, the effect of this adjustment on the financial statements is as follows:

Balance sheet	Income statement
Assets = Liabilities + Owners' equity ⟵	Net income = Revenues − Expenses

Accounts	Interest	Service
receivable	income	charge
+35.00	+28.91	−42.76

Cash	
−48.85	

Alternatively, a separate adjusting journal entry could be made for each reconciling item. The amount from this particular bank account to be included in the cash amount shown on the balance sheet for September 30 is $4,565.73. There would not be an adjusting journal entry for the reconciling items that affect the bank balance because those items have already been recorded on the company's books.

- **BUSINESS PROCEDURE CAPSULE 8**
  The Internal Control System

An organization's internal control system is made up of the policies and procedures that are designed to do the following:

1. Assure the accuracy of its bookkeeping records and financial statements
2. Protect its assets
3. Encourage adherence to the policies established by management
4. Provide for efficient operations

Internal control procedures should be designed to safeguard all of an entity's assets—cash and marketable securities; accounts and notes receivable; inventory; and property, plant, and equipment. Items 1 and 2 above are known as financial controls, and items 3 and 4 are administrative controls. Although the system of internal control is frequently discussed in the context of the firm's accounting system, it is equally applicable to every activity of the firm. Everyone in the organization should understand the need for and significance of internal controls.

Financial controls include the series of checks and balances that remove from one person the sole involvement in a transaction from beginning to end. For example, most organizations require that checks be signed by someone other than the person who prepares them. The check signer is expected to review the documents supporting the disbursement and to raise questions about unusual items. Another internal control requires the credit manager who authorizes the write-off of an account receivable to have another officer of the firm approve it. Likewise, a bank teller or cashier who has made a mistake in initially recording a transaction must have a supervisor approve the correction.

Administrative controls are frequently included in policy and procedure manuals and are reflected in management reviews of reports of operations and activities. For example, a firm's credit policy might specify that no customer is to have an account receivable balance in excess of $10,000 until the customer has had a clean payment record for at least a year. The firm's internal auditors might periodically review the accounts receivable detail to determine whether this policy is being followed.

Continued on next page.

The system of internal control does not exist because top management thinks that the employees are dishonest. Internal controls provide a framework within which employees can operate, knowing that their work is being performed in a way that is consistent with the desires of top management. To the extent that temptation is removed from a situation that might otherwise lead to an employee's dishonest act, the system of internal control provides a significant benefit.

Short-Term Marketable Securities

Recall the cash equivalents (short-term securities) that are part of Armstrong World Industries, Inc.'s, current assets. In order to increase profits and return on investment, most firms have a cash management program that involves investing cash balances in excess of those required for day-to-day operations in **short-term marketable securities**. Short-term marketable securities mature in one year or less. An integral part of the cash management program is the firm's forecast of cash receipts and disbursements. The broad objective of the cash management program is to maximize earnings by having as much cash as feasible invested for the longest possible time. Cash managers are usually interested in minimizing investment risks, and this is accomplished by investing in U.S. Treasury securities, securities of agencies of the federal government, bank certificates of deposit, and/or commercial paper. (**Commercial paper** is like an IOU issued by a very creditworthy corporation.) Securities selected for investment usually have a maturity date that is within a few months of the investment date, and that corresponds to the time when the cash manager thinks the cash will be needed.

Balance Sheet Valuation

Short-term marketable securities that will be held until they mature are reported in the balance sheet at the entity's cost, which is usually about the same as market value, because of their high quality and the short time until maturity. If an entity owns marketable securities that are not likely to be converted to cash within a few months of the balance sheet date, or securities that are subject to significant fluctuation in market value (like common stock), the balance sheet valuation and related accounting become more complex. Securities that may be traded or are available for sale are reported at market value, and any unrealized gain or loss is recognized. Reporting is an application of the matching concept since the change in market value is reflected in the fiscal period in which it occurs. The requirement that some marketable securities be reported at market value is especially pertinent to banks and other entities in the financial industry.

Interest Accrual

Interest income on short-term marketable securities should be accrued as earned so that both the balance sheet and income statement reflect more accurately the financial position at the end of the period and results of operations for the period. The asset involved is called *interest receivable*, and *interest income* is the income statement account. The accrual is made with the following adjusting entry:

Dr.	Interest receivable	xx
	Cr.	Interest income	xx

The effect of the interest accrual on the financial statements is as follows:

Balance sheet	Income statement
Assets = Liabilities + Owners' equity ⟵	Net income = Revenues – Expenses
+Interest	+Interest
receivable	income

The amount in the interest receivable account is combined with other receivables in the current asset section of the balance sheet.

Accounts Receivable

Recall from the Armstrong World Industries, Inc., balance sheet that accounts receivable is the largest current asset at December 31, 1994. Accounts receivable from customers for merchandise and services delivered are reported at **net realizable value**—the amount that is expected to be received from customers in settlement of their obligations. Two factors cause this amount to be different from the amount of the receivable originally recorded: bad debts and cash discounts.

Bad Debts/Uncollectible Accounts

Whenever a firm permits its customers to purchase merchandise or services on credit, some of the customers will not pay. Even a thorough check of a potential customer's credit rating and history of payments to other suppliers will not assure that the customer will pay in the future. Although some bad-debt losses are inevitable when a firm makes credit sales, most firms have internal control policies and procedures to keep losses at a minimum and to ensure that every reasonable effort is made to collect all amounts that are due to the firm. Some companies, however, willingly accept high-credit-risk customers and know that they will experience high bad-debt losses. These firms maximize their ROI by having a very high margin and requiring a down payment that equals or approaches the cost of the item being sold. Sales volume is higher than it would be if credit standards were stricter, so even though bad debts are relatively high, all or most of the product cost is recovered, and bad-debt losses are more than offset by the profits from greater sales volume.

Based on recent collection experience and tempered by the current state of economic affairs of the industry in which a firm is operating, credit managers can estimate with a high degree of accuracy the probable **bad debts expense** (or **uncollectible accounts expense**) of the firm. Many firms estimate bad debts based on a simplified assumption about the collectibility of all credit sales made during a period, called the percentage of sales method. Other firms perform a detailed analysis and aging of their year-end accounts receivable to estimate the net amount most likely to be collected, called the aging of receivables method. For instance, a firm may choose the following age categories and estimated collection percentages: 0–30 days (98 percent), 31–60 days (95 percent), 61–120 days (85 percent), and 121–180 days (60 percent). The firm may also have an administrative internal control policy requiring that all accounts more than six months overdue be immediately turned over to a collection agency. Such a policy is likely to increase the probability of collecting those accounts, facilitate the collection efforts for other overdue accounts, and reduce the overall costs of managing accounts receivable. The success of any bad-debts estimation technique ultimately depends on the careful application of professional judgment, coupled with the best available information.

When the amount of accounts receivable estimated to be uncollectible has been determined, a **valuation adjustment** can be recorded to reduce the **carrying value** of the asset and recognize the bad-debt expense. The adjusting entry is as follows:

Dr.	Bad debts expense	
	(or Uncollectible accounts expense)	xx
Cr.	Allowance for bad debts	
	(or Allowance for uncollectible accounts)	xx

The effect of this adjustment on the financial statement is as follows:

Balance sheet	Income statement
Assets = Liabilities + Owners' equity ⟵	Net income = Revenues – Expenses
– Allowance	– Bad
for bad debts	debts
	expense

In bookkeeping language, the **allowance for uncollectible accounts** or **allowance for bad debts** account is considered a **contra asset** because it is reported as a subtraction from an asset in the balance sheet. The debit and credit mechanics of a contra asset account are the opposite of those of an asset account; that is, a contra asset increases with credit entries and decreases with debit entries, and it normally has a credit balance. The presentation of the allowance for bad debts in the current asset section of the balance sheet (using assumed amounts) is as follows:

Accounts receivable	$10,000
Allowance for bad debts	(500)
Net accounts receivable	$ 9,500

or, as more commonly reported:

Accounts receivable, less allowance for bad debts of $500	$9,500

The allowance for bad debts account communicates to financial statement readers that an estimated portion of the total amount of accounts receivable is expected to become uncollectible. So why not simply reduce the accounts receivable account directly for estimated bad debts? The problem with this approach is that the firm has not yet determined *which* customers will not pay—only that *some* will not pay. Before accounts receivable can be reduced, the firm must be able to identify which account needs to be written off as an uncollectible account. Throughout the year, as accounts are determined to be uncollectible, they are written off against the allowance account with the following entry:

Dr.	Allowance for bad debts..................	xx	
	Cr. Accounts receivable		xx

The effect of this entry on the financial statement is as follows:

Balance sheet	Income statement
Assets = Liabilities + Owners' equity ⟵	Net income = Revenues – Expenses
−Accounts receivable	
+Allowance for bad debts	

The **write-off** of an account receivable (removing an account that is not expected to be collected) has no effect on the income statement, nor should it. The expense was recognized in the year in which the revenue from the transaction with this customer was recognized. The write-off entry removes from accounts receivable an amount that is never expected to be collected. The write-off of an account will not have any effect on the net accounts receivable reported on the balance sheet because both the asset (accounts receivable) and the contra asset (allowance for bad debts) are affected the same way (each is reduced) by the same amount. Assume that $100 of the accounts receivable in the above example was written off. The balance sheet presentation would now be as follows:

Accounts receivable................................	$9,900
Less: Allowance for bad debts.................	(400)
Net accounts receivable	$9,500

Providing for bad-debt expense in the same year in which the related sales revenue is recognized is an application of the matching concept. The allowance for bad debts (or allowance for doubtful accounts) account is a **valuation account**, and its credit balance is subtracted from the debit balance of accounts receivable to arrive at the amount of net receivables reported in the current asset section of the balance sheet. This procedure results in stating accounts receivable at the amount expected to be collected (that is, net realizable value). If an appropriate allowance for bad debts is not provided, then accounts receivable and net income will be overstated, and the ROI, ROE, and liquidity measures will be distorted. The amount of the allowance is usually reported parenthetically in the accounts receivable caption so that financial statement users can make a judgment about the credit and collection practices of the firm.

Cash Discounts

To encourage prompt payment, many firms permit their customers to deduct up to 2 percent of the amount owed if the bill is paid within a stated period—usually ten days—of the date of the sale (usually referred to as the *invoice date*). This arrangement is known as a **cash discount**. Most firms' **credit terms** provide that if the invoice is not paid within the discount period, it must be paid in full within thirty days of the invoice date. This credit term is abbreviated as 2/10, n30. The 2/10 refers to the discount terms, and the n30 means that the net amount of the invoice is due within 30 days. To illustrate, assume that Cruisers, Inc., has credit sales terms of 2/10, n30. On April 8, Cruisers, Inc., made a $5,000 sale to Mount Marina. Mount Marina has the option of paying $4,900 (5,000 − [2% × $5,000]) by April 18, or paying $5,000 on May 8.

Like most firms, Mount Marina will probably take advantage of the cash discount because it represents a high rate of return (see Business Procedure Capsule 9—Cash Discounts). The discount is clearly a cost to the seller because the selling firm will not receive the full amount of the account receivable resulting from the sale. Cash discounts on sales are usually sub-tracted from sales in the income statement to arrive at the net sales amount that is reported because the discount is in effect a reduction of the selling price.

- **BUSINESS PROCEDURE CAPSULE 9**
  Cash Discounts

Cash discounts for prompt payment represent a significant cost to the seller and a benefit to the purchaser. Not only do they encourage prompt payment, but they are also considered in the pricing decision and will be considered when evaluating the selling prices of competitors.

Converting the discount to an annual return on investment will illustrate its significance. Assume that an item sells for $100, with credit terms of 2/10, n30. If the invoice is paid by the tenth day, a $2 discount is taken, and the payor gives up the use of the $98 paid for twenty days because the alternative is to keep the money for another twenty days and then pay $100. The return on investment for twenty days is $2/$98, or slightly more than 2 percent; however, eighteen twenty-day periods are available in a year, so the annual return on investment is over 36 percent.

The step-by-step calculation is performed as follows:

$$\begin{aligned} \text{Cost of failing to take cash discount} &= \frac{\text{Discount percent}}{100\% - \text{Discount percent}} \times \frac{360}{\text{Final due date} - \text{Discount period}} \\[2mm] &= \frac{2\%}{100\% - 2\%} \times \frac{360}{30 - 10} \\[2mm] &= \frac{2\%}{98\%} \times \frac{360}{20} \\[2mm] &= \frac{2\% \times 18}{98\%} \\[2mm] &= 36.7\% \end{aligned}$$

Very few firms can earn this high of an ROI on their principal activities. Most firms have a rigidly followed internal control policy of taking all cash discounts possible.

One of the facts that credit rating agencies and credit grantors want to know about a firm when evaluating its liquidity and creditworthiness is whether the firm takes cash discounts. If it does not, that is a signal that either the management does not understand their significance or that the firm cannot afford to borrow money at a lower interest rate to earn the higher rate from the cash discount. Either of these reasons indicates a potentially poor credit risk.

> Since the purchaser's benefit is the seller's burden, why do sellers allow cash discounts if they represent such a high cost? The principal reasons are to encourage prompt payment and to be competitive. Obviously, however, cash discounts represent a cost that the firm must cover to be profitable.

On the balance sheet date, accounts receivable include the full amount of sales made in the discount period preceding the balance sheet date. In order to report accounts receivable at the amount expected to be realized as cash, accounts receivable should be reduced by the estimated cash discounts that customers will take when they pay within the discount period following the balance sheet date. These estimated cash discounts are recognized as cash discounts on sales in the fiscal period in which the sale was made. The basis for the estimate is experience with cash discounts taken. The valuation adjustment entry is as follows:

Dr.	Cash discounts on sales	xx
Cr.	Allowance for cash discounts	xx

The effect of this entry on the financial statements is as follows:

Balance sheet	Income statement
Assets = Liabilities + Owners' equity ⟵	Net income = Revenues – Expenses
– Allowance for cash discounts	– Cash discounts on sales

The allowance for cash discounts account is another contra asset, and its credit balance is subtracted from accounts receivable to determine the net amount reported in the balance sheet. The balance sheet presentation of the allowance for cash discounts is the same as previously illustrated for the allowance for bad debts. Cash discounts on sales is a contra revenue account, subtracted from sales revenue to arrive at net sales. Net sales is usually the first caption shown on the income statement. Many firms combine the amount of the allowance for cash discounts and the allowance for bad debts and report this total parenthetically in the accounts receivable caption. In the Appendix to this text's companion workbook and study guide, Armstrong World Industries, Inc., has taken this approach.

Notes Receivable

If a firm has an account receivable from a customer who has difficulties paying its accounts when due, the firm may convert that account receivable to a formal **note receivable**. The entry to reflect this transaction is as follows:

Dr.   Note receivable xx
      Cr.   Accounts receivable xx

The effect of this entry on the financial statement is as follows:

Balance sheet	Income statement
Assets = Liabilities + Owners' equity ⟵	Net income = Revenues − Expenses
− Accounts receivable	
+ Notes receivable	

One asset (an account receivable) has been exchanged for another (a note receivable). Does the entry make sense?

A note receivable differs from an account receivable in several ways. A note is a formal document that includes specific provisions with respect to its maturity date (when it is to be paid), agreements or *covenants* made by the borrower (for example, to supply financial statements to the lender or to refrain from paying dividends until the note is repaid), identification of the security or **collateral** pledged by the borrower to support the loan, penalties to be assessed if it is not paid on the maturity date, and, most important, the interest rate associated with the loan. Although some firms assess an interest charge or service charge on invoice amounts that are not paid when due, this practice is unusual for regular transactions between firms. Thus, if an account receivable is not going to be paid promptly, the seller will ask the customer to sign a note so that interest will be earned on the overdue account.

Under other circumstances a firm may lend money to another entity and take a note from that entity; for example, a manufacturer may lend money to a distributor that is also a customer or potential customer in order to help the distributor build its business. Such a transaction is another rearrangement of assets; cash is decreased, and notes receivable is increased.

Interest Accrual

If interest is to be paid at the maturity of the note (a common practice), the holder of the note should accrue interest income, usually on a monthly basis. This practice is appropriate because interest revenue has been earned, and accruing the revenue and increasing interest receivable result in more accurate monthly financial statements. The entry to do this is the same as that for interest accrued on short-term cash investments:

Dr.	Interest receivable	xx	
	Cr.	Interest income	xx

The effect of this entry on the financial statement is as follows:

Balance sheet	Income statement
Assets = Liabilities + Owners' equity ⟵	Net income = Revenues – Expenses
+Interest receivable	+Interest income

This accrual entry reflects interest income that has been earned in the period and increases current assets by the amount earned but not yet received.

Interest receivable is frequently combined with notes receivable in the balance sheet for reporting purposes. Amounts to be received within a year of the balance sheet date are classified as current assets. If the note has a maturity date beyond a year, it will be classified as a noncurrent asset.

Recognizing any probable loss from uncollectible notes and interest receivable is appropriate, just as is done for accounts receivable, and the bookkeeping process is the same. Cash discounts do not apply to notes, so there is no discount valuation allowance.

Inventories

Inventories represent the most significant current asset for many merchandising and manufacturing firms. For Armstrong World Industries, Inc., inventories account for 42 percent of current assets at December 31, 1994, and are nearly as much as the amount of accounts and notes receivable. Accounting for inventories is one of the areas in which alternative generally accepted practices can result in major differences between the assets and expenses reported by companies that might otherwise be alike in all other valuation measures.

Just as warehouse bins and store shelves hold inventory until the product is sold to the customer, the inventory accounts of a firm hold the *cost* of a product until that cost is released to the income statement to be subtracted from (matched with) the revenue from the sale. The cost of a purchased or manufactured product is recorded as an asset and carried in the asset account until the product is sold (or becomes worthless, or is lost or stolen), at which point the cost becomes an expense to be reported in the income statement. The cost of an item purchased for inventory includes not only the invoice price paid to the supplier, but also other costs associated with the purchase of the item, such as freight and material handling charges. Cost is reduced by the amount of any cash discount allowed on the purchase. The income statement caption used to report this expense is cost of goods sold (see Exhibit 2-2). The entries for purchase and sale transactions are as follows:

```
Dr.   Inventory ..............................................   xx
      Cr.   Accounts payable (or Cash) .........................   xx
            Purchase (or manufacture) of inventory
Dr.   Cost of goods sold ............................................   xx
      Cr.   Inventory ........................................................   xx
      To transfer cost of item sold to income statement
```

These transactions are illustrated in the horizontal model as follows:

Balance sheet	Income statement
Assets = Liabilities + Owners' equity ⟵	Net income = Revenues – Expenses
Purchase of Inventory:	
+Inventory +Accounts payable	
Recognize cost of goods sold:	
– Inventory	–Cost of goods sold

Recognizing cost of goods sold is a process of accounting for the *flow of costs* from the inventory (asset) account of the balance sheet to the cost of goods sold (expense) account of the income statement. T-accounts can also be used to illustrate this flow of costs, as shown in Exhibit 6-2. Of course, the sale of merchandise also generates revenue, but *recognizing revenue is a separate transaction* involving accounts receivable (or cash) and the sales revenue accounts. The following discussion focuses only on the accounting for the cost of the inventory sold.

Exhibit 6-2
Flow of Costs From Inventory to Cost of Goods Sold

Balance Sheet/Income Statement		
Inventory (asset)		**Cost of Goods Sold (expense)**
Purchases of merchandise for resale increase inventory (credit to accounts payable or cash)	When merchandise is sold, the cost flows from the inventory asset account to ⟶	the cost of goods sold expense account

Inventory Cost-Flow Assumptions

The inventory accounting alternative selected by an entity relates to the assumption about how costs flow from the inventory account to the cost of goods sold account. There are four principal alternative **cost-flow assumptions**:

1. Specific identification
2. Weighted-average
3. First-in, first-out (FIFO) (pronounced FIE-FOE)
4. Last-in, first-out (LIFO) (pronounced LIE-FOE)

These are cost-flow assumptions, and FIFO and LIFO do not refer to the physical flow of product. Thus, a firm can have a FIFO physical flow (grocery stores usually try to accomplish this) and use the LIFO cost-flow assumption.

The **specific identification** alternative links cost and physical flow. When an item is sold, the cost of that specific item is determined from the firm's records, and that amount is transferred from the inventory account to cost of goods sold. The amount of ending inventory is the cost of the items held in inventory at the end of the year. This alternative is appropriate for a firm dealing with specifically identifiable products, such as automobiles, that have an identifying serial number and are purchased and sold by specific unit. The specific identification alternative is not practical for a firm having a large number of inventory items that are not easily identified individually.

The **weighted-average** alternative is applied to individual items of inventory. It involves calculating the average cost of the items in the beginning inventory plus purchases made during the year. Then this average is used to determine the cost of goods sold and the carrying value of ending inventory. Exhibit 6-3 illustrates this method. The average cost is not a simple average of the unit costs, but is instead an average weighted by the number of units in beginning inventory and each purchase.

First-in, first-out, or **FIFO,** means that the first costs *into inventory* are the first costs *out to cost of goods sold*. The first cost in is the cost of the inventory on hand at the beginning of the fiscal year. The effect of this inventory cost-flow assumption is to transfer to the cost of goods sold account the oldest costs incurred for the quantity of merchandise sold and to leave in the inventory asset account the most recent costs of merchandise purchased or manufactured for the quantity in ending inventory. Exhibit 6-3 also illustrates this cost-flow assumption.

Exhibit 6-3
Inventory Cost-Flow Alternatives Illustrated

Situation:

On September 1, 1995, the inventory of Cruisers, Inc., consisted of five Model OB3 boats. Each boat cost Cruisers $1,500. During the year ended August 31, 1996, 40 boats were purchased on the dates and at the costs that follow. During the year, 37 boats were sold.

Required:

Determine the August 31, 1996, inventory amount, and the cost of goods sold, using the weighted-average, FIFO, and LIFO cost-flow assumptions.

Solution:

Date of Purchase	Number of Boats	Cost per Boat	Total Cost
9/1/95 (Beginning inventory)	5	$1,500	$ 7,500
11/7/95	8	1,600	12,800
3/12/96	12	1,650	19,800
5/22/96	10	1,680	16,800
7/28/96	6	1,700	10,200
8/30/96	4	1,720	6,880
Total of boats available to sell	45		$73,980
Number of boats sold	37		
Number of boats in 8/31/96 inventory ..	8		

a. *Weighted-average cost-flow assumption:*

$$\text{Weighted-average cost} = \frac{\text{Total cost of boats available to sell}}{\text{Number of boats available to sell}}$$

$$= \frac{\$73,980}{45}$$

$$= \$1,644 \text{ per boat}$$

Cost of ending inventory = $1,644 × 8 = $13,152

Cost of goods sold = $1,644 × 37 = $60,828

b. *FIFO cost-flow assumption:*

The cost of ending inventory is the cost of the 8 most recent purchases:

4 boats purchased 8/30/96 @ $1,720 ea. =	$ 6,880
4 boats purchased 7/28/96 @ $1,700 ea. =	6,800
Cost of 8 boats in ending inventory	$13,680

Continued on next page.

The cost of 37 boats sold is the sum of the costs for the first 37 boats purchased:

Beginning inventory	5 boats @	$1,500 =	$ 7,500
11/7/95 purchase	8 boats @	1,600 =	12,800
3/12/96 purchase	12 boats @	1,650 =	19,800
5/22/96 purchase	10 boats @	1,680 =	16,800
7/28/96 purchase*	2 boats @	1,700 =	3,400
Cost of goods sold			$60,300

*When the FIFO cost-flow assumption is applied, the cost of 2 of the 6 boats purchased this date is transferred from inventory to cost of goods sold.

The cost of goods sold could also have been calculated by subtracting the ending inventory amount from the total cost of the boats available for sale.

Total cost of boats available for sale	$73,980
Less cost of boats in ending inventory	(13,680)
Cost of goods sold	$60,300

c. *LIFO cost-flow assumption:*

The cost of ending inventory is the cost of the 8 oldest purchases:

5 boats in beginning inventory @ $1,500 ea. =	$ 7,500
3 boats of 11/7/95 purchase @ $1,600 ea. =	4,800
Cost of 8 boats in ending inventory	$12,300

The cost of the 37 boats sold is the sum of costs for the last 37 boats purchased:

8/30/96 purchase	4 boats @	$1,720 =	$ 6,880
7/28/96 purchase	6 boats @	1,700 =	10,200
5/22/96 purchase	10 boats @	1,680 =	16,800
3/12/96 purchase	12 boats @	1,650 =	19,800
11/7/95 purchase*	5 boats @	1,600 =	8,000
Cost of goods sold			$61,680

*When the LIFO cost-flow assumption is applied, the cost of 5 of the 8 boats purchased this date is transferred from Inventory to Cost of goods sold.

The cost of goods sold could also have been calculated by subtracting the ending inventory amount from the total cost of the boats available for sale.

Total cost of boats available for sale	$73,980
Less cost of boats in ending inventory	(12,300)
Cost of goods sold	$61,680

Last-in, first-out, or **LIFO,** is an alternative cost-flow assumption opposite to FIFO. Remember, the emphasis is on cost flow, not physical flow, and a firm can have a FIFO physical flow (like grocery stores) and still use the LIFO cost-flow assumption. Under LIFO, the most recent costs incurred for merchandise purchased or manufactured are transferred to the income statement (as cost of goods sold) when items are sold, and the inventory on hand at the balance sheet date is costed at the oldest costs, including those used to value the beginning inventory. This cost-flow assumption is also illustrated in Exhibit 6-3.

The way these cost-flow assumptions are applied depends on the inventory accounting system in use. The two systems—*periodic* and *perpetual*—are described later in this chapter. Exhibit 6-3 uses the periodic system.

Following are the results of the three alternatives presented in Exhibit 6-3:

Cost-Flow Assumption	Cost of Ending Inventory	Cost of Goods Sold
Weighted-average	$13,152	$60,828
FIFO	13,680	60,300
LIFO	12,300	61,680

Although the differences between amounts seem small in this illustration, under real-world circumstances with huge amounts of inventory, the differences become large and are material (the materiality concept was explained in Chapter 2). The differences occur because, as you have probably noticed, the cost of the boats purchased changed over time. If the cost had not changed, the ending inventory and cost of goods sold would not have differed among the three alternatives. But in practice, costs do change. The amounts resulting from the weighted-average cost-flow assumption are between those for FIFO and LIFO; this is to be expected. Weighted-average results will never be outside the range of amounts resulting from FIFO and LIFO.

The crucial point to understand about the inventory cost-flow assumption issue is the effect on cost of goods sold, operating income, and net income of the alternative assumptions. The following statement appears on page 32 of the 1994 Armstrong World Industries, Inc., annual report in the course workbook and study guide Appendix: "Approximately 49 percent in 1994 and 51 percent in 1993 of the company's total inventory is valued on a LIFO (last-in, first-out) basis. Such inventory values were lower than would have been reported on a total FIFO (first-in, first-out) basis, by $115.4 million at the end of 1994 and $109.7 million at year-end 1993." LIFO inventory values that are $115.4 million lower than FIFO mean that the cost of goods sold over the years has been $115.4 million higher and operating income has been $115.4 million lower than would have been the case under FIFO. To put this number in perspective, Armstrong World Industries, Inc.'s, inventories at December 31, 1994, totaled $293.5 million, and retained earnings at that date totaled $1,076.8 million.

The effect of LIFO on Armstrong World Industries, Inc.'s, financial position (the $115.4 million difference represetnting over 39 percent of year end 1994 inventory) and results of operations (the $115.4 million representing over 10 percent of retained earnings) has been significant, and this company is not unique (see Table 6-1). Clearly, the choice of inventory cost-flow assumption has affected Armstrong World Industries, Inc.'s, ROI, ROE, and measures of liquidity. Because of the importance of the inventory valuation to a firm's measures of profitability and liquidity, the effect of alternative cost-flow assumptions must be understood if these measures are to be used effectively in making judgments and informed decisions—especially if comparisons are made between entities.

Table 6-1

Inventory Cost-Flow Assumptions Used by 600 Publicly Owned Industrial and Merchandising Corporations—1993

	Number of Companies*
Methods:	
Last-in, first-out (LIFO)	348
First-in, first-out (FIFO)	417
Average cost	189
Other	42
Use of LIFO:	
All inventories	17
50% or more of inventories	191
Less than 50% of inventories	91
Not determinable	49
Companies using LIFO	348
*Companies may use more than one method.	

Source: Reprinted with permission from *Accounting Trends and Techniques,* Table 2-8, copyright © 1994 by American Institute of Certified Public Accountants, Inc.

The Effect of Changing Costs (Inflation/Deflation)

It is important to understand how the inventory cost-flow assumption used by a firm interacts with the direction of cost changes to affect both inventory and cost of goods sold. In times of rising costs, LIFO results in lower ending inventory and higher cost of goods sold than FIFO. These changes occur because the LIFO assumption results in the most recent, higher costs being transferred to cost of goods sold. When purchase costs are falling, the opposite is true. Exhibit 6-4 illustrates these relationships.

The graphs in Exhibit 6-4 are helpful in understanding the relative effect on cost of goods sold and ending inventory when costs move in one direction. Of course, in the real world, costs rise and fall over time, and the effect of a strategy chosen during a period of rising costs will reverse when costs decline. Thus, in the mid-1980s some firms that had switched to LIFO during a prior inflationary period began to experience falling costs. These firms reported higher profits under LIFO than they would have under FIFO.

Exhibit 6-4
Effect of Changing Costs on Inventory and Cost of Goods Sold
Under FIFO and LIFO

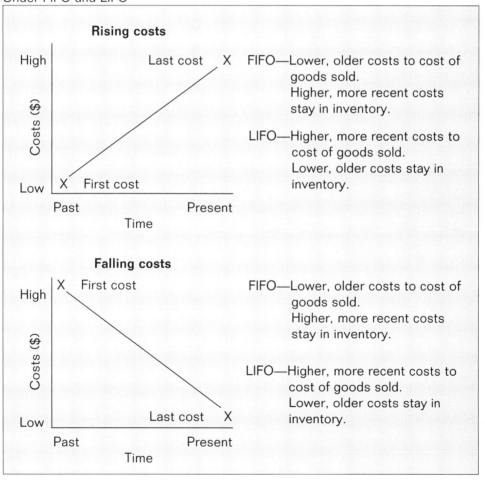

The Effect of Inventory Quantity Changes

Changes in the quantities of inventory will affect profits that depend on the cost-flow assumption used and the extent of cost changes during the year.

Under FIFO, whether inventory quantities rise or fall, the cost of the beginning inventory is transferred to Cost of Goods Sold because the quantity of goods sold during the year usually exceeds the quantity of beginning inventory. As previously explained, when costs are rising, costs of goods sold will be lower and profits will be higher than under LIFO. The opposite is true if costs fall during the year.

When inventory quantities rise during the year and LIFO is used, a layer of inventory value is added to the book value of inventories at the beginning of the year. If costs have risen during the year, LIFO results in higher cost of goods sold and lower profits than FIFO. The opposite is true if costs fall during the year.

When inventory quantities decline during the year and LIFO is used, the inventory value layers built up in prior years when inventory quantities were rising are now transferred to Cost of Goods Sold, with costs of the most recently added layer transferred first. The effect on cost of goods sold and profits of LIFO versus FIFO depends on the costs in each value layer relative to current costs of inventory if FIFO is used. Generally, costs increase over time, so inventory reductions of LIFO layers result in lower cost of goods sold and higher profits than with FIFO—just the opposite of what would normally be expected under LIFO. This process is known as a **LIFO liquidation** because the cost of old LIFO layers included in beginning inventory is removed or liquidated from the inventory account.

In recent years, many firms have sought to increase their ROI by reducing assets while maintaining or increasing sales and margin. Thus, turnover (sales/average assets) is increasing, with a resulting increase in ROI. When lower assets are achieved by reducing inventories in a LIFO environment, older and lower costs (from old LIFO layers) are released from inventory to cost of goods sold. Since revenues reflect current selling prices, which are independent of the cost-flow assumption used, profit is higher than it would be without a LIFO liquidation. In other words, net income can be increased by this unusual liquidation situation, whereby old LIFO inventory costs are matched with current sales revenues. Thus, ROI is boosted by both increased turnover and higher margin, but the margin effect occurs only in the year of the LIFO liquidation.

Selecting an Inventory Cost-Flow Assumption

What factors influence the selection of a cost-flow assumption? When rates of inflation were relatively low and the conventional wisdom was that they would always be low, most financial managers selected the FIFO cost-flow assumption because that resulted in slightly lower cost of goods sold and hence higher net income. Financial managers have a strong motivation to report higher, rather than lower, net income to the stockholders. However, when double-digit inflation was experienced, the higher net income from the FIFO assumption resulted in higher income taxes. (Federal income tax law requires that if the LIFO cost-flow assumption is used for reporting to stockholders, it must also be used for tax purposes. This tax requirement is a constraint that does not exist in other areas where alternative cost-flow assumptions are used.)

Rapidly rising costs result in **inventory profits**, or **phantom profits**, when the FIFO assumption is used because the release of older, lower costs to the income statement results in higher profits than if current costs were recognized. Since taxes must be paid on these profits and the cost of replacing the merchandise sold is considerably higher than the old cost, users of the financial statements can be misled about the firm's real economic profitability. To avoid inventory profits, many firms changed from FIFO to LIFO for at least part of their inventories during the years of high inflation. (Generally accepted accounting principles do not require that the same cost-flow assumption be used for all inventories.) This change to LIFO resulted in higher cost of goods sold than would have occurred under FIFO, lower profits, lower taxes, and (in the opinion of some analysts) more realistic financial reporting of net income. However, even though net income may better reflect a matching of revenues (which also usually rise on a per-unit basis during periods of inflation) and costs of merchandise sold, the inventory amount on the balance sheet will be reported at older, lower costs. Thus, under LIFO, the balance sheet will not reflect current costs for items in inventory. This is consistent with the original cost concept and underscores the fact that balance sheet amounts do not reflect current values of most assets.

But what about consistency, the concept that requires whatever accounting alternative selected for one year be used for subsequent financial reporting? With respect to the inventory cost-flow assumption, the Internal Revenue Service permits a one-time, one-way change from FIFO to LIFO. Since tax reporting and financial reporting must be consistent in this area, firms must change from FIFO to LIFO for financial reporting also. If they do change methods, the effect of the change on both the balance sheet inventory amount and cost of goods sold must be disclosed so that financial statement users can evaluate the effect of the change on the firm's financial position and results of operations.

Table 6-1 summarized the methods used to determine inventory cost by 600 industrial and merchandising corporations whose annual reports are reviewed and summarized by the AICPA. Significantly, many companies use at least two methods, and only seventeen companies use LIFO for all inventories. A footnote on page 32 of the 1994 Armstrong World Industries, Inc., annual report in the Appendix discloses that approximately 49 percent of the company's total inventory is valued on a LIFO basis. The mix of inventory cost-flow assumptions used in practice emphasizes the complex ramifications of selecting a cost-flow assumption.

Inventory Accounting System Alternatives

The system to account for inventory cost flow is very complex in practice because most firms have hundreds or thousands of inventory items. As mentioned earlier in the chapter, there are two principal **inventory accounting systems**: perpetual and periodic.

In a **perpetual inventory system**, a record is made of every purchase and every sale, and a continuous record of the quantity and cost of each item of inventory is maintained. Computers have made perpetual inventory systems feasible for an increasingly large number of small to medium-sized retail organizations that were previously forced to use periodic systems. Advances in the use of product bar coding and scanning devices at cash registers have lowered the costs of maintaining perpetual records. The accounting issues involved with a perpetual system are easy to understand (see Business Procedure Capsule 10) once you have learned how the alternative cost-flow assumptions are applied in a periodic system (refer to Exhibit 6-3 if you need a review).

In a **periodic inventory system**, a count of the inventory on hand (taking a **physical inventory**) is made periodically—frequently at the end of the fiscal year—and the cost of the inventory on hand, based on the cost-flow assumption being used, is determined and subtracted from the sum of the beginning inventory and purchases to determine the cost of goods sold. This calculation is illustrated by using the following **cost of goods sold model**, which uses data from the FIFO cost-flow assumption of Exhibit 6-3:

Beginning inventory	$ 7,500
Purchases	66,480
Cost of goods available for sale	$73,980
Less: Ending inventory	(13,680)
Cost of goods sold	$60,300

The examples in Exhibit 6-3 use the periodic inventory system. Although less detailed record-keeping is needed for the periodic system than for the perpetual system, the efforts involved in counting and costing the inventory on hand are still significant.

Even when a perpetual inventory system is used, periodically verifying that the quantity of an item shown by the perpetual inventory record to be on hand is the quantity actually on hand is necessary. Bookkeeping errors and theft or mysterious disappearance cause differences between the recorded and actual quantity of inventory items. When differences are found, they should be reflected as inventory losses or corrections to the inventory account, as appropriate. If the losses are significant, management would probably authorize an investigation to determine the cause of the loss and develop recommendations for strengthening the system of internal control over inventories.

• **BUSINESS PROCEDURE CAPSULE 10**
The Perpetual Inventory System

Under a perpetual inventory system, the cost-flow assumption used by the firm is applied on a day-to-day basis as sales are recorded, rather than at the end of the year (or month). A perpetual inventory system allows the firm to record increases to cost of goods sold and decreases to inventory on a daily basis. This makes sense from a matching perspective, because the *sale* of inventory is what triggers the *cost* of goods sold. The following journal entries are recorded at the point of sale:

Dr.	Accounts receivable (or Cash)		xx	
	Cr.	Sales		xx
		Purchase (or manufacture) of inventory		
Dr.	Cost of goods sold..		xx	
	Cr.	Inventory		xx

The effect of these entries on the financial statements is as follows:

Balance sheet	Income statement
Assets = Liabilities + Owners' equity ⟵	Net income = Revenues –Expenses
Record sale of goods:	
+Accounts receivable (or Cash)	+Sales
Recognize cost of goods sold:	
–Inventory	–Cost of goods sold

Thus, a continuous (or perpetual) record is maintained of the inventory account balance. Under FIFO, the periodic and perpetual systems always produce the same results for ending inventory and cost of goods sold. Why would this be the case? Even though the FIFO rules are applied at different points in time—at the end of the year (or month) with periodic, and daily with perpetual—the first-in cost will remain in inventory until the next item of inventory is sold. Once first in, always first in, and costs that flow from inventory to cost of goods sold are based strictly on the chronological order of purchase transactions. The results are the same under either system because whenever the question "What was the first-in cost?" is asked (daily or monthly), the answer is the same.

Under LIFO, when the question "What was the last-in cost?" is asked, the answer will change each time a new item of inventory is purchased. In a perpetual system, the last-in costs must be determined daily so that cost of goods sold can be recorded as sales transactions occur; the cost of the most recently purchased inventory items are assigned to cost of goods sold each day. But as soon as new items of inventory are purchased, the last-in costs are redefined accordingly. This differs from the periodic approach to applying the LIFO rules. In a periodic system, the last-in costs are assumed to relate only to those inventory items that are purchased toward the end of the year (or month), even though some of the sales transactions occurred earlier in the year (or month).

The weighted-average method becomes a "moving" average under the perpetual system. As with the LIFO method, when the question "What was the average cost of inventory?" is asked, the answer is likely to change each time new inventory items are purchased.

This discussion of accounting for inventories has focused on the products available for sale to the entity's customers. A retail firm would use the term **merchandise inventory** to describe this inventory category; a manufacturing firm would use the term **finished goods inventory**. Besides finished goods inventory, a manufacturing firm will have two other broad inventory categories: raw materials and work in process. In a manufacturing firm, the **raw materials inventory** account is used to hold the costs of raw materials until the materials are released to the factory floor, when the costs are transferred to the **work in process inventory** account. Direct labor costs (wages of production workers) and factory overhead costs (for example, factory utilities, maintenance costs for production equipment, and the depreciation of factory buildings and equipment) are also recorded in the work in process inventory account. These costs, *incurred in making the product*, as opposed to the costs of selling or of administering the company generally, are appropriately related to the inventory items being produced and become part of the product cost to be accounted for as an asset (inventory) until the product is sold.

Inventory Errors

Errors in the amount of ending inventory have a direct dollar-for-dollar effect on cost of goods sold and net income. This direct link between inventory amounts and reported profit or loss causes independent auditors, income tax auditors, and financial analysts to look closely at reported inventory amounts.

The following T-account diagram illustrates this link:

Balance Sheet/Income Statement

Inventory (asset)		Cost of Goods Sold (expense)	
Beginning balance			
Cost of goods purchased or manufactured	Cost of goods sold $\longrightarrow$	Cost of goods sold	
Ending balance			

The cost of goods sold model illustrated earlier expresses the same relationships depicted in the T-account diagram, but in a slightly different manner:

Beginning inventory	$ xxx
Cost of goods purchased or manufactured	xxx
Cost of goods available for sale	$ xxx
Less: Ending inventory	(xxx)
Cost of goods sold	$ xxx

If the beginning balance of inventory and the cost of goods purchased or manufactured are accurate, an error in the ending inventory affects cost of goods sold (in the opposite direction). For example, if the periodic inventory system is used and ending inventory is understated, then the cost of goods sold amount will be overstated. This can be seen in the model above. For any assumed amount, the goods available for sale during the period must either remain on hand as ending inventory (asset) or flow to the income statement as cost of goods sold (expense). Overstated cost of goods sold results in understated gross profit and net income. You should study the income statement shown in Exhibit 2-2 to review these relationships.

The error will also affect cost of goods sold and net income of the subsequent accounting period, but the effects of the error will be reversed because one period's ending inventory is the next period's beginning inventory. Therefore, when the periodic inventory system is used, a great deal of effort is made to have the inventory count and valuation be as accurate as possible.

Balance Sheet Valuation at the Lower of Cost or Market

Inventory carrying values on the balance sheet are reported at the **lower of cost or market**. This reporting is an application of accounting conservatism. The "market" of lower of cost or market is generally the replacement cost of the inventory on the balance sheet date. If market value is lower than cost, then a loss is reported in the accounting period in which the inventory was acquired. The loss is recognized because the decision to buy or make the item was costly, to the extent that the item could have been bought or manufactured at the end of the accounting period for less than its original cost.

The lower-of-cost-or-market determination can be made with respect to individual items of inventory, broad categories of inventory, or the inventory as a whole. A valuation adjustment will be made to reduce the carrying value of inventory items that have become obsolete or that have deteriorated and will not be salable at normal prices.

Prepaid Expenses and Other Current Assets

Other current assets are principally **prepaid expenses**, that is, expenses that have been paid in the current fiscal period but that will not be subtracted from revenue until a subsequent fiscal period. A prepaid expense is the opposite of an accrual and is referred to in accounting and bookkeeping jargon as a *deferral* or *deferred charge* (or *deferred debit*, since *charge* is a bookkeeping synonym for *debit*). An example of a **deferred charge** transaction is a premium payment to an insurance company. It is standard business practice to pay an insurance premium at the beginning of the period of insurance coverage. Assume that a one-year casualty insurance premium of $1,800 is paid on November 1, 1996. At December 31, 1996, insurance coverage for two months has been received, so the cost of that coverage should be recognized as an expense. However, the cost of coverage for the next ten months should be deferred, that is, not shown as an expense, but reported as **prepaid insurance**, an asset. Usual bookkeeping practice is to record the premium payment transaction as an increase in the prepaid insurance asset account and then to transfer the expense to the insurance expense account as the expense is incurred. The journal entries are as follows:

Nov. 1	Dr.	Prepaid insurance	1,800	
	Cr.	Cash		1,800
		Payment of one-year premium		
Dec. 31	Dr.	Insurance expense	300	
	Cr.	Prepaid insurance		300
		Insurance expense for two months incurred		

With the horizontal model, this transaction and the adjustment affect the financial statements as follows:

Balance sheet	Income statement
Assets = Liabilities + Owners' equity ←	Net income = Revenues – Expenses

Payment of premium for the year:
Cash
−1,800

Prepaid
insurance
+1,800

Recognition of expense for two months:

Prepaid insurance −300		Insurance expense −300

The balance in the prepaid insurance asset account at December 31 would be $1,500, which represents the premium for the next ten months' coverage that has already been paid and will be transferred to insurance expense over the next ten months.

Other expenses that could be prepaid and included in this category of current assets include rent, office supplies, postage, and travel expense advances to salespeople and other employees. The reason that these expenses can be or should be deferred is that they can be objectively associated with a benefit to be received in a future period. Advertising expenditures are not properly deferred because how much of the benefit of advertising occurred in the current period and how much of the benefit will be received in future periods cannot be determined objectively. As with advertising expenditures, research and development costs are not deferred, but are instead treated as expenses in the year incurred. The accountant's principal concerns are that the prepaid item be a properly deferred expense, and that it will be used up and become an expense within the one-year time frame for classification as a current asset.

Summary

This chapter discussed the accounting for and the presentation of the following balance sheet current assets and related income statement accounts:

Balance sheet	Income statement
Assets = Liabilities + Owners' equity ←	Net income = Revenues – Expenses
Cash	
Marketable securities	

Balance sheet	Income statement
Assets = Liabilities + Owners' equity ←——	Net income = Revenues – Expenses
Interest receivable.. income	Interest
Accounts receivable.. revenue	Sales
(Allowance for bad debts)... expense	Bad debts
(Allowance for cash discounts).. discounts)	(Cash
Inventory .... Cost of goods sold	
Prepaid expenses .... expenses	Operating

The amount of cash reported on the balance sheet represents the cash available to the entity as of the close of business on the balance sheet date. Cash available in bank accounts is determined by reconciling the bank statement balance with the entity's book balance. Reconciling items are necessary because of timing differences (such as deposits in transit and or outstanding checks) and errors.

Petty cash funds are used as a convenience for making small disbursements of cash.

Entities temporarily invest excess cash in short-term marketable securities in order to earn interest income. Cash managers invest in short-term, low-risk securities that are not likely to have a widely fluctuating market value. Marketable securities that will be held until maturity are reported in the balance sheet at cost; securities that may be traded or are available for sale are reported at market value.

Accounts receivable are valued in the balance sheet at the amount expected to be collected. This valuation principle, as well as the matching concept, requires that the estimated losses from uncollectible accounts be recognized in the fiscal period in which the receivable arose. A valuation adjustment recognizing bad-debt expense and the allowance for bad debts account are used to accomplish this. When an account receivable is determined to be uncollectible, it is written off against the allowance account.

Firms encourage customers to pay their bills promptly by allowing a cash discount if the bill is paid within a specified period, such as ten days. Cash discounts are classified in the income statement as a deduction from sales revenue. Accounts receivable should be reduced with an allowance for cash discounts, which accomplishes the same objectives associated with the allowance for bad debts.

Organizations have a system of internal control to ensure the accuracy of the bookkeeping records and financial statements, to protect assets, to encourage adherence to management policies, and to provide for efficient operations.

Notes receivable usually have a longer term than accounts receivable, and they bear interest. The accounting for notes receivable is similar to that for accounts receivable.

Accounting for inventories involves selecting and applying a cost-flow assumption that determines the assumed pattern of cost flow from the inventory asset account to the cost of goods sold expense account. The alternative cost-flow assumptions are specific identification; weighted-average; first-in, first-out; and last-in, first-out. The assumed cost flow will probably differ from the physical flow of the product. When price levels change, different cost-flow assumptions result in different cost of goods sold amounts in the income statement and different inventory account balances in the balance sheet. The cost-flow assumption used also influences the effect of inventory quantity changes on the balance in both cost of goods sold and ending inventory. Because of the significance of inventories in most balance sheets and the direct relationship between inventory and cost of goods sold, accurate accounting for inventories must be achieved if the financial statements are to be meaningful.

Prepaid expenses (or deferred charges) arise in the accrual accounting process. To achieve an appropriate matching of revenue and expense, amounts prepaid for insurance, rent, and other similar items should be recorded as assets (rather than expenses) until the period in which the benefits of such payments are received.

Refer to the Armstrong World Industries, Inc., balance sheet and financial review in the Appendix to this text's companion course workbook and study guide and to other financial statements you have to observe how current assets are presented.

Key Words and Phrases

administrative controls (p. 161) Features of the internal control system that emphasize adherence to management's policies and operating efficiency.

allowance for uncollectible accounts (or allowance for bad debts) (p. 165) The valuation allowance that results in accounts receivable being reduced by the amount not expected to be collected.

bad debts expense (or uncollectible accounts expense) (p. 164) An estimated expense, recognized in the fiscal period of the sale, representing accounts receivable that are not expected to be collected.

bank reconciliation (p. 158) The process of bringing into agreement the balance in the Cash account in the entity's ledger and the balance reported on the bank statement.

bank service charge (p. 158) The fee charged by a bank for maintaining the entity's checking account.

carrying value (p. 164) The balance of the ledger account (including related contra accounts, if any) of an asset, a liability, or an owners' equity account. Sometimes referred to as book value.

cash discount (p. 166) A discount offered for prompt payment.

collateral (p. 169) The security provided by a borrower that can be used to satisfy the obligation if payment is not made when due.

collect on delivery (COD) (p. 159) A requirement that an item be paid for when it is delivered. Sometimes COD is defined as *cash on delivery*.

commercial paper (p. 162) A short-term security usually issued by a large, creditworthy corporation.

contra asset (p. 165) An account that normally has a credit balance that is subtracted from a related asset on the balance sheet.

cost-flow assumption (p. 172) An assumption made for accounting purposes that identifies how costs flow from the inventory account to cost of goods sold. Alternatives include specific identification; weighted average; first-in, first-out; and last-in, first-out.

cost of goods sold model (p. 180) The way to calculate cost of goods sold when the periodic inventory system is used. The model is as follows:

Beginning inventory
+ Purchases
Cost of goods available for sale
– Ending inventory
Cost of goods sold

credit terms (p. 166) A seller's policy with respect to when payment of an invoice is due and what cash discount (if any) is allowed.

deferred charge (p. 184) An expenditure made in one fiscal period that will be recognized as an expense in a future fiscal period. Another term for a *prepaid expense*.

deposit in transit (p. 158) A bank deposit that has been recorded in the entity's cash account but that does not appear on the bank statement because the bank received the deposit after the date of the statement.

financial controls (p. 161) Features of the internal control system that emphasize accuracy of bookkeeping and financial statements, and protection of assets.

finished goods inventory (p. 182) The term used primarily by manufacturing firms to describe inventory ready for sale to customers.

first-in, first-out (FIFO) (p. 172) The inventory cost-flow assumption that the first costs in to inventory are the first costs out to cost of goods sold.

imprest account (p. 159) An asset account that has a constant balance in the ledger; cash and receipts or vouchers add up to the account balance. Used especially for petty cash funds.

internal control system (p. 158) Policies and procedures designed to:
1. Ensure the accuracy of the bookkeeping records and financial statements
2. Protect the assets
3. Encourage adherence to policies established by management
4. Provide for efficient operations of the organization

inventory accounting system (p. 180) The method used to account for the movement of items into inventory and out to cost of goods sold. The alternatives are the periodic system and the perpetual system.

inventory profits (p. 179) Profits that result from using the FIFO cost-flow assumption rather than LIFO during periods of inflation. Sometimes called *phantom profits*.

last-in, first-out (LIFO) (p. 175) The inventory cost-flow assumption that the last costs into inventory are the first costs out to cost of goods sold.

LIFO liquidation (p. 178) Under the LIFO cost-flow assumption, when the number of units sold during the period exceeds the number of units purchased or made, at least some of the costs assigned to the LIFO beginning inventory are transferred to cost of goods sold. As a result, outdated costs are matched with current revenues, and *inventory profits* occur.

lower of cost or market (p. 184) A valuation process that may result in an asset's being reported at an amount less than cost.

merchandise inventory (p. 182) The term used primarily by retail firms to describe inventory ready for sale to customers.

net realizable value (p. 163) The amount of funds expected to be received upon sale or liquidation of an asset. For accounts receivable, the amount expected to be collected from customers after allowing for bad debts and cash discounts.

note receivable (p. 169) A formal document (usually interest bearing) that supports the financial claim of one entity against another.

NSF (not sufficient funds) check (p. 158) A check returned by the maker's bank because not enough funds were in the account to cover the check.

operating cycle (p. 155) The average time it takes a firm to convert an amount invested in inventory back to cash. For most firms, the operating cycle is measured as the average number of days to produce and sell inventory, plus the average number of days to collect accounts receivable.

outstanding check (p. 158) A check that has been recorded as a cash disbursement by the entity, but that has not yet been processed by the bank.

periodic inventory system (p. 180) A system of accounting for the movement of items into inventory and out to cost of goods sold that involves periodically making a physical count of the inventory on hand.

perpetual inventory system (p. 180) A system of accounting for the movement of items in to inventory and out to cost of goods sold that involves keeping a continuous record of items received, items sold, and inventory on hand.

petty cash (p. 158) A fund used for small payments for which writing a check is inconvenient.

phantom profits (p. 179) See *inventory profits.*

physical inventory (p. 180) The process of counting the inventory on hand and determining its cost based on the inventory cost-flow assumption being used.

prepaid expenses (p. 184) Expenses that have been paid in the current fiscal period but that will not be subtracted from revenues until a subsequent fiscal period. Usually a current asset. Another term for deferred charge.

prepaid insurance (p. 184) An asset account that represents an expenditure made in one fiscal period for insurance that will be recognized as an expense in the subsequent fiscal period to which the coverage applies.

raw materials inventory (p. 182) Inventory of materials ready for the production process.

short-term marketable securities (p. 162) Investments made with cash not needed for current operations.

specific identification (p. 172) The inventory cost-flow assumption that matches cost flow with physical flow.

valuation account (p. 166) An account that reduces the carrying value of an asset to a net realizable value that is less than cost.

valuation adjustment (p. 164) An adjustment that results in an asset's being reported at a net realizable value that is less than cost.

weighted-average (p. 172) The inventory cost-flow assumption that is based on an average of the cost of beginning inventory and the cost of purchases during the year, weighted by the quantity of items at each cost.

work in process inventory (p. 182) Inventory account for the costs (raw materials, direct labor, and manufacturing overhead) of items that are in the process of being manufactured.

write-off (p. 165) The process of removing an account receivable that is not expected to be collected from the accounts receivable account. Also used generically to describe the reduction of an asset and the related recognition of an expense.

Chapter 7

Accounting for and Presentation of Noncurrent Assets

Noncurrent assets include land, buildings, and equipment; intangible assets such as leaseholds, patents, trademarks, and goodwill; and natural resources. The presentation of property, plant, and equipment and other noncurrent assets on the Consolidated Balance Sheets of Armstrong World Industries, Inc., appears straightforward on page 26 of the Appendix to the course workbook and study guide. However, several business and accounting matters are involved in understanding this presentation, and the objective of this chapter is to permit you to make sense of the noncurrent assets section of any balance sheet.

The primary issues related to the accounting for noncurrent assets are as follows:

1. Accounting for the acquisition of the asset
2. Accounting for the use (depreciation) of the asset
3. Accounting for maintenance and repair costs
4. Accounting for the disposition of the asset

Insurance producers and underwriters are interested in property values to verify consistency in property valuation and depreciation methods used. Valuation schedules can be a source of exposure identification for risk managers, underwriters, and claim specialists. The financial statement user should understand any changes in valuation or depreciation methods applied during the accounting period. Plant and equipment valuation is similarly important for exposure identification. Any changes in the valuation or depreciation method applied might indicate a change in use of the asset. Sudden changes in maintenance or repair costs for an equipment item might indicate its obsolescence, which could, in turn, lead to additional loss exposure. Claim specialists can benefit from a review of the insured's property, plant, and equipment valuation schedules in preparation for discussing a settlement offer to be able to better explain differences between the settlement offer and what the insured might expect based on the book value or original acquisition cost of the asset.

Educational Objectives

After studying this chapter, you should be able to:

1. Explain how the cost of land, buildings, and equipment is reported on the balance sheet.

2. Explain how the terms *capitalize* and *expense* are used with respect to property, plant, and equipment.

3. Describe alternative methods of calculating depreciation for financial accounting purposes and the relative effect of each on the income statement (depreciation expense) and the balance sheet (accumulated depreciation).

4. Explain why depreciation for income tax purposes is an important concern of taxpayers and how tax depreciation differs from financial accounting depreciation.

5. Describe the accounting for maintenance and repair expenditures.

6. Explain the effect on financial statements of the disposition of noncurrent assets, by abandonment, sale, or trade-in.

7. Describe the difference between an operating lease and a capital lease.

8. Describe the similarities in the financial statement effects of buying an asset and using a capital lease to acquire the rights to an asset.

9. Describe the role of present value concepts in financial reporting and their usefulness in decision making.

10. Describe various intangible assets, explain how their values are measured, and explain how their cost is reflected in the income statement.

11. Define or describe each of the Key Words and Phrases introduced in this chapter.

Land

Land owned and used in the operations of the firm is shown on the balance sheet at its original cost. All ordinary and necessary costs the firm incurs to get the land ready for its intended use are considered part of the original cost. These costs include the purchase price of the land, title fees, legal fees, and other costs related to the acquisition. If a firm purchases land with a building on it and razes the building so that a new one can be built to the firm's specifications, then the costs of the land, the old building, and razing (less any salvage proceeds) all become the cost of the land and are *capitalized* (see Business Procedure Capsule 11—Capitalizing Versus Expensing) because all of these costs were incurred to ready the land for its intended use.

Land acquired for investment purposes, or for some potential future but undefined use, is classified as a separate noncurrent and nonoperating asset. This asset is reported at its original cost. A land development company would treat land under development as inventory, and all development costs would be included in the asset carrying value. As lots are sold, the costs are transferred from inventory to cost of goods sold. Because land is never "used up," no accounting depreciation is associated with land.

When land is sold, the difference between the selling price and cost will be a gain or loss to be reported in the income statement of the period in which the sale occurred. For example, if a parcel of land on which Cruisers, Inc., had once operated a plant is sold this year for $140,000, and the land had cost $6,000 when it was acquired thirty-five years ago, the entry would be as follows:

Dr.	Cash	140,000	
Cr.	Land		6,000
Cr.	Gain on sale of land		134,000

The effect of this transaction on the financial statements is as follows:

Balance sheet	Income statement
Assets = Liabilities + Owners' equity ←	Net income = Revenues – Expenses
Cash +140,000	Gain on sale of land
Land –6,000	+134,000

Since land is carried on the books at original cost, the unrealized holding gain that had gradually occurred was ignored from an accounting perspective until Cruisers, Inc. sold the land (and realized the gain). Thus, the financial statements for each of the years between purchase and sale would *not* have reflected the increasing value of the land. Instead, the entire $134,000 gain will be reported in this year's income statement. The gain will not be included with operating income; it will be highlighted in the income statement as a nonrecurring, nonoperating item so that financial statement users will not be led to expect a similar gain in future years.

The original cost valuation of land (and all other categories of noncurrent assets discussed in this chapter) is often criticized for understating asset values on the balance sheet and for failing to provide proper matching on the income statement. The management of Cruisers, Inc., would have known that its land was appreciating in value over time, but the balance sheet would not have reflected this application. The accounting profession defends the *cost principle* based on its reliability, consistency, and conservatism. To record land at market value would involve appraisals or other subjective estimates of value that could not be verified until an exchange transaction (that is, a sale) occurred. Although approximate market value would be more relevant than original cost for decision makers, original cost is the basis for accounting for noncurrent assets. You should be aware of this important limitation of the noncurrent asset information shown in balance sheets.

• BUSINESS PROCEDURE CAPSULE 11
Capitalizing Versus Expensing

An expenditure involves using an asset (usually cash) or incurring a liability to acquire goods, services, or other economic benefits. Whenever a firm buys something, it has made an expenditure. All expenditures must be accounted for either as assets (**capitalizing** an expenditure) or as expenses (**expensing** an expenditure). Although this jargon applies to any expenditure, it is most prevalent in discussions about property, plant, and equipment.

Expenditures should be capitalized if the item acquired will have an economic benefit to the entity that extends beyond the end of the current fiscal year. However, expenditures for preventative maintenance and normal repairs, even though they are needed to maintain the usefulness of the asset over several years, are expensed as incurred. The capitalize versus expense issue is resolved by applying the matching concept, under which costs incurred in generating revenues are subtracted from revenues in the period in which the revenues are earned.

When an expenditure is capitalized (or treated as a capital expenditure), plant assets increase. If the asset is depreciable—and all plant assets except land are depreciable—depreciation expense is recognized over the estimated useful life of the asset. If the expenditure is expensed, then the full cost is reflected in the current period's income statement. It is sometimes difficult to differentiate be-

expenditures that are clearly capital and those which are obviously expenses. This gray area leads to differences of opinion that directly affect the net income reported for a fiscal period.

The materiality concept (discussed in Chapter 2) is often applied to the issue of accounting for capital expenditures. Generally speaking, most accountants expense items that are not material. Thus, the cost of a $5 wastebasket may be expensed rather than capitalized and depreciated, even though the wastebasket clearly has a useful life of many years and should theoretically be accounted for as a capital asset.

Another factor that influences the capitalize versus expense decision is the potential income tax reduction in the current year that results from expensing. Although depreciation would be claimed (and income taxes would be reduced) over the life of a capitalized expenditure, many managers prefer the immediate income tax reduction that results from expensing. The capitalize versus expense issue is another area in which accountants' judgments can have a significant effect on an entity's financial position and results of operations. Explanations in this text reflect sound accounting theory. However, in practice, there may be some deviation from theory.

Buildings and Equipment

This section will discuss the accounting for the cost of assets acquired, depreciation for financial accounting purposes, maintenance and repair expenditures, disposal of depreciable assets, and trade-in transactions.

Cost of Assets Acquired

Buildings and equipment are recorded at their original cost, which is the purchase price plus all the ordinary and necessary costs incurred to get the building or equipment ready to use in the operations of the firm. Interest costs associated with loans used to finance the construction of a building are included in the building cost until the building is put into operation. Installation and shakedown costs (costs associated with adjusting and preparing the equipment to be used in production) incurred for a new piece of equipment should be capitalized. If a firm's own employees make a piece of equipment, all of the material, labor, and overhead costs that would ordinarily be recorded as inventory costs (were the machine being made for an outside customer) should be capitalized as equipment costs. Those costs are capitalized because they are directly related to assets that the firm will use over several accounting periods and are not related only to current period earnings.

Original cost is not usually difficult to determine, but when two or more noncurrent assets are acquired in a single transaction for a lump-sum purchase price, the cost of each asset acquired must be measured and recorded separately. In such cases, an allocation of the "basket" (or combined) purchase price is made to the individual assets acquired based on relative appraisal values on the date of acquisition. Exhibit 7-1 illustrates this allocation process and the related accounting.

Exhibit 7-1
Basket Purchase Allocation Illustrated

Situation:
Cruisers, Inc., acquired a parcel of land, along with a building and some production equipment, from a bankrupt competitor for $200,000 in cash. Current values reported by an independent appraiser were land, $20,000; building, $170,000; and equipment, $60,000.

Allocation of acquisition cost:

Asset	Appraised Value	Percentage of Total*	Cost Allocation
Land	$ 20,000	8%	$200,000 × 8% = $ 16,000
Building	170,000	68%	$200,000 × 68% = 136,000
Equipment	60,000	24%	$200,000 × 24% = 48,000
	$250,000	100%	$200,000

* $20,000 / $250,000 = 8%, $170,000 / $250,000 = 68%,
$60,000 / $250,000 = 24%

Entry to record the acquisition:

Dr.	Land..	16,000	
Dr.	Building..	136,000	
Dr.	Equipment	48,000	
Cr.	Cash...		200,000

Effect of the acquisition on the financial statements:

Balance sheet	Income statement
Assets = Liabilities + Owners' equity ←	Net income = Revenues – Expenses
Land +16,000	
Building +136,000	
Equipment +48,000	
Cash –200,000	

Depreciation for Financial Accounting Purposes

In financial accounting, depreciation is an application of the matching concept. The original cost of noncurrent assets represents the *prepaid* cost of economic benefits that will be received in future years. To the extent that an asset is "used up" in the operations of the entity, a portion of the asset's cost should be subtracted from the revenues that were generated through the use of the asset. Thus, the depreciation process involves an allocation of the cost of an asset to the years in which the benefits of the asset are expected to be received. Depreciation is *not* an attempt to recognize a loss in market value or any difference between the original cost and replacement cost of an asset. In fact, the market value of noncurrent assets may actually increase as they are used—but "appreciation" is not recorded (as discussed in the land section of this chapter). Depreciation expense is recorded in each fiscal period with this adjusting entry:

Dr.	Depreciation expense	xx	
	Cr.	Accumulated depreciation	xx

The effect of this adjusting entry on the financial statements is as follows:

Balance sheet	Income statement
Asets = Liabilities + Owners' equity ⟵───	Net income = Revenues – Expenses
–Accumulated depreciation	–Depreciation expense

Accumulated depreciation is a contra asset, and the balance in this account is the cumulative total of all the depreciation expense that has been recorded over the life of the asset up to the balance sheet date. It is classified with the related asset on the balance sheet, as a subtraction from the cost of the asset. The difference between the cost of an asset and the accumulated depreciation on that asset is the **net book value** of the asset. The balance sheet presentation of a building asset and its related accumulated depreciation account (using assumed amounts) is as follows:

Building	$100,000
Less: Accumulated depreciation	(15,000)
Net book value of building	$ 85,000

or, as more commonly reported:

Building, less accumulated depreciation of $15,000	$85,000

With either presentation, the user can determine how much of the cost has been recognized as expense since the asset was acquired—which would not be

possible if the building account was directly reduced for the amount depreciated each year. This is why a contra asset account is used for accumulated
depreciation.

Cash is not involved in the depreciation expense entry. The entity's Cash account
was affected when the asset was purchased, or as it was being paid for if a
liability was incurred when the asset was acquired. The fact that depreciation
expense does not affect cash is important for understanding the statement of
cash flows, which identifies the sources and uses of a firm's cash during a fiscal
period.

There are several alternative methods of calculating depreciation expense for
financial accounting purposes. Each involves spreading the amount to be
depreciated, which is the asset's cost minus its estimated salvage value, over
the asset's estimated useful life to the entity. The depreciation method
selected will not affect the total depreciation expense to be recognized over
the life of the asset; however, different methods will result in different patterns
of depreciation expense by fiscal period. There are two broad categories of
depreciation calculation methods: the straight-line methods and accelerated
methods. Exhibit 7-2 illustrates depreciation expense patterns resulting from
these alternatives.

Exhibit 7-2
Depreciation Expense Patterns

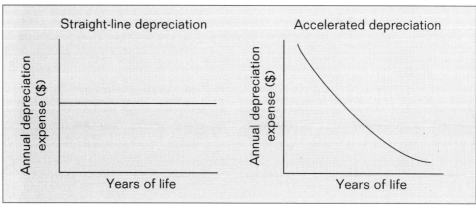

Accelerated depreciation methods result in greater depreciation expense and
lower net income than straight-line depreciation during the early years of the
asset's life. During the later years of the asset's life, annual depreciation
expense calculated by using accelerated methods is less than it would be by
using straight-line depreciation, and net income is higher.

Which method do businesses use, and why? For purposes of reporting to stockholders, most firms use the **straight-line depreciation method** because in the early years of an asset's life it results in lower depreciation expense and hence higher reported net income than accelerated depreciation. In later years, when accelerated depreciation is less than straight-line depreciation, *total* depreciation expense using the straight-line method will still be less than under an accelerated method if the amount invested in new assets has grown each year. Such a regular increase in depreciable assets is not unusual for firms that are growing, assuming that prices of new and replacement equipment are rising.

The specific depreciation calculation methods are as follows:

Straight-line

Straight-line

Units of production

Accelerated

Sum-of-the-years'-digits

Declining balance

Exhibit 7-3 illustrates each of these depreciation calculation methods.

Exhibit 7-3
Depreciation Calculation Methods

Assumptions:

Cruisers, Inc., purchased a molding machine at the beginning of 1995 for $22,000.

The machine is estimated to have a useful life to Cruisers, Inc., of five years and an estimated salvage value of $2,000.

It is estimated that the machine will produce 200 boat hulls before it is worn out.

a. **Straight-line depreciation:**

$$\text{Annual depreciation expense} = \frac{\text{Cost} - \text{Estimated salvage value}}{\text{Estimated useful life}}$$

$$= \frac{\$22,000 - \$2,000}{5 \text{ years}}$$

$$= \$4,000$$

Alternatively, a straight-line depreciation rate could be determined and multiplied by the amount to be depreciated.

$$\text{Straight-line depreciation} = \frac{1}{\text{Life in years}} = \frac{1}{5} = 20\%$$

$$\text{Annual depreciation expense} = 20\% \times \$20,000 = \$4,000$$

b. **Units-of-production depreciation:**

$$\text{Depreciation expense per unit produced} = \frac{\text{Cost} - \text{Estimated salvage value}}{\text{Estimated total units to be made}}$$

$$= \frac{\$22,000 - \$2,000}{200 \text{ hulls}}$$

$$= \$100$$

Each year's depreciation expense would be $100 multiplied by the number of hulls produced.

c. **Sum-of-the-years'-digits depreciation:**

$$\frac{\text{Annual}}{\text{depreciation expense}} = (\text{Cost} - \text{Estimated salvage value}) \times \frac{\text{Remaining life in years}}{\text{Sum-of-the-years' digits}}$$

$$\frac{1995}{\text{depreciation expense}} = (\$22,000 - \$2,000) \times \frac{5 \text{ years}}{1 + 2 + 3 + 4 + 5}$$

$$= \$20,000 \times \frac{5}{15}$$

$$= \$6,667$$

Subsequent years' depreciation expense:

$$1996 \cdots\cdots \$20,000 \times \frac{4}{15} = \$5,333$$

$$1997 \cdots\cdots \$20,000 \times \frac{3}{15} = 4,000$$

$$1998 \cdots\cdots \$20,000 \times \frac{2}{15} = 2,667$$

$$1999 \cdots\cdots \$20,000 \times \frac{1}{15} = 1,333$$

Total depreciation expense over 5 years = $20,000

d. **Declining-balance depreciation:**

Annual depreciation expense = Double the straight-line depreciation rate × Asset's net book value at beginning of year

Straight-line depreciation rate $= \dfrac{1}{\text{Life in years}} = \dfrac{1}{5} = 20\%$

Double the straight-line depreciation rate is 40%.

Year	Net Book Value at Beginning of Year		Factor	Depreciation Expense for the Year	Accumulated Depreciation	Net Book Value at End of Year
1995........	$22,000	×	0.4	= $8,800	$ 8,800	$13,200
1996........	13,200	×	0.4	= 5,280	14,080	7,920
1997........	7,920	×	0.4	= 3,168	17,248	4,752
1998........	4,752	×	0.4	= 1,901	19,149	2,851
1999........	2,851	×	0.4	= 851*	20,000	2,000

* Depreciation expense at the end of the asset's life is equal to an amount that will cause the net book value to equal the asset's estimated salvage value.

Recap of depreciation expense by year and method:

Year	Straight-Line	Sum-of-the-Years'-Digits	Declining Balance
1995.....................	$ 4,000	$ 6,667	$ 8,800
1996.....................	4,000	5,333	5,280
1997.....................	4,000	4,000	3,168
1998.....................	4,000	2,667	1,901
1999.....................	4,000	1,333	851
Total.....................	$20,000	$20,000	$20,000

The total depreciation expense for the five years is the same for each method; the pattern of the expense differs. Since depreciation is an expense, the effect on operating income of the alternative methods will be inversely related; 1995 operating income will be highest if the straight-line method is used and lowest if the declining-balance method is used.

Depreciation calculations using the straight-line, units of production, and sum-of-the-years'-digits methods involve determining the amount to be depreciated by subtracting the estimated salvage value from the cost of the asset. Salvage is considered in the declining-balance method only near the end of the asset's life when salvage value becomes the target for net book value.

The declining-balance calculation illustrated in Exhibit 7-3 is known as *double-declining balance* because the depreciation rate used was double the straight-line rate. In some instances, the rate used is 1.5 times the straight-line rate; this is referred to as *150 percent declining-balance* depreciation. Whatever rate is used, a constant percentage is applied each year to the declining balance of the net book value.

Although many firms use a single depreciation method for all of their depreciable assets, the consistency concept is applied to the depreciation method used for a particular asset acquired in a particular year. Thus, a firm could use an accelerated depreciation method for some of its assets and the straight-line method for other assets. Differences can even occur between similar assets purchased in the same or different years. In order to make sense of the income statement and balance sheet, find out from the footnotes to the financial statements which depreciation methods are used (see page 28 of the Armstrong annual report). Table 7-1 summarizes the depreciation methods used for stockholder reporting purposes by 600 large firms.

Table 7-1
Depreciation Calculation Methods Used by 600 Publicly Owned Industrial and Merchandising Corporations—1993

Methods:	Number of Companies*
Straight-line	570
Units of production	46
Declining-balance	26
Sum-of-the-years'-digits	9
Accelerated method—not specified	56
Other	9
*Companies may use more than one method.	

Source: Reprinted with permission from *Accounting Trends and Techniques*, Table 3-13, copyright © 1994 by American Institute of Certified Public Accountants, Inc.

The estimates made of useful life and salvage value are educated guesses, but accountants, frequently working with engineers, can estimate these factors with great accuracy. Those involved in the estimating process consider a firm's experience and equipment replacement practices. For income tax purposes (see Business Procedure Capsule 12), the useful life of various depreciable assets is determined by the Internal Revenue Code, which also specifies that salvage values are to be ignored.

- **BUSINESS PROCEDURE CAPSULE 12**
  Depreciation for Income Tax Purposes

  Depreciation is a deductible expense for income tax purposes. Although depreciation expense does not directly affect cash, it does reduce taxable income.

Therefore, most firms would like to have deductible depreciation expense as large an amount as possible because that would mean lower taxable income and lower taxes payable. The Internal Revenue Code has permitted taxpayers to use an accelerated depreciation calculation method for many years. Estimated useful life is generally the most significant factor (other than calculation method) affecting the amount of depreciation expense, and for many years this was a contentious issue between taxpayers and the Internal Revenue Service because the amount of depreciation expense affects the amount of tax owed.

In 1981 the Internal Revenue Code was amended to permit use of the **Accelerated Cost Recovery System (ACRS)**, frequently pronounced "acres," for depreciable assets put in service after 1980. The ACRS rules simplified the determination of useful life and allowed rapid write-off patterns similar to the declining-balance methods, so most firms started using ACRS for tax purposes. Unlike the LIFO inventory cost-flow assumption (which, if selected, must be used for both financial reporting and income tax determination purposes), "book" (that is, financial statement) and tax depreciation calculation methods need not be the same. Most firms continued to use straight-line depreciation for book purposes.

ACRS used relatively short and arbitrary useful lives and ignored salvage value. The intent was more to permit relatively quick "cost recovery" and thus encourage investment than it was to recognize traditional depreciation expense. For example, ACRS permitted the write-off of most machinery and equipment over three to five years.

However, in the Tax Reform Act of 1986, Congress changed the original ACRS provisions. The system is now referred to as the **Modified Accelerated Cost Recovery System (MACRS)**. Recovery periods were lengthened, additional categories for classifying assets were created, and the method of calculating the depreciation deduction was specified. Cost recovery periods are specified based on the type of asset and its class life, as defined by the Internal Revenue Service. Most machinery and equipment is depreciated using the double-declining-balance method, but the 150 percent declining-balance method is required for some longer-lived assets, and the straight-line method is specified for buildings.

In 1986, the IRS discouraged the use of ACRS for book depreciation because of the arbitrarily short lives involved. MACRS lives are closer to actual useful lives, but basing depreciation expense for financial accounting purposes on tax law provisions, which are subject to frequent change, is not appropriate. Yet many small to medium-sized businesses yield to the temptation to do so. Such decisions are based on the fact that tax depreciation schedules must be maintained to satisfy Internal Revenue Service rules, and therefore the need to keep separate schedules for financial reporting is avoided.

Many technical accounting challenges must be considered when calculating depreciation in practice. These include part-year depreciation for assets acquired or disposed of during a year, changes in estimated salvage value and/or useful life after the asset has been depreciated for some time, and asset grouping to facilitate the depreciation calculation. These are beyond the scope of this text; you should understand the basic calculation procedures and the different effect of each on both depreciation expense in the income statement and accumulated depreciation (and net book value) on the balance sheet.

Maintenance and Repair Expenditures

Preventative maintenance expenditures and routine repair costs are clearly expenses of the period in which they are incurred. There may be some debate with respect to some maintenance expenditures, however, because accountants' judgments may differ. If a maintenance expenditure will extend the useful life or salvage value of an asset beyond that used in the depreciation calculation, the expenditure should be capitalized, and the new net book value of the asset should be depreciated over the asset's remaining useful life.

In practice, most accountants decide in favor of expensing rather than capitalizing for several reasons. To revise the depreciation calculation data is frequently time-consuming, with little perceived benefit. Because depreciation involves estimates of useful life and salvage value to begin with, revising those estimates without overwhelming evidence that they are significantly in error is of questionable value. For income tax purposes, most taxpayers would rather have a deductible expense now (expensing) rather than later (capitalizing and depreciating). "Expensing" means recognizing the full cost of an asset as an expense in the period in which it is purchased. The asset never appears on the balance sheet. "Capitalizing and depreciating" means recognizing the asset at cost on the balance sheet, and expensing a proportional share of its value periodically (depreciation expense) over its useful life.

Because net income could be affected either favorably or unfavorably by inconsistent judgments about the accounting for repair and maintenance expenditures, auditors (both internal and external) and the Internal Revenue Service usually look closely at these expenditures when they are reviewing a firm's reported results.

Disposal of Depreciable Assets

When a depreciable asset is sold or scrapped, both the asset and its related accumulated depreciation account must be reduced by the appropriate amounts. For example, throwing out a fully depreciated piece of equipment, for which no salvage value had been estimated, would result in the following entry:

Dr.   Accumulated depreciation   xx
    Cr.   Equipment   xx

This entry does not affect *total* assets or any other parts of the financial statements as shown by the horizontal model below:

Balance sheet	Income statement
Assets = Liabilities + Owners' equity ⟵	Net income = Revenues – Expenses

–Equipment

+Accumulated
depreciation

When the asset being disposed of has a positive net book value, either because a salvage value was estimated or because it has not reached the end of its estimated useful life to the firm, a gain or loss on the disposal will result unless the asset is sold for a price that is equal to the net book value. For example, if equipment that cost $6,000 new has a net book value equal to its estimated salvage value of $900, and if it is sold for $1,200, the following entry will result:

Dr.   Cash   1,200
Dr.   Accumulated depreciation 5,100*
    Cr.   Equipment   6,000
    Cr.   Gain on sale of equipment.....................   300
    Sold equipment

        * Net book value = Cost – Accumulated depreciation

              900 = 6,000 – Accumulated depreciation

      Accumulated depreciation = 5,100

The effect of this entry on the financial statements is as follows:

Balance sheet	Income statement
Assets = Liabilities + Owners' equity ⟵	Net income = Revenues – Expenses

Cash
+1,200

Accumulated
depreciation
+5,100

Equipment
–6,000

Gain on sale
of equipment
+300

Alternatively, assume that the above equipment had to be scrapped without any salvage value. The entry would be as follows:

Dr.	Accumulated depreciation	5,100
Dr.	Loss on disposal of equipment	900
Cr.	Equipment	6,000
	Scrapped equipment	

The effect of this entry on the financial statements is as follows:

Balance sheet	Income statement
Assets = Liabilities + Owners' equity ◄───	Net income = Revenues – Expenses
Accumulated depreciation +5,100	Loss on disposal of equipment –900
Equipment –6,000	

The gain or loss on the disposal of a depreciable asset is, in effect, a correction of the total depreciation expense that has been recorded over the life of the asset. If salvage value and useful life estimates had been correct, the net book value of the asset would be equal to the **proceeds** (if any) received from its sale or disposal. Depreciation expense is never adjusted retroactively, so the significance of these gains or losses gives the financial statement user a basis for judging the accuracy of the accountant's estimates of salvage value and useful life. Gains or losses on the disposal of depreciable assets are not part of the operating income of the entity. If significant, they will be reported separately as elements of other income or expense. If not material, they will be reported with miscellaneous other income.

Trade-In Transactions

Frequently an old asset is traded in for a similar new asset. In this kind of transaction, the seller of the new equipment determines a trade-in allowance. The trade-in allowance is then subtracted from the list price of the new asset to determine the amount of cash to be paid for it.

Assume that you have an old car to trade in on a new one. Which is more important to you—the trade-in allowance on the old car or the amount you have to pay to get the new car? Probably the amount you have to pay. If you focused on the trade-in allowance, an unscrupulous dealer could offer a trade-in allowance much greater than the market value of your old car, and then work from a list price for the new car that had been inflated by an even larger amount. Because trade-in allowances are not always determined objectively, using a trade-allowance as if it were the same thing as the proceeds from the sale of an asset could lead to a fictitious gain or loss.

For income tax purposes, a trade-in transaction results in neither a gain nor a loss to the entity trading in an old asset and acquiring a new asset. Generally accepted accounting principles provide for recognizing a loss, but not a gain, on a trade-in transaction involving similar assets (an example of accounting conservatism). When no gain or loss is recognized, the cost of the new asset becomes the net book value of the old asset, plus the cash paid and/or liability assumed in the transaction. The new asset cost, less estimated salvage value, will be depreciated over the estimated useful life to the entity of the new asset. Exhibit 7-4 illustrates accounting for a trade-in transaction.

Exhibit 7-4
Trade-In Transaction Accounting Illustrated

Assumptions:

The cost of the old car was $9,300.

Accumulated depreciation on the old car is $8,100.

The new car list price is $12,800; a $2,600 trade-in allowance is given.

The buyer is going to pay $1,500 cash and sign a note for the $8,700 balance due to the new car dealer.

Accounting:

The entry to record this trade-in transaction is as follows:

Dr.	Accumulated depreciation (on old car)	8,100	
Dr.	Automobiles (cost of new car)	11,400	
	Cr.	Automobiles (cost of old car)	9,300
	Cr.	Cash	1,500
	Cr.	Note payable	8,700
		Trade of old car for new car	

The effect of this transaction on the financial statements is shown below. Notice that the income statement is not affected.

Balance sheet	Income statement
Assets = Liabilities + Owners' equity ◄——	Net income = Revenues − Expenses

Accumulated Note payable
depreciation +8,700
(on old car)
+8,100

Automobiles (cost of new car)
+11,400

Automobiles (cost of old car)
−9,300

Cash
−1,500

Continued on next page.

```
Recap of amounts:
    New car list price .........................................................   $12,800
    Old car trade-in allowance ...........................................     2,600
    Amount required from buyer to get new car...............   $10,200
    Amount paid in cash ....................................................     1,500
    Amount of note payable ..............................................   $ 8,700
    Net book value of old car ($9,300 – $8,100) .............   $ 1,200
    Amount required from buyer to get new car...............   10,200
    Cost of new car ...........................................................   $11,400
```

If the trade-in transaction involves dissimilar assets, both generally accepted accounting principles and the Internal Revenue Code consider two transactions to have occurred: the "sale" of the old asset and the purchase of a new asset. Thus, a gain or loss is recognized on the sale of the old asset, with the trade-in allowance being considered the proceeds from the sale. The cost of the new asset is the fair market value of the old asset plus the cash paid and/or liability incurred.

Assets Acquired by Capital Lease

Many firms lease, or rent, assets rather than purchase them. An **operating lease** is an ordinary, frequently short-term lease for the use of an asset that does not involve any attributes of ownership. For example, the renter (lessee) of a car from Hertz or Avis (the lessor) must return the car at the end of the lease term. Therefore, assets rented under an operating lease are not reflected on the lessee's balance sheet, and the rent expense involved is reported in the income statement as an operating expense.

A **capital lease** (or *financing lease*) results in the lessee's (renter) assuming virtually all of the benefits and risks of ownership of the leased asset. For example, the lessee of a car from an automobile dealership may sign a noncancelable lease agreement with a term of five years requiring monthly payments sufficient to cover the cost of the car, plus interest and administrative costs. A lease is a capital lease if it has *any* of the following characteristics:

1. It transfers ownership of the asset to the lessee.
2. It permits the lessee to purchase the asset for a nominal sum at the end of the lease period.

3. The lease term is at least 75 percent of the economic life of the asset.

4. The **present value** (see Business Procedure Capsule 13) of the lease payments is at least 90 percent of the fair value of the asset.

• **BUSINESS PROCEDURE CAPSULE 13**
  Present Value

Organizations and individuals are frequently confronted with the choice of paying for a purchase today or at a later date. Intuition suggests that all other things being equal, paying later is preferable, because in the meantime the cash could be invested to earn interest. This preference reflects the fact that money has value over time. Of course, other things aren't always equal, and sometimes the choice is between paying one amount—say $100—today, and a larger amount—say $110—a year later. Or in the opposite case, the choice may be between receiving $100 today or $110 a year from now. Present value analysis is used to determine which of these alternatives is financially preferable.

The present value concept is an application of compound interest—the process of earning interest on interest. If $1,000 is invested in a savings account earning interest at the rate of 10 percent compounded annually, and if the account is left alone for four years, the following results will occur:

Year	Principal at Beginning of Year	Interest Earned at 10%	Principal at End of Year
1	$1,000	$100	$1,100
2	1,100	110	1,210
3	1,210	121	1,331
4	1,331	133	1,464

This is an example of future value, and most of us think of a future amount when we think about compound interest. We understand that the future value of $1,000 invested for four years at 10 percent interest compounded annually is $1,464 because we are familiar with this aspect of the compound interest concept. This relationship can be illustrated on a time line as follows:

Today	1 year	2 years	3 years	4 years
⊢	⊢	⊢	⊢	⊣

$1,000 ⟶ invested at 10% has a future value of ⟶ $1,464

Present value analysis involves looking at the same compound interest concept from the opposite perspective. Using data in the above table, you can say that the present value of $1,464 to be received four years from now, assuming an interest rate of 10 percent compounded annually, is $1,000. On a timeline representation, the direction of the arrow indicating the time perspective is reversed.

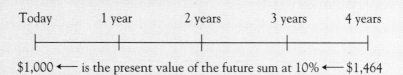

$1,000 ⟵ is the present value of the future sum at 10% ⟵ $1,464

If someone owed you $1,464 to be paid four years from now, and if you were to agree with your debtor that 10 percent was a fair interest rate for that period of time, you would both be satisfied to settle the debt for $1,000 today. Or if you owed $1,464 payable four years from now, both you and your creditor would be satisfied to settle the debt for $1,000 today (still assuming agreement on the 10 percent interest rate). That is because $1,000 invested at 10 percent interest compounded annually will grow to $1,464 in four years. Stated differently, the future value of $1,000 at 10 percent interest in four years is $1,464, and the present value of $1,464 in four years at 10 percent is $1,000.

Present value analysis involves determining the present amount that is equivalent to an amount to be paid or received in the future, recognizing that money does have value over time. The time value of money is represented by the interest that can be earned on money over an investment period. In present value analysis, **discount rate** is a term frequently used for *interest rate*. In the above example, the present value of $1,464 discounted at 10 percent for four years is $1,000. Thus, the *time value of money* in this example is represented by the $464 in interest that is being charged to the borrower for the use of money over the four-year period.

Present value analysis does not directly recognize the effects of inflation, although inflationary expectations will influence the discount rate used in the present value calculation. Generally, the higher the inflationary expectations, the higher the discount rate used in present value analysis.

The above example deals with the present value of a *single amount* to be received or paid in the future. Some transactions involve receiving or paying the same amount each period for a number of periods. This sort of receipt or payment pattern is referred to as an **annuity**. The present value of an annuity is simply the sum of the present value of each of the annuity payment amounts.

There are formulas and computer program functions for calculating the present value of a single amount and the present value of an annuity. In all cases, the amount to be received or paid in the future, the discount rate, and the number of years (or other time periods) are used in the present value calculation. Table 7-2 presents factors for calculating the present value of $1 (single amount), and Table 7-3 gives the factors for the present value of an annuity of $1 for several discount rates and for a number of periods. Glance at these tables and learn how they are constructed. For any given number of periods, the factors shown in the annuity table represent cumulative totals of the factors shown in the present value of $1 table. Check this by adding together the single amount factors for periods 1, 2, and 3 in the 4 percent column of Table 7-2 and comparing the result to the annuity factor shown for 3 periods at 4 percent in Table 7-3. In both cases, the answer should be 2.7751. Notice also (by scanning across the tables) that for any given number of periods, the higher the discount (interest) rate, the lower the present value. This makes sense when you remember that present values operate in the opposite manner from future values. The higher the interest rate, the greater the future value—and the lower the present value. Now scan down Table 7-2 and notice that for any given interest rate, the present value of $1 decreases as more periods are added. The same effects are also present in Table 7-3 but cannot be visualized because the annuity factors represent cumulative totals, yet for each additional period, a smaller amount is added to the previous annuity factor.

To find the present value of any amount, the appropriate factor from the table is multiplied by the amount to be received or paid in the future. With the data from the initial example described above, the present value of $1,464 to be received four years from now, based on a discount rate of 10 percent, can be calculated as follows:

$1,464 × 0.6830 (from the 10% column, four period row of
Table 7-2) = $1,000 (rounded)

What is the present value of a lottery prize of $1,000,000 payable in 20 annual installments of $50,000 each, assuming a discount (interest) rate of 12 percent? The time-line representation of this situation is as follows:

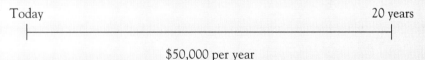

The present value of this annuity is calculated by multiplying the annuity amount ($50,000) by the annuity factor from Table 7-3. The solution is as follows:

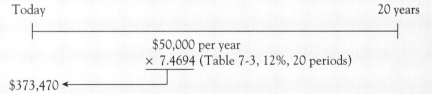

The answer of $373,470 shouldn't make the winner feel less fortunate, because she is still the winner of a sizable sum. She is just not an instant millionaire in present value terms. The lottery authority needs to deposit only $373,470 today in an account earning 12 percent interest in order to be able to pay the winner $50,000 per year for twenty years beginning a year from now. What is the present value of the same lottery prize assuming that 8 percent was the appropriate discount rate? What if a 16 percent interest rate was used?

Table 7-2

Factors for Calculating the Present Value of $1

No. of Periods	4%	6%	8%	10%	12%	14%	16%	18%	20%	22%
				Discount Rate						
1	0.9615	0.9434	0.9259	0.9091	0.8929	0.8772	0.8621	0.8475	0.8333	0.8197
2	0.9246	0.8900	0.8573	0.8264	0.7972	0.7695	0.7432	0.7182	0.6944	0.6719
3	0.8890	0.8396	0.7938	0.7513	0.7118	0.6750	0.6407	0.6086	0.5787	0.5507
4	0.8548	0.7921	0.7350	0.6830	0.6355	0.5921	0.5523	0.5158	0.4823	0.4514
5	0.8219	0.7473	0.6806	0.6209	0.5674	0.5194	0.4761	0.4371	0.4019	0.3700
6	0.7903	0.7050	0.6302	0.5645	0.5066	0.4556	0.4104	0.3704	0.3349	0.3033
7	0.7599	0.6651	0.5835	0.5132	0.4523	0.3996	0.3538	0.3139	0.2791	0.2486
8	0.7307	0.6274	0.5403	0.4665	0.4039	0.3506	0.3050	0.2660	0.2326	0.2038
9	0.7026	0.5919	0.5002	0.4241	0.3606	0.3075	0.2630	0.2255	0.1938	0.1670
10	0.6756	0.5584	0.4632	0.3855	0.3220	0.2697	0.2267	0.1911	0.1615	0.1369
11	0.6496	0.5268	0.4289	0.3505	0.2875	0.2366	0.1954	0.1619	0.1346	0.1122
12	0.6246	0.4970	0.3971	0.3186	0.2567	0.2076	0.1685	0.1372	0.1122	0.0920
13	0.6006	0.4688	0.3677	0.2897	0.2292	0.1821	0.1452	0.1163	0.0935	0.0754
14	0.5775	0.4423	0.3405	0.2633	0.2046	0.1597	0.1252	0.0985	0.0779	0.0618
15	0.5553	0.4173	0.3152	0.2394	0.1827	0.1401	0.1079	0.0835	0.0649	0.0507
16	0.5339	0.3936	0.2919	0.2176	0.1631	0.1229	0.0930	0.0708	0.0541	0.0415
17	0.5134	0.3714	0.2703	0.1978	0.1456	0.1078	0.0802	0.0600	0.0451	0.0340
18	0.4936	0.3503	0.2502	0.1799	0.1300	0.0946	0.0691	0.0508	0.0376	0.0279
19	0.4746	0.3305	0.2317	0.1635	0.1161	0.0829	0.0596	0.0431	0.0313	0.0229
20	0.4564	0.3118	0.2145	0.1486	0.1037	0.0728	0.0514	0.0365	0.0261	0.0187
21	0.4388	0.2942	0.1987	0.1351	0.0926	0.0638	0.0443	0.0309	0.0217	0.0154
22	0.4220	0.2775	0.1839	0.1228	0.0826	0.0560	0.0382	0.0262	0.0181	0.0126
23	0.4057	0.2618	0.1703	0.1117	0.0738	0.0491	0.0329	0.0222	0.0151	0.0103
24	0.3901	0.2470	0.1577	0.1015	0.0659	0.0431	0.0284	0.0188	0.0126	0.0085
25	0.3751	0.2330	0.1460	0.0923	0.0588	0.0378	0.0245	0.0160	0.0105	0.0069
30	0.3083	0.1741	0.0994	0.0573	0.0334	0.0196	0.0116	0.0070	0.0042	0.0026
35	0.2534	0.1301	0.0676	0.0356	0.0189	0.0102	0.0055	0.0030	0.0017	0.0009
40	0.2083	0.0972	0.0460	0.0221	0.0107	0.0053	0.0026	0.0013	0.0007	0.0004
45	0.1712	0.0727	0.0313	0.0137	0.0061	0.0027	0.0013	0.0006	0.0003	0.0001
50	0.1407	0.0543	0.0213	0.0085	0.0035	0.0014	0.0006	0.0003	0.0001	0.0000

Table 7-3
Factors for Calculating the Present Value of an Annuity of $1

No. of Periods	4%	6%	8%	10%	12%	14%	16%	18%	20%	22%
					Discount Rate					
1	0.9615	0.9434	0.9259	0.9091	0.8929	0.8772	0.8621	0.8475	0.8333	0.8197
2	1.8861	1.8334	1.7833	1.7355	1.6901	1.6467	1.6052	1.5656	1.5278	1.4915
3	2.7751	2.6730	2.5771	2.4869	2.4018	2.3216	2.2459	2.1743	2.1065	2.0422
4	3.6299	3.4651	3.3121	3.1699	3.0373	2.9137	2.7982	2.6901	2.5887	2.4936
5	4.4518	4.2124	3.9927	3.7908	3.6048	3.4331	3.2743	3.1272	2.9906	2.8636
6	5.2421	4.9173	4.6229	4.3553	4.1114	3.8887	3.6847	3.4976	3.3255	3.1669
7	6.0021	5.5824	5.2064	4.8684	4.5638	4.2883	4.0386	3.8115	3.6046	3.4155
8	6.7327	6.2098	5.7466	5.3349	4.9676	4.6389	4.3436	4.0776	3.8372	3.6193
9	7.4353	6.8017	6.2469	5.7590	5.3282	4.9464	4.6065	4.3030	4.0310	3.7863
10	8.1109	7.3601	6.7101	6.1446	5.6502	5.2161	4.8332	4.4941	4.1925	3.9232
11	8.7605	7.8869	7.1390	6.4951	5.9377	5.4527	5.0286	4.6560	4.3271	4.0354
12	9.3851	8.3838	7.5361	6.8137	6.1944	5.6603	5.1971	4.7932	4.4392	4.1274
13	9.9856	8.8527	7.9038	7.1034	6.4235	5.8424	5.3423	4.9095	4.5327	4.2028
14	10.5631	9.2950	8.2442	7.3667	6.6282	6.0021	5.4675	5.0081	4.6106	4.2646
15	11.1184	9.7122	8.5595	7.6061	6.8109	6.1422	5.5755	5.0916	4.6755	4.3152
16	11.6523	10.1059	8.8514	7.8237	6.9740	6.2651	5.6685	5.1624	4.7296	4.3567
17	12.1657	10.4773	9.1216	8.0216	7.1196	6.3729	5.7487	5.2223	4.7746	4.3908
18	12.6593	10.8276	9.3719	8.2014	7.2497	6.4674	5.8178	5.2732	4.8122	4.4187
19	13.1339	11.1581	9.6036	8.3649	7.3658	6.5504	5.8775	5.3162	4.8435	4.4415
20	13.5903	11.4699	9.8181	8.5136	7.4694	6.6231	5.9288	5.3527	4.8696	4.4603
21	14.0292	11.7641	10.0168	8.6487	7.5620	6.6870	5.9731	5.3837	4.8913	4.4756
22	14.4511	12.0416	10.2007	8.7715	7.6446	6.7429	6.0113	5.4099	4.9094	4.4882
23	14.8568	12.3034	10.3711	8.8832	7.7184	6.7921	6.0442	5.4321	4.9245	4.4985
24	15.2470	12.5504	10.5288	8.9847	7.7843	6.8351	6.0726	5.4509	4.9371	4.5070
25	15.6221	12.7834	10.6748	9.0770	7.8431	6.8729	6.0971	5.4669	4.9476	4.5139
30	17.2920	13.7648	11.2578	9.4269	8.0552	7.0027	6.1772	5.5168	4.9789	4.5338
35	18.6646	14.4982	11.6546	9.6442	8.1755	7.0700	6.2153	5.5386	4.9915	4.5411
40	19.7928	15.0463	11.9246	9.7791	8.2438	7.1050	6.2335	5.5482	4.9966	4.5439
45	20.7200	15.4558	12.1084	9.8628	8.2825	7.1232	6.2421	5.5523	4.9986	4.5449
50	21.4822	15.7619	12.2335	9.9148	8.3045	7.1327	6.2463	5.5541	4.9995	4.5452

• **BUSINESS PROCEDURE CAPSULE 13** *(continued)*

As these examples point out, the present value of future cash flows is directly affected by both the chosen discount rate and the relevant time frame.

Now assume that you have accepted a job from a company willing to pay you a signing bonus, and you must now choose between three alternative payment plans.

The plan A bonus is $3,000 payable today. The plan B bonus is $4,000 payable three years from today. The plan C bonus is three annual payments of $1,225 each (an annuity) with the first payment to be made one year from today. Assuming a discount rate of 8 percent, which bonus should you accept? The solution requires calculation of the present value of each bonus:

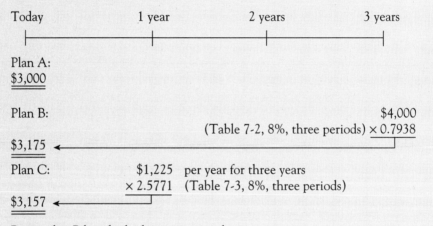

Today   1 year   2 years   3 years

Plan A:
$3,000

Plan B: $4,000
                              (Table 7-2, 8%, three periods) × 0.7938
$3,175

Plan C: $1,225   per year for three years
                  × 2.5771   (Table 7-3, 8%, three periods)
$3,157

Bonus plan B has the highest present value.

The frequency with which interest is compounded affects both future value and present value. You would prefer to have the interest on your savings account compounded monthly, weekly, or even daily rather than annually because you will earn more interest the more frequently compounding occurs. This periodic compounding is recognized in present value calculations by converting the annual discount rate to a discount rate per compounding period by dividing the annual rate by the number of compounding periods per year. Likewise, the number of periods is adjusted by multiplying the number of years involved by the number of compounding periods per year. For example, the present value of $1,000 to be received or paid six years from now, at a discount rate of 18 percent compounded annually, is $370.40 (the factor 0.3704 from the 18 percent column, six-period row of Table 7-2, multiplied by $1,000). If interest were compounded every four months, or three times per year, the present value calculation uses the factor from the 6 percent column (18 percent per year/three periods per year), and the eighteen-period row (six years × three periods per year), which is 0.3503. The present value of $1,000 to be received or paid in six years, compounding interest every four months, is $350.30:

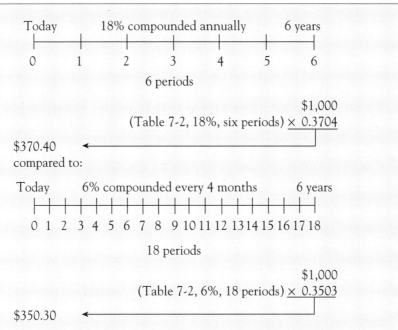

Today   18% compounded annually   6 years

0   1   2   3   4   5   6

6 periods

$1,000
(Table 7-2, 18%, six periods) × 0.3704

$370.40
compared to:

Today   6% compounded every 4 months   6 years

0 1 2 3 4 5 6 7 8 9 10 11 12 13 14 15 16 17 18

18 periods

$1,000
(Table 7-2, 6%, 18 periods) × 0.3503

$350.30

The present value of a single amount is lower when compounding is more frequent. Consider what you could do with either $370.40 or $350.30 if you were to receive the amount today rather than receiving $1,000 in six years. Each amount could be invested at 18 percent, but interest would compound on the $370.40 only once a year, and interest on the $350.30 would compound every four months. Even though you start with different amounts, you'll still have $1,000 after six years. Test your comprehension of this calculation process by verifying that the present value of an annual annuity of $100 for ten years, discounted at an annual rate of 16 percent, is $483.32, and that the present value of $50 paid every six months for ten years, discounted at the same annual rate (which is an 8 percent semiannual rate), is $490.91. The present value of an annuity is greater the more frequent the compounding because the annuity amount is paid or received sooner than when the compounding period is longer.

Many of these ideas may seem complicated to you now, but common sense will affirm the results of present value analysis. Remember that $1 in your hands today is worth more than $1 to be received tomorrow or a year from today. This explains why firms are interested in speeding up the collection of accounts receivable and other cash inflows. Of course, the opposite logic applies to cash payments, which explains why firms defer the payment of accounts payable whenever possible. The prevailing attitude is, "We're better off with the cash in our hands than in the hands of our customers or suppliers." Subsequent chapters will illustrate several applications of present value analysis to business transactions. By making the initial investment of time now, you will understand these ideas more quickly later.

The economic effect of a capital lease is no different from buying the asset outright and signing a note payable that will be paid off, with interest, over the life of the asset. Therefore, the asset and related liability should be reflected on the lessee's balance sheet. In the lessee's income statement, the cost of the leased asset will be reflected as depreciation expense, rather than rent expense, and the financing cost will be shown as interest expense.

Before a Financial Accounting Standards Board (FASB) standard issued in 1976, many companies did not record assets acquired under a capital lease because they did not want to reflect the related lease liability in their balance sheet. This practice was known as *off-balance-sheet financing* and was deemed inappropriate by FASB because it violated the full disclosure concept.

Assets acquired by capital lease are included with purchased assets on the balance sheet. The amount recorded as the cost of the asset involved in a capital lease, and as the related lease liability, is the present value of the lease payments to be made, based on the interest rate used by the lessor to determine the periodic lease payments. The entries to record capital lease transactions are as follows:

1. Date of acquisition.
    Dr.   Equipment xx
        Cr.   Capital lease liability xx
2. Annual depreciation expense.
    Dr.   Depreciation expense xx
        Cr.   Accumulated depreciation xx
3. Annual lease payments.
    Dr.   Interest expense xx
    Dr.   Capital lease liability xx
        Cr.   Cash xx

The effects of these transactions on the financial statements using the horizontal model are shown below:

Balance sheet	Income statement
Assets = Liabilities + Owners' equity ⟵	Net income = Revenues − Expenses

1. Date of Acquisition:
   +Equipment +Capital
            lease liability

2. Annual depreciation expense:
   −Accumulated   −Depreciation
     depreciation   expense

3. Annual lease payment:
   −Cash −Capital   −Interest
            lease liability   expense

The first entry/effect shows the asset acquisition and the related financial obligation that has been incurred. The second shows depreciation expense in the same way it is recorded for purchased assets. The third shows the lease payment effect on cash, reflects the interest expense for the year on the amount that has been borrowed (in effect) from the lessor, and reduces the lease liability by what is a payment on the principal of the loan from the lessor.

To illustrate the equivalence of capital lease payments and a long-term loan, assume that a firm purchased a computer system at a cost of $217,765 and borrowed the money by giving a note payable that had an annual interest rate of 10 percent and that required payments of $50,000 per year for six years. The purchase would be recorded using the following entry:

Dr.	Computer equipment...	217,765	
Cr.	Note payable		217,765

With the horizontal model, the following is the effect on the financial statements:

Balance sheet		Income statement
Assets =	Liabilities + Owners' equity ◄────	Net income = Revenues – Expenses
Computer equipment	Note payable	
+217,765	+217,765	

Each year the firm will accrue and pay interest expense on the note and make principal payments, as shown in the following table:

Year	Principal Balance at Beginning of Year	Interest at 10%	Payment Applied to Principal ($50,000 – Interest)	Principal Balance at End of Year
1...........	$217,765	$21,776	$28,224	$189,541
2...........	189,541	18,954	31,046	158,495
3...........	158,495	15,849	34,151	124,344
4...........	124,344	12,434	37,566	86,778
5...........	86,778	8,677	41,323	45,455
6...........	45,455	4,545	45,455	–0–

After six years, the note will have been fully paid.

If the firm were to lease the computer system and agree to make annual lease payments of $50,000 for six years instead of borrowing the money and buying the computer system outright, the financial statements should reflect the transaction in essentially the same way. This uniformity in valuation will happen because the present value of all of the lease payments (which include principal and interest) is $217,765. (From Table 7-3, in the 10 percent column and six-period row, the factor is 4.3553. This factor multiplied by the $50,000 annual lease payment is $217,765.) The entry at the beginning of the lease will be as follows:

Dr.	Computer equipment.....................................	217,765	
	Cr.	Capital lease liability		217,765

The following is the effect on the financial statements:

Balance sheet		Income statement	
Assets =	Liabilities + Owners' equity ◄———	Net income = Revenues – Expenses	
Computer equipment +217,765	Capital lease liability +217,765		

Each year, the principal portion of the lease payment will reduce the capital lease liability, and the interest portion will be recognized as an expense. In addition, the computer equipment will be depreciated each year. Thus, liabilities on the balance sheet and expenses in the income statement will be the same as under the borrow and purchase alternative.

Again, the significance of capital lease accounting is that the economic effect of capital leasing is no different from buying the asset outright; the effect on the financial statements should not differ either.

Intangible Assets

Intangible assets are long-lived assets that differ from property, plant, and equipment that have been purchased outright or acquired under a capital lease—either because the asset is represented by a contractual right, or because the asset results from a purchase transaction but is not physically identifiable. Examples of the first type of intangible asset are leaseholds, patents, and trademarks; the second type of intangible asset is known as *goodwill*.

Just as the cost of plant and equipment is transferred to expense over time through accounting depreciation, the cost of most intangibles is also expensed over time. **Amortization**, which means spreading an amount over time, is the term used to describe the process of allocating the cost of an intangible asset from the balance sheet to the income statement. The cost of tangible assets is depreciated; the cost of intangible assets is amortized. The terms are different, but the process is the same. Most intangibles are amortized on a straight-line basis based on useful life to the entity, but not for any period in excess of forty years. Although an accumulated amortization account is sometimes used, amortization expense is usually recorded as a direct reduction in the carrying value of the related intangible asset. Thus, periodic amortization would be recorded as follows:

```
Dr.      Amortization expense ..................................................      xx
    Cr.      Intangible asset ....................................................          xx
```

The effect of this entry on the financial statements is as follows:

Balance sheet	Income statement
Assets = Liabilities + Owners' equity ⟵	Net income = Revenues − Expenses
−Intangible asset	−Amortization expense

Amortization expense is usually included with depreciation expense in the income statement. Neither depreciation expense nor amortization expense involves a cash disbursement; cash is disbursed when the asset is acquired or, if a loan is used to finance the acquisition, when the loan payments are made.

Leasehold Improvements

When the tenant of an office building makes modifications to the office space, such as having private offices constructed, the cost of these modifications is a capital expenditure to be amortized over their useful life to the tenant or over the life of the lease, whichever is shorter. The concept is the same as the concept applying to buildings or equipment, but the terminology is different. Entities that use rented facilities extensively, such as small shops or retail store chains that operate in shopping malls, may have a significant amount of **leasehold improvements**.

Patents, Trademarks, and Copyrights

A **patent** is a monopoly license granted by the government giving the owner control of the use or sale of an invention for seventeen years. A **trademark** (or trade name), when registered with the Federal Trade Commission, can be used only by the entity that owns it, or by another entity that has secured permission from the owner. A trademark has an unlimited life, but it can be terminated by lack of use. A **copyright** is a protection granted to writers and artists that is designed to prevent unauthorized copying of printed or recorded material. A copyright is granted for the life of the writer or artist, plus fifty years.

To the extent that an entity has incurred cost in obtaining a patent, trademark, or copyright, that cost should be capitalized and amortized over its estimated remaining useful life to the entity or its statutory life, whichever is shorter. The cost of developing a patent, trademark, or copyright is not usually significant. Most intangible assets in this category arise when one firm purchases a patent, trademark, or copyright from another entity. An intangible that becomes very valuable because of the success of a product (such as "Coke") cannot be assigned a value and recorded as an asset while it continues to be owned by the entity that created it. In some cases, a firm will include a caption for trademarks or another intangible asset in its balance sheet and report a nominal cost of $1 just to communicate to financial statement users that it does have this type of asset.

License fees or royalties earned from an intangible asset owned by a firm are reported as operating revenues in the income statement. Likewise, license fees or royalty expenses incurred by a firm using an intangible asset owned by another entity are operating expenses.

Goodwill

Goodwill results from the purchase of one firm by another for a price that is greater than the fair market value of the net assets acquired. (Recall from Chapter 2 that net assets means total assets minus total liabilities.) Why would a firm be willing to pay more for a business than the fair market value of the inventory, plant, and equipment, and other assets being acquired? The purchasing firm does not consider the transaction as the purchase of assets, but instead evaluates the transaction as the purchase of *profits*. The purchaser will be willing to pay such an amount because the profits expected to be earned from the investment will generate an adequate return on the investment. If the firm being purchased has earned a greater-than-average rate of return on its invested net assets, then the owners of that firm will be able to command a price for the firm that is greater than the fair market value of its net assets. This greater-than-average return may result from excellent management, a great location, unusual customer loyalty, a unique product or service, or some other factor.

When one firm purchases another, the purchase price is first assigned to the physical net assets acquired. The cost recorded for these net assets is their fair market value, usually determined by appraisal. This cost then becomes the basis for depreciating plant and equipment, or for determining cost of goods sold if inventory is involved. To the extent that the total price exceeds the fair market value of the physical net assets acquired, the excess is recorded as goodwill. For example, assume that Cruisers, Inc., purchased a business by paying $1,000,000 in cash and assuming a note payable liability of $100,000.

The fair market value of the net assets acquired was $700,000, assigned as follows: inventory, $250,000; land, $150,000; buildings, $400,000; and notes payable, $100,000. The entry would be as follows:

Dr.		Inventory	250,000	
Dr.		Land	150,000	
Dr.		Buildings	400,000	
Dr.		Goodwill	300,000	
	Cr.	Notes payable		100,000
	Cr.	Cash		1,000,000

The effect of this transaction on the financial statements is as follows:

Balance sheet			Income statement	
Assets =	Liabilities +	Owners' equity ◄———	Net income = Revenues – Expenses	
Inventory +250,000	Notes payable +100,000			
Land +150,000				
Buildings +400,000				
Goodwill +300,000				
Cash –1,000,000				

Goodwill is an intangible asset, and it will be amortized over its expected economic life (which is the period that the expected higher than average rate of return will continue) or over forty years, whichever is less. Accounting conservatism would suggest a period of much less than forty years, but because it is difficult to determine objectively the economic life of goodwill, forty years is a frequently used amortization period. Cruisers, Inc., would make the following entry to record goodwill amortization at the end of each year for the next forty years:

Dr.	Amortization Expense	7,500	
	Cr.	Goodwill	7,500

The effect of this adjustment on the financial statements is as follows:

Balance sheet		Income statement	
Assets = Liabilities + Owners' equity ◄———		Net income = Revenues – Expenses	
Goodwill –7,500		Amortization expense –7,500	

Goodwill amortization expense is *not* an allowable expense for federal income tax purposes. Therefore, many accountants choose the forty-year amortization period to keep the expense reported in the income statement at a minimum.

Goodwill cannot be recorded by a firm simply because its management believes that goodwill exists, or even if the firm receives an offer to purchase it for more than the carrying value of its assets. Goodwill can be recorded by a purchasing firm only under the circumstances summarized above.

Another way of describing goodwill is to say that it is the present value of the greater-than-average earnings of the acquired firm, discounted for the period they are expected to last, at the acquiring firm's desired return on investment. That is, goodwill is the amount a firm is willing to pay now for expected future earnings that are greater than the earnings expected on the fair market value of the assets acquired. In fact, when analysts at the acquiring firm are calculating the price to offer for the firm to be acquired, they use present value analysis.

Some critics suggest that goodwill is a fictitious asset that should be written off against the firm's retained earnings. Others point out that it is at best a "different" asset that must be carefully evaluated when it is encountered. However, if goodwill is included in the assets used in the return on investment calculation, the rate of interest measure will reflect management's ability to earn a return on this asset.

Natural Resources

Accounting for natural resource assets, such as coal deposits, crude oil reserves, timber, and mineral deposits, parallels that for depreciable assets. **Depletion**, rather than depreciation, is the term for the using up of natural resources, but the concepts are the same, even though depletion usually involves considerably more complex estimates.

For example, when a firm pays for the right to drill for oil or mine for coal, the cost of that right and the costs of developing the well or mine are capitalized. The cost is then reflected in the income statement as depletion expense, which is matched with the revenue resulting from the sale of the natural resource. Depletion is usually recognized on a straight-line basis, based on geological and engineering estimates of the quantity of the natural resource to be recovered. Thus, if $1 million was the cost of a mine that held an estimated 20 million tons of coal, the depletion cost would be $.05 per ton. In most cases, the cost of the asset is credited or reduced directly in the depletion expense entry, instead of using an accumulated depletion account.

In practice, estimating depletion expense is complex. Depletion expense allowed for federal income tax purposes frequently differs from that recognized for financial accounting purposes because tax laws have been used to provide special incentives to develop natural resources.

Other Noncurrent Assets

Long-term investments, notes receivable that mature more than a year after the balance sheet date, and other noncurrent assets are also included as noncurrent assets. When they become current (receivable within one year), they will be reclassified to the current asset section of the balance sheet. The explanatory footnotes or financial review accompanying the financial statements will include appropriate explanations about these assets if they are significant.

Summary

This chapter discussed the accounting for and presentation of the following balance sheet noncurrent asset and related income statement accounts:

Balance sheet		Income statement	
Assets = Liabilities + Owners' equity ⟵		Net income = Revenues – Expenses	
Land		Gain on *or* sale*	Loss on sale*
Purchased .... buildings/ equipment			Repairs and maintenance expense
Leased Capital .... buildings/ lease equipment liability			Interest expense
(Accumulated .... depreciation)			Depreciation expense
Natural .... resources			Depletion expense
Intangible.. assets			Amortization expense

* For any noncurrent asset.

Property, plant, and equipment owned by the entity are reported on the balance sheet at their original cost, less (for depreciable assets) accumulated depreciation.

Expenditures representing the cost of acquiring an asset that will benefit the entity for more than the current fiscal period are capitalized. Routine repair and maintenance costs are expensed in the fiscal period in which they are incurred.

Accounting depreciation is the process of spreading the cost of an asset to the fiscal periods in which the asset is used. Depreciation does not affect cash, nor is it an attempt to recognize a loss in the market value of an asset.

Depreciation expense can be calculated several ways. The calculations result in a depreciation expense pattern that is straight-line or accelerated. Straight-line methods are usually used for book purposes, and accelerated methods (based on the Modified Accelerated Cost Recovery System, or MACRS, specified in the Internal Revenue Code) are usually used for income tax purposes.

When a depreciable asset is disposed of, both the asset and its related accumulated depreciation are removed from the accounts. A gain or loss results, depending on the relationship of any cash received in the transaction to the net book value of the asset disposed of.

When an asset is traded in on a similar asset, no gain or loss results. The cost of the new asset is the net book value of the old asset plus the cash paid and/or debt incurred to acquire the new asset.

When the use of an asset is acquired in a capital lease transaction, the asset and related lease liability are reported in the balance sheet. The cost of the asset is the present value of the lease payments, calculated using the interest rate used by the lessor to determine the periodic lease payments. The asset is depreciated, and interest expense related to the lease is recorded.

The present value concept recognizes that money has value over time. The present value of an amount to be paid or received in the future is calculated by multiplying the future amount by a present value factor based on the discount (interest) rate and the number of periods involved. An annuity is a fixed amount to be paid or received each period for some number of periods. In the calculation of the present value of an annuity, the fixed periodic amount is multiplied by the appropriate factor. The present value concept is widely used in business and finance.

Intangible assets are represented by a contractual right and are not physically identifiable. The cost of an intangible asset is spread over the useful life to the entity of the intangible asset and is called *amortization expense*. Intangible assets include leasehold improvements, patents, trademarks, copyrights, and goodwill. The cost of natural resources is recognized as *depletion expense*, which is allocated to the natural resources recovered.

Refer to the Armstrong World Industries, Inc., balance sheet and financial review in the couse workbook and study guide's Appendix and to other financial statements you have, and observe how information about property, plant, and equipment and other noncurrent assets is presented.

Key Words and Phrases

Accelerated Cost Recovery System (ACRS) (p. 205) The method prescribed in the Internal Revenue Code for calculating the depreciation deduction; applicable to the years 1981–1986.

accelerated depreciation method (p. 200) A depreciation calculation method that results in greater depreciation expense in the early periods of an asset's life than in the later periods of its life.

amortization (p. 220) The process of spreading the cost of an intangible asset over its useful life.

annuity (p. 212) The receipt or payment of a constant amount over some period of time.

capital lease (p. 210) A lease, usually long term, that has the effect of financing the acquisition of an asset. Sometimes called a *financing lease*.

capitalizing (p. 196) To record an expenditure as an asset as opposed to expensing the expenditure.

copyright (p. 221) An intangible asset represented by the legally granted protection against unauthorized copying of a creative work.

declining-balance depreciation method (p. 202) An accelerated depreciation method in which the declining net book value of the asset is multiplied by a constant rate.

depletion (p. 224) The accounting process recognizing that the cost of a natural resource asset is used up as the natural resource is consumed.

discount rate (p. 212) The interest rate used in a present value calculation.

expensing (p. 196) To record an expenditure as an expense, as opposed to capitalizing the expenditure.

goodwill (p. 222) An intangible asset arising from the purchase of a business for more than the fair market value of the net assets acquired. Goodwill is the present value of the expected earnings of the acquired business in excess of the earnings that would represent an average return on investment, discounted at the investor's required rate of return for the expected duration of the excess earnings.

intangible asset (p. 220) A long-lived asset represented by a contractual right or one that is not physically identifiable.

leasehold improvement (p. 221) A depreciable asset represented by the cost of improvements made to a leasehold by the lessee.

Modified Accelerated Cost Recovery System (MACRS) (p. 205) The method prescribed in the Internal Revenue Code for calculating the depreciation deduction; applicable to years after 1986.

net book value (p. 199) The difference between the cost of an asset and the accumulated depreciation related to the asset. Sometimes called *carrying value*.

operating lease (p. 210) A lease (usually short term) that does not involve any attribute of ownership.

patent (p. 221) An intangible asset represented by a government-sanctioned monopoly over the use of a product or process.

present value (p. 211) The value now of an amount to be received or paid at some future date, recognizing an interest (or discount) rate for the period from the present to the future date.

proceeds (p. 208) The amount of cash (or equivalent value) received in a transaction.

straight-line depreciation method (p. 201) Calculation of periodic depreciation expense by dividing the amount to be depreciated by the number of periods over which the asset is to be depreciated.

sum-of-the-years'-digits depreciation (p. 202) An accelerated depreciation method in which the amount to be depreciated is multiplied by a rate that declines each year.

trademark (p. 221) An intangible asset represented by a right to the exclusive use of an identifying mark.

units of production depreciation method (p. 202) A depreciation method based on periodic use and life expressed in terms of asset use.

Chapter 8

Accounting for and Presentation of Liabilities

Liabilities are financial obligations of the entity, or as defined by the FASB, "probable future sacrifices of economic benefits arising from present obligations of a particular entity to transfer assets or provide services to other entities in the future as a result of past transactions or events."[1] Liabilities are claims against the entity's assets by interests outside the organization. Liabilities are recorded only for *present* obligations that are the result of *past* transactions or events that will require the probable *future* sacrifice of resources. Thus, the following items would not yet be recorded as liabilities: (1) negotiations for the possible purchase of inventory, (2) increases in the replacement cost of assets due to inflation, and (3) contingent losses on unsettled lawsuits against the entity.

Most liabilities arise because credit has been obtained in the form of a loan (notes payable) or in the normal course of business—for example, when a supplier ships merchandise before payment is made (accounts payable), or when an employee works one week not expecting to be paid until the next week (wages payable). As previous chapters have illustrated, many liabilities are recorded in the accrual process that matches revenues and expenses. The term *accrued expenses* is used on some balance sheets to describe these liabilities, but this term is shorthand for *liabilities resulting from the accrual of expenses.* Remember that revenues and expenses are reported only on the income statement, and you will not be confused by this mixing of terms. Current liabilities are those that must be paid or otherwise satisfied within a year of the balance sheet date; noncurrent liabilities are those that will be paid or satisfied more than a year after the balance sheet date. Liability captions usually appearing in a balance sheet are as follows:

Current liabilities:
    Accounts payable
    Short-term debt (notes payable)
    Current maturities of long-term debt
    Unearned revenue or deferred credits
    Other accrued liabilities

Noncurrent liabilities:
    Long-term debt (bonds payable)
    Deferred income taxes
    Minority interest in subsidiaries

The order in which liabilities are presented within the current and noncurrent categories is a function of liquidity (that is, how soon the debt becomes due) and management preferences.

Review the liabilities section of the Armstrong World Industries, Inc., consolidated balance sheets on page 26 of the annual report in the Appendix to this text's companion course workbook and study guide. Three of the captions have to do with debt, and two relate to income taxes. This chapter will discuss the business and accounting practices relating to those items.

Some of the most significant and controversial issues that the FASB has addressed in recent years, including accounting for income taxes, accounting for pensions, and consolidation of subsidiaries, relate to the liability section of the balance sheet. A principal reason for the interest generated by these topics is that the recognition of a liability usually involves recognizing an expense as well. Expenses reduce net income, and lower net income means lower return on investment (ROI). Keep these relationships in mind as you study this chapter.

Educational Objectives

After studying this chapter, you should be able to:

1. Explain the difference between interest calculated on a straight basis and on a discount basis.

2. Describe the financial statement presentation of short-term debt, current maturities of long-term debt, and unearned revenues.

3. Explain the importance of making estimates for certain accrued liabilities, and explain how these items are presented in the balance sheet.
4. Describe financial leverage, and explain how it is provided by long-term debt.
5. Explain the characteristics of a bond, and describe the formal document representing most long-term debt.
6. Explain why a bond discount or premium arises and how it is accounted for.
7. Explain what deferred income taxes are and why they arise.
8. Explain what a minority interest is, why it arises, and what it means in the balance sheet.
9. Define or describe each of the Key Words and Phrases introduced in this chapter.

Current Liabilities

Current liabilities include short-term debt, current maturities of long-term debt, accounts payable, unearned revenue or deferred credits, and other accrued liabilities. This section will discuss each of these current liabilities separately.

Short-Term Debt

Most firms experience seasonal fluctuations in the demand for their products or services. For instance, a firm like Cruisers, Inc., a manufacturer of small boats, is likely to have greater demand for its product during the spring and early summer than in the winter. In order to use its production facilities most efficiently, Cruisers, Inc., plans to produce boats on a level basis during the year. This means that during the fall and winter, its inventory of boats will be increased so that it will have enough product on hand to meet spring and summer demand. In order to finance this inventory increase and be able to keep its payments to suppliers and employees current, Cruisers, Inc., will obtain a **working capital loan** from its bank. This type of short-term loan is made with the expectation that it will be repaid from the collection of accounts receivable that the sale of inventory will generate. The short-term loan usually has a **maturity date** specifying when the loan is to be repaid. Sometimes a firm will negotiate a **revolving line of credit** with its bank. The credit line represents a predetermined maximum loan amount, but the firm has flexibility in the timing and amount borrowed. There may be a specified repayment schedule or an agreement that all amounts borrowed will be repaid by a particular date. Whatever the specific loan arrangement is, the borrowing is recorded by the following entry:

```
Dr.    Cash ........................................................................    xx
    Cr.      Short-term debt................................................    xx
        Borrowed money from bank
```

The effect of this transaction on the financial statements is as follows:

Balance sheet	Income statement
Assets = Liabilities + Owners' equity ⟵	Net income = Revenues − Expenses
+Cash +Short-term debt	

The short-term debt resulting from this type of transaction is sometimes called a **note payable**. A note is a formal promise to pay a stated amount at a stated date, usually with interest at a stated rate, and sometimes secured by collateral.

Interest expense is associated with almost any borrowing, and interest expense should be recorded for each fiscal period during which the money is borrowed. Business Procedure Capsule 14—Interest Calculation Methods explains the alternative methods of calculating interest.

Prime rate is the term frequently used to express the interest rate on short-term loans. Lenders presumably establish the prime rate for their most credit-worthy borrowers, but in reality it is just a benchmark rate. The lender raises or lowers the prime rate in response to credit market forces. The borrower's rate may be expressed as "prime plus 1," for example, which means that the interest rate for the borrower will be the prime rate plus 1 percent. The interest rate may change during the term of the loan, in which case a separate calculation of interest is made for each period having a different rate.

For a loan on which interest is calculated on a straight basis (see Business Procedure Capsule 14), interest is accrued each period with the following entry:

```
Dr.    Interest expense.....................................................    xx
    Cr.      Interest payable...............................................    xx
        Accrued interest for period
```

The effect of this entry on the financial statement is as follows:

Balance sheet	Income statement
Assets = Liabilities + Owners' equity ⟵	Net income = Revenues − Expenses
+Interest payable	−Interest expense

Interest payable is a current liability because it will be paid within a year of the balance sheet date. It may be disclosed in a separate caption or included with other accrued liabilities in the current liability section of the balance sheet.

For a loan on which interest is calculated on a discount basis (see Business Procedure Capsule 14), the amount of cash **proceeds** represents the initial carrying value of the liability. With the data from the discount example in Business Procedure Capsule 14, the journal entry for the borrower is as follows:

Dr.	Cash	880	
Dr.	Discount on short-term debt	120	
	Cr.	Short-term debt		1,000

The effect of this entry on the financial statements is as follows:

Balance sheet	Income statement
Assets = Liabilities + Owners' equity ⟵	Net income = Revenues − Expenses

Cash	Short-term
+880	debt
	+1,000
	Discount on
	short-term
	debt
	−120

The discount on short-term debt account is a **contra liability**, classified as a reduction of short-term debt on the balance sheet. As interest expense is incurred, the discount on short-term debt is amortized as follows:

Dr.	Interest expense	xx	
	Cr.	Discount on short-term debt	xx

The effect of this entry on the financial statements is as follows:

Balance sheet	Income statement
Assets = Liabilities + Owners' equity ⟵	Net income = Revenues − Expenses
+Discount on	−Interest
short-term debt	expense

The amortization of the discount to interest expense affects neither cash nor interest payable. Net income decreases as interest expense is recorded, and the carrying value of short-term debt increases as the discount is amortized.

• **BUSINESS PROCEDURE CAPSULE 14**
  Interest Calculation Methods

Lenders calculate interest on either a straight (simple interest) basis or on a discount basis. The straight calculation involves charging interest on the money actually available to the borrower for the length of time it was borrowed. Interest on a **discount loan** is based on the principal amount of the loan, but the interest is subtracted from the principal, and only the difference is made available to the borrower. In effect, the borrower pays the interest in advance. Assume that $1,000 is borrowed for one year at an interest rate of 12 percent.

Straight Interest

The **interest calculation—straight basis** is made as follows:

$$\text{Interest} = \text{Principal} \times \text{Rate} \times \text{Time (in years)}$$
$$= \$1,000 \times 0.12 \times 1$$
$$= \$120$$

At the maturity date of the note, the borrower will repay the principal of $1,000 plus the interest owed of $120. The borrower's *effective interest rate—* the **annual percentage rate (APR)**— is 12%:

$$\text{APR} = \text{Interest paid/Money available to use} \times \text{Time (in years)}$$
$$= \$120 / \$1,000 \times 1$$
$$= 12\%$$

This is another application of the present value concept described in Chapter 7. The amount of the liability on the date the money is borrowed is the present value of the amount to be repaid in the future, calculated at the effective interest rate—which is the rate of return desired by the lender. To illustrate, the amount to be repaid in one year is $1,120, the sum of the $1,000 principal plus the $120 of interest. From Table 7-2, the factor in the 12 percent column and one-period row is 0.8929; $1,120 × 0.8929 = $1,000 (rounded). These relationships are illustrated on the following time line:

1/1/96		12/31/96
$1,000 Principal borrowed	Interest = $1,000 × 0.12 × 1 year = $120	$1,120 Principal and interest repaid

Discount

The **interest calculation—discount basis** is made as illustrated above, except that the interest amount is subtracted from the loan principal, and the borrower receives the difference. In this case, the loan proceeds would be $880 ($1,000 – $120). At the maturity of the note, the borrower will pay just the principal of $1,000 because the interest of $120 has already been paid—it was subtracted from the principal amount when the loan was obtained. These relationships are illustrated on the following time line:

1/1/96   12/31/96

|——|

$880   Interest = $1,000 × 0.12 × 1 year = $120 $1,000
Proceeds   Principal
borrowed   paid

Because the full principal amount is not available to the borrower, the effective interest rate (APR) on a discount basis is much higher than the rate used in the lending agreement to calculate the interest:

APR = Interest paid/Money available to use × Time (in years)

= $120 / $880 × 1

= 13.6%

When present value analysis is applied, the carrying value of the liability on the date the money is borrowed represents the amount to be repaid, $1,000, multiplied by the present value factor for 13.6 percent for one year. The factor is 0.8803, and although it is not explicitly shown in Table 7-2, it can be derived approximately by **interpolating** between the factors for 12 percent and 14 percent.

An *installment loan* is repaid periodically over the life of the loan, so only about half of the proceeds (on average) are available for use throughout the life of the loan. Thus, the effective interest rate is about twice that of a *term loan* requiring a lump-sum repayment of principal at the maturity date.

In the final analysis, whether interest is calculated using the straight method or the discount method or whether an installment loan or term loan is arranged is not important; what is important is the APR, or effective interest rate. The borrower's objective is to keep the APR (which must be disclosed in accordance with federal truth in lending laws) to a minimum.

Current Maturities of Long-Term Debt

When funds are borrowed on a long-term basis (a topic to be discussed later in this chapter), principal repayments are commonly required on an installment basis; every year a portion of the debt matures and is to be repaid by the borrower. Any portion of a long-term borrowing that is to be repaid within a year of the balance sheet date is reclassified from the noncurrent liability section of the balance sheet to the **current maturities of long-term debt** account. These amounts are reported in the current liability section but separately from short-term debt because the liability arose from a long-term borrowing transaction. Interest payable on long-term debt is classified with other interest payable and may be combined with other accrued liabilities for reporting purposes.

Accounts Payable

Amounts owed to suppliers for goods and services that have been provided to the entity on credit are the principal components of **accounts payable**. Unlike accounts receivable, which are reported net of estimated cash discounts expected to be taken, accounts payable to suppliers that permit a cash discount for prompt payment are not usually reduced by the amount of the cash discount expected to be taken. The materiality concept supports this treatment, because the amount involved is not likely to have a significant effect on the financial position or results of the operations of the firm. However, accounts payable for firms that record purchases net of anticipated cash discounts will be reported at the amount expected to be paid.

Purchase transactions for which a cash discount is allowed are recorded by using either the *gross* or *net* method. The difference between the two is the timing of the recognition of the cash discount. The gross method results in recognizing the cash discount only when the invoice is paid within the discount period. The net method recognizes the cash discount when the purchase is initially recorded, under the assumption that all discounts will be taken; an expense is then recognized if the discount is not taken. Business Procedure Capsule 15 evaluates these methods.

To illustrate and contrast the gross and net methods of recording purchases on account, assume that a $1,000 purchase is made with terms 2/10, n30. The journal entries under each method are as follows:

			Method Used		
			Gross		Net
1.	Record purchase:				
	Dr.	Inventory	1,000		980
		Cr. Accounts payable		1,000	980
2.	Pay within the discount period:				
	Dr.	Accounts payable	1,000		980
		Cr. Cash		980	980
		Cr. Purchase discounts		20	
3.	Pay after the discount period:				
	Dr.	Purchase discounts lost			20
	Dr.	Accounts payable	1,000		980
		Cr. Cash		1,000	1,000

• **BUSINESS PROCEDURE CAPSULE 15**

Gross and Net Methods of Recording Purchases

Because cash discounts represent such a high return on investment (see Business Procedure Capsule 9 in Chapter 6), most firms follow a rigid internal control policy of taking all cash discounts possible. Thus, many firms use the net method, which assumes that cash discounts will be taken. Under the net method, if a discount is missed because an invoice is paid after the cash discount date, the expense purchase discounts lost is recorded. This expense highlights in the financial statements that a discount was missed, and management can then take the appropriate action to eliminate or minimize future missed discounts. Thus, the net method has the advantage of strengthening the firm's system of internal control because any breakdown in the policy of taking every possible cash discount is highlighted. The net method is easy to apply in practice because no special accounts are involved in recording payments made within the discount period—which is the usual case.

The gross method treats cash discounts taken by the firm as a reduction of the cost of goods sold reported in the income statement but does not report any cash discounts that were missed. Thus, management cannot easily determine how well its internal control policy is being followed. Although the gross method involves more bookkeeping because the purchase discounts account is affected each time a cash discount is recorded, many firms use the gross method.

The financial statement effects of each method are as follows:

Balance sheet	Income statement
Assets = Liabilities + Owners' equity ⟵	Net income = Revenues − Expenses

A. Gross method

1. Record purchase:

Inventory	Accounts
+1,000	payable
	+1,000

2. Pay within the discount period:

Cash	Accounts		Purchase
−980	payable		discounts*
	−1,000		+20

*(A reduction of cost of goods sold)

3. Pay after the discount period:

Cash	Accounts
−1,000	payable
	−1,000

Balance sheet	Income statement
Assets = Liabilities + Owners' equity ⟵	Net income = Revenues − Expenses

B. Net method

1. Record purchase:

Inventory	Accounts
+980	payable
	+980

2. Pay within the discount period:

Cash	Accounts
−980	payable
	−980

3. Pay after the discount period:

Cash	Accounts		Purchase
−1,000	payable		discounts
	−980		lost
			−20

Unearned Revenue or Deferred Credits

Customers often pay for services or products before the service or product is delivered. An entity collecting cash before earning the related revenue records an **unearned revenue**, or a **deferred credit**, which is included in current liabilities. Unearned revenues must then be allocated to the fiscal periods in which the services are performed or the products are delivered, in accordance with the matching concept. Chapter 4 discussed the accounting for revenue received before being earned. To illustrate, assume that a magazine publisher requires a subscriber to pay in advance for a subscription. The entry to record this transaction is as follows:

Dr.   Cash   xx
    Cr.   Unearned subscription revenue   xx

The adjusting entry to record the revenue earned during the fiscal period would be as follows:

Dr.   Unearned subscription revenue..............................   xx
    Cr.   Subscription revenue   xx

The financial statement effects of this transaction and adjustment are as follows:

Balance sheet	Income statement
Assets = Liabilities + Owners' equity ⟵	Net income = Revenues – Expenses

Cash received with subscription:

+Cash   +Unearned
        subscription
        revenue

Adjustment in fiscal period in which revenue is earned (that is, magazines are delivered):

–Unearned   +Subscription
 subscription   revenue
 revenue

This situation is the opposite of the prepaid expense/deferred charge transaction described in Chapter 6. In that kind of transaction, cash was *paid* in the current period, and *expense* was recognized in subsequent periods. Unearned revenue/deferred credit transactions involve the *receipt* of cash in the current period and the recognition of *revenue* in subsequent periods.

Deposits received from customers are also accounted for as deferred credits. If the deposit is an advance payment for a product or service, the deposit is transferred from a liability account to a revenue account when the product or service is delivered. Or, for example, if the deposit is received as security for a returnable container, when the container is returned, the refund of the customer's deposit reduces (is a credit to) cash and eliminates (is a debit to) the liability.

An interesting issue is the accounting for deposits that will never be claimed. For example, a soft drink bottler receives more deposits for containers from customers than it will repay, because some of the containers will be broken and others will be permanently lost. What accounting makes sense in this situation? Based on experience and estimates, an adjusting entry is made to transfer some of the deposit liability to a revenue account. This adjustment offsets some of the cost of the lost containers. Although the deposit amount is usually less than the cost of the container, the bottler has in effect "sold" the container for the deposit amount.

Unearned revenues/deferred credits are usually classified with other accrued liabilities in the current liability section of the balance sheet.

Other Accrued Liabilities

Included in the caption "Other Accrued Liabilities" are liabilities for accrued payroll, accrued payroll taxes (which include the employer's share of Social Security taxes and federal and state unemployment taxes), accrued property taxes, accrued interest (if not reported separately), and other accrued expenses. These are other applications of the matching principle. Each of these items represents an expense that has been incurred but not yet paid. The expense is recognized and the liability is shown so that the financial statements present a more complete summary of the results of operations (income statement) and financial position (balance sheet) than would be presented without the accrual. To illustrate the accrual of property taxes, assume that Cruisers, Inc., operates in a city in which real estate tax bills for one year are not issued until April of the following year and are payable in July. Thus, an adjusting entry must be made to record the estimated property tax expense for the year. The adjusting entry is as follows:

Dr.	Property tax expense	xx	
	Cr.	Property taxes payable	xx

The effect of this adjustment on the financial statements is as follows:

Balance sheet	Income statement
Assets = Liabilities + Owners' equity ⟵	Net income = Revenues − Expenses
+Property taxes payable	−Property tax expense

When Cruisers receives the tax bill in April, the payable account must be adjusted to reflect the amount actually owed in July. However, this adjustment does not cause Cruisers, Inc., to restate the liability and expense amounts it reported in the previous year because the estimate was based on the best information available at the time.

A firm's estimated liability under product warranty or performance guarantees is another example of an accrued liability. The estimated warranty expense that will be incurred on a product should be recognized in the same period in which the revenue from the sale is recorded. Although the expense and liability must be estimated, experience and statistical analysis can be used to develop very accurate estimates. The following entries are made in the fiscal periods in which the product is sold, and when the warranty is honored.

To accrue the estimated warranty liability in the fiscal period in which the product is sold, the entry is as follows:

Dr.	Warranty expense	xx	
	Cr.	Estimated warranty liability	xx

To record actual warranty cost in the fiscal period in which the warranty is honored, the entry is as follows:

Dr.	Estimated warranty liability	xx	
	Cr.	Cash (or Repair parts inventory)	xx

The effect of warranty accounting on the financial statements is as follows:

Balance sheet	Income statement
Assets = Liabilities + Owners' equity ⟵	Net income = Revenues – Expenses

Fiscal period in which product is sold:

+Estimated warranty liability	–Warranty expense

Fiscal period in which warranty is honored:

–Cash and/or repair parts inventory	–Estimated warranty liability

One accrued liability that is usually shown separately, because of its significance, is the accrual for income taxes. The current liability for income taxes is related to the long-term liability for deferred taxes; both are discussed later in this chapter.

Noncurrent Liabilities

Noncurrent liabilities include long-term debt, deferred income taxes, and other long-term liabilities.

Long-Term Debt

A corporation's *capital structure* is the mix of debt and owners' equity that is used to finance the firm's assets. For many nonfinancial firms, **long-term debt** accounts for up to half of the firm's capital structure. One of the advantages of using debt is that interest expense is deductible in calculating taxable income, whereas dividends (distributions of earnings to stockholders) are not tax-deductible. Thus, debt usually has a lower economic cost to the firm than owners' equity. For example, assume that a firm has an average tax rate of 30 percent, and that it issues long-term debt with an interest rate of 10 percent. The firm's after-tax cost of debt is only 7 percent, which is probably less than the return sought by stockholders. Another reason for using debt is to obtain favorable **financial leverage**. Financial leverage refers to the difference between the rate of return earned on assets or return on investment (ROI) and the rate of return earned on owners' equity (ROE). This difference results from the fact that the interest cost of debt is usually a fixed percentage, which is not a function of the return on assets. Thus, if the firm can borrow money at an interest cost of 10 percent and use that money to buy assets on which it earns a return greater than 10 percent, then the owners will have a greater return on their investment or ROE than if they had provided all of the funds themselves. In other words, financial leverage relates to the use of borrowed money to enhance the return to owners.

Exhibit 8-1 illustrates the concept of financial leverage. If a firm earns a lower return on investment than the interest rate on borrowed funds, financial leverage will be negative, and ROE will be less than ROI. Financial leverage adds risk to the firm, because if the firm does not earn enough to pay the interest on its debt, the debtholders can force the firm into bankruptcy.

Chapter 14 will discuss financial leverage in greater detail. For now, understand that the use of long-term debt with a fixed interest cost usually results in ROE being different from ROI. Whether financial leverage is good or bad for the stockholders depends on the relationship between ROI and the interest rate on long-term debt.

Exhibit 8-1
Financial Leverage

> **Assumptions:**
> Two firms have the same assets and operating income. Current liabilities and income taxes are ignored for simplification. The firm without financial leverage has, by definition, no long-term debt. The firm with financial leverage has a capital structure that is 40% long-term debt, with an

interest rate of 10%, and 60% owners' equity. Return on investment and return on equity are shown below for each firm.

The return-on-investment calculation has been modified from the model introduced in Chapter 3. ROI is based on income from operations and total assets, rather than net income and total assets. Income from operations (which is net income before interest expense) is used because the interest expense reflects a financing decision, not an operating result. Thus, ROI becomes an evaluation of the operating activities of the firm.

Firm Without Leverage		*Firm With Leverage*	
Balance sheet:		Balance sheet:	
Assets	$10,000	Assets	$10,000
Liabilities	0	Liabilities (10%)	$ 4,000
Owners' equity	10,000	Owners' equity	6,000
Total liabilities and		Total liabilities and	
owners' equity	$10,000	owners' equity	$10,000
Income statement:		Income statement:	
Income from		Income from	
operations	$ 1,200	operations	$ 1,200
Interest expense	0	Interest expense	400
Net income	$ 1,200	Net income	$ 800

ROI and ROE Calculations:

Return on investment (ROI = Income from operations/Assets)

ROI = $1,200 / $10,000   ROI = $1,200 / $10,000
      = 12%   = 12%

Return on equity (ROE = Net income/Owners' equity)

ROE = $1,200 / $10,000   ROE = $800 / $6,000
      = 12%   = 13.3%

Analysis:

In this case, ROI is the same for both firms because the operating results did not differ—each firm earned 12% on the assets it had available to use. What differed was the way in which the assets were financed (that is, capital structure). The firm with financial leverage has a higher return on owners' equity because it was able to borrow money at a cost of 10% and use the money to buy assets on which it earned 12%. ROE is higher than ROI for a firm with positive financial leverage. The excess return on borrowed funds is the reward to owners for taking the risk of borrowing money at a fixed cost.

Recall the discussion and illustration of capital lease liabilities in Chapter 7. Lease payments that are due more than a year from the balance sheet date are included in long-term debt and recorded at the present value of future lease payments.

Most long-term debt, however, is issued in the form of bonds. A **bond** or **bond payable** is a formal document, usually issued in denominations of $1,000. Bond prices, both when issued and later when they are bought and sold in the market, are expressed as a percentage of the bond's **face amount**—the principal amount printed on the face of the bond. A $1,000 face amount bond that has a market value of $1,000 is priced at 100. (This means 100 percent; usually the term *percent* is neither written nor stated.) A $1,000 bond trading at 102.5 can be purchased for $1,025; such a bond priced at 96 has a market value of $960. When a bond has a market value greater than its face amount, it is trading at a premium; the amount of the **bond premium** is the excess of its market value over its face amount. A **bond discount** is the excess of the face amount over market value.

Accounting and financial reporting considerations for bonds can be classified into three categories: the original issuance of bonds, the recognition of interest expense, and the accounting for bond retirements or conversions.

If a bond is issued at its face amount, the journal entry and the effect on the financial statements are straightforward:

```
Dr.    Cash ........................................................................    xx
    Cr.    Bonds payable.................................................        xx
           Issuance of bonds at face amount
```

The effect of the issuance of a bond on the financial statements is as follows:

Balance sheet	Income statement
Assets = Liabilities + Owners' equity ⟵	Net income = Revenues − Expenses
+Cash +Bonds payable	

As was the case with short-term notes payable, the bonds payable liability is reported at the present value of amounts to be paid in the future with respect to the bonds, discounted at the return on investment desired by the lender (the bondholder). For example, assume that a 10 percent bond with a ten-year maturity is issued to investors who desire a 10 percent return on their investment. The issuer of the bonds provides two cash flow components to the investors in the bonds: the annual interest payments and the payment of principal at maturity. The interest cash flow is an annuity because the same amount is paid each period. Using present value factors from Tables 7-2 and 7-3, the present values are as follows:

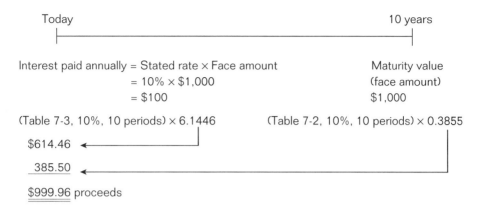

The present value of the liability is the sum of the discounted principal and interest payments. Except for a rounding difference in the present value factors, this sum is the same as the face amount of the bonds.

Because of the mechanics involved in a bond issue, there is usually a time lag between the establishment of the interest rate to be printed on the face of the bond and the actual issue date. During this time lag, market interest rates will fluctuate, and the market rate on the issue date will probably differ from the **stated rate** (or **coupon rate**) used to calculate interest payments to bondholders. This difference in interest rates causes the proceeds (the cash received) from the sale of the bonds to be more or less than the face amount; the bonds are issued at a premium or discount, respectively. Exhibit 8-2 illustrates the reason for this.

Exhibit 8-2
Bond Discount and Premium

> The interest paid by a borrower to its bondholders each period is fixed; that is, the same amount of interest (equal to the stated or coupon rate multiplied by the face amount of the bond) will be paid on each bond in each period regardless of what happens to market interest rates. When an investor buys a bond, he or she is entitled to an interest rate that reflects market conditions at the time the investment is made. Because the amount of interest the investor is to receive is fixed, the only way the investor can earn an effective interest rate different from the stated rate is to buy the bond for more or less than its face amount (that is, to buy the bond at a premium or discount). In other words, since the stated interest rate cannot be adjusted, the selling price of the bond must be adjusted to reflect the changes that have occurred in market interest rates since the stated interest rate was established. As already illustrated, the amount the investor is willing to pay for the bond is the present value of the cash flows

Continued on next page.

to be received from the investment, discounted at the investor's desired rate of return (that is, the market interest rate).

Assumptions:

Cruisers, Inc., issues a 10%, $1,000 bond when market interest rates are 12%. The bond will mature in eight years. Interest is paid semiannually.

Required:

Calculate the proceeds from the bond issue and the premium or discount to be recognized.

Solution:

The solution involves calculating the present value of the cash flows to be received by the investor, discounted at the investor's desired rate of return, which is the market interest rate. The cash flows have two components: the semiannual interest payments and the payment of principal at maturity. The interest is an annuity because the same amount is paid each period. Because the interest is paid semiannually, semiannual compounding should be recognized in the present value calculation. This is accomplished by using the number of semiannual periods in the life of the bonds. Since the bonds mature in eight years, there are sixteen semiannual periods. However, the interest rate per semiannual period is half of the annual interest rate. To be consistent, the same approach is used to calculate the present value of the principal. Thus, the solution uses factors from the 6% column (one-half the investors' desired ROI) and the sixteen-period row (twice the term of the bonds) of the present value tables. (If interest were paid quarterly, the annual ROI would be divided by four, and the term of the bonds in years would be multiplied by four.) With the present value factors from Tables 7-2 and 7-3, the present values are as follows:

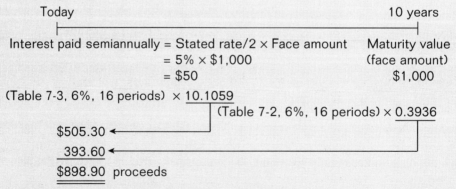

The proceeds received by Cruisers, Inc., as well as the amount invested by the buyer of the bond, are the sum of the present value of the interest payments and the present value of the principal amount. Since this sum is less than the face amount, the bond is priced at a discount.

This illustration demonstrates two important points about the process of calculating the proceeds from a bond issue:

1. The *stated interest rate* of the bond is used to calculate the amount of interest paid each payment period; this is the annuity amount used in the calculation of the present value of the interest.

2. The *market interest rate* (or the investors' desired ROI), adjusted for the compounding frequency, is the discount rate used in the present value calculations.

In this illustration, the market interest rate is higher than the bond's stated interest rate; thus, the investor would pay sufficiently less than the face amount of the bond so that the $50 to be received each six months and the $1,000 to be received at maturity will provide a market rate of return.

The issuance of the $1,000 bond by Cruisers, Inc., will be recorded with the following entry:

Dr.	Cash	898.90	
Dr.	Discount on bonds payable	101.10	
Cr.	Bonds payable		1,000.00
	Issued bond at a discount		

The effect of this entry on the financial statements is as follows:

Balance sheet	Income statement
Assets = Liabilities + Owners' equity ←	Net income = Revenues – Expenses

Cash	Bonds payable
+898.90	+1,000
	Discount on bonds payable −101.10

If market rates are less than the stated interest rate on the bond, the opposite will be true (that is, the investor will be willing to pay a premium over the face amount of the bond). Use the above model to prove to yourself that if the market interest rate is 12%, then a 13% stated rate, $1,000 face amount, ten-year bond on which interest is paid semiannually would be issued for $1,057.34 (that is, the bond would be issued at a premium of $57.34).

This exhibit illustrates the fundamental reason for bonds being issued for a price (or having a market value) that is different from the face amount. The actual premium or discount is a function of the magnitude of the difference between the stated interest rate of the bond and the market interest rate, and the number of years to maturity, because present value factors reflect the time value of money. For any given difference between the bond's stated interest rate and the market interest rate, the closer a bond is to maturity, the smaller the premium or discount will be.

Because bond premium or discount arises from a difference between the bond's stated interest rate and the market interest rate, the premium or discount should affect the issuing firm's interest expense. Bond discount represents additional interest expense to be recognized over the life of the bonds. The interest that will be paid (based on the stated rate) is less than the interest that would be paid if it were based on the market rate at the date the bonds were issued. Bond discount is a deferred charge that is amortized to interest expense over the life of the bond. The amortization increases interest expense over the amount actually paid to bondholders. Bond discount is classified in the balance sheet as a contra account to the bonds payable liability. Bond premium is a deferred credit that is amortized to interest expense, and its effect is to reduce interest expense below the amount actually paid to bondholders. Bond premium is classified in the balance sheet as an addition to the Bonds payable liability. The journal entries to record the interest accrual, interest payment, and discount or premium amortization are as follows:

Interest accrual (each fiscal period, perhaps monthly):

Dr.	Interest expense	xx	
	Cr.	Interest payable		xx

Interest payment (periodically, perhaps semiannually):

Dr.	Interest payable	xx	
	Cr.	Cash		xx

Amortization of discount (each time interest is accrued):

Dr.	Interest expense	xx	
	Cr.	Discount on bonds payable		xx

Amortization of premium (each time interest is accrued):

Dr.	Premium on bonds payable	xx	
	Cr.	Interest expense		xx

The effects of these transactions on the financial statements are as follows:

Balance sheet	Income statement
Assets = Liabilities + Owners' equity ⟵	Net income = Revenues − Expenses

Interest accrual (each fiscal period, perhaps monthly):

+Interest payable	−Interest expense

Interest payment (periodically, perhaps semiannually):

−Cash −Interest payable	

Amortization (each time interest is accrued):

Discount:

+Discount on bonds payable	−Interest expense (An increase in interest expense)

Premium:

–Premium	+Interest
on bonds	expense
payable	(A reduction in interest expense)

Discount or premium is usually amortized on a straight-line basis over the life of the bonds because the amounts involved are often immaterial. However, it is more appropriate to use a compound interest method that results in amortization related to the carrying value (face amount plus unamortized premium or minus unamortized discount) of the bonds. Using this accelerated method, amortization is largest in the first year of the bonds' life, and it decreases in subsequent years.

Bonds payable are reported on the balance sheet at their carrying value. Sometimes this amount is referred to as the **book value** of the bonds. As discount is amortized over the life of a bond, the carrying value of the bond increases. At the maturity date, the bond's carrying value is equal to its face amount because the bond discount has been fully amortized. Likewise, as premium is amortized, the carrying value of the bond decreases until it equals the face amount at maturity. Thus, when bonds are paid off (or retired) at maturity, the journal entry is as follows:

```
Dr.     Bonds payable .......................................................     xx
   Cr.     Cash ..............................................................          xx
           Retirement of bonds at maturity
```

The effect of this transaction on the financial statements is as follows:

Balance sheet	Income statement
Assets = Liabilities + Owners' equity ⟵	Net income = Revenues – Expenses
–Cash　–Bonds	
payable	

Most bonds are **callable bonds**; this means the issuer may pay off the bonds before the scheduled maturity date. Bonds will be called if market interest rates have dropped below the rate being paid on the bonds and the firm can save interest costs by issuing new bonds at a lower rate. Or if the firm has cash that will not be needed in operations in the immediate future, it can redeem the bonds and save more interest expense than could be earned (as interest income) by investing the excess cash. A **call premium** is usually paid to bondholders if the bond is called; that is, bondholders receive more than the face amount of the bond because they must reinvest the proceeds, usually at a lower interest rate than was being earned on the called bonds.

If the bonds are called or redeemed before maturity, the unamortized balance of premium or discount should be written off as part of the transaction. Since a call premium is usually involved in an early retirement of bonds, a loss on the retirement will usually be recognized—although a gain on the retirement is possible. The journal entry to record an early retirement of bonds having a book value of $95,000 by redeeming them for a total payment of $102,000 is as follows:

Dr.		Bonds payable	100,000	
Dr.		Loss on retirement of bonds	7,000	
	Cr.	Cash		102,000
	Cr.	Discount on bonds payable		5,000

The effect of this transaction on the financial statements is as follows:

Balance sheet		Income statement
Assets = Liabilities + Owners' equity ⟵		Net income = Revenues − Expenses
Cash Bonds payable		Loss on
−102,000 −100,000		retirement
		of bonds
Discount on		−7,000
bonds payable		
+5,000		

The loss or gain on the retirement of the bonds is reported as an extraordinary item (explained in more detail in Chapter 10) in the income statement. The loss or gain is not considered part of operating income or interest expense. The firm is willing to retire the bonds and recognize the loss because it will save, in future interest expense, more than the loss incurred.

A discussion of bonds involves much specialized terminology, and although students do not need to master all of it to understand the financial statement effect of bond transactions, it is relevant to understanding bonds.

Bond Terminology

The contract between the issuer of the bonds and the bondholders is the **bond indenture**, and it is frequently administered by a third party, the **trustee of bonds**—often a bank trust department. Bonds are issued in one of two forms: **registered bonds** and **coupon bonds**.

The issuer knows the name and address of the owner of a registered bond, and interest payments are mailed to the bondholder on a quarterly or semiannual basis, as called for in the indenture. The issuer does not know the owner of a coupon bond; the bondholder receives interest by clipping a coupon on the interest payment date and depositing it in his or her bank account. The coupon is then sent to the trustee and is honored as if it were a check. Coupon bonds are no longer issued because federal income tax regulations have been changed to require interest payers to report the name and Social Security number of payees, but coupon bonds issued before that regulation are still outstanding.

Bonds are also classified according to the security, or collateral, that the issuer pledges. **Debenture bonds** (or **debentures**) are bonds that are secured only by the general credit of the issuer. **Mortgage bonds** are secured by a lien against real estate owned by the issuer. **Collateral trust bonds** are secured by the pledge of securities or other intangible property.

Another classification of bonds relates to when the bonds mature. **Term bonds** require a lump-sum repayment of the face amount of the bond at the maturity date. **Serial bonds** are repaid in installments. The installments may or may not be equal in amount; the first installment is usually scheduled for a date several years after the issuance of the bonds. **Convertible bonds** may be converted into stock of the issuer corporation at the option of the bondholder. The number of shares of stock into which a bond is convertible is established when the bond is issued, but the conversion feature may not become effective for several years. If the stock price has risen substantially while the bonds have been outstanding, bondholders may elect to receive shares of stock with the anticipation that the stock will be worth more than the face amount of the bonds when the bonds mature.

The specific characteristics, the interest rate, and the maturity date are usually included in a bond's description. For example, for the hypothetical company, Cruiser, Inc.'s, long-term debt is described as 12 percent convertible debentures due in 2005, callable after 1996 at 102, or its 12.5 percent First Mortgage Serial Bonds with maturities from 1998 to 2008.

Deferred Income Taxes

Deferred income taxes are a long-term liability and represent income taxes that are expected to be paid more than a year after the balance sheet date. For many firms, deferred income taxes are one of the most significant liabilities shown on the balance sheet. These amounts arise from the accounting process of matching revenues and expenses; a liability is recognized for the probable future tax consequences of events that have taken place up to the balance sheet date. For example, some revenues that have been earned and recognized for accounting (book) purposes during the current fiscal year may not be taxable until the following year. Likewise, some expenses (such as depreciation) may be deductible for tax purposes before they are recorded in determining book income. These temporary differences between book income and taxable income cause deferred tax liabilities that are postponed until future years.

The most significant temporary difference item for most firms relates to depreciation expense. As previously explained, a firm may use straight-line depreciation for financial reporting and the Modified Accelerated Cost Recovery System (prescribed by the Internal Revenue Code) for income tax determination. Thus, depreciation deductions for tax purposes are taken earlier than depreciation expense is recognized for book purposes. Of course, this temporary difference will eventually reverse; over the life of the asset, the same total amount of book and tax depreciation will be reported. To calculate the amount of the current liability to be recorded as income taxes payable, the company's actual tax liability is determined each year. A deferred income tax liability is then calculated by multiplying the temporary differences (such as those related to depreciation) by the income tax rates expected to apply in the taxable years in which these differences will reverse. Income tax expense on the income statement is the sum of the current taxes payable plus the increase (or less the decrease) in the deferred tax liability from the beginning to the end of the fiscal period. Although the calculations involved are complicated, the adjusting journal entry to accrue income taxes is straightforward:

Dr.	Income tax expense	....	xx	
	Cr.	Income taxes payable	....	xx
	Cr.	Deferred income taxes	....	xx
		To accrue current and deferred income taxes		

The effect of this adjustment on the financial statements is as follows:

Balance sheet	Income statement
Assets = Liabilities + Owners' equity ⟵	Net income = Revenues − Expenses
+Income taxes payable	−Income tax expense
+Deferred income taxes	

If income tax rates do not decrease, the deferred income tax liability of most firms will increase over time. As firms grow, more depreciable assets are acquired, and price-level increases cause costs for (new) replacement assets to be higher than the cost of (old) assets being replaced. Thus, the temporary difference between book and tax depreciation grows each year because the excess of book depreciation over income tax depreciation for older assets is more than offset by the excess of tax depreciation over book depreciation for newer assets. Accordingly, some accountants have questioned the appropriateness of showing deferred taxes as a liability, since in the aggregate the balance of this account has grown increasingly larger for many firms and therefore never seems to actually become payable. They argue that deferred tax liabilities—if recorded at all—should be recorded at the present value of future cash flows discounted at an appropriate interest rate. Otherwise, the amounts shown on the balance sheet will overstate the obligation to pay future taxes.

Most deferred income taxes result from the temporary difference between book and tax depreciation expense, but there are other temporary differences as well. When the temporary difference involves an expense that is recognized for financial accounting purposes before it is deductible for tax purposes, a deferred tax asset can arise. For example, an estimated warranty liability is shown on the balance sheet, and warranty expense is reported in the income statement in the year the firm sells a warranted product, but the tax deduction is not allowed until an actual warranty expenditure is made. Because this temporary difference will cause taxable income to be lower in future years, a deferred tax asset is reported.

The accounting for deferred tax items is an extremely complex issue that has caused a great deal of debate within the accounting profession. The accounting described here is based on a standard about accounting for income taxes issued by the FASB in 1992, referred to as FAS 109. This standard was the result of an extensive review of past pronouncements and suggestions for change. FAS 109 superseded FAS 96, and the adoption of the new standard was mandatory for fiscal 1993. FAS 96 had been announced in 1987, but its implementation was postponed three times because of heavy pressure from businesses about the complexity of the standard and the cost of implementing it. As illustrated by the recent history of accounting for deferred taxes, accounting standards have evolved over time in response to the needs of financial statement users.

Other Long-Term Liabilities

Frequently included in the balance sheet category "Other Long-Term Liabilities" are obligations to pension plans and other employee benefit plans, including deferred compensation and bonus plans. Expenses of these plans are accrued and reflected in the income statement of the fiscal period in which the employee earns the benefit. Because benefits are frequently conditional upon continued employment, future salary levels, and other factors, actuaries and other experts estimate the expense to be reported in a given fiscal period. The employer's pension expense will also depend on the ROI earned on funds invested in the pension or other benefit plan trust accounts over a period of time. Because of the large number of significant factors that must be estimated in the expense and liability calculations, accounting for pension plans is a complex and controversial topic. In 1985, the FASB issued an accounting standard to increase the uniformity of accounting for pensions. One of the significant provisions of the standard requires the recognition of a minimum liability on the balance sheet if the fair market value of the pension plan assets is less than the accumulated benefit obligation to pension plan participants.

An issue closely related to pensions is the accounting for postretirement benefit plans other than pensions. These plans provide medical, hospitalization, life insurance, and other benefits to retired employees. Before 1992, the cost of these plans was generally reported as an expense in the fiscal period in which payments were made to the plans that provide the benefits, and an entity's liabilities under these plans were not reflected in the balance sheet. After several years of study and much controversy, in 1992 the FASB issued a standard that requires the recognition of the accumulated liability and accrual of costs during the employees' working years when the benefits are earned. Thus, the concept of matching revenues and expenses is to be applied on the same basis as for pension plans. One major difference between pension plans and other postretirement benefit plans is that very few firms had funded their other postretirement benefit plans. This means that the liabilities to be recognized are very large—in some cases more than half of a firm's owners' equity. The FASB standard gives firms the choice of recognizing the expense and accumulated liability all at once or deferring the expense and recognizing it over twenty years (or the remaining service life of the covered employees, if longer).

Another item included with other long-term liabilities of some firms is the estimated liability under lawsuits in progress and/or product warranty programs. The liability is reflected at its estimated amount, and the related expense is reported in the income statement of the period in which the expense was incurred or the liability was identified. Sometimes the term *reserve* is used to describe these items, as in "reserve for product warranty claims." However, the term *reserve* is misleading because this amount refers to an estimated liability, not an amount of money that has been set aside to meet the liability.

The last caption in the long-term liability section of many balance sheets is **minority interest in subsidiaries**. A subsidiary is a corporation that is more than 50 percent owned by the firm for which the financial statements have been prepared. (See Business Procedure Capsule 4 in Chapter 2 for more discussion about subsidiaries.) The financial statements of the parent company and its subsidiaries are combined through a process known as *consolidation*. The resulting financial statements are referred to as the **consolidated**

financial statements of the parent and its subsidiaries. In consolidation, most of the assets and liabilities of the parent and subsidiary are added together. Reciprocal amounts (for example, a parent's account receivable from a subsidiary and the subsidiary's account payable to the parent) are eliminated or offset. The parent's investment in the subsidiary (an asset) is offset against the owners' equity of the subsidiary. Minority interest arises if the subsidiary is not 100-percent owned by the parent company because the parent's investment will be less than the owners' equity of the subsidiary. Minority interest is the equity of the other (that is, minority) stockholders in the owners' equity of the subsidiary. This amount does not represent what the parent company would have to pay to acquire the rest of the stock of the subsidiary, nor is it a liability in the true sense of the term. The minority interest reported on a consolidated balance sheet is included because the subsidiary's assets and liabilities (except those eliminated to avoid double counting) have been added to the parent company's assets and liabilities, and the parent's share of owners' equity of the subsidiary is included in consolidated owners' equity. To keep the balance sheet in balance, the equity of the minority stockholders in the owners' equity of the subsidiary must be shown.

Although usually included with noncurrent liabilities, some accountants believe that minority interest should be shown as a separate item between liabilities and owners' equity because this amount is not a liability of the consolidated entity.

Summary

This chapter discussed the accounting for and presentation of the following liabilities and related income statement account (contra liabilities and reductions of expense accounts are shown in parentheses):

Balance sheet	Income statement
Assets = Liabilities + Owners' equity ⟵	Net income = Revenues – Expenses

Current Liabilities:

Short-term debt	Interest expense
(Discount on short-term debt)	Interest expense
Accounts payable	(Purchase discounts)

Balance sheet		Income statement
Assets = Liabilities + Owners' equity ◄———		Net income = Revenues – Expenses
or, alternatively		
Accounts payable		Purchase discounts lost
Unearned revenue		Revenue
Other accrued liabilities		Various expenses
Long-Term Liabilities:		
Bonds payable		Interest expense
(Discount on .... bonds payable)		Interest expense
Premium on... bonds payable		(Interest expense)
Deferred income .... taxes		Income tax expense

Liabilities are an entity's obligations. Most liabilities arise because funds have been borrowed or because an obligation is recognized as a result of the accrual accounting process. Current liabilities are those expected to be paid within a year of the balance sheet date. Noncurrent or long-term liabilities are expected to be paid more than a year after the balance sheet date.

Short-term debt, such as a bank loan, is obtained to provide cash for seasonal buildup of inventory. The loan is expected to be repaid when the inventory is sold and the accounts receivable from the sale are collected. The interest cost of short-term debt is sometimes calculated on a discount basis. A discount basis results in a higher annual percentage rate than straight interest because the discount is based on the maturity value of the loan, and the proceeds available to the borrower are calculated as the maturity value minus the discount. A discount is recorded as a contra liability and is amortized to interest expense. The amount of discounted short-term debt shown as a liability on the balance sheet is the maturity value minus the unamortized discount.

Long-term debt principal payments that will be made within a year of the balance sheet date are classified as a current liability.

Accounts payable represent amounts owed to suppliers of inventories and other resources. Some accounts payable are subject to a cash discount if paid within a time frame specified by the supplier. The internal control system of most entities tries to encourage adherence to the policy of taking all cash discounts offered.

Unearned revenue and other deferred credits, and other accrued liabilities, arise primarily because of accrual accounting procedures that result in the recognition of expenses in the fiscal period in which they are incurred. Many of these liabilities are estimated because the actual liability is not known when the financial statements are prepared.

Long-term debt is a significant part of the capital structure of many firms. Owners borrow rather than invest funds when the firm expects to take advantage of the financial leverage associated with debt. If borrowed money can be invested to earn a higher return (ROI) than the interest cost, the return on the owners' investment (ROE) will be greater than ROI. However, the opposite is also true. Leverage adds to the risk associated with an investment in an entity.

Long-term debt is frequently issued in the form of bonds payable. Bonds have a stated interest rate (that is almost always a fixed percentage), a face amount or principal, and a maturity date when they must be paid. Because the interest rate on a bond is fixed, changes in the market rate of interest result in fluctuations in the market value of the bond. As market interest rates rise, bond prices fall, and vice versa. The market value of a bond is the present value of the interest payments and maturity value, discounted at the market interest rate. When bonds are issued and the market rate at the date of issue is different from the stated rate of the bond, a premium or discount results. Both bond premium and discount are amortized to interest expense over the life of the bond. Premium amortization reduces interest expense below the amount of interest paid. Discount amortization increases interest expense over the amount of interest paid. A bond is sometimes retired before its maturity date because market interest rates have dropped significantly below the stated interest rate of the bond. Early retirement of bonds can result in a gain, but usually results in a loss.

Deferred income taxes result from temporary differences between book and taxable income. The most significant temporary difference is caused by the different depreciation expense calculation methods used for each purpose. The amount of deferred income tax liability is the amount of income tax expected to be paid in future years, based on tax rates expected to apply in future years multiplied by the total amount of temporary differences.

Other long-term liabilities may relate to pension obligations, other postretirement benefit plan obligations, warranty obligations, or estimated liabilities under lawsuits in process. Also included in this caption in the balance sheet of some companies is the equity of minority stockholders in the net assets of less than wholly owned subsidiaries, all of whose assets and liabilities are included in the entity's consolidated balance sheet.

Refer to the Armstrong World Industries, Inc., balance sheet and financial review in the Appendix to this text's companion course workbook and study guide and to other financial statements you have to observe how information about liabilities is presented.

Key Words and Phrases

accounts payable (p. 236) A liability representing an amount payable to another entity, usually because of the purchase of merchandise or a service on credit.

annual percentage rate (APR) (p. 234) The effective (true) annual interest rate on a loan.

bond or **bond payable** (p. 244) A long-term liability with a stated interest rate and maturity date, usually issued in denominations of $1,000.

bond discount (p. 244) The excess of the face amount of a bond issued over the market value of a bond or the proceeds of the issue.

bond indenture (p. 250) The formal agreement between the borrower and investors in bonds.

bond premium (p. 244) The excess of the market value of a bond or the proceeds of a bond issue over the face amount of a bond or the bonds issued.

book value (p. 249) The balance of the ledger account (including related contra accounts, if any) for an asset, a liability, or an owners' equity account. Sometimes referred to as *carrying value*.

call premium (p. 249) An amount paid in excess of the face amount of a bond when the bond is repaid before its established maturity date.

callable bonds (p. 249) Bonds that can be redeemed by the issuer, at its option, before the maturity date.

collateral trust bond (p. 251) A bond secured by the pledge of securities or other intangible property.

consolidated financial statements (p. 254) Financial statements resulting from the combination of parent and subsidiary company's financial statements.

contra liability (p. 233) An account that normally has a debit balance that is subtracted from a related liability on the balance sheet.

convertible bonds (p. 251) Bonds that can be converted to preferred or common stock of the issuer at the bondholder's option.

coupon bond (p. 250) A bond for which the owner's name and address are not known by the issuer and/or trustee. Interest is received by clipping interest coupons that are attached to the bond and submitting them to the issuer.

coupon rate (p. 245) The rate used to calculate the interest payments on a bond. Sometimes called the *stated rate*.

current maturities of long-term debt (p. 236) Principal payments on long-term debt that are scheduled to be paid within one year of the balance sheet date.

debenture bonds or **debentures** (p. 251) Bonds secured by the general credit of the issuer.

deferred credit (p. 238) An account with a credit balance that will be recognized as a revenue (or as an expense reduction) in a future period. See *unearned revenue*.

deferred income taxes (p. 251) A long-term liability that arises because of temporary differences between when an item (principally depreciation expense) is recognized for book purposes and tax purposes.

discount loan (p. 234) A loan on which interest is paid at the beginning of the loan period.

face amount (p. 244) The principal amount of a bond.

financial leverage (p. 242) The use of debt (with a fixed interest rate) that causes a difference between return on investment and return on equity.

interest calculation—discount basis (p. 235) Interest calculation in which the interest (called *discount*) is subtracted from the principal to determine the amount of money (the proceeds) made available to the borrower. Only the principal is repaid at the maturity date because the interest is in effect prepaid.

interest calculation—straight basis (p. 234) Interest calculation in which the principal is the amount of money made available to the borrower. The borrower repays principal and interest at the maturity date.

interpolating (p. 235) A mathematical term to describe the process of *interpreting* and *relating* two factors from a (present value) table to approximate a third factor not shown in the table.

long-term debt (p. 242) A liability that will be paid more than one year from the balance sheet date.

maturity date (p. 231) The date when a loan is scheduled to be repaid.

minority interest in subsidiaries (p. 254) An account that arises in the preparation of consolidated financial statements when some subsidiaries are less than 100 percent owned by the parent company.

mortgage bond (p. 251) A bond secured by a mortgage on real estate.

note payable (p. 232) Usually a short-term liability that arises from issuing a note; a formal promise to pay a stated amount at a stated date, usually with interest at a stated rate, and sometimes secured by collateral.

prime rate (p. 232) The interest rate charged by banks on loans to large and most creditworthy customers; a benchmark interest rate.

proceeds (p. 233) The amount of cash received in a transaction.

registered bond (p. 250) A bond for which the owner's name and address are recorded by the issuer and/or trustee.

revolving line of credit (p. 231) A loan on which regular payments are to be made, but that can be increased to a predetermined limit as additional funds must be borrowed.

serial bond (p. 251) A bond that is to be repaid in installments.

stated rate (p. 245) The rate used to calculate the amount of interest payable on a bond. Sometimes called the *coupon rate*.

term bond (p. 251) A bond that is to be repaid in one lump sum at the maturity date.

trustee of bonds (p. 250) The agent who coordinates activities between the bond issuer and the investor in bonds.

unearned revenue (p. 238) A liability arising from receipt of cash before the related revenue has been earned. See *deferred credit*.

working capital loan (p. 231) A short-term loan that is expected to be repaid from collections of accounts receivable.

Chapter Note

1. Financial Accounting Standards Board, *Statement of Financial Accounting Concepts No. 6*, "Elements of Financial Statements," para. 35.

Chapter 9

Accounting for and Presentation of Owners' Equity

Owners' equity is one of the primary categories of balance sheet information examined by insurance professionals. Owners' equity, also called net assets, is the remainder amount of total assets after liabilities are subtracted. If this amount increases over time, it is an indication of an entity's increasing value to its owners. Owners' equity is the total of paid-in capital (common stock, preferred stock, and additional paid-in capital) and retained earnings. This chapter explains the basic characteristics of the components of owners' equity and provides some of the reasons corporations might have a particular mix of paid-in capital and retained earnings.

Owners' equity is the claim of the entity's owners to the assets shown in the balance sheet. Neither the liabilities nor the elements of owners' equity are specifically identifiable with particular assets, although certain assets may be pledged as collateral for some liabilities. When users of financial statements review an entity's balance sheet, they typically look for changes in owners' equity over time, how it is distributed among paid-in capital and retained earnings, how that distribution changes over time, and whether the trends identified reflect changes in risk characteristics of the firm. Insurance professionals must regularly assess the risk characteristics of the business entities they insure to evaluate the assumed loss exposure and price adequacy. Much of the discussion in this chapter will focus on the owners' equity section of the balance sheets of Racers, Inc., in Exhibit 9-1.

Exhibit 9-1
Owners' Equity Section of Racers, Inc.
Balance Sheets at August 31, 1996 and 1995

	August 31	
	1996	*1995*
Owners' equity:		
Paid-in capital:		
Preferred stock, 6%, $100 par value, cumulative, callable at $102, 5,000 shares authorized, issued, and outstanding	$ 500,000	$ 500,000
Common stock, $2 par value, 1,000,000 shares authorized, 244,800 shares issued at August 31, 1996, and 200,000 shares issued at August 31, 1995	489,600	400,000
Additional paid-in capital	3,322,400	2,820,000
Total paid-in capital	$4,312,000	$3,720,000
Retained earnings	2,828,000	2,600,000
Less: Common stock in treasury, at cost; 1,000 shares at August 31, 1996	(12,000)	—
Total owners' equity	$7,128,000	$6,320,000

The specific terminology used to identify owners' equity depends on the form of the entity's legal organization. For an individual proprietorship, the term **proprietor's capital**, or *capital*, perhaps combined with the owner's name, is frequently used. For example, in the balance sheet of a single proprietorship owned by Mary Powers, owner's equity would be labeled Mary Powers, Capital. For a partnership, the term **partners' capital** is used, and sometimes the capital account balance of each partner is shown on the balance sheet. In both proprietorships and partnerships, no distinction is made between invested (or paid-in) capital and retained earnings (or earned capital).

Because the corporate form of organization is used for firms that account for most of the business activity in the U.S. economy, this text focuses on corporation owners' equity. As explained in Chapter 2, corporation owners' equity has two principal components: paid-in capital and retained earnings. The financial statements of many small businesses that use the corporate form of organization are likely to show in owners' equity only capital stock (which is paid-in capital) and retained earnings. However, as shown by the shareholders' equity section of the Consolidated Balance Sheets of Armstrong World Industries, Inc., on page 26 of the Appendix to this text's companion workbook and study guide, the owners' equity section can become complex. The owners' equity section of the balance sheets in other annual reports that you have may appear equally complex.

Owners' equity captions usually seen in a balance sheet are as follows:

- Paid-in capital:
    Common stock
    Preferred stock (optional)
    Additional paid-in capital
- Retained earnings (Deficit if negative)
- Cumulative foreign currency translation adjustment
- Less: Treasury stock

The objective of this chapter is to help you to make sense of the owners' equity presentation of any balance sheet. You will also learn about many characteristics of owners' equity that are relevant to personal investment decisions.

Educational Objectives

After studying this chapter, you should be able to:

1. Explain the characteristics of common stock, and describe how common stock is presented in the balance sheet.
2. Describe the characteristics of preferred stock, and explain its advantages and disadvantages to the corporation.
3. Compare the relative advantage to an investor of investing in preferred or common stock.
4. Illustrate how preferred stock is presented in the balance sheet.
5. Explain the accounting for a cash dividend and the dates involved in dividend transactions.
6. Describe stock dividends and stock splits, and explain their use.
7. Explain what treasury stock is, why it is acquired, and how treasury stock transactions affect owners' equity.
8. Explain the cumulative foreign currency translation adjustment and why it appears in owners' equity.
9. Describe how owners' equity transactions for the year are reported in the financial statements.
10. Define or describe each of the Key Words and Phrases introduced in this chapter.

Paid-In Capital

The captions shown in the paid-in capital category of owners' equity (that is, common stock, preferred stock, and additional paid-in capital) represent amounts invested in the corporation by stockholders and are sometimes referred to as *contributed capital*. On the other hand, the retained earnings (or earned capital) category of owners' equity represents the entity's cumulative earnings (that is, net income over the life of the entity) less any dividends paid. Naturally, stockholders are interested in the relationship between paid-in capital and retained earnings. The higher the retained earnings account balance is relative to paid-in capital amounts the better, because retained earnings reflect, in part, management's ability to earn a return on invested (paid-in) amounts. However, a large retained earnings balance may also lead stockholders to pressure management and the board of directors to pay higher dividends. Remember the distinction between paid-in capital and retained earnings when interpreting the owners' equity section of any balance sheet.

Common Stock

As already explained, **common stock** (called **capital stock** at times, especially when no other classes of stock are authorized) represents residual ownership. Common stockholders are the ultimate owners of the corporation; they have claim to all assets that remain in the entity after all liabilities and preferred stock claims (described in the next section) have been satisfied. In the case of bankruptcy or forced liquidation, this residual claim may not have any value because the liabilities and preferred stock claims may exceed the amount realized from the assets in liquidation. In this severe case, the liability of the common stockholders is limited to the amount they have invested in the stock; common stockholders cannot be forced by creditors and/or preferred stockholders to invest additional amounts to make up their losses. In the more positive (and usual) case, common stockholders prosper because the profits of the firm exceed the fixed claims of creditors (interest) and preferred stockholders (preferred dividends). All of these profits accrue to common stockholders—there is no upper limit to the value of their ownership interest. Of course, the market value of common stock reflects the profitability (or lack thereof) and ultimate dividend-paying capability of the corporation. However, as residual owners, common stockholders are not entitled to receive any specific dividend amount and may not receive any dividends at all in some years.

Common stockholders have the right and obligation to elect members to the corporation's board of directors. The election process can take one of two forms, as described in Business Procedure Capsule 16—Electing Directors. The board of directors hires corporate officers, and the officers execute strategies for achieving corporate objectives. Some officers may also be directors (**inside directors**), but current practice is to have most boards made up primarily of **outside directors** (not employed by the firm) who can bring an outside viewpoint to the considerations and deliberations of the board.

Common stockholders must also approve changes to the corporate charter (for example, when the number of shares of stock authorized is changed so that additional shares can be sold to raise more capital) and may have to approve transactions such as mergers or divestitures.

Common stock can have **par value** or can be of a no-par-value variety. When it is used, par value is usually a nominal amount assigned to each share when the corporation is organized. In today's business world, par value has virtually no financial reporting or economic significance with respect to common stock. In most states, the par value of the issued shares represents the **legal capital** of the corporation. Most state corporation laws provide that stock with par value cannot be issued for a price less than par value, and they provide that total owners' equity cannot be reduced to less than legal capital by dividends or the purchase from stockholders of previously issued shares of stock. If the stock has par value, the amount reported in the balance sheet will be the par value multiplied by the number of shares issued. Any difference between par value and the amount realized from the sale of the stock is recorded as additional paid-in capital. Some firms assign a **stated value** to the common stock, which is essentially par value by another name. If a firm issues true no-par-value stock, then the total amount received from the sale of the shares is recorded as common stock.

A survey of the annual reports for 1993 of 600 publicly owned merchandising and manufacturing companies indicated that only 62 companies had no-par-value common stock. Of those 62 companies, 13 had an assigned or stated value per share.[1]

To illustrate the sale of common stock, assume that during the year ended August 31, 1996, Racers, Inc., sold 40,000 additional shares of its $2 par value common stock at a price of $13 per share. The journal entry to record this transaction was as follows:

Dr.		Cash (40,000 shares × $13)	520,000	
	Cr.	Common stock (40,000 shares × $2)		80,000
	Cr.	Additional paid-in capital		
		(40,000 shares $11)		440,000

The effect of this stock issue on the financial statements of Racers, Inc., was as follows:

Balance sheet			Income statement	
Assets =	Liabilities +	Owners' equity	◄── Net income =	Revenues – Expenses

Cash	Common stock
+520,000	+80,000
(40,000 shares × $13)	(40,000 shares × $2)

Additional paid-in
capital
+440,000
(40,000 shares × $11)

Exhibit 9-1 shows that common stock and additional paid-in capital increased during 1996 (the remaining portion of these increases will be explained in the stock dividends section of this chapter).

On the balance sheet, the number of shares *authorized, issued,* and *outstanding* will be disclosed. The number of **authorized shares** is stated in the corporate charter that is filed with the state according to its laws regarding corporate organization. This represents the maximum number of shares that the corporation is legally approved to issue; increases in the number of authorized shares requires shareholder approval. The number of **issued shares** is the number of shares of stock that have actually been transferred from the corporation to shareholders.

The number of **outstanding shares** will differ from the number of issued shares if the firm has **treasury stock**. As explained in more detail later in this chapter, treasury stock is a firm's own stock that the firm has acquired from stockholders. Exhibit 9-2 summarizes the relationship between these terms and the balance sheet disclosure required for each. The difference between the number of shares authorized and the number of shares issued represents the potential for additional shares to be issued. The common stock of many firms provides a **preemptive right**, which gives present shareholders the right to purchase shares from any additional share issuances in proportion to their present percentage of ownership. The preemptive right is usually most significant in smaller, closely held corporations (that is, those with only a few stockholders) in which existing stockholders want to prevent their ownership interest from being diluted. Even though they are not ordinarily bound by a preemptive right provision, many large corporations offer existing stockholders the right to purchase additional shares when more capital is needed. This maintains stockholder loyalty and can be a relatively inexpensive way to raise capital.

- **BUSINESS PROCEDURE CAPSULE 16**
  Electing Directors

Directors are elected by a **cumulative voting** procedure or on a slate basis. Under cumulative voting, each stockholder is entitled to cast a number of votes equal to the number of shares owned multiplied by the number of directors to be elected. Thus, if five directors are to be elected, the owner of 100 shares of common stock is entitled to 500 votes: all 500 can be cast for one candidate, 100 can be cast for each of five candidates, or they can be cast in any combination between these extremes. In **slate voting**, the common stockholder is entitled to one vote for each share owned, but each vote is for an entire slate of candidates.

In most cases, the voting method doesn't affect the outcome. A committee of the board of directors nominates director candidates (equal to the number of directors to be elected), a proxy committee made up of members of the board seeks proxies from the stockholders, and the required number of nominees are duly elected. Occasionally, however, an outside group challenges the existing board; under these circumstances, the election can be exciting. Each group nominates director candidates and solicits stockholder votes. Under slate voting, the successful group will be the one that gets a majority of the vote; that group's entire slate will be elected. Of course, controlling 50.1 percent of the voting shares will ensure success in the election. Under cumulative voting, however, a minority group of stockholders can concentrate their votes on one or two of their own candidates, thus making it easier to secure representation on the board of directors. For example, if five directors are to be elected, the votes of approximately 17 percent of the outstanding common stock are required to elect one director.

Many people, especially proponents of corporate democracy, favor cumulative voting. Some states require corporations organized under their laws to have cumulative voting for directors. Yet corporations often prefer to maintain a slate voting practice because this method makes getting a seat on the board more difficult for corporate raiders who desire control of the corporation and others. Another tactic designed to reduce an outsider's chance of securing a director position is to provide for rolling terms. For example, for a nine-member board, three directors will be elected each year for a three-year term. Thus, even with cumulative voting, the votes of many more shares are required to elect one director than would be required if all nine directors were elected each year.

Exhibit 9-2
Balance Sheet Disclosure for Shares of Stock

Terminology	Number of Shares Disclosed	Dollar Amount Disclosed
Shares authorized	Number specified in the corporate charter (maximum approved to be issued)	None
Shares issued	Number of shares that have been issued to stockholders (usually sale)	Number of shares × par or stated value or If no par or stated value, total amount received from sale of shares
Shares outstanding	Number of shares still held by stockholders (shares issued less treasury shares)	None
Treasury stock	Number of issued shares purchased by the corporation from stockholders and not formally retired	Cost of treasury stock owned by corporation

Preferred Stock

Preferred stock is a class of paid-in capital that differs from common stock in that preferred stock has several debt-like features and a limited claim on assets in the event of liquidation. Also, in most cases, holders of preferred stock do not have a voting privilege. (Common stock represents residual equity—it has claim to all assets remaining after the liabilities and preferred stock claims have been met in the liquidation of the corporation.) Preferred stock has been viewed as having less risk than common stock. In the early years of the Industrial Revolution, when firms sought to raise the large amounts of capital required to finance factories and railroads, investors were more willing to acquire preferred stock in a firm than take the risks associated with common stock ownership. As firms have prospered and many investors have experienced the rewards of common stock ownership, preferred stock has become a less significant factor in the capital structure of many manufacturing, merchandising, and service-providing firms. However, utilities and financial corporations continue to issue preferred stock.

The advantages of preferred stock, relative to common stock, relate to dividends and to the priority of claims on assets in the event of liquidation of the corporation, or redemption of the preferred stock. A **dividend** is a distribution of the earnings of the corporation to its owners. The dividend requirement of preferred stock must be satisfied before a dividend can be paid to the common stockholders. Most preferred stock issues call for a quarterly or semiannual dividend, which must be kept current if there is to be a dividend on the common stock. The amount of the dividend is expressed in dollars and cents or as a percentage of the par value of the preferred stock. As shown in Exhibit 9-1, the preferred stock of Racers, Inc., is referred to as "6%, $100 par value." This means that each share of preferred stock is entitled to an annual dividend of $6 (6% × $100). The same dividend result could have been accomplished by creating a $6 cumulative preferred stock. The terms of the stock issue specify whether the dividend is to be paid at the rate of $1.50 per quarter, $3 semiannually, or $6 annually. Preferred stock issues, including that of Racers, Inc., usually provide a **cumulative dividend**, which means that if a dividend payment is not made, missed dividends (or dividends *in arrears*) must be paid before any dividend can be paid to the common stockholders. Occasionally, preferred stock issues have **participating dividends**, which means that after the common stockholders have received a specified dividend, the preferred and common stockholders share any further dividends in a specified ratio. Exhibit 9-3 illustrates the calculation of preferred stock dividend amounts.

Exhibit 9-3
Illustration of Preferred Stock Dividend Calculation

Case 1

6%, $100 par value cumulative preferred stock 50,000 shares authorized, issued, and outstanding. Dividend payable semiannually, no dividends in arrears.

Semiannual preferred dividend amount:

   6% × $100 × 50,000 shares outstanding × 1/2 year = $150,000

Case 2

$4.50, $75 par value cumulative preferred stock, 50,000 shares authorized and issued, 40,000 shares outstanding (10,000 shares of treasury stock). Dividend payable quarterly, no dividend in arrears.

Quarterly preferred dividend amount:

      $4.50 × 40,000 shares outstanding × 1/4 year = $45,000

Continued on next page.

Case 3

$4, $50 par value cumulative preferred stock, 100,000 shares authorized, 60,000 shares issued, 54,000 shares outstanding (6,000 shares of treasury stock). Dividend payable annually. Dividends were not paid in prior two years.

Dividend required in current year to pay prior years' and current year's preferred dividend:

$4 × 54,000 shares outstanding × 3 years = $648,000

Case 4

$2, $25 par value cumulative participating preferred stock, 30,000 shares authorized, 25,000 shares issued and outstanding. Dividend payable annually. Dividends were not paid in the prior two years. After preferred stockholders are paid for arrears and their current year preference, common stockholders receive a base dividend of $2 per share. Preferred and common stockholders are to share equally on a per-share basis in any additional dividends. The company has 100,000 shares of common stock outstanding, and dividends for the year total $410,000.

	Preferred	Common	Remaining Balance
Allocation:			
Total amount declared			$410,000
Pay preferred dividend in arrears ($2 × $25,000 shares × 2 years)	$100,000		310,000
Pay current year's preferred dividend ($2 × 25,000 shares)	50,000		260,000
Pay common stock base dividend ($2 × 100,000 shares)		$200,000	60,000
Allocate $60,000 available for participation*	12,000	48,000	0
Total dividends paid	$162,000	$248,000	

*25,000 preferred shares/125,000 total shares = 20% × $60,000 = $12,000.

100,000 common shares/125,000 total shares = 80% × $60,000 = $48,000.

A preferred stock issue's claim on the assets in the event of liquidation (**liquidating value**) or redemption (**redemption value**) is an amount specified when the preferred stock is issued. If the preferred stock has a par value, the liquidating value or redemption value is usually equal to the par value, or it is equal to the par value plus a slight premium. If the preferred stock has no par value, then the liquidating value or redemption value is a stated amount. In either case, the claim in liquidation must be fulfilled before the common stockholders receive anything. However, once the liquidating claim is met, the preferred stockholders will not receive any additional amounts.

Callable preferred stock is redeemable (usually at a slight premium over par or liquidating value) at the option of the corporation. **Convertible preferred stock** may be exchanged for common stock of the corporation at the option of the stockholder at a conversion rate (for example, six shares of common stock for each share of preferred stock) established when the preferred stock is authorized. For many firms, the call and conversion features of preferred stock cannot be exercised for a number of years after the authorization (or issue) date of the stock; such restrictions are specified in the stock certificate. Note in Exhibit 9-1 that the preferred stock of Racers, Inc., is callable at a price of $102.

Preferred stock has some of the same characteristics as bonds payable. Exhibit 9-4 summarizes the principal similarities and differences of the two. The tax deductibility of interest expense causes many financial mangers to prefer debt to preferred stock. After all, they reason, if a fixed amount is going to have to be paid out regularly, it might as well be in the form of deductible interest rather than nondeductible preferred dividends. (As explained in Chapter 7, the after-tax cost of bonds paying 10 percent interest is only 7 percent for a corporation with an average tax rate of 30 percent.) Most investors also prefer bonds because the interest owed to them is a fixed claim that must be paid, but preferred stock dividends may be skipped, even though any arrearage may have to be paid before dividends can be paid on common stock. Of 600 publicly owned industrial and merchandising companies whose annual reports for 1993 that the AICPA reviewed, 438 had no preferred stock outstanding.[2]

From the creditors' point of view, preferred stock reduces the risk associated with financial leverage (introduced in Chapter 8). Financial firms (such as banks, insurance companies, and finance companies) and utilities often have a significant portion of their owners' equity represented by preferred stock. This is because a significant proportion of the capital requirements of these firms is provided by investors who prefer the relative security of preferred stock rather than debt and/or common stock.

The balance sheet disclosures for preferred stock include the following:

- The par value and dividend rate (or the amount of the annual dividend requirement)
- The liquidating or redemption value
- The number of shares authorized by the corporate charter
- The number of shares issued
- The number of shares outstanding

Exhibit 9-4
Comparison of Preferred Stock and Bonds Payable

Preferred Stock	Bonds Payable
Similarities	
Dividend is (usually) a fixed claim to income.	Interest is a fixed claim to income.
Redemption value is a fixed claim to assets.	Maturity value is a fixed claim to assets.
Is usually callable and may be convertible.	Is usually callable and may be convertible.
Differences	
Dividend may be skipped, even though it usually must be caught up if dividends are to be paid on the common stock.	Interest must be paid or firm faces bankruptcy.
No maturity date.	Principal must be paid at maturity.
Dividends are not an expense and are not deductible for income tax purposes.	Interest is a deductible expense for income tax purposes.

Any difference between the number of shares issued and the number of shares outstanding is caused by shares held in the firm's treasury, or treasury stock. In addition, the amount of any preferred dividends that have been missed (that are in arrears) is disclosed in the balance sheet.

Additional Paid-In Capital

As has already been illustrated, **additional paid-in capital** is an owners' equity category that reflects the excess of the amount received from the sale of preferred or common stock over par value. (Remember that the amount in the common or preferred stock account is equal to the par value multiplied by the number of shares issued, or the total amount received from the sale of no-par-value stock.) The additional paid-in capital account is also used for other relatively uncommon capital transactions that cannot be reflected in the common or preferred stock accounts or that should not be reflected in retained earnings. **Capital in excess of par value** (or stated value) and *capital surplus* are terms sometimes used to describe additional paid-in capital. The latter term was widely used many years ago before the term *surplus* fell into disfavor because of its connotation of something "extra" and because uninformed financial statement readers might think that this amount was available for dividends.

The paid-in capital of a corporation represents the amount invested by the owners, and if par value stock is involved, paid-in capital includes par value and additional paid-in capital. If no-par-value stock is issued, paid-in capital represents the owners' investment.

Retained Earnings

The **retained earnings** account reflects the cumulative earnings of the corporation that have been retained for use in the business rather than disbursed to the stockholders as dividends. *Retained earnings is not cash!* Retained earnings is increased by the firm's net income, and the accrual basis of accounting results in a net income amount that is different from the cash increase during a fiscal period. To the extent that operating results increase cash, that cash may be used for operating, investing, or financing activities.

Virtually the only factors affecting retained earnings are net income or loss reported on the income statement and dividends. (Remember that all revenue, expense, gain, and loss accounts reported on the income statement are indirect changes to the retained earnings account on the balance sheet. As these items are recorded throughout the year, retained earnings are, in effect, increased for revenues and gains and decreased for expenses and losses.) Under certain very restricted circumstances, generally accepted accounting principles permit direct adjustments of retained earnings for the correction of errors (referred to as *prior period adjustments*). For example, if a firm neglected to include a significant amount of inventory in its year-end physical count and this error was not discovered until the following year, a direct adjustment to inventory and retained earnings would be appropriate. However, new information about an estimate made in a prior year (for example, for depreciation or bad debts) does not warrant a direct entry to retained earnings, because the amounts reported would have reflected the best information available at the time. Accounting principles emphasize that the income statement is to reflect all transactions affecting owners' equity, except for the following:

1. Dividends to stockholders (which are a reduction in retained earnings)
2. Transactions involving the corporation's own stock (which are reflected in the paid-in capital section of the balance sheet)
3. A cumulative foreign currency translation adjustment (which is accounted for in a separate owners' equity account, as will be explained later in this chapter)
4. Unrealized gain or loss, net of related income taxes, on certain marketable securities that are reported at market value rather than cost

If the retained earnings account has a negative balance because cumulative losses and dividends have exceeded cumulative net income, this account is referred to as **deficit**.

Cash Dividends

For a corporation to pay a cash dividend, it must meet several requirements: The firm must have retained earnings, the board of directors must declare the dividend, and the firm must have enough cash to pay the dividend. If the firm has agreed in a bond indenture or other contract to maintain certain minimum standards of financial health (for example, a current ratio of at least 2.5:1), the dividend must not cause any of these measures to fall below their agreed-upon level. From both the corporation's and the stockholders' perspectives, several key dates are related to the dividend (see Business Procedure Capsule 17—Dividend Dates). Once the board of directors has declared the dividend, it becomes a legally enforceable liability of the corporation. The journal entries to record the declaration and subsequent payment of a cash dividend are as follows:

On the declaration date:

Dr.	Retained earnings	xx
Cr.	Dividends payable	xx

On the payment date:

Dr.	Dividends payable	xx
Cr.	Cash	xx

The effects on the financial statements of these entries are as follows:

Balance sheet	Income statement
Assets = Liabilities + Owners' equity ⟵	Net income = Revenues − Expenses

Declaration date:
      +Dividends −Retained
        payable   earnings
Payment date:
−Cash   −Dividends
 payable payable

Dividends are not an expense and do not appear on the income statement. Dividends are a distribution of earnings of the corporation to its stockholders and are treated as a direct reduction of retained earnings. If a balance sheet is issued between the date the dividend is declared and the date it is paid, the dividends payable account will be included in the current liability section of the balance sheet.

Stock Dividends and Stock Splits

In addition to a cash dividend, or sometimes instead of a cash dividend, a corporation may issue a **stock dividend**. A stock dividend is the issuance of additional shares of common stock to the existing stockholders in proportion to the number of shares each currently owns. It is expressed as a percentage; for example, a 5 percent stock dividend would result in the issuance of 5 percent of the currently outstanding shares. A stockholder who owns 100 shares would receive 5 additional shares of stock, but his or her proportionate ownership interest in the firm would not change. (Fractional shares are not issued, so an owner of ninety shares would receive four shares and cash equal to the market value of half of a share.)

The motivation for a stock dividend is usually to maintain the loyalty of stockholders when the firm does not have enough cash to pay (or increase) the cash dividend. Although many stockholders like to receive a stock dividend, such a distribution is not income to the stockholders. To understand why there is no income to stockholders, consider the effect of the stock dividend from the issuing corporation's point of view. A stock dividend does not cause any change in either assets or liabilities; therefore, it cannot affect *total* owners' equity. However, additional shares of stock are issued, and the common stock account must reflect the product of the number of shares issued multiplied by par value. Because the issuance of shares is called a *dividend*, retained earnings should also be reduced. The amount of the reduction in retained earnings is the number of dividend shares issued multiplied by the market price per share. Any difference between market price and par value is recorded in the additional paid-in capital account. If the shares are without par value, then the common stock account is increased by the market value of the dividend shares issued.

During the year ended August 31, 1996, Racers, Inc., issued a 2 percent stock dividend on its $2 par value common stock when the market price was $15 per share. (The stock dividend occurred at some point after the additional 40,000 shares of common stock had been issued.) Thus, 4,800 dividend shares were issued (2% × 240,000 shares outstanding). The journal entry to record this transaction was as follows:

Dr.	Retained earnings	72,000	
Cr.	Common stock....................................		9,600
Cr.	Additional paid-in capital		62,400

With the horizontal model, the effect of the financial statements was as follows:

Balance sheet	Income statement
Assets = Liabilities + Owners' equity ◄———	Net income = Revenues – Expenses

Retained earnings
(4,800 shares × $15)
−72,000

Common stock
(4,800 shares × $2)
+9,600

Additional paid-in
capital
(4,800 shares × $13)
+62,400

The stock dividend affects *only* the owners' equity of the firm. **Capitalizing retained earnings** is the term sometimes used to refer to the effect of a stock dividend transaction because the dividend results in the permanent transfer of some retained earnings to paid-in capital. The income statement is not affected because the transaction is between the corporation and its stockholders (who own the corporation); no gain or loss can result from a capital transaction.

If the stock dividend percentage is more than 20 to 25 percent, only the par value or stated value of the additional common shares issued is transferred from retained earnings to common stock.

What happens to the market value of a share of stock when a firm issues a stock dividend? Is the shareowner any wealthier? As already explained, nothing happens to the firm's assets, liabilities, or earning power as a result of the stock dividend; therefore, the *total* market value of the firm should not change. Since more shares of stock are now outstanding and the total market value of all the shares remains the same, the market value of each share will drop. This is why the stock dividend does not represent income to stockholders. However, under some circumstances the market value per share of the common stock will not settle at its theoretically lower value. This anomaly will occur especially if the cash dividend per share is not adjusted to reflect the stock dividend. Thus, if the firm had been paying a cash dividend of $1.00 per share before the stock dividend and the same cash dividend rate is continued, the dividend rate has effectively increased, and the stock price will probably rise to reflect this.

- **BUSINESS PROCEDURE CAPSULE 17**
  Dividend Dates

Three dates applicable to every dividend are the declaration date, the record date, and the payment date. In addition, an ex-dividend date will apply to companies whose stock is publicly traded. The declaration, record, and payment dates for a closely held company can be the same date.

The **declaration date** is the date on which the board of directors declares the dividend. The **record date** is used to determine who receives the dividend; the person listed on the stockholder records of the corporation on the record date is considered the owner of the shares. The owner of record is the person to whom the check is made payable and mailed to on the **payment date**. If shares have been sold but the ownership change has not yet been noted on the corporation's records, the prior owner (the one in the records) receives the dividend (and may have to settle with the new owner, depending on their agreement with respect to the dividend). The **ex-dividend date** relates to this issue of who receives the dividend. When the stock of a publicly traded company is bought or sold, the seller has a settlement period of three business days in which to deliver the stock certificate. The buyer also has three business days to pay for the purchase. Thus, the stock trades "ex-dividend" three business days before the record date to give the corporation a chance to increase the accuracy of its ownership records. On the ex-dividend date, the stock trades without the dividend (that is, the seller retains the right to receive the dividend if the stock is sold on or after the ex-dividend date). If the stock is sold before the ex-dividend date, then the buyer is entitled to receive the dividend. All other things being equal, the price of the stock in the market falls by the amount of the dividend on the ex-dividend date.

No specific requirement deals with the number of days that should elapse between the declaration, record, and payment dates for publicly traded stocks. Two to four weeks commonly elapse between each date.

Sometimes the managers of a firm want to lower the market price of the firm's common stock by a significant amount because they believe that a stock trading in a price range of $20 to $50 per share is a more popular investment than a stock priced at more than $50 per share. A **stock split** will accomplish this objective. A stock split involves issuing additional shares to existing stockholders and, if the stock has a par value, reducing the par value proportionately. For example, if a firm had 60,000 shares of $10 par value stock outstanding, with stock trading in the market at a price of $80 per share, a 4-for-1 stock split would involve issuing three additional shares to each stockholder for each share owned. Then a stockholder who had owned 200 shares would receive an additional 600 shares, bringing the total shares owned to 800. As in the case of a stock dividend, nothing has happened to the assets or liabilities of the firm, so nothing can happen to owners' equity. The total market value of the company would not change, but the market price of each share would fall. (Compare the results of 60,000 shares × $80 to 240,000 shares × $20. The results are equivalent.) No accounting entry is required for a stock split. The common stock caption of owners' equity indicates the drop in par value per share and the proportionate increase in the number of shares authorized, issued, and outstanding. If the corporation has used no-par-value stock, only the number of shares changes.

Sometimes a stock split is accomplished in the form of a very large (for example, 100 percent) stock dividend. As explained earlier, when this happens, only the par or stated value of the additional shares issued is transferred from retained earnings to the common stock account. The par value of the stock is not adjusted.

Treasury Stock

Many corporations occasionally purchase shares of their own stock. The corporation can acquire as treasury stock any class of stock that is outstanding. Rather than being retired, this stock is held for future use for employee stock purchase plans, for acquisitions of other companies, or even to be resold for cash if additional capital is needed. Sometimes treasury stock is acquired as a defensive move to thwart a takeover by another company, and frequently a firm buys treasury stock with excess cash because the market price is low and the company's own stock is thought to be a good investment. Whatever the motivation, the purchase of treasury stock is in effect a partial liquidation of the firm, because the firm's assets are used to reduce the number of shares of stock outstanding. For this reason, treasury stock is not reflected in the balance sheet as an asset; it is reported as a contra owners' equity account (that is, treasury stock is deducted from the sum of paid-in capital and retained earnings).

Because treasury stock transactions are capital transactions (between the corporation and its stockholders), the purchase or sale of treasury stock never affects the income statement. When treasury stock is acquired, it is recorded at cost. When treasury stock is sold or issued, any difference between its cost and the consideration received is recorded in the additional paid-in capital account. As can be seen in Exhibit 9-1, Racers, Inc., purchased 1,000 shares of its own common stock at a total cost of $12,000 during the year ended August 31, 1996. The journal entry to record this purchase is as follows:

```
Dr.    Treasury stock.........................................................    12,000
    Cr.    Cash .............................................................        12,000
        Purchase 1,000 shares of treasury stock at a cost of $12 per share
```

The effect of this transaction on the financial statements is as follows:

Balance sheet		Income statement
Assets = Liabilities + Owners' equity	◄───	Net income = Revenues – Expenses

Cash	Treasury stock
–12,000	(A contra owners'
	equity account)
	–12,000)

If 500 shares of this treasury stock were sold at a price of $15 per share in fiscal 1997, the journal entry to record the sale would be as follows:

```
Dr.    Cash ........................................................................    7,500
    Cr.    Treasury stock ..................................................        6,000
    Cr.    Additional paid-in capital .....................................        1,500
        Sale of 500 shares of treasury stock at a price of $15 per share
```

The effect of this transaction on the financial statements is as follows:

Balance sheet		Income statement
Assets = Liabilities + Owners' equity	◄───	Net income = Revenues – Expenses

Cash	Treasury stock
+7,500	+6,000
	Additional paid-in
	+1,500

Cash dividends are not paid on treasury stock. However, stock dividends are issued on treasury stock, and stock splits affect treasury stock.

Cumulative Foreign Currency Translation Adjustment

When the financial statements of a foreign subsidiary are consolidated with those of its U.S. parent company, the financial statements of the subsidiary, originally expressed in the currency of the country in which it operates, must be converted to U.S. dollars. The conversion process is referred to as *foreign currency translation*. Because of the mechanics used in the translation process and because exchange rates fluctuate over time, a debit or credit difference between the translated value of the subsidiary's assets and liabilities and the translated value of the subsidiary's owners' equity arises in the translation and consolidation process. Before 1983, this debit or credit difference was reported as a loss or gain in the consolidated income statement. Because of large changes in exchange rates, a firm might have reported a large translation gain in one year and an equally large translation loss in the next year. The translation gain or loss had a material effect on reported results but did not have a significant economic effect because the gain or loss was never actually realized. The difference between the value of the subsidiaries as measured in U.S. dollars versus foreign currency units will *never* be converted to cash unless the foreign subsidiaries are sold. Therefore, the FASB issued an accounting standard that requires firms to report the translation gain or loss as a separate account within owners' equity rather than as a gain or loss in the income statement. The effect of this accounting standard was to make reported net income more meaningful and to highlight as a separate item in owners' equity the cumulative translation adjustment. To the extent that exchange rates of the U.S. dollar rise and fall relative to the foreign currencies involved, the amount of this **cumulative foreign currency translation adjustment** will fluctuate over time. This treatment of the translation adjustment is consistent with the going-concern concept because as long as the entity continues to operate with foreign subsidiaries, the translation adjustment will not be realized.

Reporting Changes in Owners' Equity Accounts

The reasons for changes to any owners' equity account during a fiscal period should be presented in the balance sheet, in a separate statement of changes in owners' equity, or in the footnotes or financial review accompanying the financial statements. One possible format for a statement of changes in owners' equity is presented for Racers, Inc., in Exhibit 9-5. Alternative formats may be used.

Even if the paid-in capital accounts do not change and there is no treasury stock or foreign subsidiary, an analysis of retained earnings is presented. This can be done in a separate statement, as illustrated for Racers, Inc., in Exhibit 9-6, or by appending the beginning balance, dividend, and ending balance information to the bottom of the income statement, which then becomes a combined statement of income and retained earnings.

In the Armstrong World Industries, Inc., Annual Report in the Appendix to this text's companion workbook and study guide, changes in shareholders' equity are presented in a footnote located on page 38. What approach is used in the other annual reports that you have?

Exhibit 9-5
Statement of Changes in Owners' Equity

RACERS, INC.
Statement of Changes in Owners' Equity
For the Year Ended August 31, 1996

	Preferred Stock		Common Stock		Additional Paid-in Capital	Retained Earnings	Common Treasury Stock	
	No. of Shares	$	No. of Shares	$	$	$	No. of Shares	$
Balance, Aug. 31, 1995	5,000	500,000	200,000	400,000	2,820,000	2,600,000	—	—
Sale of common stock			40,000	80,000	440,000			
Purchase of common treasury stock							1,000	12,000
Net income						390,000		
Cash dividends:								
Preferred stock						(30,000)		
Common stock						(60,000)		
Stock dividend:								
2% on 240,000 shares when market value was $15 per share			4,800	9,600	62,400	(72,000)		
Balance, August 31, 1996	5,000	500,000	244,800	489,600	3,322,400	2,828,000	1,000	12,000

Exhibit 9-6
Statement of Changes in Retained Earnings

RACERS, INC. Statement of Changes in Retained Earnings For the Year Ended August 31, 1996	
Retained earnings balance, beginning of year	$2,600,000
Add: Net income	390,000
Less: Cash dividends:	
Preferred stock	(30,000)
Common stock	(60,000)
2% stock dividend on common stock	(72,000)
Retained earnings balance, end of year	$2,282,000

Summary

This chapter described the accounting for and presentation of owners' equity accounts. Except for the fact that net income is added to retained earnings, transactions affecting owners' equity do not affect the income statement.

Owners' equity is also referred to as net assets. For single proprietorships and partnerships, the term capital is frequently used instead of owners' equity. For a corporation, the components of owners' equity are paid-in capital, retained earnings, treasury stock, and possibly the cumulative foreign currency translation adjustment and/or an unrealized loss on certain marketable securities.

Paid-in capital always includes common stock and may include preferred stock and additional paid-in capital. Common stock represents the basic ownership of the corporation. Common stock may have a par value or may be no par value. Additional paid-in capital represents the difference between the par (or stated) value of common stock issued and the total amount paid in to the corporation when the stock was issued. Additional paid-in capital is sometimes given the more descriptive caption "capital in excess of par (or stated) value." If no-par-value common stock has no stated value, the total amount paid in to the corporation when the stock was issued is reported as the dollar amount of common stock. The principal right and obligation of the common stockholders are to elect the board of directors of the corporation. Voting for directors can be on either a cumulative basis or a slate basis.

Preferred stock is different from common stock in that preferred has a prior claim to dividends and a prior claim on assets when the corporation is liquidated. In most cases, preferred stock does not have a voting privilege. Preferred stock is in some respects similar to bonds payable. However, the most significant difference between the two is that interest on bonds is a tax-deductible expense, and dividends on preferred stock are a nondeductible distribution of the corporation's earnings.

Retained earnings represent the cumulative earnings reinvested in the business. If earnings are not reinvested, they are distributed to stockholders as dividends. Retained earnings is not cash. The retained earnings account is increased by net income and decreased by dividends (and by a net loss).

Dividends are declared by the board of directors and paid to owners of the stock on the record date. Although cash dividends can be paid with any frequency, quarterly or semiannual dividend payments are most common in practice. Stock dividends represent the issuance of additional shares of stock to stockholders in proportion to the number of shares owned on the record date. Stock dividends do not affect the assets, liabilities, or total owners' equity of the firm but do result in the transfer of an amount of retained earnings to paid-in capital. Stock dividends are expressed as a percentage of the number of predividend shares outstanding and are usually relatively small (that is, less than 20 percent).

Stock splits also involve issuing additional shares of stock to stockholders in proportion to the number of shares owned on the record date but usually result in at least doubling the number of shares held by each stockholder. Stock splits are expressed as a ratio of the number of shares held after the split to the number held before the split (for example, two for one). The reason for (and effect of) a stock split is to reduce the market value per share of the stock.

Treasury stock is the corporation's own stock that has been purchased from stockholders and is being held in the treasury for future reissue. Treasury stock is reported as a contra owners' equity account. When treasury stock is reissued at a price different from its cost, no gain or loss is recognized, but paid-in capital is affected.

The cumulative foreign currency translation adjustment is an amount reported in owners' equity of corporations having foreign subsidiaries. The adjustment arises in the process of translating the financial statements of subsidiaries (expressed in foreign currency units) to U.S. dollars. Because exchange rates can fluctuate widely, net income could be distorted if this adjustment were reported in the income statement. To avoid this distortion, the adjustment is reported in owners' equity.

Owners' equity captions usually seen in a balance sheet are as follows:

- Paid-in capital:
    Common stock
    Preferred stock (optional)
    Additional paid-in capital
- Retained earnings (Deficit if negative)
- Cumulative foreign currency translation adjustment
- Less: Treasury stock

A firm may have only common stock (sometimes called capital stock) and retained earnings as components of owners' equity.

Changes in owners' equity are usually reported in a comprehensive statement that summarizes the changes of each element of owners' equity. However, if paid-in capital accounts have not changed significantly, a statement of changes in retained earnings may be presented by itself. Sometimes the statement of changes in retained earnings is combined with the income statement.

Refer to the Armstrong World Industries, Inc., balance sheet, the shareholders' equity analysis in the financial review in the Appendix to this text's companion workbook and study guide, and to other financial statements you have, and observe how information about owners' equity is presented.

Key Words and Phrases

additional paid-in capital (p. 272) The excess of the amount received from the sale of stock over the par (or stated) value of the shares sold.

authorized shares (p. 266) The number of shares of a class of stock authorized by the corporation's charter. The maximum number of shares the corporation can legally issue.

callable preferred stock (p. 271) Preferred stock that can be redeemed by the corporation at its option.

capital in excess of par value (p. 264) Another term for *additional paid-in capital.*

capital stock (p. 264) The aggregate par (or stated) value of the company's issued stock outstanding. Capital stock can be either common or preferred.

capitalizing retained earnings (p. 276) The transfer of retained earnings to paid-in capital that occurs when a stock dividend is declared.

common stock (p. 264) The class of stock that represents residual ownership of the corporation.

convertible preferred stock (p. 271) Preferred stock that can be converted to common stock of the corporation at the option of the stockholder.

cumulative dividend (p. 269) A feature of preferred stock that requires that any missed dividends be paid before dividends can be paid on common stock.

cumulative foreign currency translation adjustment (p. 280) A component of owners' equity arising from the translation of foreign subsidiary financial statements included in the consolidated financial statements.

cumulative voting (p. 267) A system of voting for the directors of a firm in which the number of votes that can be cast for one or more candidates is equal to the number of shares of stock owned multiplied by the number of directors to be elected.

declaration date (p. 277) The date a dividend is declared by the board of directors.

deficit (p. 274) Retained earnings with a negative (debit) balance.

dividend (p. 269) A distribution of earnings to the owners of a corporation.

ex-dividend date (p. 277) The date on and after which the buyer of a publicly traded stock will not receive a dividend that has been declared.

inside director (p. 265) A member of the firm's board of directors who is also an officer or employee of the firm.

issued shares (p. 266) The number of shares of a class of stock that has been issued (usually sold) to stockholders.

legal capital (p. 265) The amount associated with the capital stock that has been issued by a corporation. Legal capital is generally the par value or stated value of the shares issued.

liquidating value (p. 270) The stated claim of preferred stock if the corporation is liquidated. Sometimes called *redemption value.*

outside director (p. 265) A member of the firm's board of directors who is not also an officer or employee of the firm.

outstanding shares (p. 266) The number of shares of a class of stock held by stockholders.

par value (p. 265) An arbitrary value assigned to a share of stock when the corporation is organized. Sometimes used to refer to the stated value or face amount of a security.

participating dividend (p. 269) A feature of preferred stock that provides a right to preferred stockholders to receive additional dividends at a specified ratio after a base amount of dividends has been paid to common stockholders.

partners' capital (p. 262) The owners' equity in a partnership.

payment date (p. 277) The date a dividend is paid.

preemptive right (p. 266) The right of a stockholder to purchase shares from any additional share issuances in proportion to the stockholder's present percentage of ownership.

preferred stock (p. 268) The class of stock representing an ownership interest with certain preferences relative to common stock, usually including a priority claim to dividends.

proprietor's capital (p. 262) The owners' equity of an individual proprietorship.

record date (p. 277) The date used to determine the stockholders who will receive a dividend.

redemption value (p. 270) The stated claim of preferred stock if the corporation is liquidated. Sometimes called *liquidating value*.

retained earnings (p. 273) Cumulative net income that has not been distributed to the owners of a corporation as dividends.

slate voting (p. 267) A system of voting for the directors of a firm in which votes equal to the number of shares owned are cast for a single slate of candidates.

stated value (p. 265) An arbitrary value assigned to shares of no-par-value stock.

stock dividend (p. 275) A distribution of additional shares to existing stockholders in proportion to their existing holdings. The additional shares issued usually amount to less than 20 percent of the previously issued shares.

stock split (p. 277) A distribution of additional shares to existing stockholders in proportion to their existing holdings. The additional shares issued usually amount to 100 percent or more of the previously issued shares.

treasury stock (p. 266) Shares of a firm's stock that the firm has reacquired.

Chapter Notes

1. AICPA, *Accounting Trends and Techniques* (New York, NY: AICPA, 1994), Table 2-33.
2. AICPA, Table 2-32.

Chapter 10

Accounting for Revenues and Expenses

The income statement answers some of the most important questions that users of the financial statements have: What were the financial results of the entity's operations for the fiscal period? How much profit (or loss) did the firm have? Are sales increasing relative to cost of goods sold and other operating expenses? Chapters 6 through 9 introduced many income statement accounts and explained transactions also affecting asset and liability accounts. However, because of the significance of the net income figure to managers, stockholders, potential investors, and others, focusing on the form and content of this financial statement is appropriate.

Insurance professionals often need to assess the financial performance of prospective or existing insureds as part of the underwriting process to determine insurability, or as part of the claim process to determine a claim's validity and the amount of loss. Just as evaluating an entity's current assets related to its current liabilities provides a measure of the entity's liquidity or ability to meet current obligations, evaluating the amount by which an entity's revenue exceeds its expenses provides a measure of the entity's profitability or the effectiveness of asset use. This chapter focuses on the income statement and the statement of cash flows for noninsurance entities, and Chapter 11 examines those statements as they would be prepared by an insurance entity.

The income statement of Armstrong World Industries, Inc., is on page 25 of the annual report provided in the Appendix of this text's companion course workbook and study guide. That page of the annual report has been reproduced as Exhibit 10-1, which contains comparative statements for the years ended December 31, 1994, 1993, and 1992. A comparative statement, reporting two or more years' financial information together, permits the reader of the statement to assess quickly the recent trend of these important data. Armstrong has used an alternative name for the income statement—the statement of operations.

Exhibit 10-1
Income Statement

ARMSTRONG WORLD INDUSTRIES, INC., AND SUBSIDIARIES
Consolidated Statements of Operations
(millions except for per share data)

	Year Ended December 31		
	1994	*1993*	*1992*
Net sales	$2,752.7	$2,525.4	$2,549.8
Cost of goods sold	1,904.7	1,819.2	1,903.8
Gross profit	$ 848.0	$ 706.2	$ 646.0
Selling, general, and administrative expenses	514.8	493.6	506.6
Restructuring charges	—	89.9	165.5
Operating income (loss)	$ 333.2	$ 122.7	$ (26.1)
Interest expense	28.3	38.0	41.6
Other expense (income), net	.4	(6.0)	(7.3)
Earnings (loss) before income taxes	$ 304.5	$ 90.7	$ (60.4)
Income taxes	94.1	27.2	(.5)
Earnings (loss) before cumulative effect of accounting changes	$ 210.4	$ 63.5	$ (59.9)
Cumulative effect of changes in accounting for:			
Postretirement benefits, net of income tax benefit of $84.9	—	—	(135.4)
Postemployment benefits, net of income tax benefit of $20.9	—	—	(32.4)
Net earnings (loss)	$ 210.4	$ 63.5	$ (227.7)
Dividends paid on Series A convertible preferred stock	19.0	19.2	19.3
Tax benefit on dividends paid on unallocated preferred shares	4.9	5.3	5.5
Net earnings (loss) applicable to common stock	$ 196.3	$ 49.6	$ (241.5)

	Year Ended December 31		
	1994	*1993*	*1992*
Per share of common stock:			
Primary:			
Earnings (loss) before cumulative effect of accounting changes	$ 5.22	$ 1.32	$ (1.98)
Cumulative effect of changes in accounting for:			
Postretirement benefits	—	—	(3.64)
Postemployment benefits	—	—	(.87)
Net earnings (loss)	$ 5.22	$ 1.32	$ (6.49)
Fully diluted:			
Earnings (loss) before cumulative effect of accounting changes	$ 4.64	$ 1.26	$ (1.98)
Cumulative effect of changes in accounting for:			
Postretirement benefits	—	—	(3.64)
Postemployment benefits	—	—	(.87)
Net earnings (loss)	$ 4.64	$ 1.26	$ (6.49)

Armstrong's income statement includes several subtotals between "net sales" (revenues) and what is popularly referred to as the *bottom line*, which on this statement is labeled "net earnings." The principal objective of the first part of this chapter is to help you to make sense of the components of any income statement.

The second part of this chapter explores the statement of cash flows in more detail than presented in Chapter 2. Remember that this statement explains the change in the entity's cash from the beginning to the end of the fiscal period by summarizing the cash effects of the firm's operating, investing, and financing activities during the period.

Armstrong's comparative statements of cash flows are presented on page 27 of the companion workbook's Appendix for each of the past three years. The subtotal captions describe the activities—operating, investing, and financing—that caused cash to be provided and used during these years. Pay more attention to these three big-picture items than to the detailed captions and amounts within each category. Notice, however, that Armstrong uses a substantial amount of cash each year to purchase property, plant, and equipment (an investing activity) and to pay cash dividends (a financing activity). As explained later, these are both signs of a financially healthy firm, especially if the firm can cover these payments from its cash flows provided by operating activities. Did Armstrong have sufficient funds from its operating activities to cover its investing and financing activities for each year presented?

The income statement and statement of cash flows report what has happened for a *period of time* (usually, but not necessarily, for the fiscal year ended on the balance sheet date). The balance sheet is focused on a single *point in time*—usually the end of the fiscal year—but one can be prepared as of any date.

Educational Objectives

After studying this chapter, you should be able to:

1. Explain what revenue is and what the two criteria are that permit revenue recognition.

2. Explain how cost of goods sold is determined under both perpetual and periodic inventory accounting systems.

3. Explain the significance of gross profit (or gross margin) and how the gross profit (or gross margin) ratio is calculated and used.

4. Identify the principal categories of "other operating expenses," and explain how these items are reported on the income statement.

5. Describe how "income from operations" is determined, and explain why this income statement subtotal is significant to managers and financial analysts.

6. Describe the nature of the items that make up "other income and expenses."

7. Identify the components of the earnings per share calculation, and explain the reasons for some of the refinements made in that calculation.

8. Describe the unusual items that may appear on the income statement, including:
   - Discontinued operations
   - Extraordinary items
   - Minority interest in earnings of subsidiaries

9. Describe the alternative income statement presentation models.

10. Describe the purpose and general format of the statement of cash flows.

11. Explain why the statement of cash flows is significant to financial analysts and investors who rely on the financial statements for much of their evaluative data.

12. Define or describe each of the Key Words and Phrases introduced in this chapter.

Income Statement

As explained in Chapter 2, the purpose of the income statement is to answer this question: "Did the entity operate at a profit for the period of time under consideration?" The answer to that question is determined by subtracting from the entity's revenues the expenses incurred in generating those revenues.

Revenues

The FASB defines **revenues** as "inflows or other enhancements of assets of an entity or settlements of its liabilities (or a combination of both) from delivering or producing goods, rendering services, or other activities that constitute the entity's ongoing major or central operations."[1] In its simplest application, this definition means that when a firm sells a product or provides services to a client or customer and receives cash, creates an account receivable, or satisfies an obligation, the firm has revenue. Most revenue transactions fit this straightforward situation. Revenues are generally measured by the amount of cash received or expected to be received from the transaction. If the cash is not expected to be received within a year, then the revenue is usually measured by the present value of the amount expected to be received.

In *Concepts Statement No. 5*, the FASB expands on the above definition of revenues to provide guidance in applying the fundamental criteria involved in recognizing revenue. To be recognized, revenues must be realized or realizable and earned. Sometimes one of these criteria is more important than the other.

Realization means that the product or service has been exchanged for cash, claims to cash, or an asset that is readily convertible to a known amount of cash or claims to cash. Thus, the expectation that the product or service provided by the firm will result in a cash receipt has been fulfilled.

Earned means that the entity has completed or substantially completed the activities it must perform to be entitled to the revenue benefits (that is, the increase in cash or some other asset, or the satisfaction of a liability).

The realization and earned criteria for recognizing revenue are usually satisfied when the product or merchandise being sold is delivered to the customer or when the service is provided. Thus, revenue from selling and servicing activities is commonly recognized when the sale is made, which means when the product is delivered or when the service is provided to the customer.

An example of a situation in which the earned criterion is more significant than the realization criterion concerns a magazine publishing company that receives cash at the beginning of a subscription period. In this case, revenue is recognized as earned when the magazine is delivered. On the other hand, if a product is delivered or a service is provided without any expectation of receiving cash or satisfying a liability (that is, when a donation is made), no revenue is to be recognized because the realization criterion has not been fulfilled.

When revenues are related to the use of assets over a period of time—such as the renting of property or the lending of money—they are earned as time passes and recognized based on the contractual prices that had been established in advance.

Some agricultural products, precious metals, and marketable securities have readily determinable prices and can be sold without significant effort. If this is the case, revenues (and some gains or losses) may be recognized when production is completed or when prices of the assets change.

Because of the increasing complexity of many business activities and other newly developed transactions, several revenue recognition problems have arisen. Therefore, the FASB and its predecessors within the American Institute of Certified Public Accountants have issued numerous pronouncements about revenue recognition issues for various industries and transactions. As a result, revenue recognition is straightforward an overwhelming proportion of the time. However, since they are the key to the entire income statement, revenues that are misstated (usually on the high side) can lead to significantly misleading financial statements. Accordingly, management and internal auditors often design internal control procedures to help promote the accuracy of the revenue recognition process.

Sales is the term used to describe the revenues of firms that sell purchased or manufactured products. In the normal course of business, some sales transactions will be subsequently voided because the customer returns the merchandise for credit or for a refund. In some cases, rather than have a shipment returned (especially if it is only slightly damaged or defective and is still usable by the customer), the seller will make an allowance on the amount billed and reduce the account receivable from the customer for the allowance amount. If the customer has already paid, a refund is made. These **sales returns and allowances** are accounted for separately for internal control and analysis purposes but are subtracted from the gross sales amount to arrive at *net* sales. In addition, if the firm allows cash discounts for prompt payment, total cash discounts are also subtracted from gross sales for reporting purposes. A fully detailed income statement prepared for use within the company might have the following revenue section captions:

Sales	$
Less: Sales returns and allowances	( )
Less: Cash discounts	( )
Net sales	$

Net sales is the first caption usually seen in the income statement of a merchandising or manufacturing company (as illustrated in Exhibit 10-1). Many companies provide the detailed calculation of the net sales amount in the accompanying notes or financial review section of the annual report.

Firms that generate significant amounts of revenue from providing services in addition to (or instead of) selling a product label the revenue source appropriately in the income statement. Thus, a leasing company might report rental and service revenues as the lead item on its income statement, or a consulting service firm might show fee revenues, or simply fees. If a firm has several types of revenue, the amount of each could be shown if each amount is significant and the accountant concludes that it would increase the usefulness of the income statement.

From a legal perspective, the sale of a product involves the passing of title (that is, ownership rights) to the product from the seller to the purchaser. The point at which title passes is usually specified by the shipment terms (see Business Procedure Capsule 18—Shipping Terms). This issue becomes especially significant in two situations. The first involves shipments made near the end of a fiscal period. The shipping terms will determine whether revenue is recognized in the period in which the shipment was made or in the subsequent period if that is when the customer received the shipment. Achieving an accurate "sales cutoff" may be important to the accuracy of the financial statements if the period-end shipments are material in amount. The second situation relates to any loss or damage of the merchandise while it is in transit from the seller to the buyer. The legal owner of the merchandise, as determined by the shipping terms, is the one who suffers the loss. Of course, this party may then seek to recover the amount of the loss from the party responsible for the damage (usually a third-party shipping company).

<table>
<tr><td>

• **BUSINESS PROCEDURE CAPSULE 18**
  Shipping Terms

Many products are shipped from the seller to buyer instead of being picked up by the buyer at the time of sale. **Shipping terms** define the owner of products while they are in transit. **FOB destination** and **FOB shipping point** are the terms used to indicate that the product is owned by the party to whom it is being shipped or by the party from whom it was shipped, respectively. (FOB stands for *free on board* and is jargon that has carried over from the days when much merchandise was shipped by boat.) When an item is shipped FOB destination, the seller owns the product until the buyer accepts it at the buyer's designated location. Thus, title to merchandise shipped FOB destination passes from seller to buyer when the buyer receives the merchandise. FOB shipping point means that the buyer accepts ownership of the product at the seller's shipping location.

Shipping terms also describe which party to the transaction is to *incur* the shipping cost. The *seller* incurs the freight cost for shipments made FOB destination; the *buyer* incurs the cost for shipments made FOB shipping point. *Payment* of the freight cost is another issue, however. The seller pays the freight cost for products shipped **freight prepaid**; when a shipment arrives **freight collect**, the buyer pays the freight cost. Ordinarily, items shipped FOB destination will have freight prepaid, and items shipped FOB shipping point will be shipped freight collect. However, depending on freight company policies or other factors, an item having shipping terms of FOB destination may be shipped freight collect, or vice versa. If this happens, the firm paying the freight subsequently collects the amount paid to the freight company from the other firm, which *incurred* the freight cost under the shipping terms.

</td></tr>
</table>

For certain sales transactions, a firm may take more than a year to construct the item being sold (for example, a shipbuilder or a manufacturer of complex custom machinery). In these circumstances, delaying revenue recognition until the product has been delivered may result in the reporting of misleading income statement information for several years. Because these items are being manufactured under a contract with the buyer that specifies a price, revenue (and costs and profits) can be recognized under what is known as the **percentage-of-completion method**. If, based on engineers' analyses and other factors, 40 percent of a job has been completed in the current year, 40 percent of the expected revenue (and 40 percent of the expected costs) will be recognized in the current year.

Companies should disclose any unusual revenue recognition methods, such as the percentage-of-completion method, in the notes or financial review accompanying the financial statements. Because revenue directly affects profits, the user of the financial statements must be alert to and understand the effect of any revenue recognition method that differs from the usual and generally accepted practice of recognizing revenue when the product or service has been delivered to the customer.

Gains, which are increases in an entity's net assets resulting from incidental transactions or nonoperating activities, are usually not included with revenues at the beginning of the income statement. Gains are reported as other income after the firm's operating expenses have been shown and income from operations has been reported. Interest income is an example of an "other income" item. The reporting of gains will be explained in more detail later in this chapter.

Expenses

The FASB defines **expenses** as "outflows or other using up of assets or incurrences of liabilities (or a combination of both) from delivering or producing goods, rendering services, or carrying out other activities that constitute the entity's ongoing major or central operations."[2] Some expenses (cost of goods sold is an example) are recognized concurrently with the revenues to which they relate. This is another application of the **matching concept**, introduced in Chapter 2. Some expenses (administrative salaries, for example) are recognized in the period in which they are incurred because the benefit of the expense is used up simultaneously or soon after incurrence. Other expenses (depreciation, for example) result from an allocation of the cost of an asset to the periods that are expected to benefit from its use. In each of these categories, expenses are recognized in accordance with the matching principle because they are incurred to support the revenue-generating process. The amount of an expense is measured by the cash or other asset used up to obtain the economic benefit it represents. When the outflow of cash related to the expense will not occur within a year, the present value of the future cash flow should be recognized as the amount of the expense.

The identification of expenses to be recognized in the current period's income statement is usually straightforward. Cost of goods sold, compensation of employees, uncollectible accounts receivable, utilities consumed, and depreciation of long-lived assets are all examples of expenses easily identifiable for current period recognition. In other cases (research and development costs and advertising expense, for example), the effect of the expenditure on the revenues of future periods is not readily determinable. For those types of expenditures, there is no sound method of matching the expenditure with the revenues that may be earned over several periods. To avoid the necessity of making arbitrary allocations, all advertising and research and development expenditures are recorded as expenses in the period incurred. This approach is justified by the objectivity and conservatism concepts.

Other types of expense involve complex recognition and measurement issues. Income tax expense and pension expense are just two examples. Chapter 7 discussed the liabilities related to those expenses.

Losses, which are decreases in an entity's net assets resulting from incidental transactions or nonoperating activities, are not included with expenses. Losses are included with other income and expenses reported after income from operations, as discussed later in this chapter.

The discussion of expenses in this chapter follows the sequence in which expenses are presented in most income statements.

Cost of Goods Sold

Cost of goods sold is the most significant expense for many manufacturing and merchandising companies. Recall from the discussion of the accounting for inventories in Chapter 6 that the **inventory cost-flow assumption** that the firm uses (FIFO, LIFO, or weighted-average) affects this expense. **Inventory shrinkage,** the term that describes inventory losses from obsolescence, errors, and theft, is usually included in cost of goods sold unless the amount involved is material. In that case, the inventory loss would be reported separately as a loss after operating income has been reported.

Determination of the cost of goods sold amount is a function of the inventory cost-flow assumption and the inventory accounting system (periodic or perpetual) used to account for inventories. Recall that under a perpetual system, a record is made of every purchase and every sale, and a continuous record of the quantity and cost of each item is maintained. When an item is sold, its cost (as determined according to the cost-flow assumption) is transferred from the inventory asset to the cost of goods sold expense with the following entry:

Dr.	Cost of goods sold	xx
Cr.	Inventory	xx

The effect of this entry on the financial statements is as follows:

Balance sheet	Income statement
Assets = Liabilities + Owners' equity ←	Net income = Revenues – Expenses
–Inventory	–Cost of goods sold

The key point about a perpetual inventory system is that cost is determined when the item is sold. A perpetual inventory system requires much data processing but can give management a great deal of information about which inventory items are selling well and which are not. Computers have enabled many firms to adopt a perpetual inventory system. Regular counts of specific inventory items are made on a cyclical basis during the year, and actual quantities on hand are compared to the computer record of the quantity on hand. This is an internal control procedure designed to determine whether the perpetual system is operating accurately and to trigger an investigation of significant differences.

In a periodic inventory system, a count of the inventory on hand (a physical inventory) is made periodically—frequently at the end of a fiscal year—and the cost of inventory on hand (determined according to the cost-flow assumption) is determined. This cost is then subtracted from the sum of the cost of the beginning inventory (that is, the ending inventory of the prior period) and the cost of the merchandise purchased during the current period. (For a manufacturing firm, the cost of goods manufactured is used rather than purchases.) This **cost of goods sold model** is illustrated below using 1994 data from the Armstrong World Industries, Inc., financial statements in the Appendix to the workbook. Can you find the inventory amounts in the Appendix? All amounts are in millions of dollars.

	Cost of beginning inventory	$ 286.2
+	Net purchases	1,912.0
=	Cost of goods available for sale	$2,198.2
−	Cost of ending inventory...............................	(293.5)
=	Cost of goods sold	$1,904.7

The amounts shown for cost of goods sold, inventory, and net purchases include the price paid to the supplier plus all ordinary and necessary costs related to the purchase transaction (such as freight and material handling charges). Cost is reduced by the amount of any cash discount allowed on the purchase. When the periodic inventory system is used, freight charges, purchases discounts, and **purchases returns and allowances** (the purchaser's side of the sales return and allowance transaction) are usually recorded in separate accounts, and each account balance is classified with purchases. Thus, the net purchases amount is made up of the following:

Purchases	$
Add: Freight charges	
Less: Purchase discounts	( )
Less: Purchase returns and allowances	( )
Net purchases	$

Although the periodic system may require a less complicated record-keeping system than the perpetual system, the need to take a complete physical inventory to determine accurately the cost of goods sold is a disadvantage. Also, although it can be estimated or developed from special analysis, inventory shrinkage (losses from theft, errors, and so forth) is not really known when the periodic system is used because these losses are included in the total cost of goods sold.

Selling expenses (discussed later in the "Other Operating Expenses" section of this chapter) are *not* included as part of cost of goods sold.

Gross Profit or Gross Margin

The difference between sales revenue and cost of goods sold is **gross profit**, or **gross margin**. With data from Exhibit 10-1, the income statement for Armstrong World Industries, Inc., to this point is as follows:

ARMSTRONG WORLD INDUSTRIES, INC., AND SUBSIDIARIES
Consolidated Statements of Operations
(dollars in millions)

	Years Ended December 31		
	1994	1993	1992
Net sales	$2,752.7	$2,525.4	$2,549.8
Cost of goods sold	1,904.7	1,819.2	1,903.8
Gross profit	$ 848.0	$ 706.2	$ 646.0

When the amount of gross profit is expressed as a percentage of the sales amount, the resulting **gross profit ratio** (or **gross margin ratio**) is an especially important statistic for managers of merchandising firms. Exhibit 10-2 illustrates the calculation of the gross profit ratio for Armstrong World Industries, Inc., for 1994.

Because the gross profit ratio is a measure of the amount of each sales dollar that is available to cover operating expenses and profit, one of its principal uses is to estimate whether the firm is operating at a level of sales that will lead to profitability in the current period. If the firm is to be profitable, a certain gross profit ratio and level of sales must be achieved. Sales can be determined on a daily basis from cash register tapes or sales invoice records, and that amount can then be multiplied by the estimated gross profit ratio to determine the estimated gross profit amount. This amount can be related to estimated operating expenses to estimate the firm's income from operations. In many cases just knowing the amount of sales is enough to be able to estimate whether the firm has reached profitability. This is especially true for firms that have virtually the same gross profit ratio for every item sold. However, if the gross profit ratio differs by class of merchandise, as it usually does, then the proportion of the sales of each class to total sales (the **sales mix**) must be considered when estimating total gross profit. For example, if Armstrong World Industries, Inc., has a 20 percent gross profit ratio on floor coverings and a 40 percent gross profit ratio on furniture, and if the proportion of floor coverings and furniture sold each month changes, then the sales of both product categories must be considered to estimate total gross profit anticipated for any given month.

Exhibit 10-2
Gross Profit Ratio

ARMSTRONG WORLD INDUSTRIES, INC.
Gross Profit Ratio—1994
(dollars in millions)

Net sales	$2,752.7
Cost of goods sold	1,904.7
Gross profit (or gross margin)	$ 848.0

Gross profit ratio = Gross profit/Net sales
= $848.0 / $2,752.7
= 30.8%

The gross profit ratio can be used to estimate cost of goods sold and ending inventory for periods in which a physical inventory has not been taken. As illustrated in Exhibit 10-3, this is the process used to estimate the amount of inventory lost in a fire, a flood, or another natural disaster. The key to the calculation is the estimated gross profit ratio. Many firms prepare quarterly (or monthly) income statements for internal reporting purposes and use this estimation technique to avoid the cost and business interruptions associated with an inventory count.

Another important use of the gross profit ratio is to set selling prices. If the gross profit ratio required to achieve profitability at a given level of sales is known, the cost of the item can be divided by the complement of the gross profit ratio (or the cost of goods sold ratio) to determine the selling price. Exhibit 10-4 illustrates the relationship between sales and the gross profit ratio. Of course, competitive pressures, the manufacturer's recommended selling price, and other factors also influence the price finally established, but the desired gross profit ratio and the item's cost are frequently the starting points in the pricing decision.

Exhibit 10-3
Using the Gross Profit Ratio To Estimate
Ending Inventory and Cost of Goods Sold

Assumptions:

A firm expects to have a gross profit ratio of 30% for the current fiscal year. Beginning inventory is known because it is the amount of the physical inventory taken at the end of the prior fiscal year. Net sales and net purchases are known from the accounting records of the current fiscal period.

The model (with known data entered):

Net sales	$100,000	100%
Cost of goods sold:		
Beginning inventory	$ 19,000	
Net purchases	63,000	
Cost of goods available for sale	$ 82,000	
Less: Ending inventory	?	
Cost of goods sold	$?	
Gross profit	$?	30%

Calculation of Estimated Ending Inventory:

Gross profit = 30% × $100,000 = $30,000
Cost of goods sold = $100,000 − $30,000 = $70,000
Ending inventory = $82,000 − $70,000 = $12,000

Exhibit 10-4
Using Desired Gross Profit Ratio To Set Selling Price

Assumption:

A retail store's cost for a particular carpet is $8 per square yard. What selling price per square yard should be established for this product if a 20% gross profit ratio is desired?

Selling price = Cost of product / (1 − Desired gross profit ratio)
= $8 / (1 − 0.2)
= $10

Proof:

Calculated selling price...............................	$10 per square yard
Cost of product...	8 per square yard
Gross profit...	$ 2

$$\text{Gross profit ratio} = \text{Gross profit} / \text{Selling price}$$
$$= \$2 / \$10$$
$$= 20\%$$

The gross profit ratio required to achieve profitability varies among firms as a result of their operating strategies. For example, discount stores seek a high sales volume and a low level of operating expenses, so they expect a relatively low gross profit ratio. Boutiques, on the other hand, have a relatively low sales volume and higher operating expenses and need a relatively high gross profit ratio to achieve profitability.

Even though managers often use gross profit and the gross profit ratio, many companies do not present gross profit as a separate item in their published income statements. However, cost of goods sold is usually shown as a separate item. Thus, users of the income statement can make the calculation for comparative and other evaluation purposes.

Other Operating Expenses

The principal categories of other **operating expenses** frequently reported on the income statement are as follows:

- Selling expenses
- General and administrative expenses
- Research and development expenses

These categories can be combined in a variety of ways for financial reporting purposes. For instance, Armstrong World Industries, Inc., uses the single category "Selling, general, and administrative expenses."

The financial statement footnotes, or financial review, sometimes provide detailed disclosure of the nature and amount of expense items that are combined with others in the income statement. However, management often reports certain operating expenses as separate items to highlight their significance. Common examples include repairs and maintenance, research and development, and advertising. Total depreciation and amortization expense is frequently reported (or disclosed) as a separate item because these expenses do not result in the disbursement of cash. The total of depreciation and amortization expense also appears in the statement of cash flows, as will be illustrated later in this chapter.

Income From Operations

The difference between gross profit and operating expenses represents **income from operations** (or **operating income**), as shown in the following partial income statement from Exhibit 10-1:

ARMSTRONG WORLD INDUSTRIES, INC., AND SUBSIDIARIES
Consolidated Statements of Operations
(dollars in millions)

	Years Ended December 31		
	1994	1993	1992
Net sales	$2,752.7	$2,525.4	$2,549.8
Cost of goods sold	1,904.7	1,819.2	1,903.8
Gross profit	$ 848.0	$ 706.2	$ 646.0
Selling, general, & administrative expenses	514.8	493.6	506.6
Restructuring charges	—	89.9	165.5
Operating income (loss)	$ 333.2	$ 122.7	$ (26.1)

Although only an intermediate subtotal on the income statement, income from operations is frequently interpreted as the most appropriate measure of management's ability to use the firm's operating assets. Income from operations *excludes* the effects of interest expense, interest income, gains and losses, income taxes, and other nonoperating transactions. Thus, many investors prefer to use income from operations data (rather than net income data) to make a "cleaner" assessment of the firm's profitability trend. As discussed in Chapter 3, income from operations is frequently used in the return on investment calculation, which relates operating income to average operating assets.

Although operating income is commonly used as a proxy for net income, investors must pay careful attention to the items that are included in the determination of this important subtotal. In its 1994 annual report, Armstrong World Industries, Inc., reclassified the "restructuring charges" for 1992 and 1993 as an operating expense item. (These amounts were subtracted in the determination of operating income (loss) in Exhibit 10-1.) However, the restructuring charges were originally reported in the "other income and expense" category during 1992 and 1993 and thus were *not* subtracted in the determination of operating income during those years. Because these expenses were material in amount, the reclassification within the income statement had a significant effect on the *trend* of operating income over the three-year period. How much would Armstrong report as operating income for 1992 and 1993 if the restructuring charges were added back? What effect would this have on your evaluation of the 1994 results?

Managers of firms that do not report income from operations as a separate item believe that other income and expense items (that is, gains and losses) should receive as much attention in the evaluation process as revenues and expenses from the firm's principal operations. After all, nonoperating items do exist and do affect overall profitability. There is no single best presentation method for all firms; this is another area in which the accountant's judgment is used to select among equally acceptable financial reporting alternatives.

Other Income and Expenses

Other income and expenses are reported after income from operations. These nonoperating items include interest expense, interest income, gains, and losses.

Interest expense is the item of other income and expenses most frequently identified separately. Most financial statement users want to know the amount of this expense because it represents a contractual obligation that cannot be avoided. As discussed in Chapter 8, interest expense is associated with financial leverage. The more a firm borrows, the more interest expense it incurs, and the higher its financial leverage. Although increased financial leverage may lead to a greater return on equity (ROE) for stockholders, it also increases the riskiness of their investment.

Interest income earned from excess cash that has been temporarily invested is not ordinarily subtracted from interest expense. Interest income is reported as a separate item if it is material in amount relative to other nonoperating items. The full disclosure principle is applied to determine the extent of the details reported in this section of the income statement. Significant items that would facilitate the reader's understanding of net income or loss are separately identified, either in the statement itself or in the footnotes or financial review. Items that are not significant are combined in an "other" or "miscellaneous" category. Examples of nonoperating gains or losses are those resulting from litigation, the sale or disposal of depreciable assets (including plant closings), and inventory obsolescence losses.

Income Before Income Taxes and Income Tax Expense

The income statement usually has a subtotal labeled "**Income before income taxes**," followed by the caption "Income taxes" or "Provision for income taxes" and the amount of this expense. Some income statements do not use the "Income before income taxes" caption; income taxes are listed as another expense in these statements. There will almost always be a footnote or financial review disclosure of the details of the income tax expense calculation.

Net Income and Earnings per Share

Net income (or net loss), sometimes called *the bottom line*, is the sum of the revenues and gains minus the expenses and losses. Because net income increases retained earnings, which is a necessary prerequisite for dividends, stockholders and potential investors are especially interested in net income. Refer to Exhibit 10-1, and study the structure of income statements in other annual reports you have.

To facilitate interpretation of net income (or loss), it is also reported on a per-share of common stock basis. In its simplest form, **earnings per share (EPS)** is calculated by dividing net income by the average number of shares of common stock outstanding during the year. Two principal complications in the calculation should be understood. First, a weighted-average number of shares of common stock is used. This makes sense because if shares are issued early in the year, the proceeds from their sale have been used longer in the income-generating process than the proceeds from shares issued later in the year. The weighting basis usually used is the number of months that each block of shares has been outstanding. Exhibit 10-5 illustrates the weighted-average calculation.

The other complication in the EPS calculation arises when a firm has preferred stock outstanding. Preferred stockholders are entitled to their dividends before dividends can be paid on common stock. Because of this prior claim to earnings, the amount of the preferred stock dividend requirement is subtracted from net income to arrive at the numerator in the calculation of earnings per share of common stock outstanding. Dividends are not expenses, so the preferred stock dividend requirement is not shown as a deduction in the income statement. To illustrate the EPS calculation, assume that Cruisers, Inc., had net income of $1,527,000 for the year ended August 31, 1994, and had 80,000 shares of a 7 percent, $50 par value preferred stock outstanding during the year.

Exhibit 10-5
Weighted-Average Shares Outstanding Calculation

Assumptions:

On September 1, 1995, the beginning of its fiscal year, Cruisers, Inc., had 200,000 shares of common stock outstanding.

On January 3, 1996, 40,000 additional shares were issued for cash.

On June 25, 1996, 15,000 shares of common stock were acquired as treasury stock (and are no longer outstanding).

Weighted-average calculation:

Period	Number of Months	Number of Shares Outstanding	Months × Shares
9/1 - 1/3	4	200,000	800,000
1/3 - 6/25	6	240,000	1,440,000
6/25 - 8/31	2	225,000	450,000
Totals	12		2,690,000

Weighted-average number of shares outstanding = 2,690,000 / 12
= 224,167

With the weighted-average number of shares of common stock outstanding from Exhibit 10-5, the earnings per share of common stock would be calculated as follows:

Net income	$1,527,000
Less preferred stock dividend requirement (7% × $50 par value × 80,000 shares outstanding)	280,000
Net income available for common stock	$1,247,000

$$\text{Earnings per share of common stock outstanding} = \frac{\text{Net income available for common stock}}{\text{Weighted-average number of shares of common stock outstanding}}$$

$$= \frac{\$1,247,000}{224,167}$$

$$= \$5.56$$

In addition to the two principal complications just discussed, several other issues (not discussed here) can add to the complexity of the EPS calculation. The result of the calculation illustrated above is called *primary earnings per share.* Because of its significance, primary earnings per share of common stock outstanding is reported on the income statement just below the amount of net income. Note the presentation of primary earnings per share information in Exhibit 10-1.

In addition to primary earnings per share, a firm may be required to report *fully diluted earnings per share.* If the firm has issued long-term debt or preferred stock that is convertible to common stock, the conversion of the debt or preferred stock could result in a lower earnings per share of common stock outstanding. This can happen because the increase in net income available to the common stock (if interest expense is reduced, or if preferred dividends are not required) is proportionately less than the number of additional common shares issued in the conversion. The reduction in earnings per share of the common stock is referred to as **dilution.** If significant, the effect of the potential dilution is reported on the income statement by showing the fully diluted earnings per share of common stock as well as the primary earnings per share. Fully diluted earnings per share are calculated under the assumption that the convertible debt and/or preferred stock had been converted at the beginning of the year.

The income statement presentation of net income and EPS when potential dilution exists is shown below. (Data are from the previous Cruisers, Inc., illustrations, with an assumed fully diluted earnings per share amount.)

Net income	$1,527,000
Earnings per share of common stock:	
Primary	$5.56
Fully diluted	$4.98

As illustrated in the Armstrong World Industries, Inc., income statement in Exhibit 10-1, if any *unusual items* are reported on the income statement (discussed later in this chapter), the per-share amount of each item is disclosed, and EPS is the sum of EPS before the unusual items and the per-share amounts of the unusual items. This is done for both primary and fully diluted EPS data.

Income Statement Presentation Alternatives

There are two principal alternative presentations of income statement data: the **single-step format** and the **multiple-step format.** Exhibit 10-6 illustrates both using hypothetical data for Cruisers, Inc., for fiscal years 1995 and 1996. (Examples of the unusual items that may appear on the income statement will be discussed in the next section of this chapter and illustrated in Exhibit 10-7.) The single-step format does not provide subtotals for gross profit and income from operations, as are provided by the multiple-step format.

Exhibit 10-6
Income Statement Format Alternatives

I. Single-step format

CRUISERS, INC., AND SUBSIDIARIES
Consolidated Income Statement
For the Years Ended August 31, 1996, and 1995
(000 omitted)

	1996	*1995*
Net sales	$77,543	$62,531
Cost of goods sold	48,077	39,870
Selling expenses	13,957	10,590
General and administrative expenses	9,307	7,835
Interest expense	3,378	2,679
Other income (net)	385	193
Minority interest [explained later]	432	356
Income before taxes	$ 2,777	$ 1,394
Provision for income taxes	1,250	630
Net income	$ 1,527	$ 764
Earnings per share of common stock outstanding	$5.56	$2.42

II. Multiple-step format

CRUISERS, INC., AND SUBSIDIARIES
Consolidated Income Statement
For the Years Ended August 31, 1996, and 1995
(000 omitted)

	1996	*1995*
Net sales	$77,543	$62,531
Cost of goods sold	48,077	39,870
Gross profit	$29,466	$22,661
Selling, general, and administrative expenses	23,264	18,425
Income from operations	$ 6,202	$ 4,236
Other income (expense):		
Interest expense	(3,378)	(2,679)
Other income (net)	385	193
Minority interest	(432)	(356)
Income before taxes	$ 2,777	$ 1,394
Provision for income taxes	1,250	630
Net income	$ 1,527	$ 764
Earnings per share of common stock outstanding	$5.56	$2.42

Continued on next page.

The principal difference between these two formats is that the multiple-step format provides subtotals for gross profit and income from operations. As previously discussed, each of these amounts is useful in evaluating the performance of the firm, and proponents of the multiple-step format believe that these amounts should be highlighted.

You may notice an inconsistency in the use of parentheses in the single-step and multiple-step formats in Exhibit 10-6. No parentheses are used in the single-step format; the user is expected to know by reading the captions which items to add and which to subtract in the calculation of net income. In the multiple-step format, the caption for "Other income (expense)" indicates that *in this section of the statement*, items without parentheses are added and items in parentheses are subtracted. In other parts of the statement, the caption indicates the arithmetic operation. With either format, the reader must be alert to make sense of the information presented.

The recent trend has been for more companies to use the multiple-step income statement format. A survey of the annual reports for 1993 of 600 publicly owned industrial and merchandising companies indicated that only 199 companies continued to use the single-step format (as compared to 240 companies in the 1988 survey and 295 in 1984).[3] This trend apparently reflects the increasing complexity of business activities and the demand for more detailed information.

Unusual Items Sometimes Seen on an Income Statement

One of the ways that investors and potential investors use the income statement is to predict probable results of future operations from the results of current operations. Nonrecurring transactions that affect the predictive process are highlighted and reported separately from the results of recurring transactions. The reporting of unusual items also facilitates users' comparisons of net income for the current year with that of prior years. Two of the more frequently encountered unusual items relate to discontinued operations and extraordinary items. Other captions sometimes seen on an income statement relate to the cumulative effect of a change in the application of an accounting principle, or to the earnings of subsidiaries. *When any of these items affects income tax expense, the amount disclosed in the income statement is the amount of the item net of the income tax effect.*

Discontinued Operations

When a segment or major portion of a business is disposed of, the effect that the discontinued operation has had on the current operations of the firm should be disclosed separately. This separate disclosure is made to help users of the financial statements understand how future income statements may differ because the firm will be operating without the disposed business segment. This is accomplished by reporting the income or loss, after income taxes, of the discontinued operation separately after a subtotal amount labeled **income from continuing operations**. Income from continuing operations is the income after income taxes of continuing operations. The effect of this reporting is to exclude all of the effects of the discontinued operation from the revenues, expenses, gains, and losses of continuing operations. Exhibit 10-7 illustrates this presentation. Earnings per share data are also reported separately for discontinued operations.

Exhibit 10-7
Income Statement Presentation of Unusual Items

Under either the single-step or multiple-step format (see Exhibit 10-6), the "Income before taxes" caption would be shown as "Income *from continuing operations* before taxes," and the rest of the income statement would appear as follows:

	1996	1995
Income from continuing operations before taxes ...	$2,777	$1,394
Provisions for income taxes	1,250	630
Income from continuing operations	$1,527	$ 764
Discontinued operations, net of income taxes:		
Loss from operations	(162)	—
Loss on disposal	(79)	—
Loss from discontinued operations	$ (241)	—
Earnings before extraordinary item	$1,286	$ 764
Extraordinary item:		
Gain on termination of pension plan, net of income taxes	357	—
Net income	$1,643	$ 764
Earnings per share of common stock outstanding:		
Continuing operations	$ 5.56	$ 2.42
Discontinued operations:		
Loss from operations	(.72)	—
Loss on disposal	(.35)	—
Extraordinary item	1.59	—
Net income	$ 6.08	$ 2.42

Note: The cumulative effect of a change in accounting principle would appear after extraordinary items and would be reported net of tax. EPS disclosure would also be required.

Extraordinary Items

A transaction that is unusual in nature and occurs infrequently qualifies for reporting as an **extraordinary item** if the amount involved has a significant after-tax income statement effect. The reason for such separate reporting is to emphasize that the item is extraordinary and that the income statements for subsequent years are not likely to include this kind of item. Examples of extraordinary items are gains or losses from early repayment of long-term debt, pension plan terminations, some litigation settlements, and the use of tax loss carryforwards (see Business Procedure Capsule 19—Tax Loss Carryovers).

When an extraordinary item is reported, earnings per share of common stock outstanding are reported for income before the extraordinary item, for the extraordinary item, and for net income (after the extraordinary item). Exhibit 10-7 also illustrates this presentation.

Minority Interest in Earnings of Subsidiaries

As explained in Chapter 7, the financial statements of a subsidiary are consolidated with those of the parent even if the parent owns less than 100 percent of the stock of the subsidiary. The consolidated income statement includes all of the revenues, expenses, gains, and losses of the subsidiary. However, only the parent company's equity in the subsidiary's earnings is included in consolidated net income. The minority share owners' equity in the subsidiary's earnings is reported in the consolidated income statement as a deduction from income after income taxes when this minority interest is significant. When the **minority interest in the earnings of the subsidiary** is not significant, this deduction is included with other income and expense.

Cumulative Effect of a Change in Accounting Principle

A change from one generally accepted principle or method to another (from straight-line to accelerated depreciation, for example) is permitted only if a standard-setting body (such as the FASB) has promulgated a change, or if the change can be justified by the entity based on its current economic circumstances. The cumulative effect of the change on the reported net income of prior years, net of any income tax effect, is reported in the income statement for the year of the change. This amount is reported at the bottom of the income statement, after income from continuing operations and any other unusual items. Income statements of prior years that are presented for comparative purposes are not revised to reflect the change; however, the effect that the change would have had on those years is disclosed in the explanatory notes to the financial statements (see Chapter 12). An exception to this procedure occurs for some changes mandated by the FASB, for which restatement of prior years' financial statements is required. In these cases, the cumulative effect of the change is reflected in the beginning retained earnings balance of the earliest year presented in the comparative financial statements. Note in Exhibit 10-1 that Armstrong World Industries, Inc., reported the cumulative effect of a change in accounting for postretirement and postemployment benefits that occurred in 1992. The change reflected the requirements of new financial accounting standards issued by the FASB that Armstrong World Industries, Inc., had implemented. (The new financial accounting standards were discussed in Chapter 7, in the section on other long-term liabilities.)

• **BUSINESS PROCEDURE CAPSULE 19**
  Tax Loss Carryovers

The Internal Revenue Code provides that a business that experiences an operating loss in any year can offset that loss against profits that have been earned in the past or that may be earned in the future. Accordingly, the firm can recover the income taxes that were paid in the past or escape taxation on the future profits. Generally speaking, losses can be carried back three years and carried forward for fifteen years. To illustrate, assume the following pattern of operating income and losses for a firm that began business in 1991:

	1991	1992	1993	1994	1995
Operating income (loss)	$50,000	$30,000	$(100,000)	$(40,000)	$70,000

The corporation would have paid taxes in 1991 and 1992 based on its income in those years. In 1993, no taxes would be payable because the firm operated at a loss. Under the **tax loss carryover** rules, $50,000 of the 1993 loss would be carried back to 1991, $30,000 of the 1993 loss would be carried back to 1992, and the taxes previously paid in each of those years would be refunded to the corporation. The remaining $20,000 of "unused" loss from 1993 would be carried forward to be offset against profits of the next fifteen years. No taxes would be payable in 1994 because of the loss in that year, but there would be no carryback of that loss because the 1993 carryback absorbed the 1991 and 1992 profits; the 1994 loss would be carried forward. In 1995, the $70,000 of profits would be reduced by the $20,000 loss carryforward from 1993 and the $40,000 loss carryforward from 1994, so only $10,000 of 1995 profits would be subject to tax.

In the income statement, it is desirable to relate income tax expense, or recovery of income taxes previously paid, to results from operations. Thus, for the firm in the example, income tax expense for 1991 and 1992 would be reported in the usual way, as illustrated below. In the 1993 income statement,

Continued on next page.

the income tax refund from 1991 and 1992 would be shown as an income tax recovery, or negative tax expense. The potential income tax reduction in the future from the carryforward is not reflected in the financial statements because it will not be realized unless profits are earned in the future. The 1994 income statement will not show either expense or potential future reduction of income taxes. The 1995 income statement will reflect income tax expense based on pre-tax income of $70,000; then, the tax reduction because of the $60,000 of loss carryover would be reported as an extraordinary item in 1995.

The income tax expense (recovery) for each year would be reported as follows, assuming an income tax rate of 40%:

	1991	1992	1993	1994	1995
Operating income (loss) before taxes ..	$50,000	$30,000	$(100,000)	$(40,000)	$70,000
Income tax expense/ (recovery)	20,000	12,000	(32,000)	—	28,000
Net income (loss)	$30,000	$18,000	$ (68,000)	$(40,000)	$42,000
For 1995 only: Extraordinary item: Utilization of tax loss carryforward					24,000
Net income					$66,000

(Note: The income statement caption for the $42,000 amount reported in 1995 would be "Earnings before extraordinary item.")

Statement of Cash Flows

Chapter 2 described the purpose of the statement of cash flows as to identify an entity's sources and uses of cash during the year. The following discussion explains the development of the statement of cash flows and two approaches to presenting an entity's cash flow information.

Content and Format of the Statement

The **statement of cash flows** (and its predecessor, the statement of changes in financial position) is a relatively new financial statement that illustrates how accounting evolves to meet the requirements of users of financial statements. The importance of understanding an entity's cash flows has been increasingly emphasized over the years. The accrual basis income statement is not designed to present cash flows from operations, and, except for related revenues and expenses, it shows no information about cash flows from investing and financing activities.

In the early 1960s, some companies began presenting information about changes in balance sheet items. In 1963, the Accounting Principles Board of the AICPA recommended that this statement be called the *statement of source and application of funds*. The term *funds* usually meant working capital (that is, current assets minus current liabilities), and this statement explained the change in working capital that had occurred between the dates of the balance sheets presented in the annual report. In 1971, the Accounting Principles Board made the statement mandatory and gave it the title "Statement of Changes in Financial Position." In 1987, the FASB issued a standard requiring the presentation of a statement of cash flows, which has replaced the statement of changes in financial position.

The primary purpose of the statement of cash flows is to provide relevant information about the cash receipts and cash payments of an enterprise during a period.[4] The statement shows why cash (including short-term investments that are essentially equivalent to cash) changed during the period by reporting net cash provided or used by operating activities, investing activities, and financing activities.

There are two alternative approaches to presenting the statement of cash flows—the *direct-method presentation* and the *indirect-method presentation*. The direct method involves listing each major class of cash receipts transactions and cash disbursements transactions for each of the three activity areas. The operating activity transactions include cash received from customers, cash paid to merchandise or raw material suppliers, cash paid to employees for salaries and wages, cash paid for other operating expenses, cash payments of interest, and cash payments for taxes. Section I of Exhibit 10-8 contains a direct-method statement of cash flows. Under the direct method, each of the captions reported on the statement explains how much cash was received or paid during the year for that item. For this reason, the FASB standard encourages enterprises to use the direct method.

Exhibit 10-8
Statement of Cash Flows

I. Direct method

CRUISERS, INC., AND SUBSIDIARIES
Consolidated Statements of Cash Flows
For the Years Ended August 31, 1996, and 1995
(000 omitted)

	1996	1995
Cash flows from operating activities:		
Cash received from customers..................	$14,929	$13,021
Cash paid to suppliers	6,784	8,218
Payment for compensation of employees .	2,137	1,267
Other operating expenses paid.................	1,873	1,002
Interest paid..	675	703
Taxes paid...	1,037	532
Net cash provided by operating activities .	$ 2,423	$ 1,299
Cash flows from investing activities:		
Proceeds from sale of land	$ —	$ 200
Investment in plant and equipment	(1,622)	(1,437)
Net cash used for investing activities	$ (1,622)	$ (1,237)
Cash flows from financing activities:		
Additional long-term borrowing	$ 350	$ 180
Payment of long-term debt	(268)	(53)
Purchase of treasury stock	(37)	(26)
Payment of dividends on capital stock	(363)	(310)
Net cash used for financing activities.......	$ (318)	$ (209)
Increase (Decrease) in cash...........................	$ 483	$ (147)
Cash balance, August 31, 1995, and 1994	276	423
Cash balance, August 31, 1996, and 1995	$ 759	$ 276
Reconciliation of net income and		
net cash provided by operating activities:		
Net income	$ 1,390	$ 666
Add (Deduct) items not affecting cash:		
Depreciation expense	631	526
Minority interest....................................	432	356
Gain on sale of land	—	(110)
Increase in accounts receivable	(30)	(44)
Increase in inventories	(21)	(168)
Increase in current liabilities	16	66
Other (net)	5	7
Net cash provided by operating activities	$ 2,423	$ 1,299

II. Indirect method

CRUISERS, INC., AND SUBSIDIARIES
Consolidated Statements of Cash Flows
For the Years Ended August 31, 1996, and 1995
(000 omitted)

	1996	1995
Cash flows from operating activities:		
Net income	$ 1,390	$ 666
Add (Deduct) items not affecting cash:		
Depreciation expense	631	526
Minority interest.................................	432	356
Gain on sale of land	—	(110)
Increase in accounts receivable	(30)	(44)
Increase in inventories	(21)	(168)
Increase in current liabilities	16	66
Other (net)	5	7
Net cash provided by operating activities .	$ 2,423	$ 1,299
Cash flows from investing activities:		
Proceeds from sale of land	$ —	$ 200
Investment in plant and equipment	(1,622)	(1,437)
Net cash used for investing activities	$(1,622)	$(1,237)
Cash flows from financing activities:		
Additional long-term borrowing	$ 350	$ 180
Payment of long-term debt	(268)	(53)
Purchase of treasury stock	(37)	(26)
Payment of dividends on capital stock	(363)	(310)
Net cash used for financing activities........	$ (318)	$ (209)
Increase (Decrease) in cash	$ 483	$ (147)
Cash balance, August 31, 1995, and 1994	276	423
Cash balance, August 31, 1996, and 1995	$ 759	$ 276

The indirect method explains the change in cash by explaining the change in each of the noncash accounts in the balance sheet. A statement of cash flows prepared this way shows net income as the first source of operating cash. However, net income is determined on the accrual basis and must be adjusted for revenues and expenses that do not affect cash. The most significant noncash income statement items are usually total depreciation and amortization expense. Recall the journal entries to record these items:

Dr.		Depreciation expense...	xx	
	Cr.	Accumulated depreciation		xx

and

Dr.		Amortization expense	xx	
	Cr.	Intangible asset		xx

The effects of these transactions on the financial statements are as follows:

Balance sheet	Income statement
Assets = Liabilities + Owners' equity ◄——	Net income = Revenues – Expenses
–Accumulated depreciation	–Depreciation expense
and	
–Intangible asset	–Amortization expense

Therefore, the depreciation and amortization expense amounts reported on the income statement are added back to net income to determine more accurately the amount of cash generated from operations. Other income statement items that need to be considered in a similar way are the following:

- Income tax expense not currently payable (that is, deferred income taxes resulting from temporary differences in the recognition of revenues and expenses for book and tax purposes).

- Gains or losses on the sale or abandonment of assets. The *proceeds* from the sale, not the gain or loss, affect cash. Losses are added back to net income, and gains are subtracted from net income. The sale proceeds are reported as an investing activity, described below.

- Increases (or decreases) to interest expense that result from the amortization of discount (or premium) on bonds payable. Discount amortization is added back to net income, and premium amortization is subtracted from net income.

Changes in the noncash accounts must also be shown. Thus, increases in current assets and decreases in current liabilities are reported as operating uses of cash. Conversely, decreases in current assets and increases in current liabilities are reported as operating sources of cash. Section II of Exhibit 10-8 illustrates an indirect-method statement of cash flows.

Investing activities relate to the purchase and sale of noncurrent assets. Cash is often used for the acquisition of assets such as land, buildings, or equipment during the year (these investments are sometimes called *capital additions*). Investments in debt or equity securities of other entities are also shown as investing uses. Likewise, cash received from the sale of noncurrent assets is shown as an investing source of cash.

Financing activities relate to changes during the year in noncurrent liabilities (such as bonds payable) and in owners' equity accounts. Thus, the issuance of bonds or common stock will result in a financing source of cash, and the retirement of bonds will be reported as a financing use. Cash dividends and treasury stock transactions are also reported as financing activities because they affect owners' equity.

The difference between the two methods is in the presentation of cash flows from operating activities. When the direct-method format is used, a separate schedule reconciling net income reported on the income statement with net cash provided by operating activities is required. This reconciliation is in the form of the indirect-method presentation of net cash provided by operating activities. A survey of the 1993 annual reports of 600 publicly owned merchandising and manufacturing companies indicated that 585 firms used the indirect-method presentation, and 15 companies used the direct-method presentation.[5] Business Procedure Capsule 20 explains the cash flow relationships under the indirect method in more detail.

Interpreting the Statement of Cash Flows

The statement of cash flows focuses on cash receipts and cash payments during the period, so the first question to be answered is, "Did the company's cash balance increase or decrease during the year?" The answer is usually found near the bottom of the statement. In the annual report of a publicly owned corporation, comparative statements for the most recent and prior two years are presented, and the change in each of the three years can be noted. If the change in the cash balance during a year has been significant (more than 10 percent of the beginning cash balance), the financial statement user will try to understand the reasons for the change by focusing on the relative totals of each of the three categories of cash flows—operating activities, investing activities, and financing activities. Even if the change in the cash balance during a year is not significant, the user will observe the relationship between these broad categories.

- **BUSINESS PROCEDURE CAPSULE 20**
  Understanding Cash Flow Relationships—Indirect Method

As the AICPA study indicated, most firms report the statement of cash flows using the indirect method. Most statements of changes in financial position prepared before 1988 also used the indirect method. The primary reason for this preference is that no separate accounting procedures are needed for companies to accumulate cash flows data when the indirect method is used. The statement

---

Continued on next page.

of cash flows is normally prepared by using balance sheet and income statement data and other information readily available in the company's accounting records. However, the operating activities information reported under the direct method is not so readily determinable, and the cost of generating this information can be prohibitive.

The primary objective of the operating activities section of the statement of cash flows (indirect method) is to determine the net cash provided by operating activities. Although net income is determined on an accrual basis, it is ordinarily the most accurate proxy for operating cash flows and thus serves as the starting point in the calculation of this important amount. *However, none of the adjustments shown in the operating activities section (indirect method) explain how much cash was actually received or paid during the year.* The only operating activity items that convey independent meaning are the amounts shown for net income and net cash provided by operating activities. Review the operating activities section of Exhibit 10-8 for the indirect method. Notice, for example, that accounts receivable increased during both years presented. Does this explain how much cash was received from the collection of accounts receivable during these years? (No, but the direct method shows these amounts.) Once you understand this, the adjustment process for the indirect method is very straight-forward.

Net income is initially assumed to generate operating cash, and this assumption is then adjusted for the effects of noncash (or nonoperating) income statement items. As already explained, the amounts shown for depreciation and amortization expense will be added back to net income each year because cash is never paid for these expenses. Similar adjustments would be made to remove the effects of noncash revenues or to remove the effects of most nonoperating transactions included in net income. Once these income statement adjustments are made, the current (that is, *operating*) accounts on the balance sheet must be analyzed to determine their effects on cash during the year. To simplify the analysis, assume that all changes in account balances from the beginning to the end of the year are attributable to cash transactions. If inventory (a current asset) increased during the year, then cash must have decreased (to pay for the increase in inventory). The assumed transaction would be as follows:

Dr.	Inventory	xx	
	Cr.	Cash	xx

Likewise, if short-term debt (a current liability) increased during the year, then cash must have increased (for the receipt of the loan proceeds), as follows:

Dr.	Cash	xx	
	Cr.	Short-term debt	xx

The financial statement effects of these assumed transactions would be as follows:

Balance sheet	Income statement
Assets = Liabilities + Owners' equity ⟵	Net income = Revenues – Expenses

Increase in the Inventory account balance:
+Inventory
–Cash

Increase in the Short-term account balance:
+Cash   +Short-term
             debt

In a similar way, decreases in current asset accounts are assumed to increase cash (for example, the collection of an accounts receivable), and decreases in current liability accounts are assumed to decrease cash (for example, the payment of an account payable). Of course, these are only assumptions, but by assuming that cash is involved on the opposite side of every transaction, you will understand the nature of each of the adjustments made within the operating activities section of the statement of cash flows.

A firm should have a positive cash flow provided by operating activities. If operating activities do not generate cash, the firm will have to seek outside funding to finance its day-to-day activities, as well as its investment requirements. Although negative cash flow from operating activities might apply to a firm just starting up, it would be a sign of possible financial weakness for a mature company.

Virtually all financially healthy firms have growth in revenues as a financial objective. This growth usually requires increasing capacity to manufacture or sell products, or to provide services. Thus, a principal investing activity is the acquisition of plant and equipment. The total cash used for investing activities should be compared to the total cash provided by operating activities as a test that cash provided by operating activities exceeds cash used for investing activities. If total cash from operating activities exceeds total cash used for investing activities, the indication is that the firm is generating the cash it needs to finance its growth, and that is probably positive. If the cash used for investing activities exceeds the cash provided by operating activities, the difference will have to be provided by financing activities or come from the cash balance carried forward from the prior year. This is not necessarily negative, because investment requirements in any one year may be unusually high. If, however, cash used for investing activities exceeds cash provided by operating activities year after year and the difference is provided from financing activities, a question about the firm's ability to generate additional funds from financing activities must be raised.

Financing activities include the issue and repayment of debt, the sale of stock and purchase of treasury stock, and the payment of dividends on stock (although some companies report cash dividends separately in the reconciliation of beginning and ending cash). Most companies want to have the cash dividend covered by the excess of cash provided from operating activities over cash used for investing activities.

The details of each category of cash flows contain clues that will explain any overall change. For example, if cash flows provided by operating activities are less than cash used for investing activities, or if operating cash flows are decreasing even though profits are increasing, accounts receivable and/or inventories may be increasing at a higher rate than sales. This is a signal that the firm may have liquidity problems that would not necessarily be reflected by the change in working capital, the current ratio, or the acid-test ratio. These liquidity measures include other items besides cash, and the firm's inability to collect its accounts receivable and/or sell its inventory may artificially increase current assets and distort these relationships. Of course, other interpretations of this same trend might also be possible, but the trend itself might not have been observed without a careful analysis of cash flow data.

The details of an entity's investing activities frequently describe its growth strategy. Besides investing in more plant and equipment, some firms acquire capacity by purchasing other companies or by investing in the securities of other companies. Occasionally a firm will sell some of its plant and equipment, in which case cash is provided. The reasons for and consequences of such a sale of assets are of interest to financial statement users.

To illustrate these interpretation techniques, refer to the Armstrong World Industries, Inc., Consolidated Statements of Cash Flows on page 27 of the annual report in the Appendix to this text's companion course workbook and study guide. Even though the company suffered a substantial net loss in 1992, the cash flows provided by operating activities were positive. Note the large add-backs to the 1992 net loss for noncash expenses and losses (that is, depreciation and amortization expense, loss from restructuring activities, and loss from cumulative effect of changes in accounting). Although reporting these expenses and losses on the accrual-based income statement was appropriate, the company did not incur out-of-pocket costs for these items. In fact, the cash provided by operating activities exceeded cash used for investing activities in all three years—a relationship generally considered desirable. In

1994, the company purchased considerably more property, plant, and equipment than in either of the previous two years. In all three years, financing activities resulted in a net use of cash, with the repayment of short-term debt being a significant use in 1993 and 1994. In 1992 short-term debt increased, but this was more than offset by the reduction of long-term debt. Cash dividends were paid in all three years, and the overall picture for Armstrong World Industries, Inc., is good. Cash provided by operating activities is covering investment requirements and cash dividends.

The statement of cash flows provides useful information for owners, managers, employees, suppliers, potential investors, and others interested in the economic activities of the entity. This statement provides information that is difficult, if not impossible, to obtain from the other three financial statements alone.

Summary

This chapter described the income statement and the statement of cash flows. The income statement summarizes the results of the firm's profit-generating or loss-generating activities for a fiscal period. The statement of cash flows explains the change in the firm's cash from the beginning to the end of the fiscal period by summarizing the cash effects of the firm's operating, investing, and financing activities during the period.

Revenues are reported at the beginning of the income statement. Revenues result from the sale of a product or the provision of a service, not necessarily from the receipt of cash. The revenues of most manufacturing and merchandising firms are called sales. Net sales, which is gross sales minus sales returns and allowances and cash discounts, is usually the first caption of the income statement. Service entities describe the source of their revenues (for example, rental fees or consulting fees).

Expenses are subtracted from revenues in the income statement. A significant expense for many firms is cost of goods sold. The actual calculation of cost of goods sold is determined by the system used to account for inventories. With a perpetual inventory system, cost can be determined and recognized when a product is sold. With a periodic inventory system, cost of goods sold is calculated at the end of the fiscal period using beginning and ending inventory amounts and the purchases (or cost of goods manufactured) amount. Sometimes cost of goods sold is reported separately and subtracted from net sales to arrive at gross profit or gross margin in what is called a multiple-step income statement presentation. Other firms include cost of goods sold with operating expenses in a single-step income statement presentation.

Gross profit (or gross margin) is frequently expressed as a ratio. The gross profit ratio can be used to monitor profitability, to set selling prices, or to estimate ending inventory and cost of goods sold.

Selling, general, and administrative expenses are the costs of operating the firm. They are deducted from gross profit to arrive at operating income, an important measure of management performance.

Interest expense is usually shown as a separate item in the other income and expense category of the income statement. Other significant gains or losses are also identified.

Income before income taxes is frequently reported as a subtotal before income tax expense is shown because this expense is a function of all income statement items reported to that point in the statement.

Net income, or net earnings, is reported in total and on a per share of outstanding common stock basis. If there is a significant potential dilution from convertible debt or preferred stock, earnings per share on a fully diluted basis are also reported.

To facilitate users' comparisons of net income with that of prior years and to provide a basis for future expectations, income or loss from discontinued operations and extraordinary items are reported separately in the income statement.

The determination of cash flows from operating activities is essentially a conversion of the accrual accounting income statement to a cash basis income statement. The principal reasons net income does not affect cash directly are that not all accounts receivable from sales are collected in the fiscal period of the sale and that not all of the expenses reported in the income statement result in the disbursement of cash in the fiscal period in which the expenses are incurred.

Investing activities include purchases of plant and equipment, investments in other companies, and possibly the sale of noncurrent assets.

Financing activities include issuance and redemption of bonds and stock, including treasury stock transactions, and cash dividends on stock.

The statement of cash flows shows the change in cash during the year and reports cash provided from or used by operating activities, investing activities, and financing activities.

There are two presentation formats for the statement of cash flows, the direct method and the indirect method. The difference between the two is primarily in the presentation of cash flows from operating activities. Most entities use the indirect method.

Interpretation of the statement of cash flows involves observing the relationship between the three broad categories of cash flows (operating activities, investing activities, and financing activities) and the change in the cash balance for the year. Cash should be provided from operating activities that is equal to or greater than cash used for investing activities, although large investment requirements in any one year may reduce the beginning-of-the-year cash balance. Cash can also be raised from financing activities to offset large investment requirements. The detailed activities of each cash flow category are reviewed to assess their effect on the overall cash position of the firm. The statement of cash flows provides important information that is not easily obtained from the other financial statements.

Refer to the income statement and statement of cash flows for Armstrong World Industries, Inc., in the Appendix to this text's course workbook and study guide and to these statements in other annual reports you have to observe content and presentation alternatives.

Key Words and Phrases

cost of goods sold (p. 296) Cost of merchandise sold during the period; an expense deducted from net sales to arrive at gross profit.

cost of goods sold model (p. 297) The formula for calculating cost of goods sold by adding beginning inventory and purchases and subtracting ending inventory.

dilution (p. 306) The reduction in "earnings per share of common stock" that may occur if convertible securities are actually converted to common stock.

earned (p. 291) A revenue recognition criterion that relates to completion of the revenue-generating activity.

earnings per share (EPS) (p. 304) Net income available to common stockholders divided by the average number of shares of common stock outstanding during the period.

expenses (p. 295) Outflows or other using up of assets or incurrences of liabilities during a period from delivering or producing goods, rendering services, or carrying out other activities that constitute the entity's major operations.

extraordinary item (p. 310) A gain or loss from a transaction that both is unusual and occurs infrequently; it is reported separately in the income statement.

FOB destination (p. 294) The shipping term that means that title passes from seller to buyer when the merchandise arrives at its destination.

FOB shipping point (p. 294) The shipping term that means that title passes from seller to buyer when the merchandise leaves the seller's premises.

freight collect (p. 294) A freight payment alternative meaning that freight is payable when the merchandise arrives at its destination.

freight prepaid (p. 294) A freight payment alternative meaning that the shipper pays freight.

gains (p. 295) Increases in net assets from incidental transactions and other events affecting an entity during a period, except those that result from revenues or investments by owners.

gross margin (p. 298) Another term for *gross profit*.

gross margin ratio (p. 298) Another term for *gross profit ratio*.

gross profit (p. 298) The difference between net sales and cost of goods sold. Sometimes called *gross margin*.

gross profit ratio (p. 298) The ratio of gross profit to net sales. Sometimes called *gross margin ratio*.

income before income taxes (p. 304) An income statement subtotal on which income tax expense is based.

income from continuing operations (p. 309) An income statement subtotal that is presented before income or loss from discontinued operations.

income from operations (p. 302) The difference between gross profit and operating expenses. Also called *operating income*.

inventory cost-flow assumption (p. 296) The application of FIFO, LIFO, weighted-average, or specific identification procedures to determine the cost of goods sold.

inventory shrinkage (p. 296) Inventory losses resulting from theft, deterioration, and record-keeping errors.

losses (p. 296) Decreases in net assets from incidental transactions and other events affecting an entity during a period, except those that result from expenses or distributions to owners.

matching concept (p. 295) Results in a fair presentation of the results of a firm's operations during a period by requiring the deduction of all expenses incurred in generating that period's revenues from the revenues earned in the period.

minority interest in earnings of subsidiary (p. 310) An income statement item representing the minority stockholders' share of the earnings of a subsidiary that have been included in the consolidated income statement.

multiple-step format (p. 306) An income statement format that includes subtotals for gross profit, operating income, and income before taxes.

net income (p. 304) The excess of revenues and gains over expenses and losses for a fiscal period.

operating expenses (p. 301) Expenses, other than cost of goods sold, incurred in the day-to-day activities of the entity.

operating income (p. 302) The difference between gross profit and operating expenses. Also referred to as *earnings from operations*.

other income and expenses (p. 303) An income statement category that includes interest expense, interest income, and gain or loss items not related to the principal operating activities of the entity.

percentage-of-completion method (p. 294) A method of recognizing revenue based on the completion percentage of a long-term construction project.

purchases returns and allowances (p. 297) Reductions in purchases from products returned to the supplier, or adjustments in the purchase cost.

realization (p. 291) A revenue recognition criterion that relates to the receipt of cash or a claim to cash in exchange for the product or service.

revenues (p. 291) Inflows of cash or increases in other assets, or settlement of liabilities during a period, as a result of delivering or producing goods, rendering services, or performing other activities that constitute the entity's major operations.

sales (p. 292) Revenues resulting from the sale of product.

sales mix (p. 299) The proportion of total sales represented by various products or categories of products.

sales returns and allowances (p. 293) Reductions in sales from product returns or adjustments in selling price.

shipping terms (p. 294) The description of when title passes from seller to buyer.

single-step format (p. 306) An income statement format that excludes subtotals such as gross profit and operating income.

statement of cash flows (p. 313) The financial statement that explains why cash changed during a fiscal period. Cash flows from operating, investing, and financing activities are shown in the statement.

tax loss carryover (p. 311) A loss for tax purposes for the current year that can be carried back or forward to offset taxable income of other years.

Chapter Notes

1. FASB, *Statement of Financial Accounting Concepts No. 6*, "Elements of Financial statements" (Stamford, CT, 1985), para. 78. Copyright © by the Financial Accounting Standards Board, High Ridge Park, Stamford, CT 06905, U.S.A. Quoted with permission. Copies of the complete document are available from the FASB.

2. Ibid., para. 80.

3. AICPA, *Accounting Trends and Techniques* (New York, NY, 1994, 1989, and 1985), Table 3-2.

4. FASB, *Statement of Financial Accounting Standards No. 95*, "Statement of Cash Flows" (Stamford, CT, 1985), para. 78. Copyright © by the Financial Accounting Standards Board, High Ridge Park, Stamford, CT 06905, U.S.A. Quoted with permission. Copies of the complete document are available from the FASB.

5. AICPA, *Accounting Trends and Techniques* (New York, NY, 1994), Table 3-2.

Chapter 11

How To Interpret Property-Liability Insurer Financial Statements

Chapters 6 through 10 provided an in-depth discussion of accounting for and presentation of assets, liabilities, owners' equity, revenues, and expenses for noninsurance business entities. This chapter explores accounting for and presentation of those items for property-liability insurers.

The discussion focuses on SAP-based financial reporting practices, comparing them to GAAP-based reporting practices when appropriate to identify differences between the two presentation methods. SAP is not an alternative accounting system, but merely a group of exceptions to accounting practices set forth in GAAP. The chapter will provide illustrations to explain how these exceptions are perceived as being compatible with the regulatory objectives of protecting policyholders by safeguarding insurer solvency.

In addition to describing the accounts most frequently found in insurer financial statements, this chapter explains methods used to value those items and provides basic transaction analysis of common insurance transactions for insurance sales (premium receipts), loss reserving, and settlement. Appendix A to this chapter shows the effect of reinsurance on an insurer's statutory financial statements, and Appendix B summarizes the premium and loss transactions presented throughout the chapter.

Review questions and recommended problems are provided in the companion course workbook and study guide to help students gain familiarity with insurer financial statements and to develop their analytical skills for insurance-related problem solving. The workbook also contains key statements and exhibits from a SAP-based Annual Statement for use in solving insurer-related problems for this chapter, similar to those provided for noninsurance entities in previous chapters. To gain additional practice in reading and analyzing insurer financial statements, students are encouraged to obtain a statutory Annual Statement from an insurer with which they are familiar.

Educational Objectives

After studying this chapter, you should be able to:

1. Describe the composition of a property-liability insurer's statutory balance sheet, and explain how it differs from that insurer's GAAP-based balance sheet.

2. Explain the significance of conservative surplus valuation and how it is accomplished through statutory accounting principles.

3. Explain why a property-liability insurance company's assets are valued differently than those of a noninsurance business entity for statutory accounting purposes.

   In support of the above objective, you should be able to:

   • Explain how various admitted assets are valued for statutory accounting purposes.

   • Describe those assets which are not admitted to an insurance company's statutory balance sheet, and justify their exclusion.

4. Describe the liability items that typically appear on an insurer's balance sheet.

   In support of the above objective, you should be able to:

   • Describe how reserves for losses and unearned premiums are valued.

   • Explain the significance of liabilities, other than reserve items, that appear on the statutory balance sheet for a typical property-liability insurer.

5. Describe the principal components of policyholders' surplus.

6. Describe the method required by regulatory authorities for accounting for and presentation of revenues and expenses for a property-liability insurer.

   In support of the above objective, you should be able to:

   • Explain the application of the matching principle in statutory accounting for property-liability insurers.

   • Explain how investment gains and losses affect the income statement and balance sheet of a property-liability insurer.

7. Use horizontal transaction analysis to describe the accounting for typical insurance transactions including:

    *   Premium receipts and earned premium
    *   Paid losses and loss reserves

8. Define or describe each of the Key Words and Phrases introduced in this chapter.

Statutory Accounting Principles (SAP)

Statutory accounting principles (SAP) are designed to meet unique financial reporting required by insurance regulators. The focus of reporting under SAP is on the solvency of the insurance organization.

Most insurance companies prepare two financial statements: one based on SAP and another based on GAAP. Publicly traded insurance companies prepare SAP financial statements for insurance regulators and GAAP financial statements for investors. Mutual insurance companies prepare SAP financial statements for insurance regulators but do not necessarily prepare separate GAAP financial statements.

Chapter 5 distinguished between the going-concern and liquidation perspectives of accounting. The going-concern perspective is fundamental to financial accounting and reporting under GAAP because investors and creditors, concerned with future cash flows, expect the organization to continue into the future. SAP differs from GAAP because it is based on the liquidation perspective, with the focus of financial accounting and reporting on the liquidation values of an insurer's assets and liabilities.

When compared with GAAP, SAP appears to understate assets and overstate liabilities. This conservative orientation of SAP can be explained by referring to valuation rules and the matching concept. Chapter 2 introduced both concepts in the context of GAAP. Below, each concept is discussed on a SAP basis.

Valuation Rules Under SAP

Valuation rules under SAP are designed to satisfy two criteria:

1. Valuation should *result in a conservative statement of policyholders' surplus.*

2. Valuation should *prevent sharp fluctuations in policyholders' surplus.*

A conservative valuation of policyholders' surplus is consistent with the liquidation perspective of accounting and provides a buffer to help prevent a financially troubled insurer from becoming insolvent.

Conservative Statement of Policyholders' Surplus

To understand how SAP valuation rules promote a conservative statement of policyholders' surplus, refer to the basic accounting equation (balance sheet equation), introduced in Chapter 2:

Assets = Liabilities + Owners' equity

Under SAP, the term "policyholders' surplus" is substituted for owners' equity to reflect the priority given policyholders' claims over any claims of owners. If this substitution is made and owners' equity is placed on the left side of the equation, the result is as follows:

Policyholders' surplus = Assets – Liabilities

Policyholders' surplus is conservatively stated when the *lowest* of several values is selected for each asset and/or the *highest* of several values is selected for each liability. This chapter will mention several SAP valuation rules that promote a conservative valuation of policyholders' surplus.

An example of a liability that is conservatively valued under SAP is loss reserves for certain lines of business. In the first three years after a policy is issued, the value placed on loss reserves attributed to that policy is subject to a minimum determined by multiplying a prescribed percentage by the policy's earned premium. If the estimated loss amount is first valued below the statutory prescribed minimum, the loss reserve under SAP would need to be increased to comply with the requirements, but under GAAP the reserve would not be increased.

An example of an asset that is conservatively valued under SAP is balances receivable that are *more than ninety days overdue* to an insurer from its agents. This receivable is generally considered an asset under GAAP, but it is not allowed as a balance sheet asset under SAP, effectively assigning it a zero value.

Preventing Sharp Fluctuations in Policyholders' Surplus

Sharp fluctuations in policyholders' surplus are prevented by selecting asset and liability values that change the least from period to period. Again, if asset and liability values on the balance sheet are stable, then policyholders' surplus will also be stable. If asset values, such as stocks and bonds, are sharply fluctuating, then policyholders' surplus will also fluctuate sharply. The same concept applies to liabilities.

An example of how SAP prevents sharp fluctuations in policyholders' surplus is the way in which it values bonds, a major invested asset category for insurers. The market value of bonds can change dramatically from period to period depending on the overall level of market interest rates. If, during a period of rising or falling interest rates, bonds are carried at market value on an insurer's balance sheet, the level of that insurer's policyholders' surplus could change sharply because of the change in market value of the bonds.

To prevent sharp fluctuations in policyholders' surplus, SAP values bonds at amortized cost rather than market value. For an individual bond, amortized cost steadily increases or decreases from when an insurer purchases the bond to when it redeems the bond. Therefore, when bonds are valued at amortized cost, policyholders' surplus does not vary erratically (or randomly) with changes in the market value of bonds.

Often, an insurer purchases a bond at a price above (at a premium) or below (at a discount) its par value (the amount the bond issuer will pay when the insurer redeems the bond). In these cases, the premium or discount is amortized, which means that the reported value of the bond is gradually adjusted over time so that it ultimately equals the par value at the bond's maturity. This gradual adjustment in reported value stabilizes the bonds on an insurer's balance sheet and prevents sharp fluctuations in policyholders' surplus. A later section of this chapter will discuss bond valuation, including amortization of premiums and discounts, in detail.

Matching Concept

Chapter 2 described the matching concept, whereby expenses are matched to the revenues they help produce to provide a realistic measure of net income on the income statement for a specific period. Under statutory accounting, the expenses associated with issuing an insurance policy, called *policy acquisition costs*, are generally incurred before the associated premium income is earned. For example, an insurer generally must pay commissions to its agents for producing a policy near the beginning of the policy term even though the premium revenue associated with the policy is earned evenly over the policy's term. The matching concept of GAAP dictates that, since the premium revenue is earned evenly over the policy term, the policy acquisition costs, the expenses associated with issuing that policy, should also be recognized evenly over the policy term to provide a realistic net income figure at any point in time.

SAP violates the matching concept by charging policy acquisition costs as an expense when they are incurred rather than evenly throughout the policy term. However, one benefit of this mismatch is that it promotes a conservative valuation of policyholders' surplus (and net income) because policy acquisition costs are prematurely charged as an expense, reducing net income and therefore policyholders' surplus. The matching concept is further discussed in the section of this chapter adressing the income statement.

Statutory Balance Sheet for Property-Liability Insurers

The statutory balance sheet for a property-liability insurer is based on SAP and includes many of the assets and liabilities found on the balance sheet of any business. For example, cash and real estate are included as assets. The statutory balance sheet also includes many assets and liabilities unique to insurance operations, such as premiums due from agents (an asset) and reserves for unpaid losses (a liability).

Exhibit 11-1 shows a statutory balance sheet for Acme Insurance. (To simplify the presentation, some of the balance sheet items typically having smaller account balances are not included.) Acme's statutory balance sheet will be used throughout this section to discuss the various balance sheet items appearing on it.

Assets of Property-Liability Insurers

For statutory accounting purposes, an insurer's assets are classified as either admitted or nonadmitted assets. **Admitted assets** are assets permitted to be shown on a company's Annual Statement balance sheet. **Nonadmitted assets** are assets that are not permitted to be shown on a company's Annual Statement balance sheet, mainly because they are illiquid. The concept of admitting only certain assets because they are liquid supports the valuation rules under SAP that policyholders' surplus should be stated conservatively and that sharp fluctuations should be prevented.

An asset's liquidity is measured in two dimensions. First, the less time needed to convert the asset to cash, the more liquid is the asset. Second, the greater the certainty of what value will be realized when the asset is converted to cash, the more liquid is the asset. The uncertainties about the time required to convert to cash or the value realized on liquidation exclude certain assets from insurance company balance sheets. Assets such as automobiles, leasehold improvements, furniture, certain types of equipment, and supplies are nonadmitted because of their low liquidity characteristics.

For Acme Insurance, admitted assets equal $784 million, as shown in Exhibit 11-1. Examples of admitted assets are investment-grade stocks and bonds. Examples of nonadmitted assets are receivables from agents that are over ninety days past due and furniture and equipment owned by the insurer. These items would not be shown as assets on a statutory balance sheet.

An insurer's admitted assets are divided into three main categories: invested assets, receivables, and "other assets."

Exhibit 11-1
Acme Insurance Company Balance Sheet

Acme Insurance Company
Statutory Balance Sheet
as of December 31
($millions)

Admitted Assets		Liabilities and Surplus*	
Bonds—at amortized cost	$554	Loss reserves (unpaid losses)	$340
Stocks	60	Loss adjustment expense reserves	67
Real estate	17	Excess of statutory reserves over statement reserves	10
Mortgage loans on real estate	6	Unearned premium reserve	118
Short-term investments	12	Funds held by company under reinsurance treaties	5
Cash on hand and on deposit	29	Provision for reinsurance	2
Cash and invested assets	$678	Other liabilities	24
Agents' balances (less than 90 days overdue)	94	Total liabilities	$566
		Common and preferred capital stock	25
Reinsurance recoverable on loss and loss adjustment expenses	3	Gross paid in and contributed surplus	50
Accrued interest, dividends, and real estate income	5	Unassigned funds	142
Other assets	4	Special surplus funds	1
Total admitted assets	$784	Total liabilities and surplus	$784

* All loss and premium liability figures are net of reinsurance.

Invested Assets

For most property-liability insurers, invested assets, such as bonds and common stocks, make up the largest share of admitted assets.

Bonds

Bonds are typically the largest single invested asset category for a property-liability insurer. Many insurers, especially small insurers, invest a high proportion of their total assets in bonds. Property-liability insurers consider bonds a safe long-term investment, and bonds provide them with a stable source of investment income. Acme Insurance has $554 million, or 71 percent, of its admitted assets in bonds.

State insurance regulations limit the amount that an insurance company can invest in certain types of bonds. Although limitations vary by state, in general they prohibit an insurance company from investing more than a certain percentage of its assets in any one permitted category of bonds, such as medium or lower grade (below investment grade) obligations, as classified by the National Association of Insurance Commissioner's Securities Valuation Office (SVO). Investments in excess of those limitations are classified as nonadmitted assets. The excess amount is charged directly to policyholders' surplus in the year in which the excess occurs. Charging an account means making a debit entry to that account. When policyholders' surplus is *charged*, it decreases because a debit entry decreases an owners' equity account.

Although the market price of bonds can vary widely over time as interest rates change, insurers are allowed to show bonds at amortized value on their Annual Statement balance sheets. Consequently, an insurer's policyholders' surplus is not severely affected by sudden change in the market price of its bonds unless the bonds are sold. This supports the rule under SAP that valuation should prevent sharp fluctuations in policyholders' surplus.

To understand how amortized value stabilizes the value of a bond shown on a statutory Annual Statement, one must understand how a bond is amortized. Assume that Acme purchases a bond having a $10,000 par value that matures in three years. The bond pays interest of 8 percent, or $800 per year. The current market rate of interest for bonds with comparable quality and maturity is 6 percent. Because of the added value attributable to this interest rate differential, Acme must pay a premium (that is, more than $10,000) to purchase the bond in the open market. Assume that Acme pays $10,534.60, or a premium of $534.60 over the par value of the bond. The book value of the bond, which is the amount shown on Acme's balance sheet, is $10,534.60, which is Acme's cost for the bond. The premium of $534.60 is amortized over the remaining life of the bond, and the book value of the bond on Acme's balance sheet is reduced each year until it equals the par value of $10,000 that Acme receives when the bond matures in three years.

Exhibit 11-2 shows the amortized premium for the bond over the three-year period.[1] The amortized premium is subtracted from the actual coupon payment each year to calculate the *effective* coupon payment. The amortized portion of the actual coupon payment can be thought of as an annual return to the purchaser of a portion of the bond's cost, and the effective coupon payment can be thought of as an approximation of the market return on the bond.

Exhibit 11-2
Amortization of a Bond Purchased at a Premium

End of Year	(1) Actual Coupon Payment	(2) Amortized Premium	(1 – 2) Effective Coupon Payment
1	$ 800.00	$178.20	$ 621.80
2	800.00	178.20	621.80
3	800.00	178.20	621.80
Totals	$2,400.00	$534.60	$1,865.40

Exhibit 11-3 shows the amortized book value each year, which is calculated by taking the initial cost of $10,534.60 and subtracting amortized premium each year. The amortized book value at the end of year three, which is also the bond's maturity date, equals the $10,000 par value of the bond.

Exhibit 11-3
Amortized Book Value of a Bond Purchased at a Premium

End of Year	(1) Beginning of Year Book Value	(2) Amortized Premium	(1 – 2) End of Year Book Value
1	$10,534.60	$178.20	$10,356.40
2	10,356.40	178.20	10,178.20
3	10,178.20	178.20	10,000.00

To summarize, Acme paid a premium of $534.60 over the par value of the bond because the coupon rate on the bond was higher than the current market rate of interest. This premium is divided by the number of years remaining on the bond, and the result is used to reduce the book value of the bond each year. In this way, the value of the bond on Acme's balance sheet is steadily declining each year until it reaches the par value amount when the bond matures.

If Acme purchased a bond at less than par value, because the market rate of interest is greater than the coupon rate on the bond, the discount would be amortized. The procedure would be the opposite of that shown in Exhibit 11-2 because the amortized discount each year would be *added* to the actual coupon payment (instead of subtracted) so that the effective coupon payment is higher. The value of the bond on Acme's balance sheet would increase steadily each year until it reaches the par value of $10,000 at maturity.

To understand how amortization stabilizes the value of bonds shown on Acme's balance sheet, compare the amortized value of a bond to its market value. Assume that for the three-year remaining life of the bond illustrated in Exhibit 11-2 and Exhibit 11-3, interest rates fall by the end of year one and then increase dramatically by the end of year two. Because the market value of a bond is inversely related to the level of market interest rates, at the end of year one, the market value of Acme's bond would increase well above its amortized book value of $10,356.40. Conversely, at the end of year two, the market value would be well below its amortized book value of $10,178.20. If, as with GAAP, Acme were required to use market value rather than amortized book value on its balance sheet, the value of bonds on its balance sheet would vary considerably depending on fluctuations in the level of market interest rates. Since bonds are generally the largest invested asset of a property-liability insurer, this variability in bond values could contribute significantly to sharp fluctuations in policyholders' surplus.

Exhibit 11-4 compares month-end market values to amortized values over a three-year period of a bond with a par value of $10,000 and coupon rate of 8 percent. Use of market values can create instability in the reported value of the bond throughout the period it is held.

For insurance companies with cash flows sufficient to cover operating expenditures without liquidating bond investments, amortized cost valuation has the advantage of shielding policyholders' surplus from bond market fluctuations. One disadvantage of amortized cost valuation is that insurance companies unable to meet operating expenditures from current cash flow fail to disclose their hazardous financial condition when they value bonds at amortized cost in excess of market value.

Stocks

Stocks are the second largest asset category for property-liability insurers. In the case of Acme Insurance, stocks are valued at $60 million, well below the value of Acme's bonds. (Insurance companies might also own preferred stock, which has dividend right priority over common stock and is often convertible into common stock.)

Exhibit 11-4
Comparison of Market Values to Amortized Values of a $10,000 Bond
Purchased at a Premium

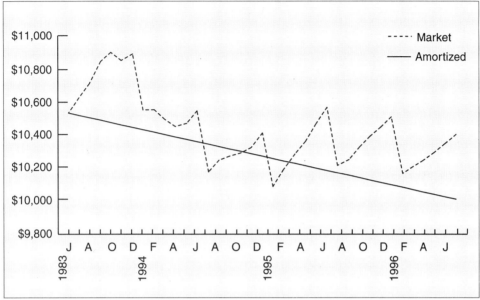

Most states have regulations that restrict investments in common stocks. In general, these regulations limit the percentage of admitted assets that an insurer can hold in a single stock. They might also limit the percentage an insurer can hold of the total outstanding stock of a single issuer. These regulations serve two purposes:

1. They encourage portfolio diversification.
2. They discourage insurance companies from obtaining proprietary interests in noninsurance-related activities.

If an insurance company's investment exceeds these limitations, the excess amount is a nonadmitted asset.

Stocks are valued at their *association* values, which are values prescribed by the Securities Valuation Office (SVO) of the National Association of Insurance Commissioners. Association values are usually the market price for each stock at the close of the last trading day of the prior year. Thus, unlike bonds, the statutory statement value of common stocks reflects market variations in common stock prices.

However, the SVO does have the authority to adjust stock prices to prevent sharp fluctuations in policyholders' surplus. For example, near the close of trading on the last day of the calendar year, a company might announce a new business venture or dividend policy that causes its closing price to climb or fall drastically. Because a stock's year-end closing price can be artificially high or low when compared with its underlying value, the SVO often provides *adjusted* stock prices that insurance companies must use in their Annual Statements. Placing these values on its SAP balance sheet for stock investments helps an insurer prevent sharp fluctuations in its policyholders' surplus.

State regulations that limit stock investments and the authority vested in the SVO to adjust stock values support SAP valuation rules. GAAP does not have these same provisions relating to stock valuation.

Real Estate

Insurance companies own real estate either as an investment or as office space for normal business activities. Real estate is reflected in statutory annual statements at original cost, plus additions or improvements, less depreciation and encumbrances on the real estate. GAAP values real estate in the same manner. However, if the market value of real estate drops below its book value, the real estate must be shown at its market value. For Acme Insurance, real estate is valued on its statutory Annual Statement at $17 million. Mortgage loans on real estate, a separate category from real estate assets, are valued at $6 million.

An insurance company that owns the building housing its own operating space must charge itself rent for statutory financial statement purposes. The rent should be a fair and reasonable amount based on what the company would normally have to pay if it did not own the building. Since the company offsets the rent charged to itself by a corresponding revenue from rent entry, its net income is not affected.

Short-Term Investments

Typically, the third largest category of invested assets for property-liability insurers is short-term investments. Acme has short-term investments valued at $12 million.

This category is a catchall item because it includes bills, notes, commercial paper, certificates of deposit, and shares in money market funds. All short-term investments have a maturity period of one year or less. They are generally targeted to provide funds for liabilities that the insurer must pay within a year, such as loss reserves for short-tail (quick loss development) lines of business such as fire and other property lines.

Receivables

Two major categories of receivables for property-liability insurers are balances due from agents and amounts due from reinsurers for losses and loss adjustment expenses already paid by the insurer.

Agents' Balances

Agents' balances, or uncollected premiums, represent the sum of insurance premiums due from agents, policyholders, or other insurance companies. Most agency contracts specify the period of time an agent has to collect premiums and to pay the insurance company. (That time is typically within thirty to forty-five days after the policy is recorded.) Agents generally remit premiums to the insurer net of commissions, and the insurance company usually records any uncollected premium net of commission. Companies that bill policyholders directly typically have uncollected premiums outstanding at year end.

Uncollected premiums or agents' balances more than ninety days overdue are nonadmitted assets and therefore reduce policyholders' surplus. Therefore, insurers must collect premiums due within the ninety-day period to include them as admitted assets.

Requiring that agents' balances more than ninety days overdue be classified as nonadmitted assets contributes to a conservative valuation of assets and therefore policyholders' surplus. To understand the effect of this requirement, assume that Acme Insurance has total agents' balances due of $97 million, of which $3 million is more than ninety days overdue. Only $94 million of its agents' balances would appear in its SAP balance sheet, as shown in Exhibit 11-1. Therefore, assets and policyholders' surplus are each reduced by $3 million. GAAP allows agents' balances more than ninety days overdue as assets unless there is evidence that they will not be collected.

The effect on Acme's financial statements of not allowing agents' balances more than ninety days overdue is as follows:

Balance sheet		Income statement
Assets = Liabilities + Policyholders' surplus	←	Net income = Revenues – Expenses
Agents' balances –3,000,000	Policyholders' surplus –3,000,000	

Both assets and policyholders' surplus are decreased by $3 million. The income statement is not affected because disallowed agents' balances are a direct adjustment to policyholders' surplus and bypass the income statement.

Reinsurance Recoverable on Loss and Loss Adjustment Expenses

An insurer's statutory balance sheet shows amounts recoverable from reinsurers for loss and loss adjustment expenses already paid by the insurer. It does not include any amount that will be recoverable on future payments. Acme Insurance has $3 million due from reinsurers for loss and loss adjustment expenses it has already paid.

Under certain circumstances, when reinsurance recoverable is more than ninety days overdue, an insurer must post a liability on its balance sheet equal to 20 percent of the amount overdue. This provision for reinsurance recoverables is covered in more detail in the liabilities section of this chapter.

Accrued Interest, Dividends, and Real Estate Income

Chapter 4 described accruals as transactions for which cash has not yet been received or paid, but the effect of which must be recorded in the accounts in order to accomplish a matching of revenues and expenses. Just as with noninsurance entities, any interest, dividends, or other income that has been earned by the insurer but not yet paid to it must be accrued and recorded as a receivable on the balance sheet and credited to income on the income statement. The accounting treatment for these items is the same under GAAP as it is under SAP. In the case of Acme Insurance, $5 million is accrued for interest, dividends, and real estate income that it has already earned but not yet been paid.

Other Assets

Other assets of a property-liability insurer include items such as federal income tax recoverable, electronic data processing equipment, and equity in pools and associations. Acme Insurance has $4 million in other assets.

Liabilities of Property-Liability Insurers

A property-liability insurer's major liabilities include reserves for losses and loss adjustment expenses, and unearned premiums. An insurer must recognize an additional liability when loss reserves for certain lines of business are less than a specified minimum amount. Liabilities must also be recognized when an insurer withholds funds from reinsurers or when reinsurers are slow in paying the amounts they owe.

Loss Reserves

Loss reserves are generally the largest and most important liability on a property-liability insurer's balance sheet. An insurer's **loss reserves** are estimates of the dollar amounts necessary to satisfy all unsettled policy claims against the insurer, regardless of the year in which the loss occurred. Thus, loss reserves include estimates of the amount necessary to satisfy unpaid claims for losses from the current year and *all previous years.*

Loss reserves are divided into two components: case loss reserves and incurred-but-not-reported reserves. A **case loss reserve** is the estimated amount needed to pay a claim. Case loss reserves are based on the judgment of adjusters and claims department personnel responsible for settling a claim. **Incurred-but-not-reported (IBNR) reserves** are the estimated amounts to be paid on incurred losses if the claim has not yet been reported. For example, a worker exposed to a harmful chemical might not show signs of injury for several years and therefore not report a claim to the insurer until several years after the exposure to the harmful substance. Based on experience, the insurer might set up a reserve during the current period for this claim. Loss reserves as reported on an insurer's balance sheet include both case and IBNR reserves:

Loss reserves = Case reserves + IBNR reserves

On average, case loss reserves for reported claims tend to increase over time, particularly for liability lines of insurance. After the initial reporting of a claim, facts are often discovered that necessitate an increase in the loss reserve. For example, a claimant might discover that his injury is worse than initially thought, or a lawsuit might be filed for a claim that the insurer initially thought could be settled quickly for a small amount. This tendency for loss reserves to increase over time is called **loss development.**

Sometimes, IBNR loss reserves include not only reserves for losses that have occurred and will be reported in the future, but also reserves for the estimated development of case loss reserves. Thus, when analyzing reserves, users of financial statements should find out what is included in a particular IBNR loss reserve figure.

In the case of Acme Insurance, loss reserves are equal to $340 million. This is an estimate of the unpaid losses for the current and *all prior years.* Acme's loss reserves include an estimate for the development of case reserves and an estimate of the amount that will be needed to pay for IBNR losses.

To explain the composition of current loss reserves on Acme's balance sheet, the illustration in Exhibit 11-5 shows the makeup of the $340 million loss reserve figure. As losses are paid out to claimants, the loss reserve decreases by an equal amount. Periodically, loss reserves are adjusted when new information is discovered on claims. It takes many years for all losses from a particular year to be fully paid. However, as time passes, total paid losses for a particular year tend to increase and loss reserves tend to decrease. Thus, the bulk of

Acme's current $340 million loss reserve figure is probably derived from the more recent years.

Exhibit 11-5 shows the amount paid and the amount reserved as of December 31 for each of the past ten years for Acme Insurance.

Exhibit 11-5
Acme Insurance—Total Paid and Reserved Losses for the Past Ten Years as of December 31 (millions)

Year	Total Amount Paid	Case and IBNR Reserves (Total Amount Unpaid)	Total Amount of Loss
91	$ 95	$ 1	$ 96
92	114	1	115
93	125	5	130
94	110	8	118
95	130	13	143
96	140	20	160
97	115	35	150
98	120	45	165
99	99	72	171
00	37	140	177
Totals	$1,085	$340	$1,425

A higher percentage of total losses is paid for each earlier year. For Acme Insurance, total case and IBNR reserves equal $340 million, which is the amount that appears on Acme's balance sheet as a liability. Of the $340 million in loss reserves, $140 million is from the current year, and the balance is from previous years. In general, the valuation of loss reserves is the same under SAP as under GAAP. For tax purposes, the Tax Reform Act of 1986 requires that loss and loss adjustment expense reserves be discounted to their present value.

Loss Adjustment Expense Reserves

Loss reserves usually are estimates of the amount required to pay claims but not the associated loss adjustment expenses, which cover the costs of investigating and processing losses. Insurers establish reserves for anticipated future loss adjustment expenses that will be required to settle losses that have occurred regardless of whether the losses occurred during the current year or previous years. These reserves are shown on a separate line titled "loss adjustment expenses." For Acme Insurance, loss adjustment expense reserves equal $67 million. Reserves for loss adjustment expenses can be estimated by applying a percentage, based on experience, to either earned premiums or incurred losses.

Excess of Statutory Reserves Over Statement Reserves

Statutes of the various states require that minimum reserves be established for auto liability, medical malpractice, other liability (including general liability), and workers compensation. Minimum reserves are required for these lines because they are characterized by long delays between reporting and settlement (that is, they have *long tails*), which can lead to an underestimation of loss reserves, particularly in the early years after a loss occurs. When the statutory minimum reserve exceeds the insurer's reserve estimates reported on its statutory Annual Statement, the excess liability is reported as *Excess of statutory over statement reserves*. For Acme Insurance, this figure is $10 million.

The minimum loss reserve requirement applies for three years from the policy year in which losses are incurred. To calculate the minimum loss reserve requirement, a minimum loss ratio percentage is calculated and applied to earned premium. For example, the minimum loss ratio percentage for general liability is 60 to 75 percent of earned premiums, depending on the loss experience of the insurer.

For Acme Insurance, assume that excess of statutory over statement reserves arises only from general liability and that the minimum loss ratio percentage applied to Acme's earned general liability premiums is 60 percent. Excess of statutory over statement reserves is calculated in three steps:

1. The percentage loss ratio is applied to Acme's earned premium for the past three years to calculate statutory minimum loss amounts.
2. Paid losses are subtracted from these figures to determine the statutory minimum reserves.
3. The results are then compared to statement reserves.

Exhibits 11-6 and 11-7 show these calculations.

Acme's total excess of statutory reserves over statement reserves (from Exhibit 11-7) is equal to $10 million, which is the same number that appears on Acme's balance sheet.

Exhibit 11-6

Acme Insurance—Calculation of Statutory Minimum Reserve for
General Liability

Year	(1) Earned Premium	(2) Statutory Minimum Loss Ratio	(3) = (1) × (2) Statutory Minimum Incurred Losses and Loss Expense	(4) Loss and Loss Expense Payments	(3) – (4) Statutory Minimum Reserve
98	$70,000,000	60%	$42,000,000	$26,000,000	$16,000,000
99	80,000,000	60%	48,000,000	20,000,000	28,000,000
00	90,000,000	60%	54,000,000	10,000,000	44,000,000

Exhibit 11-7

Acme Insurance—Excess of Statutory Reserves Over Statement Reserves for
General Liability

Year	(1) Statutory Minimum Reserve	(2) Statement Reserve	(1) – (2) Excess of Statutory Reserves Over Statement Reserves
98	$16,000,000	$14,000,000	$ 2,000,000
99	28,000,000	25,000,000	3,000,000
00	44,000,000	39,000,000	5,000,000
Total	**$88,000,000**	**$78,000,000**	**$10,000,000**

The effect of requiring excess statutory reserves on Acme's balance sheet is as
follows:

Balance sheet		Income statement
Assets = Liabilities + Policyholders' surplus	←	Net income = Revenues – Expenses

Excess	Policyholders'
reserves	surplus
+10,000,000	–10,000,000

When excess statutory reserves are necessary, they bypass the income statement and are charged directly to policyholders' surplus. Thus, loss expenses on
the income statement do not include excess statutory reserve amounts.

The statutory minimum reserve requirement promotes a conservative valuation of policyholders' surplus because if statement reserves are not at a certain minimum amount, SAP requires that an amount be added to bring them up to that minimum amount. GAAP has no such requirement.

Unearned Premium Reserve

The unearned premium reserve is typically about one-quarter of the total liabilities in a property-liability insurer's balance sheet. (For companies that write primarily property insurance, the unearned premium reserve can be the largest liability. This is because loss reserves for property insurance are usually relatively small compared to loss reserves for liability insurance.) For Acme Insurance, the unearned premium reserve is $118 million.

To understand the meaning of the unearned premium reserve, you must understand the meaning of the term **unearned premium**. Premium is not immediately earned when a policy is written; instead, the premium is earned over the term of the policy. When a policy is written, the entire premium is recorded as premiums written. A liability called an **unearned premium reserve** must be posted on the primary insurer's balance sheet to indicate the portion of the premium not yet earned (resulting from an adjusting entry to premiums written).

The unearned premium reserve liability represents, at least in theory, the portion of the premium that an insurer would need to return to each policyholder should the insurer go out of business or cancel all of its outstanding policies. The unearned premium can also be thought of as the amount required to cover losses and expenses during the unexpired term of a policy. Yet another way to interpret the reserve is to consider it as the approximate amount that an insurance company would have to pay a reinsurer to assume the insurer's obligation under the contract.

Assume that a one-year property policy was issued on October 1 with an annual premium of $200. If financial statements were prepared at the close of the business day on which the policy was issued, the $200 premium would be shown in the liability section of the balance sheet as unearned. The entire premium is unearned even though the insurance company had to use a portion of the premium revenue immediately to pay for the expenses associated with writing the policy. On December 31, the insurer reports one-quarter of the policy's advance premium, $50, as earned premium for the year and the remaining three-quarters, $150, as an unearned premium reserve.

The unearned premium reserve is calculated in the same manner under both SAP and GAAP, following the revenue recognition principle. There are different ways to estimate the unearned premium reserve, depending on whether the unearned premium is determined separately for each policy or for a group of policies in the aggregate.

Funds Held by Company Under Reinsurance Treaties

Acme Insurance has a liability of $5 million for funds held under reinsurance treaties. This item represents funds that belong to Acme's reinsurers but that Acme Insurance withholds to secure recoverables from reinsurers.

A primary insurer must withhold funds or obtain a letter of credit from the reinsurer when the primary insurer purchases reinsurance from an *unauthorized* reinsurer. This is because the insurer would otherwise have to post a liability on its Annual Statement for reinsurance ceded to the unauthorized reinsurer.[2]

The term **authorized reinsurer** refers to a reinsurer that is authorized to do business in the insurer's state of domicile. Authorized reinsurers include licensed reinsurers and reinsurers otherwise authorized to do business in a state. **Unauthorized reinsurers**, which are not licensed or otherwise authorized, are usually alien reinsurers doing business in the U.S.

When an insurer purchases reinsurance from an authorized (licensed) reinsurer, it can take credit on its Annual Statement for losses and unearned premiums ceded to that reinsurer. Thus, loss reserves and unearned premium reserves are shown on the balance sheet *net* of the amounts ceded to authorized reinsurers.

When an insurer purchases reinsurance from an unauthorized reinsurer, loss reserves and unearned premium reserves are also shown net on the balance sheet. However, the insurer might be required to post an additional liability for these amounts under its "provision for reinsurance," as explained below.

Provision for Reinsurance

An insurer might be required to make an adjusting entry resulting in a credit to a liability account called **provision for reinsurance**. Acme's provision for reinsurance is $2 million. The circumstances under which an entry must be made to this account differ depending on whether the reinsurer is authorized or unauthorized.

When an insurer has undisputed balances due for losses and loss adjustment expenses that are more than ninety days overdue from an *authorized* reinsurer, 20 percent of the overdue amount must be added to the insurer's liability provision for reinsurance. This is referred to as the **ninety-day rule**. Assume Acme Insurance has receivables of $10 million from a single authorized reinsurer that are overdue by more than ninety days. Twenty percent of this amount, or $2 million, would be reported in Acme's provision for reinsurance.

When an insurer does not require an *unauthorized* reinsurer to deposit funds or provide a letter of credit to cover the insurer's losses and unearned premiums that are reinsured, the insurer must include in its *provision for reinsurance* an amount equal to the entire amount of losses and unearned premiums that are reinsured with that unauthorized reinsurer. Because this is a significant penalty, insurers should always require deposit funds or a letter of credit from unauthorized reinsurers. Acme requires its unauthorized reinsurers to deposit funds or a letter of credit, as evidenced by Acme's $5 million liability for *funds held by company under reinsurance treaties*.

The provision for reinsurance required under SAP promotes a conservative valuation of policyholders' surplus. Just as with agents' balances over ninety days and excess of statutory reserves over statement reserves, the provision for reinsurance liability is directly charged to policyholders' surplus and bypasses the income statement.

GAAP statements do not include a provision for reinsurance. Thus, GAAP does not require that 20 percent of receivables from authorized reinsurers that are ninety days or more overdue be posted as a liability. Also, regardless of whether an unauthorized reinsurer provides the primary insurer a cash deposit or a letter of credit to secure losses and unearned premiums, under most circumstances GAAP does not require that these amounts be included as a liability.

Other Liabilities

Other liabilities that appear on a statutory annual statement balance sheet include such items as taxes payable, dividends payable, and amounts payable to a firm's parent, subsidiaries, and affiliates. For Acme Insurance, other liabilities amount to $24 million. These items would be reported at the same value on SAP-based financial statements as on GAAP-based financial statements.

Policyholders' Surplus

Under statutory accounting, the capital and surplus of an insurance company are collectively referred to as *surplus as regards policyholders* or policyholders' surplus. Policyholders' surplus, which is equivalent to owners' equity for a noninsurance entity, is equal to net admitted assets, or admitted assets minus liabilities. Using the term *policyholders' surplus* instead of *owners' equity* emphasizes the priority given to satisfying policyholder obligations.

State statutes specify the minimum amount of policyholders' surplus that an insurer must maintain to continue writing business. The required amount varies depending on the lines of business the company writes.

If the insurer's policyholders' surplus drops below the required minimum amount, the insurer is considered **technically insolvent**, even though the insurer's net worth might be positive (that is, admitted assets exceed total liabilities). Noninsurance entities are considered insolvent when owners' equity drops below zero.

Chapter 9 referred to the components of owners' equity for a noninsurance entity, including common capital stock, preferred capital stock, additional paid-in capital, and retained earnings. Exhibit 11-8 shows equivalent components for policyholders' surplus.

Exhibit 11-8
Comparison Between Owners' Equity and Policyholders' Surplus

Owners' Equity Component	Policyholders' Surplus Equivalent
Common capital stock	Common capital stock
Preferred capital stock	Preferred capital stock
Additional paid-in capital	Gross paid-in and contributed surplus
Retained earnings	Unassigned funds

Common and Preferred Capital Stock

Capital stock, both common and preferred, is the aggregate par or stated value of the company's capital stock outstanding (*par value* and *stated value* were defined in Chapter 9). Although capital stock can be either common or preferred, most stock insurers exclusively issue common stock. The aggregate par value of Acme's common stock is $25 million.

Gross Paid-In and Contributed Surplus

Gross paid-in and contributed surplus results from selling stock for an amount in excess of the stock's par or stated value and from any subsequent contributions of funds from stockholders. Thus, if a $5.00 par value common share is issued for $7.50, $2.50 is credited to the gross paid-in and contributed surplus account. The gross paid-in and contributed surplus is equivalent to additional paid-in capital for a noninsurance entity. Acme's gross paid-in and contributed surplus is $50 million.

Unassigned Funds

Unassigned funds (surplus) is retained earnings less dividends paid since the inception of the company and, to that extent, is equivalent to the retained earnings account of a noninsurance entity. Unassigned funds include all adjustments to surplus, such as the change in the provision for reinsurance, change in the excess of statutory reserves over statement reserves, changes in nonadmitted assets, and unrealized capital gains or losses on investments. The amount of unassigned surplus funds limits the amount that can be distributed as nonliquidating dividends to policyholders or stockholders. Unassigned funds for Acme Insurance equal $142 million.

Some states allow insurance companies to borrow funds, usually to meet minimum surplus requirements. These so-called **surplus notes** are reported in the policyholders' surplus section of the balance sheet, have strict interest and principal repayment provisions, and are subordinate to all other obligations of the insurer.[3]

Special Surplus Funds

The only component of policyholders' surplus not mentioned in Exhibit 11-8 is **special surplus funds**, which are funds that the board of directors has authorized for a specific purpose. For example, an insurance company writing lines of business that have widely fluctuating loss ratios might decide to establish a specially earmarked subdivision of policyholders' surplus and call it *reserve for extraordinary losses*. That reserve is sometimes equal to the deductible amount in the company's catastrophe reinsurance contract. However, using the term *reserve* to classify a portion of surplus does not change that surplus into a liability. In the policyholders' surplus section of the balance sheet, reserve is used in the traditional GAAP context—to allocate, or set aside, a portion of the surplus (owners' equity) account for a specific purpose.

Special surplus accounts are often created to deal with underwriting loss and investment value fluctuations. Assessments made by post-insolvency insurance company guaranty funds are often handled by creating a special surplus fund. Insurers might also assign portions of their surplus for potential income taxes on unrealized capital gains, policyholder dividends not yet declared, or other contingencies. Regardless of their intended purpose, special surplus funds restrict the amount of funds available for stockholder or policyholder dividends.[4] Acme has established a special surplus fund of $1 million.

Statutory Income Statement for Property-Liability Insurers

The income statement for a property-liability insurer serves the same purpose as an income statement for a noninsurance entity. It shows an organization's net income over a period of time after all expenses are subtracted from revenues. Income statements covering several years can be used to examine trends in revenues and expenses.

An insurer's statutory income statement highlights certain items that are important for the reader to understand the insurer's financial results. Although it differs in format from an income statement for a noninsurance entity, the statutory income statement reports much of the same financial information. For example, instead of net sales, an insurer reports premiums earned as the principal revenue item. Also, since an insurer does not sell or manufacture physical products, cost of goods sold does not appear. Instead, incurred losses and loss adjustment expenses are the principal expense categories. Chapter 10 defined losses as decreases in an entity's net assets resulting from incidental transactions or nonoperating activities; as used here, losses are a principal expense item for an insurer. The statutory income statement shows separate income and expenses for both underwriting and investment activities.

Exhibit 11-9 shows the income statement for Acme Insurance. It will be used throughout this section to explain the major components of a property-liability insurer's statement of income, which is what this statement is called in the Annual Statement. Many of the concepts discussed in this section were introduced in the previous section on the statutory balance sheet.

Underwriting Income

Underwriting is the major operating activity of insurers. Underwriting income is measured by calculating the remainder of premiums earned after deducting underwriting losses and expenses incurred for a specific period of time.

Premiums

Premium is the major revenue item for insurers. *Concepts Statement No. 5* of the FASB requires that, in order to be recognized, revenues must be realized or realizable and earned. A premium is usually paid to the insurer at the beginning of a policy period, and thus it is realized at that time. However, because the insurer provides coverage over the policy period, the premium is not earned when it is paid. The insurer earns the premium evenly throughout the policy period.

To recognize premiums properly, an insurer must set up the written premium account, and make periodic adjusting entries to determine earned premium, and unearned premium amounts. **Written premium** is the amount of premium billed to insureds less premiums returned. As premium is written, the entire premium amount is unearned. (The section of this chapter on the statutory balance sheet explained the term *unearned premium* and how an unearned premium reserve is calculated.) As policies age, the unearned premium amount decreases, and written premiums become premiums earned.

For example, assume that Acme Insurance company receives a $600 premium at the beginning of a one-year policy period. Acme would record the following:

Dr.	Cash	$600	
Cr.	Premiums written		$600

The effect on Acme's financial statements is as follows:

Balance sheet	Income statement
Assets = Liabilities + Policyholders' surplus ⟵	Net income = Revenues – Expenses
Cash	Premiums
+600	written
	+600

Exhibit 11-9
Acme Insurance Company Statement of Income

Acme Insurance Company
Statement of Income
for the Year Ended December 31
(all figures in millions)

Underwriting Income

Premiums earned	$322
Losses incurred	177
Loss expenses incurred	61
Other underwriting expenses incurred	80
Total underwriting deductions	$318
Net underwriting gain	$ 4

Investment Income

Net investment income earned	$ 41
Net realized capital gains or (losses)	7
Net investment gain or (loss)	$ 48
Net income before dividends to policyholders and federal income tax	$ 52
Dividends to policyholders	22
Net income before federal income tax	$ 30
Federal income tax	9
Net income	$ 21

If the premium were billed directly to the customer or to the agent's account, a debit entry would be made to the appropriate premium receivable account instead of to cash.

When Acme prepares its financial reports, an adjusting entry is made to recognize unearned premium for all of its in-force policies. For example, assume that when Acme prepares its financial statements, nine months of the policy mentioned above have elapsed. Then, $150 (3/12) of the premium is unearned, and $450 is earned. The adjusting entry would be as follows:

Dr.   Premiums written $150
   Cr.   Unearned premium reserve $150

The effect on Acme's financial statements is as follows:

Balance sheet	Income statement
Assets = Liabilities + Policyholders' surplus ⟵	Net income = Revenues − Expenses
Unearned premium reserve +150	Premiums written −150

Thus, premium not yet earned is recognized as a liability. The balance of the premiums written account represents premiums earned. A closing entry would be made to transfer those premiums earned to policyholders' surplus under the unassigned funds account.

For income statement purposes, "premiums earned" is calculated by taking unearned premiums at the beginning of the period, adding premiums written during the period, and subtracting unearned premiums at the end of the period:

$$\text{Premiums earned} = \text{Unearned premiums at beginning of period} + \text{Premiums written during period} - \text{Unearned premiums at end of period}$$

For Acme Insurance, premiums earned are shown in the following formula:

$$\text{Premiums earned (millions)} = \$105 + \$335 - \$118$$
$$= \$322$$

The unearned premium figure of $118 million at the end of the period is shown on Acme's balance sheet in Exhibit 11-1, and the earned premium of $322 million for the period is shown in Acme's income statement in Exhibit 11-9.

Barring premium rate changes, if an insurance company writes the same mix of business and the same premium volume each year, premiums written and premiums earned will be equal, and the unearned premium reserve will remain constant. A company that is growing will experience an increasing unearned premium reserve, causing earned premiums to be less than written premiums, as in the case of Acme Insurance. Conversely, a company whose written premiums are declining will experience a decreasing unearned premium reserve, causing earned premiums to exceed written premiums.

Losses and Loss Adjustment Expenses Incurred

Losses incurred for a specific period are the total amounts paid by the insurer for losses that have occurred plus changes in the loss reserves for payments that are expected to be made in the future for those losses.

When a loss occurs, a reserve amount is set up for the estimated amount that the insurer will pay on that loss by the time it is closed out. As the insurance company pays loss-related items such as medical expenses and settlements, losses paid increase and loss reserves decrease by the same amount, leaving "losses incurred" unchanged.

Assume Acme Insurance is notified of a claim and sets up a reserve of $10,000. The entry would be as follows:

Dr.	Losses incurred (expense)	$10,000
Cr.	Loss reserves	$10,000

The effect on Acme's financial statements is as follows:

Balance sheet	Income statement
Assets = Liabilities + Policyholders' surplus ←	Net income = Revenues – Expenses
Loss reserves +10,000	Losses incurred +10,000

Assume Acme pays $2,000 in medical expenses on the claim. Acme would record the following:

Dr.	Loss reserves..	$2,000
Cr.	Cash (paid losses)	$2,000

The effect on Acme's financial statements is as follows:

Balance sheet	Income statement
Assets = Liabilities + Policyholders' surplus ←	Net income = Revenues – Expenses
Cash −2,000 Loss reserves −2,000	

Acme's income statement is not affected when an amount is paid on a claim that has already been reserved. This is because when a loss is paid, the amount of payment is taken from the loss reserves; thus, the total incurred loss stays the same. At any point in time, the total incurred loss amount for the claim is the total amount paid plus the loss reserve for that claim.

Calculating "losses incurred" for a property-liability insurer's income statement includes *all* loss transactions that occurred during the period of the income statement, *even transactions related to outstanding losses that occurred in prior years.* For example, an insurer might discover that loss reserves must be increased for a loss that occurred in a prior accounting period. Since the income statement for the previous period has already been produced, the increase in outstanding loss reserves will be reflected in the income statement for the current period.

For example, assume that Acme Insurance discovers that the loss reserve for a loss that occurred two years ago must be increased by $5,000. The entry would be as follows:

Dr.	Losses incurred (expense) $5,000	
	Cr. Loss reserves	$5,000

The effect on Acme's *current* financial statements is as follows:

Balance sheet	Income statement
Assets = Liabilities + Policyholders' surplus ⟵	Net income = Revenues – Expenses
Loss reserves +5,000	Losses incurred –5,000

Assume that during the current period, an insurer learns of an adverse court decision related to coverage for environmental losses. Based on this decision, the insurer decides that it must increase its loss reserves by $20 million for covered environmental losses that occurred in prior periods. This $20 million increase in loss reserves would be added to "losses incurred" for the current period's income statement and reduce net income for the current period by $20 million.

For income statement purposes, "losses incurred" is calculated by taking the difference in loss reserves from the beginning to the end of the accounting period and adding losses paid during the period:

$$\text{Losses incurred} = \frac{\text{Losses paid}}{\text{during period}} + \frac{\text{Loss reserves}}{\text{at end of period}} - \frac{\text{Loss reserves}}{\text{at beginning of period}}$$

For Acme Insurance, losses incurred for the current period can be calculated from Exhibit 11-5, as shown in the following formula:

$$\text{Losses incurred (millions)} = \$37 + \$340 - \$200$$
$$= \$177$$

The $37 million figure is the amount paid during the current year (year 00) in Exhibit 11-5, and the $340 million figure is the total loss reserves at the end of the current year.

The $200 million for loss reserves at the beginning of the current year assumes that the loss reserves for previous years did not change during the current year. If loss reserves for previous years did change during the current year, then incurred losses for the current year would be affected. For example, assume that loss reserves at the beginning of the current year were $180 million and that, during the current year, the insurer decides it must increase its loss reserves by $20 million for environmental losses it covered that occurred in prior periods. Losses incurred would be calculated as follows:

$$\text{Losses incurred (millions)} = \$37 + \$340 - \$180$$
$$= \$197$$

Incurred losses for the current period have increased by $20 million based on environmental losses that occurred in previous periods. Incurred losses for the current period would decrease if loss reserves from previous years were decreased.

For financial reporting purposes, loss reserves must be estimated for each financial statement period. This requirement stems from the matching concept mentioned previously whereby expenses should be matched to the revenues they help produce. If estimated loss reserves are inaccurate, then loss expenses are not correctly matched with the premium revenue generated for a particular period, and net income is either understated or overstated. However, loss reserves is a difficult figure to estimate, and insurers must frequently adjust their loss reserve figures.

Loss adjustment expenses are treated in a manner similar to the treatment of losses. A reserve is established for anticipated future loss adjustment expenses required to settle losses (both reported and IBNR) that occurred before the close of the current accounting period. As loss adjustment expenses are paid, the loss adjustment expense reserve is reduced. "Loss adjustment expenses incurred" on an insurer's income statement is calculated in a manner similar to the calculation of losses incurred.

Underwriting Expenses

Underwriting expenses include all of the expenses associated with underwriting, except losses, loss adjustment expenses, and investment expenses. Major categories of underwriting expenses include commissions and brokerage paid, salaries, advertising, rent, equipment, postage, and state premium taxes paid.

As mentioned in Chapter 5, an insurer's income statement under SAP follows a conservative approach by charging all policy acquisition costs immediately as an expense. Much of an insurer's underwriting expense amount falls into the category of policy acquisition costs.

GAAP recognizes policy acquisition costs proportionally to match them to the related premium income. Policy acquisition costs that have not yet been charged as an expense are shown as a prepaid asset (deferred policy acquisition costs) on the GAAP balance sheet.

To demonstrate the effect of not matching revenues and expenses, assume Acme Insurance issues a one-year policy for a $600 premium and immediately incurs policy acquisition costs of $120. Acme earns the premium at the rate of $50 per month for this policy. Under GAAP, the $120 of acquisition costs would be charged proportionately over the policy term at $10 per month; under SAP, the $120 would be charged at the beginning of the policy term. At the end of the first month, the revenue and expenses (assuming no losses) for the policy under GAAP and SAP would be as follows:

GAAP		SAP	
Earned premium	$50	Earned premium	$ 50
Policy acquisition costs	10	Policy acquisition costs	120
Net income or loss	$40	Net income or loss	$(70)

As shown above, SAP would record a $70 loss, and GAAP would record a $40 profit.

Investment Income

Since insurers invest a large portion of their assets, substantial investment earnings can result. In 1995, for instance, the net investment income of property and liability insurance companies amounted to approximately $36.8 billion, and underwriting operations produced a loss of approximately $14.2 billion. The resulting net operating income was $22.6 billion.[5] Net operating income typically does not include realized capital gains that are included when calculating net investment gain or (loss), as shown below:

$$\text{Net investment gain or (loss)} = \text{Net investment income earned} + \text{Net realized capital gains or (losses)}$$

Net Investment Income Earned

The statement of income of the statutory Annual Statement shows net investment income earned, which is the amount of investment income earned less investment expenses. For Acme Insurance, net investment income earned equals $41 million.

Investment income consists of interest, dividends, and real estate earnings. Interest income is derived mainly from bonds, and dividends are derived from stocks. Real estate income is derived from mortgage loans and rental income. The investment income includes the amounts accrued for interest, dividend, and real estate income on an insurer's balance sheet.

Amortization of an asset can affect the amount of interest income. As shown in Exhibit 11-2, if the premium or discount on a bond is amortized, the amortization amount is used to adjust the interest earned on the bond. When the purchase price of a mortgage loan differs from the unpaid balance, statutory rules also require amortization of the difference. That amortization is an adjustment to mortgage interest earned.

Real estate income usually consists of the amount charged for occupancy of an insurance company's own buildings plus any rents received from tenants. The amount charged for occupancy of its own buildings is both investment income and rental expense to the various areas of operational activity.

Certain investment expenses, such as salaries of investment officers and real estate taxes, are charged directly to investment expense accounts (allocations are made to other expense accounts according to expense allocation rules). In addition to investment expenses, other expenses, such as depreciation of real estate and interest on borrowed funds, are deducted from interest, dividends, and real estate income to determine net investment income.

Net Realized Capital Gains or (Losses)

The income statement of the statutory Annual Statement shows net realized capital gains or (losses). A gain or loss is said to be *realized* when an asset is sold above or below its book value on the balance sheet. For Acme Insurance, net realized capital gains or losses equals $7 million.

Net realized capital gains or (losses) is calculated by taking the profits minus the losses generated by the sale of invested assets. Included in the invested asset category are bonds, stocks, short-term investments, and real estate. Exhibit 11-10 shows how the net realized gain or loss is calculated for Acme Insurance.

The $7 million net realized gain is the same as the $7 million net realized capital gain on Acme's income statement.

Unrealized Capital Gains or (Losses)

When an unsold asset, such as a stock, appreciates in value above its book value on the balance sheet, the gain in value is said to be *unrealized*. When an asset with an unrealized gain or (loss) is shown at market value on the balance sheet, a corresponding adjustment must be made to either the income statement or policyholders' surplus to reflect periodic changes in the asset's unrealized gain or loss. For a property-liability insurer, the adjustment is made directly to policyholders' surplus. For example, stocks are shown at market value on the statutory balance sheet. When the market value of a stock changes, resulting in a corresponding change in its unrealized gain or loss, a direct adjustment is made to policyholders' surplus.

Exhibit 11-10
Calculation of the Net Realized Gain or (Loss) for Acme Insurance
(All figures in millions)

	(a) +	(b) =	(c)
	Gain on Sale or Maturity	(Loss) on Sale or Maturity	Net Realized Gain or (Loss)
Bonds	$10	$ (7)	$3
Stocks	11	(3)	8
Short-term investments	1	(4)	(3)
Real estate	0	(1)	(1)
Total	$22	$(15)	$7

Statement of Cash Flows

The statement of cash flows, which was introduced in Chapter 2 and discussed in detail in Chapter 10, provides useful information that cannot be obtained from the other financial statements. On the statutory Annual Statement, a cash flow statement follows directly after the statement of income.

Cash flows in the Annual Statement are calculated using the direct method (as opposed to the indirect method) by listing the insurer's major cash receipts and disbursements. As with the statement of cash flows under GAAP, the statement shows separate calculations for cash from operating activities, cash from investing activities, and cash from financing activities.

The items shown on the SAP statement of cash flows reflect the items shown in the SAP financial statements. For example, cash from operating activities includes premiums collected net of reinsurance (an inflow) and loss and loss adjustment expenses paid (an outflow). Cash from investing activities includes proceeds from investments sold (an inflow) and cost of acquired investments (an outflow). Cash from financing activities includes cash provided by surplus notes and borrowed funds (inflows) and dividends and borrowed funds repaid (outflows).

An analysis of the statement of cash flows can provide useful information about the financial operations of an insurer. For example, a positive cash flow from operating activities is a sign of a healthy insurer, and a negative cash flow from operating activities means that the insurer must sell some investments or seek additional sources of financing.

Other Supporting Schedules

The summary financial statements contained in the statutory annual statement are followed by supporting materials such as exhibits, schedules, and a comprehensive questionnaire of general interrogatories. Those supporting materials analyze premium writings, loss payments, unearned premium calculations, assumed and ceded reinsurance, and loss reserve provisions by line of coverage. Those supporting materials also show detailed calculations of special statutory loss and loss adjustment expense reserves and the development or maturation of losses to indicate whether the insurer has established proper loss reserves.

Summary

This chapter described statutory accounting principles (SAP) and how they differ from GAAP. It also described the statutory balance sheet, income statement, and statement of cash flows for property-liability insurers, all of which are based on SAP.

The statutory balance sheet includes many assets and liabilities unique to insurance operations, such as premiums due from agents and reserves for unpaid losses. It also includes policyholders' surplus, which is equivalent to owners' equity on a GAAP balance sheet. The statutory income statement contains revenue and expense items unique to insurers, such as earned premium and incurred losses.

Valuation rules under SAP are designed to provide a conservative statement of and prevent sharp fluctuations in policyholders' surplus. When compared with GAAP, SAP appears to understate assets and overstate liabilities. The following chart summarizes the SAP rules discussed throughout this chapter that promote a conservative valuation of policyholders' surplus.

SAP Rules That Promote a Conservative Valuation of Policyholders' Surplus	

SAP Rule	Decrease in Assets/Increase in Liabilities (when compared with GAAP)
Some assets are **nonadmitted assets**, which means they are not allowed as assets on a SAP balance sheet. Nonadmitted assets include bonds in default and agents' balances more than 90 days overdue.	Decrease in assets
Insurer must have loss reserves that are at least a certain minimum level (called **statutory minimum reserves**).	Increase in liability (if statement reserves are less than statutory requirement)
When an **authorized reinsurer** has undisputed balances more than 90 days overdue or when an **unauthorized reinsurer** does not provide a cash deposit or letter of credit to cover losses and unearned premium that are reinsured, an insurer must post a **provision for reinsurance** on its balance sheet.	Increase in liabilities
SAP requires that policy acquisition costs be charged as an expense when incurred, rather than charged proportionately as the corresponding premium is earned. This violates the **matching concept**.	Decrease in asset ("deferred policy acquisition costs," as explained in Chapter 5)

Sharp fluctuations in policyholders' surplus are prevented by selecting asset and liability values that change the least from period to period. Any premium or discount paid for a bond is amortized as part the bond's cost over the life the bond so that the balance sheet value (book value) of the bond is fairly stable over time and does not fluctuate with changes in market values. The Securities Valuation Office has the authority to adjust stock prices to prevent their sharp fluctuations from affecting policyholders' surplus. Real estate is valued in a statutory balance sheet at original cost less depreciation, which shields its book value from changes in its market value.

Policyholders' surplus on a property-liability insurer's balance sheet is equal to net admitted assets, which is admitted assets minus liabilities. The components of policyholders' surplus are roughly equivalent to the components of owners' equity, except for special surplus funds, which are funds on a statutory balance sheet that the board of directors of an insurer has authorized for a specific purpose.

Premiums and losses are treated in a similar manner on both a SAP and GAAP basis. Insurers must accurately estimate loss reserves for each financial statement period. Otherwise, losses are not properly matched with their associated premium revenue because any changes in loss reserves for losses that occurred in previous periods will affect the current period's net income.

Investment income is an important part of an insurance company's total revenues. It consists of net investment income earned and net realized capital gains or losses. Unrealized capital gains and losses do not flow through the income statement, but they are charged directly to policyholders' surplus.

Statutory accounting principles as well as the statutory balance sheet and income statement are designed to meet the unique financial reporting needs of insurance organizations and their regulators. This chapter described how statutory accounting focuses on the liquidity of an insurance organization to measure the ability of an insurer to pay claims.

Key Words and Phrases

admitted assets (p. 332) Assets meeting minimum standards of liquidity that are allowed to be reported on an insurer's balance sheet prepared in accordance with statutory accounting principles.

agents' balances (p. 339) Represents the sum of insurance premiums due from agents, policyholders, and other insurance companies. Also referred to as uncollected premiums.

authorized reinsurer (p. 346) A reinsurer that is granted authority to do business in the primary insurer's state of domicile.

capital stock (p. 348) The aggregate par (or stated) value of the company's issued stock outstanding. Capital stock can be either common or preferred.

case loss reserve (p. 341) Based on the judgment of adjusters and claims department personnel, the estimated amount needed to pay a claim.

excess-of-loss contract (p. 364) A reinsurance contract under which the insurer retains all of the loss up to a stated amount, after which the reinsurer pays the balance of the loss (or 80 to 90 percent of the balance) up to the contract limit.

gross paid in and contributed surplus (p. 348) The amount realized from the sale of capital stock when issued that exceeds the stock's par or stated value.

incurred-but-not-reported (IBNR) reserves (p. 341) The estimated amounts needed to make future payments on losses that have occurred but that have not yet been reported to the insurer.

loss development (p. 341) The tendency for loss reserves to change over time. Quantifiably, the difference between the loss reserve amount at a particular date and the total of payments on those losses plus any amount still unpaid for those losses at the development date.

losses incurred (p. 353) The total amounts paid by an insurer for losses that have occurred plus changes in the loss reserve for payments that are expected to be made in the future for those losses.

loss reserves (p. 340) Estimate of the amount needed to satisfy all unsettled policy claims against the insurer, regardless of the year in which the loss occurred.

ninety-day rule (p. 346) Requirement that 20 percent of loss and loss adjustment expense amounts beyond ninety days overdue from authorized reinsurers be added to the primary insurer's provision for reinsurance.

nonadmitted assets (p. 332) Assets excluded from an insurer's statutory balance sheet because of their relative illiquidity.

premium capacity (p. 364) The total amount of premium an insurer can write in a year given its financial condition, based on policyholders' surplus.

pro rata contract (p. 364) A reinsurance contract under which both the ceding company (primary insurer) and the reinsurer share the premium and losses on a proportional basis.

provision for reinsurance (p. 346) A statutory Annual Statement balance sheet liability item that consists of reinsurance penalties resulting from (1) unauthorized reinsurance that is inadequately secured by withheld funds or letters of credit and (2) overdue recoverables from either authorized or unauthorized reinsurers.

special surplus funds (p. 349) Funds that the insurer's board of directors has authorized for a special purpose.

surplus notes (p. 349) Amount reported in the policyholders' surplus section of an insurer's statutory balance sheet representing borrowed funds. Surplus notes have strict interest and principal repayment provisions and are subordinate to all other financial obligations of the insurer.

surplus relief (p. 364) An action resulting from a primary insurer's use of reinsurance that increases the insurer's policyholders' surplus.

technically insolvent (p. 348) When an insurer's policyholders' surplus falls below the required minimum amount, even though the insurer's net worth might be positive (that is, admitted assets exceed total liabilities).

unassigned funds (surplus) (p. 348) The total of an insurer's retained earnings, less dividends paid, since the inception of the company.

unauthorized reinsurers (p. 346) Reinsurers that are not licensed or otherwise authorized to do business in a primary insurer's state of domicile.

unearned premium (p. 345) The portion of an insurer's written premium that has not yet been earned or that is attributable to unexpired coverage. The portion of an insurer's written premium that has not yet been earned, for which service under the policies is yet to be provided.

unearned premium reserve (p. 345) A liability (reserve account) representing an estimate of the total of unearned premiums that would have to be refunded if all in-force policies were canceled.

written premium (p. 350) The amount of insurance premium billed to insureds less premiums returned.

Chapter Notes

1. This example of bond amortization has been simplified for illustrative purposes. Other, more sophisticated methods exist for amortizing the book value of a bond.

2. Michael W. Elliott, Bernard L. Webb, Howard N. Anderson, and Peter R. Kensicki, *Principles of Reinsurance*, vol. 2 (Malvern, PA: American Institute for CPCU, 1995), pp. 124-125.

3. D. Keith Bell, "Other Liabilities, Capital and Surplus," *Property-Casualty Insurance Accounting*, 6th ed. (Durham, NC: Insurance Accounting and Systems Association, 1994), p. 6:15.

4. Terrie E. Troxel and George E. Bouchie, *Property-Liability Insurance Accounting and Finance*, 4th ed. (Malvern, PA: American Institute for CPCU, 1995), pp. 126-128.

5. A.M. Best, *Best's Aggregates & Averages: Property-Casualty, 1996 Edition* (Oldwick, NJ: A.M. Best Company, 1996), p. 96.

Appendix A: → *Compare this analysis w/the one in the Reinsurance 141 Book.*
Reinsurance Transactions

Reinsurance is a contractual arrangement under which one insurer (the ceding company) buys insurance from another insurer (the reinsurer or assuming company). The reinsurance arrangement covers some or all of the losses incurred by the ceding company.

Reinsurance can be categorized by the method used to spread the loss between the ceding company and the reinsurer. Under a **pro rata contract**, both the insurer and reinsurer share the premium and losses on a proportional basis. Under an **excess-of-loss contract**, the insurer retains all of the loss up to a stated amount, after which the reinsurer pays the balance of the loss (or 80 to 90 percent of the balance) up to the contract limit. Pro rata reinsurance is the preferred method for increasing the capacity of an insurer.

Pro rata reinsurance has the advantage of providing additional premium capacity to the ceding insurer. **Premium capacity** is the total amount of premium an insurer can write in a year. Gross premium capacity is a function of both the policyholders' surplus and reinsurance protection arranged by the insurer. Net premium capacity is a function of the insurer's policyholders' surplus alone.

An insurer's net written premiums (that is, net of reinsurance) should not exceed a multiple of its policyholders' surplus. Financial analysts, regulators, and insurance rating organizations become concerned when the net written premiums of an insurer are more than three times its policyholders' surplus. Some analysts suggest that a ratio of four-to-one might be acceptable for some lines of business, and a three-to-one ratio might be excessive for others. Regardless of the proper ratio, any form of reinsurance that increases policyholders' surplus causes a corresponding increase in premium capacity. The action of increasing the policyholders' surplus of an insurer is called **surplus relief**.

Pro rata reinsurance can increase policyholders' surplus and thus provide surplus relief. This occurs because premium is transferred to the reinsurer, which pays a ceding commission to the insurer to offset the insurer's policy acquisition costs. The premium capacity of the insurer is increased not only because of an increase in policyholders' surplus, but also because a portion of the insurer's premium has been ceded to a reinsurer. Thus, the insurer's net premiums are lowered.

The following example illustrates the idea of surplus relief. Assume that an insurer writes $20 million of premium evenly throughout a year and incurs $4 million in policy acquisition costs. To simplify the analysis, assume the insurer is new and has no unearned premiums and no loss and loss adjustment expense reserves at the beginning of the year. However, the insurer does have $9 million in assets and $9 million in policyholders' surplus. The loss and loss adjustment expense reserves incurred during the first year of operations are equal to the earned premium, and 50 percent of the premium is earned at the end of the first year. No losses are paid during the first year.

The balance sheet for the insurer at the beginning of the year is shown below:

Insurer Balance Sheet
Beginning of Year
(All figures in $millions)

Assets		Liabilities & Policyholders' Surplus	
Cash & Invested assets	$9	Unearned premium	$0
		Loss and Loss adjustment expense reserves	0
		Policyholders' surplus	9
Total assets	$9	Total Liab. & Surplus	$9

If the insurer did not purchase pro rata reinsurance, it would have written premium of $20 million, policy acquisition costs of $4 million, an unearned premium reserve of $10 million, and loss and loss adjustment reserves of $10 million. The balance sheet at the end of the year would be as follows:

Insurer Balance Sheet
End of Year—No Reinsurance
(All figures in $millions)

Assets		Liabilities & Policyholders' Surplus	
Cash & Invested assets	$25	Unearned premium	$10
		Loss and Loss adjustment expense reserves	10
		Total liabilities	$20
		Policyholders' surplus	5
Total assets	$25	Total Liab. & Surplus	$25

Assets increased by the $20 million in premium and decreased by the $4 million in acquisition costs. The policyholders' surplus fell from $9 million to $5 million, which is equal to the $4 million in policy acquisition costs incurred. The written premium to surplus ratio for the year is 4:1 ($20 million divided by $5 million).

The balance sheet numbers would have changed, including an increase in policyholders' surplus, if the insurer purchased pro rata reinsurance. Assume the insurer cedes 75 percent of the premium (and losses) to a reinsurer. Also assume that the reinsurer pays the insurer a 30 percent ceding commission. The insurer would cede $15 million in premium (75 percent of written premium) to the reinsurer and would receive a $4.5 million ceding commission (30 percent), so the insurer's assets at the end of the year would equal $14.5 million ($9.0 million assets + $5.0 million premium + $4.5 million ceding commission – $4.0 million policy acquisition costs). The insurer's liabilities would also be 25 percent of what they would be without reinsurance, so both the unearned premium reserve and the loss and loss adjustment expense reserve would be reduced by 75 percent. The following balance sheet shows the result of the purchase of the pro rata reinsurance:

Insurer Balance Sheet
End of Year—With Pro Rata Reinsurance
(All figures in $millions)

Assets		Liabilities & Policyholders' Surplus	
Cash & Invested assets	$14.5	Unearned premium	$ 2.5
		Loss and Loss adjustment expense reserves	2.5
		Total liabilities	$ 5.0
		Policyholders' surplus	9.5
Total assets	$14.5	Total Liab. & Surplus	$14.5

The most significant result of this balance sheet reconfiguration is that the policyholders' surplus has increased by the $4.5 million in ceding commission, from $5.0 million to $9.5 million. In addition to the increase in policyholders' surplus, pro rata reinsurance decreased the ratio of net written premiums to policyholders' surplus. It fell from 4:1 to more than 0.5:1 ($5 million divided by $9.5 million).

This benefit would not be as large in a real-world situation because, for simplification reasons, this example shows no investment income earned on the assets. Without reinsurance, the insurer would have higher assets and would be able to earn more investment income than if reinsurance were purchased. This would offset a small part of the benefit of purchasing the pro rata reinsurance.

Appendix B: Summary of Accounting Entries for Insurance Transactions

Following is a summary of the accounting entries for premium and loss transactions covered in this chapter.

Sale of Insurance

Dr.	Cash	xx
	Cr. Premiums written	xx

Adjusting Entry for Earned Premiums

Dr.	Premiums written	xx
	Cr. Premiums earned	xx
	Cr. Unearned premium reserve	xx

Reserving a Loss

Dr.	Losses incurred	xx
	Cr. Loss reserves	xx

Paying a Loss

Dr.	Loss reserves	xx
	Cr. Cash	xx

Part III

Tools for Analytical Decision Making

Chapter 12

Reading Financial Statements in Context: What's Behind the Numbers?

Financial statements can provide an almost limitless amount of information. Sudden changes in item amounts from one period to the next might indicate that abnormal or problematic conditions exist. However, such changes might instead be the result of changes in accounting practices or valuation methods employed by the reporting entity. When analyzing a firm's financial condition, experienced analysts do not consider their examination of financial statements complete without also reviewing the notes to those statements. In addition to the notes, analysts might review the entity's Form 10-K filed with the Securities and Exchange Commission and reports from independent financial rating services such as A. M. Best's for insurers and Standard & Poor's or Dun & Bradstreet for noninsurers. When conducting a ratio analysis of the entity's financial statements, analysts often compare the results of their calculations with benchmarks provided for similar companies within an industry segment.

Because of the complexities related to financial reporting and because of the number of alternative generally accepted accounting principles that can be used, **explanatory notes to the financial statements** are included as an integral part of the financial statements. As explained in Chapter 2, the full disclosure concept means that companies are required to report all necessary information to prevent a reasonably astute user of the financial statements from being misled. The explanatory notes, or **financial review**, are referred to on each individual financial statement and are presented immediately after the financial statements. In the Armstrong World Industries, Inc., report provided in the Appendix to this text's course workbook and study guide, the financial review appears on pages 28 through 42.

At first glance the notes to the financial statements can appear intimidating because they frequently require more pages than the financial statements themselves, contain a great deal of detailed information, and include much financial management terminology. However, the reader cannot fully understand the financial statements without referring to the notes.

Financial statements of companies whose securities are publicly traded must be audited by independent auditors, and the annual reports of those companies must include disclosures required by the Securities and Exchange Commission. An understanding of the auditors' report and a review of the other disclosures lead to a more complete picture of a company's financial condition, results of operations, and cash flows.

When a user needs to gain information about a company's financial condition or operating performance and its financial statements are not readily available, outside reporting sources can be consulted that provide summaries of an entity's financial statement data, evaluations of the company's performance, and ratings of its debt and equity issues, or key financial ratios for competing firms or the firm's industry segment. These sources exist for both insurance and noninsurance business entities.

The principal objective of this chapter is to permit you to make sense of the explanatory notes and other financial information found in most corporate annual reports. A secondary objective of this chapter is expose you to the types of information summaries and evaluation reports available from financial reporting services.

Educational Objectives

After studying this chapter, you should be able to:

1. Explain why the explanatory notes should be considered an integral part of the financial statements.
2. Identify the kinds of significant accounting policies that are explained in the notes.
3. Describe the nature and content of typical disclosures relating to:

- Accounting changes
- Business combinations
- Contingencies and commitments
- Events occurring after the balance sheet date
- Effects of inflation
- Segment information

4. Describe the role of the Securities and Exchange Commission, and identify some of its reporting requirements.

5. Explain why a statement of management's responsibility is included with the notes.

6. Describe the purpose and content of the "management's discussion and analysis" (MD&A) section of a corporation's Form 10-K filing with the Securities and Exchange Commission.

7. Describe what is included in the five-year (or longer) summary of financial information contained in most corporate annual reports.

8. Describe the content of the independent auditor's report and explain the importance of this report to financial statement users.

9. Describe the financial information that is available from the following financial reporting services:
   - Standard & Poor's
   - Dun & Bradstreet
   - A. M. Best Company
   - Publishers of industry ratios

10. Define or describe each of the Key Words and Phrases introduced in this chapter.

Organization of the Explanatory Notes

The explanatory notes that refer to specific financial statement items are generally presented in the same sequence as the financial statements and in the same sequence that items appear within the individual statements. The financial statement sequence is usually as follows:

1. Income statement
2. Balance sheet
3. Statement of cash flows

Placement of the statement of changes in owners' equity usually depends on the complexity of that statement. If paid-in capital has not changed during the year, a statement of changes in retained earnings may be presented after the income statement and may even be combined with it because net income is the principal item affecting retained earnings. If several capital stock transactions have occurred during the year, a full statement of changes in owners' equity, which includes changes in retained earnings, would be presented separately after the balance sheet. Some companies, including Armstrong World Industries, Inc., present the statement of changes in owners' equity as part of the notes or financial review (see page 38 of the Armstrong World Industries, Inc., report in the Appendix to the course workbook and study guide).

In addition to the notes or financial review, many annual reports include a narrative section called **management's discussion and analysis (MD&A)**. This is a description of the firm's activities for the year, including comments about its financial condition and results of operations. Also included in most annual reports is a comparative summary of key financial data for several years. Both of these components can be helpful to annual report users.

Explanatory Notes (or Financial Review)

The explanatory notes section of an entity's financial statements, sometimes called the "financial review" section, provides valuable information about significant changes in accounting policy, valuation methods, and contingencies and commitments that might have affected the development or presentation of statement content. The notes help to ensure that financial statements provide full disclosure of that information needed by current and potential investors, creditors, and other users to make informed business decisions.

Significant Accounting Policies

As emphasized in earlier chapters, management must make several choices among alternative accounting practices that are generally acceptable. Because these choices differ among firms, disclosure of the specific practices being followed by any firm is necessary for readers to make sense of that firm's financial statements. Users also need information about **significant accounting policies** in order to make intelligent comparisons of the financial position and results of operations of different firms in the same industry. The following discussion highlights the importance of many of these accounting policy disclosures. The comments in italics refer to the 1994 Annual Report of Armstrong World Industries, Inc., in the course workbook and study guide's Appendix.

Depreciation method—The method (straight-line, units-of-production, sum-of-the-years'-digits, or declining-balance) being used for financial reporting purposes and the range of useful lives assumed for broad categories of asset types are usually disclosed. The amount of depreciation expense may also be disclosed in the notes, although it is also reported in the statement of cash flows as an add back to net income. *Armstrong generally uses straight-line depreciation for financial reporting purposes (see page 28). How much depreciation and amortization expense did Armstrong report for 1994?*

Inventory valuation method—The method (weighted-average, FIFO, or LIFO) being used is disclosed. If different methods are being used for different categories of inventory, the method used for each category is disclosed. When LIFO is used, a comparison of the cumulative difference in the balance sheet inventory valuation under LIFO with what it would have been under FIFO is usually disclosed. *What percentage of Armstrong's 1994 inventory is valued on a LIFO basis (see page 32)? How much inventory would Armstrong report on its balance sheet for 1994 on a total FIFO basis?*

Basis of consolidation—A brief statement confirms that the consolidated financial statements include the financial data of all subsidiaries—or if not, why not.

Income taxes—A reconciliation of the statutory income tax rate (currently about 35 percent) with the effective tax rate (indicated by the firm's income tax expense as a percentage of pre-tax income) is provided. Reasons for this difference include tax credits (for example, for investment in new plant and equipment) and other special treatment given certain items for income tax purposes. *Armstrong reports a table that reconciles its statutory and effective tax rates for each of the past three years (see page 31). Notice that the 34 percent statutory tax benefit of the 1992 operating loss was virtually eliminated as a result of restructuring charges and other tax effects reported in that year. You can verify Armstrong's effective tax rate for each year by dividing the "Income taxes" reported on the income statement by "Earnings (loss) before income taxes." Try this with the income statement data reported on page 25.*

An explanation is also made of the deferred taxes resulting from temporary differences between the fiscal year in which an expense (or revenue) is reported for book purposes and the fiscal year in which it is reported for tax purposes. As already discussed, the principal factor in deferred taxes is the use of straight-line depreciation for book purposes and accelerated depreciation for tax purposes. However, many firms also report significant deferred tax items related to postretirement and postemployment benefits because of the adoption of two recent FASB standards (also discussed in Chapter 8). *Armstrong reports a detailed table of deferred income tax assets and liabilities for the past two years (see page 33). The deferred tax assets related to postretirement and postemployment benefits (and other asset items) offset the deferred tax liabilities related to depreciation methods (and other liability items). A separate footnote disclosure explains Armstrong's "Income tax benefits" in considerably less detail (see page 32).*

Employee benefits—The cost of employee benefit plans included as an expense in the income statement is disclosed. The significant actuarial assumptions made with respect to funding pension plans may be discussed, and certain estimated future pension liabilities may be disclosed. The two elements of pension expense are current service cost and prior service cost. Current service cost is the actuarially determined cost to provide future pension benefits based on employees' earnings and service in the current year. Prior service cost is the actuarially determined cost of providing future pension benefits based on employees' earnings and service in past years. Prior service cost arises when a pension plan is started or modified and the future pension benefit will be affected by the employees' earnings and service in past years. Since prior service cost is recognized in future income statements over several years, the amortization process is most significant in understanding the firm's current and probable future pension expense. Many firms have a significant unfunded prior service liability that is not reflected separately on the balance sheet but is disclosed in the explanatory notes. *Details of Armstrong's pension costs and related items are disclosed on pages 29–30. The first table reports the elements of "Total pension (credit) cost" for each of the past three years; separate tables are provided to show the details of the "Net pension credit" for U.S. plans and of the "Net pension cost" for non-U.S. plans reported as elements of "Total pension cost." The tables describing the "Funded status" of Armstrong's pension plans indicate that the U.S. plans are overfunded ("Prepaid pension cost" is an asset) and that the non-U.S. plans are underfunded ("Accrued pension cost" is a liability).*

Amortization of intangible assets—If the balance sheet includes the intangible asset goodwill, the method of amortizing this intangible asset and the amount of amortization expense recorded in the current year are disclosed. The maximum amortization period allowed by generally accepted accounting principles is forty years, but many firms use a shorter period. As discussed in Chapter 7, accounting for goodwill is a problem for accountants. *Armstrong's "Depreciation and amortization" footnote indicates that intangible assets are amortized over periods of three to forty years (see page 28).*

Earnings per share of common stock—An explanation of the calculation, perhaps including the details of the calculation of the weighted-average number of shares outstanding, and the adjustments to net income for preferred stock dividends are provided. The potential dilution of the earnings per share (EPS) figure resulting from convertible bonds or convertible preferred stock if conversions had taken place during the year are also explained. *Armstrong describes its EPS calculation process, including the effect of preferred stock dividends and convertible preferred stock, in a brief footnote on page 28.*

Stock option and stock purchase plans—Many firms have a **stock option plan** under which officers and key employees are given an option to buy a certain number of shares of stock at some time in the future, but at a price equal to the market value of the stock when the option is granted. The stock option presumably provides an incentive to increase the profitability of the firm so that the stock price will rise. Then, when the option is exercised, the owner has an immediate profit that is, in effect, additional compensation for a job well done. *Armstrong reports that 1,367,100 option shares are exercisable at the end of the year. The $36.82 average price of these option shares (see the table on page 37) is less than the $38.50 year-end market value per share of common stock (reported in the Nine-Year Summary on page 52).*

Under a stock purchase plan, the employees can purchase shares of the company's common stock at a slight discount from market value. The objective is to permit the employees to become part owners of the firm, and thus to have more of an owner's attitude about their jobs and the company. *Armstrong has an employee stock ownership plan (ESOP) in which all employees are eligible to participate (see page 31). In addition, certain key executives are entitled to "Performance restricted shares" of Armstrong's common stock if the company meets certain predetermined performance goals. How many of these shares were outstanding at the end of 1994 (see page 37)?*

From the employees' point of view, stock option and stock purchase plans are usually good fringe benefits. From the investors' point of view, the shares that are issuable under these plans represent potential dilution of equity. Thus, the nature of these plans is described, and the potential dilution is disclosed.

Details of Other Financial Statement Amounts

Many firms include in the explanatory notes the details of amounts that are reported as a single amount in the financial statements. For example, the amount of research and development expenses included in a broader income statement operating expense category, the details of the "other income" category of the income statement, or details of the cost and accumulated depreciation of plant and equipment that are reported in total on the balance sheet may be provided. Long-term debt, frequently reported as a single amount on the balance sheet, is usually made up of several obligations. A descriptive listing of the obligations, including a schedule of the principal payments required for each of the next five years, is usually reported. The firm's financial officers decide the extent of such detail to be reported, generally based on their judgment of the benefit of such detail to the broad audience that will receive the financial statements. In some cases, disclosure requirements of the Securities and Exchange Commission and the desire to conform the stockholders' report with the report required to be filed with the SEC (see Business Procedure Capsule 21) result in these details.

Other Disclosures

The notes to financial statements provide other disclosures not related to significant accounting policy changes. For example, changes in accounting principles, contingencies and commitments because of the firm's involvement with litigation, or the effect of inflation can materially affect comparability of the current period's financial statements with those prepared for previous periods.

Accounting Change

An **accounting change** is a change in an accounting principle that has a material effect on the comparability of the current period financial statements with those of prior periods. The effects of recently adopted accounting changes must be disclosed. For example, if a firm changes its inventory cost-flow assumption from FIFO to LIFO, this change and the dollar effect of the change on both the income statement and balance sheet must be disclosed. Likewise, a change in depreciation methods, a change in the method of accounting for pension costs, or any other change having a significant effect on the financial statements must be disclosed.

Sometimes the accounting change is the result of a FASB pronouncement. The most common changes reported in the AICPA survey of the 1993 annual reports of 600 corporations were of this variety. They included changes in the accounting for income taxes (by 233 firms), pension costs (224), postretirement benefits (176), and postemployment benefits (87).[1] The financial review in the Armstrong World Industries, Inc., 1994 Annual Report mentions the company's accounting changes for the last two items. These changes are still included in the financial review because the comparative income statements and statements of cash flows include 1992 data.

Business Combinations

If the firm has been involved in a **business combination** (that is, a merger, an acquisition, or a disposition), the transactions involved are described and the effect on the financial statements are explained. In the case of the disposition of part of the business, the income statement will segregate the effect on the current year's results of discontinued operations.

Most mergers and acquisitions are accounted for by using **purchase accounting**. Under purchase accounting, the assets acquired are recorded by the acquiring company at their *fair market value* at the date of acquisition. Any amount paid for the acquired assets (or company) in excess of the fair market value of the assets is recorded as goodwill—an intangible asset that is then amortized to expense over a period of time. An alternative accounting method, **pooling of interests accounting**, can be used in certain circumstances. Under pooling, the assets acquired are recorded by the acquiring company at the *book value* at which the acquired company carries them. Likewise, the stock issued in the merger is recorded at the book value of the acquired company, not the market value of the shares issued. This accounting alternative eliminates any necessity for goodwill but usually results in the acquired assets being recorded by the acquiring company at less than fair market value. The notes explain the accounting method used in the merger or acquisition. In the AICPA survey of the 1993 annual reports of 600 corporations, 200 firms reported business combinations under the purchase method, and only 21 firms reported pooling of interests.[2]

- **BUSINESS PROCEDURE CAPSULE 21**
  Reporting to the Securities and Exchange Commission

The Securities and Exchange Commission (SEC) was created by the Securities and Exchange Act of 1934 to administer the provisions of that act and the Securities Act of 1933. Later, Congress assigned to the SEC the authority and responsibility for administering other securities laws. Securities issued by corporations (principally stocks and bonds) that are offered for sale to more than a very few investors must be registered with the SEC. The basic objective of this registration is to provide potential investors a full and fair disclosure of the securities being issued, the issuer's business activities and financial position, and an explanation of the use to be made of the proceeds of the security issue. Registration does not result in a seal of approval or a guarantee against loss. Investors must decide for themselves whether their objectives are likely to be achieved. Registration is required for additional issues of previously unregistered securities (for example, if the corporation wants to raise capital by selling additional shares of stock) and for issues of newly created securities (for exam-

Continued on next page.

ple, bonds that will be offered to the public). A **prospectus** summarizing the complete registration statement must be provided to investors before or concurrent with purchase of the security. A prospectus is provided by the company or the broker through whom the securities are being sold.

Registered securities can be traded publicly on a stock exchange or in the over-the-counter market. Firms that issue these securities are required to file an annual report with the SEC. This report is referred to as *Form 10-K*. The requirements of Form 10-K have had a significant effect on the scope of material included in the annual report to stockholders. Most companies include in their annual report all of the financial statement information required in the Form 10-K.

Form 10-K requires some information not usually found in the financial statements, including data about executive compensation and ownership of voting stock by directors and officers. This information is also included in the proxy statement sent to stockholders along with the notice of the annual meeting and a description of the items expected to be acted upon by the stockholders at that meeting. Stockholders who do not expect to attend the annual meeting are invited to return a **proxy**. Although the proxy gives another person (usually a director of the corporation) the right to vote the stockholder's shares, the owner can indicate his or her preference for how the shares are to be voted on the indicated issues.

The registration statement, prospectus, Form 10-K, and proxy statement are public documents, and copies can be obtained from the corporation or the SEC.

Contingencies and Commitments

Firms are commonly involved in litigation, the results of which are not known when the financial statements are prepared. If a firm is denying liability in a lawsuit in which it is a defendant, it should disclose the fact of the lawsuit to readers of the financial statements. Of course, the concept of matching revenue and expense requires the recognition of any anticipated cost of verdicts that the company expects to have to pay. An expense or a loss and a related liability should be reported in the period affected. Even if the lawsuit is one that management and counsel believe will not result in any liability to the company, the fact of the potential loss and liability should be disclosed. The nature of the legal action, the potential damages, and a statement to the effect that the claims against the company are not likely to be sustained are included in the notes. *Armstrong continues to update its extensive "Litigation" footnote each year (see pages 39–42). Most of the personal injury lawsuits against the company involve alleged exposure to asbestos-containing products used, manufactured, or sold by the company—even though Armstrong has not sold any such products since 1969.*

In some cases a firm or one of its subsidiaries may act as a guarantor of the indebtedness of another entity. In those cases, the amount of the potential liability and a brief description of the circumstances should be disclosed in the notes. *Armstrong's ESOP loan guarantee is reported on the balance sheet as a separate noncurrent liability and as a reduction of stockholders' equity. Essentially, the company has guaranteed the repayment of a loan taken out by a separate, but related, entity (the ESOP). The proceeds of this loan were used to purchase a new series of the company's own preferred stock on behalf of the employees participating in the ESOP plan (see page 31).*

If the firm has committed to purchase a significant amount of plant and equipment or to pay significant amounts of rent on leased property for several years into the future, these commitments are disclosed. This is because the commitment is like a liability but is not recorded on the balance sheet because the actual purchase transaction has not yet occurred.

A firm may have other kinds of **contingencies** and **commitments**. Most will have a negative effect on the financial position of the firm or its results of operations if they materialize. The purpose of disclosing them is to provide full disclosure to the user of the financial statements.

Events After the Balance Sheet Date

If, after the balance sheet date, a significant event occurs that has a material effect on the balance sheet or income statement, the subsequent event and its probable effect on future financial statements should be explained. Examples of such significant events include the issuance of a large amount of long-term debt, the restructuring of long-term debt, a business combination, the issuance of a large amount of capital stock, and the sale of a significant part of the company's assets.

Effect of Inflation

Financial statements do not reflect the effect of inflation. The original cost concept and the objectivity principle result in assets being recorded at their historical cost to the entity, based on current dollars when the transactions are recorded. In 1979, because of the significant inflation that the United States had experienced in the prior decade, the FASB required large companies to report certain inflation-adjusted data in the explanatory notes to the financial statements. This was done on a trial basis for five years. In effect, the income statement, earnings per share of common stock, and total net assets were adjusted based on two methods of reflecting the effect of changing prices: a price index method and a current replacement cost method. The effect of each of these methods was usually to reduce reported earnings, because higher amounts would be reported for depreciation expense and cost of goods sold.

Depreciation expense was greater than recorded because asset values had increased. For firms that used the FIFO cost-flow assumption, cost of goods sold also increased because inventory replacement costs were higher than the historical cost used in traditional accounting. Firms that used LIFO did not experience as much of a cost of goods sold increase because LIFO releases more current costs to the income statement. Net assets were generally increased significantly under each method of reflecting inflation. In 1986 the FASB rescinded the requirement, and now firms are merely encouraged to report the effects of inflation.

Reporting the effects of inflation is a controversial and complex area of accounting. If the economy experiences high rates of inflation in the future, efforts to reflect the effect of inflation directly in the financial statements will likely be renewed.

Segment Information

Most large corporations operate in several lines of business and in several international areas. In addition, some firms have major customers (frequently the U.S. government) that account for a significant part of the total business. A **business segment** is a group of the firm's business activities that have a common denominator. Management identifies and defines the components of each business segment. Segments may reflect the company's organizational structure, manufacturing processes, product-line groups, or industries served. The required disclosure of segment, geographic, and major customer information is designed to permit financial statement users to make judgments about the effect on the firm of factors that might influence specific lines of business, geographic areas, or major customers.

Data shown for each segment include sales to unaffiliated customers, operating profit, capital expenditures, depreciation and amortization expense, and identifiable assets. From these data, a DuPont Model return-on-investment calculation can be performed, and for each segment a simple statement of cash flows can be prepared showing cash flows from operating activities (net income plus depreciation expense), minus cash used for investing activities (capital expenditures). This simple statement of cash flows omits financing activities (such as long-term debt and dividend transactions), but it does highlight the principal cash flows related to each segment. Although these segment measures cannot be combined to equal the total company's ROI or cash flows (because assets and expenses applicable to the corporation as a whole have not been arbitrarily allocated to segments), segment trends over time can be determined. Exhibit 12-1 illustrates this estimation process with the data disclosed for Armstrong's "Floor coverings" industry segment on page 37 of the 1994 annual report in the Appendix to the course workbook.

Exhibit 12-1
Approximate ROI and Cash Flows for the Floor Coverings Segment of
Armstrong World Industries, Inc.—1994

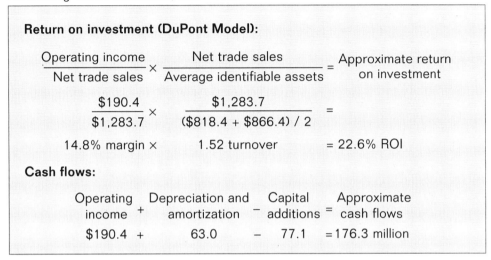

Return on investment (DuPont Model):

$$\frac{\text{Operating income}}{\text{Net trade sales}} \times \frac{\text{Net trade sales}}{\text{Average identifiable assets}} = \frac{\text{Approximate return}}{\text{on investment}}$$

$$\frac{\$190.4}{\$1,283.7} \times \frac{\$1,283.7}{(\$818.4 + \$866.4) / 2} =$$

14.8% margin ×   1.52 turnover   = 22.6% ROI

Cash flows:

$$\frac{\text{Operating}}{\text{income}} + \frac{\text{Depreciation and}}{\text{amortization}} - \frac{\text{Capital}}{\text{additions}} = \frac{\text{Approximate}}{\text{cash flows}}$$

$190.4 +   63.0   −   77.1   =176.3 million

Sales to unaffiliated customers, operating profits, and identifiable assets are also reported by geographic areas in which the firm operates. For example, the areas in the geographic breakdown used by many firms with international operations are the United States, Europe, Africa, Pan America, and the Pacific. ROI calculations can also be made based on geographic areas, but cash flow information cannot be approximated because the required geographic disclosures do not include capital expenditures or depreciation and amortization expense.

If a firm has a major customer that accounts for more than 10 percent of its total sales, this fact should be disclosed to financial statement users so that a judgment about the influence of that customer on the firm's continued profitability can be made.

Management's Statement of Responsibility

Many firms include in the explanatory notes **management's statement of responsibility**, which explains that the responsibility for the financial statements lies with the management of the firm, not the external auditors/certified public accountants who express an opinion about the fairness with which the financial statements present the financial condition and results of operations of the company. The statement of responsibility usually refers to the firm's system of internal controls, the internal audit function, the audit committee of the board of directors, and other policies and procedures designed to ensure that the company operates at a high level of ethical conduct. Armstrong includes this statement on page 43 of its annual statement.

Management's Discussion and Analysis

For many years, the SEC has required companies that must file a Form 10-K annual report with the SEC to include in the report a discussion by management of the firm's activities during the year and its financial condition and results of operations. This discussion is being included in more and more annual reports to stockholders. Management's discussion and analysis (MD&A) should enhance disclosure to the public of information about the corporation. It is a part of the annual report that current and potential investors should read. In the Armstrong World Industries, Inc., report, management's discussion and analysis of financial condition and results of operations appear on pages 45 through 51.

Five-Year (or Longer) Summary of Financial Data

Most corporate annual reports present a summary of financial data for at least the five most recent years. Many firms report these data for longer periods, and at least one firm reports for every year since it was organized. Included in the summary are key income statement data or even the entire income statement in condensed form. In addition to amounts, significant ratios such as earnings as a percentage of sales, average assets, and average owners' equity are included. Earnings and dividends per share, the average number of shares outstanding each year, and other operating statistics may be reported. Year-end data from the balance sheet such as working capital; property, plant, and equipment (net of accumulated depreciation); long-term debt; and owners' equity are usually reported. Book value per share of common stock and the year-end market price of common stock are frequently reported. When stock dividends or stock splits have occurred, the per share data of prior years are adjusted retroactively so that the per share data are comparable.

As an illustration of the adjustment of per share data for stock dividends or stock splits, assume that Cruisers, Inc., reported earnings per share and cash dividends per share of $4.50 and $2.00, respectively, for fiscal 1994. Assume also that in 1995 the firm had a 2-for-1 stock split. In the annual report for

1995, earnings and dividends for 1994 should reflect that because of the split, now twice as many shares of common stock are outstanding as were when 1994 amounts were first reported. Therefore, in the 1995 annual report, 1994 earnings per share and dividends per share will be reported at $2.25 and $1.00, respectively. Assume further that in 1996 Cruisers had a 10 percent stock dividend that resulted in 110 shares outstanding for every 100 shares that were outstanding before the stock dividend. The 1996 annual report will report 1994 earnings per share and dividends per share as $2.05 ($2.25 / 1.10) and $.91 ($1.00 / 1.10), respectively.

The **five-year summary** is not included in the scope of the outside auditors' work, nor does their opinion relate to the summary. Therefore, the summary appears in the annual report *after* the outside auditors' opinion. Likewise, the summary is not a part of the explanatory notes to the financial statements; it is a supplementary disclosure. Armstrong World Industries, Inc.'s, annual report includes a nine-year summary on page 52.

Independent Auditors' Report

The independent auditors' report is a brief (usually three paragraphs) often easily overlooked report that relates to the financial statements and the accompanying explanatory notes. The SEC requires an audit of the financial statements of a publicly owned company. Many privately owned firms have an audit of their financial statements to support their bank loan negotiations.

The first three paragraphs of the independent auditors' report for Armstrong World Industries, Inc. (which is on page 43 of the annual report in the Appendix of the course workbook and study guide), are reproduced in Exhibit 12-2. This report format has been standardized by the Auditing Standards Board of the AICPA and is almost universal. Armstrong World Industries, Inc., received an *unqualified*, or "clean," audit opinion, meaning that its financial statements were "present[ed] fairly, in all material respects . . . in conformity with generally accepted accounting principles." This is by far the most commonly presented opinion in annual reports because most firms prefer to make the necessary "auditor-suggested adjustments" to financial statement amounts and footnote disclosures than to receive a *qualified* audit opinion.

The report is usually addressed to the board of directors and stockholders of the corporation. The first or *introductory paragraph* identifies the financial statements that were audited and briefly describes the responsibilities of both management and the auditors with respect to the financial statements. Management is responsible for the financial statements; the auditors' task is to express an opinion about them.

Exhibit 12-2
Independent Auditors' Report

> The Board of Directors and Shareholders,
> Armstrong World Industries, Inc.:
>
> We have audited the consolidated balance sheets of Armstrong World
> Industries, Inc., and subsidiaries as of December 31, 1994, and 1993, and
> the related statements of earnings and cash flows for each of the years in
> the three-year period ended December 31, 1994. These consolidated
> financial statements are the responsibility of the company's management.
> Our responsibility is to express an opinion on these consolidated financial
> statements based on our audits.
>
> We conducted our audits in accordance with generally accepted auditing
> standards. Those standards require that we plan and perform the audit to
> obtain reasonable assurance about whether the financial statements are
> free of material misstatements. An audit includes examining, on a test
> basis, evidence supporting the amounts and disclosures in the financial
> statements. An audit also includes assessing the accounting principles
> used and significant estimates made by management, as well as evaluating
> the overall financial statement presentation. We believe that our audits
> provide a reasonable basis for our opinion.
>
> In our opinion, the consolidated financial statements referred to above
> present fairly, in all material respects, the financial position of Armstrong
> World Industries, Inc., and subsidiaries, at December 31, 1994, and 1993,
> and the results of their operations and their cash flows for each of the
> years in the three-year period ended December 31, 1994, in conformity
> with generally accepted accounting principles.

The second paragraph is the *scope paragraph,* and it describes the nature and extent of the auditor's work. The auditor's concern is with obtaining reasonable assurance about whether the financial statements are free of material misstatements, and their work involves tests to gain that confidence. Auditors give no guarantee that the financial statements are free from fraudulent transactions or from the effects of errors. The accuracy of the financial statements is the responsibility of management, not of the auditors. However, generally accepted auditing standards do require extensive audit procedures as a means of obtaining reasonable assurance that the financial statements are free from material misstatements.

The third paragraph is the *opinion paragraph,* and in that sense it is the most important. The benchmark is fair presentation in all material respects. If, during the course of the audit, the auditor determines that the financial statements taken as a whole do not "present fairly," the auditor will require a change in the presentation or withdraw from the audit. The latter action is very rare.

The name of the auditing firm, sometimes presented as a facsimile signature, and the date of the report are shown. The date of the report is the date the audit work was completed, and a required audit procedure is to review transactions after the balance sheet date up to the date of the report. As discussed earlier in this chapter, unusual transactions that occur during this period must be disclosed in the financial statements or in the explanatory notes.

Occasionally the auditors' report includes an explanatory paragraph that describes a situation that does not affect fair presentation but that should be disclosed to keep the financial statements from being misleading. Items that require additional explanation include the following:

1. Basing the opinion in part on the work of another auditor
2. Uncertainties about the outcome of certain events that would have affected the presentation if the outcome could be estimated
3. Substantial doubt about the entity's ability to continue as a going concern
4. A material change between periods in an accounting principle or its method of application

The fourth paragraph of the auditors' report on page 43 of the Armstrong annual report refers to two of these items.

The auditor can issue a qualified opinion if the scope of the audit was restricted and essential audit work could not be performed, or if a material departure from generally accepted accounting principles affects only part of the financial statements. The reason for the qualification is explained in the report, and the opinion about fair presentation is restricted to the unaffected parts of the financial statements. Qualified opinions rarely occur in practice.

The financial statement reader should review the independent auditors' report and determine the effect of any departure from the standard report.

Financial Statement Compilations

Accounting firms also perform services for client organizations whose debt and equity securities are not publicly traded (and whose financial statements are not required by the SEC to be audited). Many small businesses use an outside accounting firm to prepare the necessary tax returns and to assemble financial information into conventional financial statements. The accounting firm may prepare financial statements to submit to banks and other major suppliers for purposes of obtaining commercial credit. Because the accounting firm is not engaged in an audit, a report must be issued that clearly communicates that the accounting firm is not providing any form of assurance as to the fairness of the financial statements. Such a report, called a compilation report, is shown in Exhibit 12-3.

Exhibit 12-3
Compilation Report

The Board of Directors and Shareholders,
Cruisers, Inc.:

We have compiled the accompanying balance sheet of Cruiser's, Inc., as of December 31,1996, and the related statements of income and retained earnings and cash flows for the year then ended, in accordance with standards established by the American Institute of Certified Public Accountants.

A compilation is limited to presenting in the form of financial statements information that is the representation of management. We have not audited or reviewed the accompanying financial statements and, accordingly, do not express an opinion or any other form of assurance on them.

Management has elected to omit substantially all of the disclosures required by generally accepted accounting principles. If the omitted disclosures were included in the financial statements, they might influence the user's conclusions about Cruisers, Inc.'s, financial condition, results of operations, cash flows, and changes in financial position. Accordingly, these financial statements are not designed for those who are not informed about such matters.

(Accounting firm's signature, address, and date)

Users of financial statements should be aware that the compilation report is an unaudited statement based on management provided information. If the firm's need for capital is great and it borrows substantial amounts from its bank, the bank may reject compilations and insist on financial statements that have been audited by an independent accountant. Having an audit will usually cause the firm's accounting costs to rise significantly.

Other Sources of Financial Information

Investors, creditors, and other financial statement users often need information in addition to that provided by current-period financial statements when evaluating an entity's financial condition, operating performance, or value. Insurance producers, underwriters, or claim adjusters may need an industry or underwriting class performance standard against which current or prospective risks can be compared or a source of basic account balance relationships that can be used to reconstruct accounting records that have been damaged in a loss.

Although most business clients with whom insurance professionals transact business are not evaluated or reported on by rating services (because stock of the companies is not publicly traded on exchanges), most business clients can be evaluated by comparing their performance to an industry standard or market leader. Insurance producers can also use reports from outside rating services to evaluate the insurers with which they do business.

An important part of any financial analysis is comparing the performance results of the entity being analyzed to that of a benchmark. A **benchmark** is a predetermined standard used in financial analysis, against which some measure of an entity's operations or financial condition is compared to determine the entity's relative performance. Benchmarks can be as simple as rules of thumb or as complex as the financial ratio results of a competitor or industry segment.

Many analysts do not have access to a firm's current financial statements and therefore must rely on financial summaries or ratings of a firm's condition or its debt and equity issues provided by an independent rating service. Current and future investors often refer to published stock and bond reports to make quick assessments of the financial condition and value of the firms in which they might invest. When using outside information sources, one must be able to rely on the accuracy of the information provided to gain information beneficial to decision making.

Numerous sources of financial information outside of an entity's own financial statements can benefit analysts. The following sections identify popular sources of financial information and performance ratings, with a brief description of the information each provides. For brevity, only excerpts of the reports of these sources are provided. Each source should be consulted individually to obtain a full description of the information available and the basis on which it is reported before it is used in any analysis or decision-making activity.

A. M. Best's Ratings of Insurance Companies

The oldest insurance company rating service is the A.M. Best Company, which annually publishes ratings for life-health and property-liability insurance companies. The system used by Best's to rate property-liability insurers is described here based on the information provided in the introductory pages of both the 1996 editions of *Best's Key Rating Guide, Property-Casualty* and *Best's Insurance Reports, Property-Casualty*. Best's develops a rating based on factors that affect an insurer's overall performance, competitive market position, and ability to meet policyholder obligations. Best's rates insurers by using both quantitative and qualitative criteria. Quantitative evaluation criteria include the following:

1. Profitability
2. Leverage and capitalization
3. Liquidity

The qualitative evaluation includes the following eight criteria:

1. Assessment of the insurer's spread of risk
2. Quality and appropriateness of the reinsurance program
3. Quality and diversification of assets
4. Adequacy of loss reserves
5. Adequacy of surplus
6. Capital structure and holding company
7. Management experience and objectives
8. Market presence

Best's assigns ratings ranging from A++ to F, or a Financial Performance Rating (FPR) from 9 to 2. The following table summarizes rating definitions provided by A.M. Best in the *Key Rating Guide*:

Rating Designation	Rating Definition
A++ and A+	Companies have demonstrated *superior* overall performance and have a *very strong* ability to meet their obligations to policyholders over a long period of time.
A and A–	Companies have demonstrated *excellent* overall performance and have a *strong ability* to meet their obligations to policyholders over a long period of time.
B++ and B+	Companies have demonstrated *very good* overall performance and have a *good ability* to meet their obligations to policyholders over a long period of time.
B and B–	Companies have demonstrated *adequate* overall performance and have an *adequate ability* to meet their obligations to policyholders, but their financial strength is *vulnerable* to unfavorable changes in underwriting or economic conditions.

C++ and C+	Companies have demonstrated *marginal* overall performance and have a *current ability* to meet their obligations to policyholders, but their financial strength is *vulnerable* to unfavorable changes in underwriting or economic conditions.
C and C–	Companies have demonstrated *marginal* overall performance and have a *current ability* to meet their obligations to policyholders, but their financial strength is *very vulnerable* to unfavorable changes in underwriting or economic conditions.
D	Companies have demonstrated *poor* overall performance and have a *current ability* to meet their obligations to policyholders, but their financial strength is *extremely vulnerable* to unfavorable changes in underwriting or economic conditions.
E	Companies have been placed by a state insurance regulatory authority under any form of *supervision*, control, or restraint, such as conservatorship or rehabilitation, but not liquidation.
F	Companies have been placed under an order of *liquidation* by a court of law, or owners have voluntarily agreed to liquidate. Note: Companies that voluntarily liquidate or dissolve their charters are generally not insolvent.

In 1996, A.M. Best reported on 3,191 property-liability insurers. Of that number, lettered ratings were assigned to 2,079. The remaining 1,112 insurers were categorized into one of four classes of "no rating opinions." NR-1 is assigned to small companies that did not provide a copy of their NAIC Annual Statement. NR-2 is assigned to companies that do not meet A.M. Best's minimum size and/or operating experience requirements. NR-3 is assigned to companies for which Best's normal rating categories do not apply because of the company's unique operations. NR-4 is assigned to companies that request their ratings not be published. Exhibit 12-4 provides a summary of the distribution of Best's ratings for the 3,191 companies on which it reported in 1996.

Best's Insurance Reports

Best's Insurance Reports, Property-Casualty provides a brief summary of key financial statement items, including an abbreviated balance sheet and investment schedule. This information is accompanied by an executive summary describing the insurer's ownership structure and dates of organization, a brief history of the company's development, and a one- or two-paragraph synopsis of the insurer's current operations and future outlook based on its current liquidity and surplus position.

Exhibit 12-4
A.M. Best's 1996 Ratings of Property-Casualty Insurers

1996 Property/Casualty Rating Distribution*
Based on Individual Companies

Best's Rating/FPR Level	Category	Number	Percentage
	Secure Ratings		
A++	Superior	141	6.8%
A+	Superior	301	14.5
FPR = 9	Strong	0	0.0
	Subtotal	**442**	**21.3**
A	Excellent	547	26.3
A–	Excellent	475	22.8
FPR = 8	Strong	1	0.0
FPR = 7	Above Average	8	0.4
	Subtotal	**1,031**	**49.6**
B++	Very Good	161	7.8
B+	Very Good	143	6.9
FPR = 6	Above Average	19	0.9
FPR = 5	Average	51	2.5
	Subtotal	**374**	**18.0**
	Secure Ratings	**1,847**	**88.8%**
	Vulnerable Ratings		
B	Adequate	75	3.6%
B–	Adequate	33	1.6
FPR = 4	Average	43	2.1
	Subtotal	**151**	**7.3**
C++	Fair	12	0.6
C+	Fair	11	0.5
FPR = 3	Below average	16	0.8
	Subtotal	**39**	**1.9**
C	Marginal	12	0.6
C–	Marginal	2	0.1
FPR = 2	Below Average	5	0.2
	Subtotal	**19**	**0.9**

D	Very Vulnerable	5	0.2
E	Under State Supervision	14	0.7
F	In Liquidation	4	0.2
	Vulnerable Ratings	**232**	**11.2%**
	Total Rating Opinions	**2,079**	**100.0%**

——————————————— No Rating Opinions ———————————————

NR-1	Limited Data Filing	771	69.3%
NR-2	Less Than Minimum Size/		
	Operating Experience	126	11.3
NR-3	Rating Procedure Inapplicable	196	17.6
NR-4	Company Request	19	1.7
S	Rating Suspended	0	0.0
	Subtotal-No Rating Opinions	**1,112**	**100.0%**
	Total Reported Companies	**3,191**	

*As of June 24, 1996

Best's Key Rating Guide

The *Key Rating Guide* also provides Best's ratings of property-liability insurers. Features that distinguishing this publication from *Best's Insurance Reports* are the standardized tabular format of presentation that allows quick comparison among reported companies' results and the five-year summary of key financial information and ratios that allows analysts to identify performance trends. Exhibit 12-5 provides the *Key Rating Guide* report segment for Argonaut Insurance Group. This report provides a five-year summary on a consolidated basis for the Argonaut group of six insurance companies.

Best's reports that the Argonaut Group writes approximately 82.7 percent of its total business in workers compensation and writes primarily in California (22.6 percent of total business), Hawaii (10.0 percent), Illinois (9.3 percent), Pennsylvania (7.4 percent), and Washington, D.C. (4.7 percent). Policyholders' surplus has increased by 48.8 percent (($625,948 – $420,786) / $420,786), but net written premiums has decreased by 51.4 percent (($370,286– $180,016) / $370,286), over the five-year period from 1991 to 1995. Return on policyholders' surplus has decreased from 21.7 percent in 1991 to 15.9 percent in 1995. A.M. Best measures return on policyholders' surplus as the sum of after-tax net income and unrealized capital gains divided by the average policyholders' surplus for the period.

Exhibit 12-5

1996 Best's *Key Rating Guide*—Property-Casualty Edition Annual Statement
Data For Years 1991-1995

Company Name
Rating Unit Name
Group Affiliation

Principal Officer
Mailing Address
Dom.: Began Bus.: Struct.: Mktg
Specialty
Phone #
AMB #   NAIC #

ARGONAUT GROUP
Argonaut Group
Argonaut Group
Charles E. Rinisch, CEO
250 Middlefield Road
Menlo Park, CA 94025-3507
CA : Consol : Agency
Workers Comp
415-326-0900
AMB#04019

Rating / Balance Sheet / Operations

Data Year	Best's Rating/FPR & FSC	Modifier Effective Date	Cash & Short Term Investments (%)	Stocks and Bonds (%)	All Other Assets (%)	Total Admitted Assets ($000)	Loss Res. (%)	Unearned Prem. (%)	All Other Liab. (%)	Total Liab. ($000)	Policyholders' Surplus ($000)	Direct Prem. Written ($000)	Net Prem. Written ($000)	Bus. Net Ret (%)	Net Underwriting Income ($000)	Net Investment Income ($000)	Pretax Operating Income ($000)	Net Income ($000)
'91	A+		1.0	87.8	11.2	1,822,040	91.9	2.1	6.0	1,401,254	420,786	386,910	370,286	87.0	-53,096	130,382	78,518	77,275
'92	A+		0.6	86.5	12.9	1,816,240	88.8	5.6	5.6	1,353,721	462,520	270,759	322,594	103.6	-30,002	119,597	89,937	88,781
'93	A+		1.9	82.5	15.6	1,888,271	81.4	5.6	13.0	1,360,606	527,665	285,210	284,314	94.5	3,999	114,545	118,205	98,074
'94	A+		3.5	82.1	14.4	1,810,851	80.4	5.7	13.9	1,258,210	552,641	250,707	248,853	92.7	-16,996	107,480	90,260	79,783
'95	A+	X 06/24/96	2.9	82.7	14.4	1,732,866	80.7	5.5	13.8	1,106,918	625,948	196,684	180,016	85.5	-40,828	100,038	59,300	58,133

Principal Lines: Workers' Comp 82.7%, Com'l MultiPeril 11.2%, Oth Liab Occur 5.9%, All Other 0.3%   Principal States: CA 22.6%; HI 10.0%; IL 9.3%;PA 7.4%; DC 4.7%

Profitability Tests / Leverage Tests / Liquidity Tests / Loss Reserve Tests

Data year	Loss Ratio (X)	Expense Ratio (X)	Combined Ratio After Pol. Div. (X)	Operating Ratio (X)	Pretax ROR (%)	Yield on Invested Assets (%)	Return on PHS (%)	Change in NPW (%)	NPW to PHS (X)	Net Leverage (X)	Gross Leverage (X)	Rein. Recoverables to PHS (%)	BCAR (X)	Quick Liquidity (%)	Current Liquidity (%)	Overall Liquidity (%)	Operating Cash Flow ($000)	Class 3-6 Bonds (% of PHS)	Development to PHS (%)	Loss Reserves to PHS (%)
'91	86.7	20.1	114.3	78.8	21.4	8.1	21.7	-18.2	0.9	4.1	4.9	58.4	---	41.8	119.2	133.5	-35,371	7.1	12.2	306.0
'92	83.9	21.6	109.5	73.1	27.4	7.6	18.9	-12.9	0.7	3.5	4.0	47.6	---	52.3	121.1	137.6	19,416	6.3	2.7	259.9
'93	72.7	26.5	101.4	65.0	37.5	7.3	23.6	-11.9	0.5	2.9	3.3	42.8	---	72.6	126.5	144.7	26,705	5.6	-1.1	209.9
'94	74.1	28.9	109.3	70.8	32.3	6.9	16.1	-12.5	0.5	2.6	3.1	40.8	187.2	86.4	132.1	153.8	-22,845	2.9	0.5	183.0
'95	73.4	38.0	124.8	76.7	28.5	6.7	15.5	-27.7	0.3	2.0	2.3	32.0	228.4	100.2	140.5	165.1	-56,835	2.6	---	142.6

Other Insurer Rating Services

Although no other insurance company rating service rates as many companies as the A.M. Best Company, there are other very reliable rating services in the industry. Standard & Poor's, a company well established in the specialty field of stocks and bonds reports for many years, also provides executive summary-type reports of major insurance companies. Following a text format very similar to that of the A.M. Best reports, Standard & Poor's provides a statement of "Rationale" prefacing the letter rating assigned to a particular insurer. The rating hierarchy of Standard & Poor's is very similar to that used by A.M. Best Company. Within the executive summary are provided a five-year summary of selected financial statistics and by-line distribution of premium volume, and a schedule of standard performance measures such as return measures, loss ratios, and expense ratios. Standard & Poor's Ratings Services are also accessible on the Internet.

Services Rating Noninsurance Companies

Several independent organizations provide credit reports on individuals and business organizations. Underwriters recognize this type of service as a useful source of information about a firm's financial capacity and debt-paying ability. Creditworthiness is a factor that has long been included in the set of criteria used to evaluate risks assumed by insurers. With the help of financial and credit analysis, experienced underwriters can assess various types of data as indicators of the following:[3]

- Moral and morale hazards
- Ability to pay premiums
- Financial strength and soundness of management

One of the most popular reporting services used by property and liability underwriters is Dun & Bradstreet (D&B). Reports provided by D&B (1) report on the history of the company and the background of its owners and managers; (2) describe, in detail, the method of operation; (3) outline the company's paying record; (4) analyze financial status, operating results, and trends; and (5) assign composite credit ratings.[4]

Insurance company guidelines are usually explicit about how underwriters should use financial reporting services. The guidelines might require that each applicant be researched in the *Dun & Bradstreet Reference Book*. If the applicant is not listed, not rated, or rated "fair" or "limited," or if the rating has dropped for an existing policyholder, then one of the more extensive reporting services offered by D&B should be used.

STANDARD &POOR'S
STOCK REPORTS

Home Depot

1149

NYSE Symbol **HD**

In S&P 500

20-DEC-96 | **Industry:** Retail Stores | **Summary:** HD operates a chain of over 470 retail warehouse-type stores, selling a wide variety of home improvement products for the do-it-yourself and home remodeling markets.

S&P Opinion: Buy (★★★★★)	

Quantitative Evaluations

Outlook
(1 Lowest—5 Highest)
• **4+**

Fair Value
• **61⅝**

Risk
• **Average**

Earn./Div. Rank
• **A+**

Technical Eval.
• **Bullish** since 12/95

Rel. Strength Rank
(1 Lowest—99 Highest)
• **23**

Insider Activity
• **Neutral**

Recent Price • 49⅞
52 Wk Range • 59½-41½

Yield • 0.5%
12-Mo. P/E • 27.6

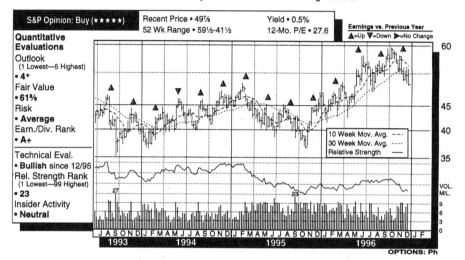

Earnings vs. Previous Year
▲=Up ▼=Down ▶=No Change

10 Week Mov. Avg. – – –
30 Week Mov. Avg. - - - -
Relative Strength —

OPTIONS: Ph

Overview - 20-DEC-96

Revenue growth of this leading home improvement retailer should be in the 25% range in FY 98, mainly fueled by the company's ongoing aggressive expansion program. Some 125 new units are planned for FY 98. Same unit sales should rise about 6%. Operating income should increase in 24% range. HD has continued room for growth in the highly fragmented $134 billion do-it-yourself home improvement industry, with only a 12% share of the market. The industry is projected to grow at an annual 5% rate through the end of this decade. The bulk of the growth should come from the estimated 75 million older homes that will need to be repaired. The company plans to operate 900 stores by the end of 1999. The $1 billion proceeds from the October 1996 sale of 3.25% convertible subordinated notes were used to repay outstanding commercial paper obligations and will be used to finance a portion of the company's capital expenditure program, including store expansions and renovations.

Valuation - 20-DEC-96

Following the 16% drop in price from the year high, we upgraded the shares to a "strong buy" recommendation. With plans to expand the company's store base by 25% annually over the next few years, Home Depot is building substantially on its already dominant position in the do-it-yourself market. As a result, earnings per share should continue to grow in the 23% to 25% range over the next few years. The shares warrant a premium P/E multiple to the market in line with the company's outstanding earnings record and well-defined growth prospects.

Key Stock Statistics

S&P EPS Est. 1997	1.90	Tang. Bk. Value/Share	11.71
P/E on S&P Est. 1997	26.3	Beta	0.81
S&P EPS Est. 1998	2.35	Shareholders	66,000
Dividend Rate/Share	0.24	Market cap. (B)	$ 24.4
Shs. outstg. (M)	480.3	Inst. holdings	57%
Avg. daily vol. (M)	1.930		

Value of $10,000 invested 5 years ago: $ 39,438

Fiscal Year Ending Jan. 31

	1997	1996	1995	1994	1993	1992
Revenues (Million $)						
1Q	4,362	3,569	2,872	2,180	1,640	1,187
2Q	5,293	4,152	3,287	2,454	1,856	1,353
3Q	4,922	3,998	3,240	2,317	1,834	1,298
4Q	—	3,752	3,077	2,287	1,818	1,299
Yr.	—	15,470	12,477	9,239	7,148	5,137
Earnings Per Share ($)						
1Q	0.41	0.34	0.31	0.34	0.18	0.13
2Q	0.56	0.45	0.39	0.30	0.23	0.17
3Q	0.46	0.37	0.31	0.23	0.19	0.13
4Q	E0.48	0.39	0.32	0.25	0.21	0.16
Yr.	E1.90	1.54	1.32	1.01	0.81	0.60

Next earnings report expected: mid February

Dividend Data (Dividends have been paid since 1987.)

Amount ($)	Date Decl.	Ex-Div. Date	Stock of Record	Payment Date
0.050	Feb. 22	Mar. 06	Mar. 08	Mar. 22 '96
0.060	May. 29	Jun. 07	Jun. 11	Jun. 25 '96
0.060	Aug. 27	Sep. 10	Sep. 12	Sep. 26 '96
0.060	Nov. 13	Dec. 03	Dec. 05	Dec. 19 '96

A Division of The McGraw-Hill Companies

Standard & Poor's NYSE Stock Reports

Information released December 27, 1996

STANDARD &POOR'S STOCK REPORTS

The Home Depot, Inc.

1149

20-DEC-96

Business Summary - 20-DEC-96

Home Depot operates retail warehouse-type stores selling a wide assortment of building materials and home improvement products primarily to the do-it-yourself and home remodeling markets. At August 13, 1996, it was operating 433 stores in 28 states, mostly in California, Florida and Texas, and 23 stores in Canada.

Sales by product group in FY 96 (Jan.) were: plumbing, heating, lighting and electrical supplies (28%); building materials, lumber, and floor and wall coverings (34%); hardware and tools (13%); seasonal and specialty items (14%); and paint and other (11%).During FY 96, the company opened restaurants in certain stores; operators vary by market.

Stores average 105,000 sq. ft., plus 20,000 to 28,000 sq. ft. of garden center and storage space. They stock 40,000 to 50,000 product items.

HD's strategy is to provide a broad range of merchandise at competitive prices, utilizing knowledgeable service personnel and aggressive advertising.

In 1994, HD acquired a 75% interest in Canada's Aikenhead's Home Improvement Warehouse chain from Molson Cos. Ltd., for $160 million. Beginning in the year 2000, it has the right to acquire the remaining 25%. The chain, known as Home Depot Canada, currently operates 23 warehouse-style stores in Canada.

EXPO Design Centers, with about 144,000 sq. ft. of selling space, market upscale interior design products. The company currently operates four EXPO stores.

HD also operates two prototype Home Depot Crossroads, which carry traditional merchandise as well as catering to the needs of rural customers, such as farmers and ranchers. In December 1995, the company announced plans to integrate Crossroads into its existing Home Depot division; the company anticipated benefiting from cost efficiencies and greater name recognition.

Important Developments

Nov. '96—In the third quarter of FY 97 (Jan.), total sales rose 23%, year to year; same-store sales were up 7%. Sales per square foot increased 3% and the average customer sale increased 1%. Annualized inventory turnover was 5.7 through the first nine months of FY 97, level with a year ago. During the third quarter HD opened 22 Home Depot stores and one EXPO Design Center. During FY 97, the company expects to open a total of 90 to 95 new stores and relocate six existing units. The company also plans to expand its store openings to 127 units in FY 98.

Capitalization

Long Term Debt: $1,247,208,000 (10/27/96).

Per Share Data ($) (Year Ended Jan. 31)	1996	1995	1994	1993	1992	1991	1990	1989	1988	1987
Tangible Bk. Val.	10.27	7.40	6.22	5.15	3.95	1.87	1.42	1.07	0.89	0.49
Cash Flow	1.91	1.54	1.20	0.96	0.73	0.54	0.38	0.26	0.20	0.12
Earnings	1.54	1.32	1.01	0.82	0.60	0.45	0.32	0.22	0.17	0.09
Dividends	0.19	0.15	0.12	0.08	0.05	0.04	0.02	0.02	0.01	Nil
Payout Ratio	12%	11%	12%	10%	9%	8%	8%	7%	5%	Nil
Cal. Yrs.	1995	1994	1993	1992	1991	1990	1989	1988	1987	1986
Prices - High	50	48¼	50⅞	51½	35⅛	14½	8½	4¾	4⅛	2 3/16
- Low	36⅝	36½	35	29¾	11⅝	7⅝	4¼	2⅝	1¾	1 1/16
P/E Ratio - High	32	48	50	63	58	32	27	21	25	24
- Low	24	36	35	36	19	17	13	12	11	12
Income Statement Analysis (Million $)										
Revs.	15,470	12,477	9,239	7,148	5,137	3,815	2,759	2,000	1,454	1,011
Oper. Inc.	1,361	1,117	793	615	434	300	205	141	109	67.0
Depr.	181	130	85.9	65.6	52.3	34.4	20.5	14.4	10.6	8.4
Int. Exp.	25.0	53.5	44.6	48.6	24.0	31.1	18.3	4.5	6.0	15.1
Pretax Inc.	1,195	980	737	576	396	260	182	126	96.0	47.0
Eff. Tax Rate	39%	38%	38%	37%	37%	37%	39%	39%	43%	49%
Net Inc.	732	605	457	363	249	163	112	77.0	54.0	24.0
Balance Sheet & Other Fin. Data (Million $)										
Cash	108	58.0	431	414	395	137	135	16.0	26.0	17.0
Curr. Assets	2,672	2,133	1,967	1,562	1,158	714	566	337	257	198
Total Assets	7,354	5,778	4,701	3,932	2,510	1,640	1,118	699	528	395
Curr. Liab.	1,416	1,214	973	755	534	413	292	194	147	107
LT Debt	720	983	882	844	271	531	303	108	52.0	117
Common Eqty.	4,988	3,442	2,814	2,304	1,691	683	512	383	321	163
Total Cap.	5,822	4,496	3,724	3,164	1,969	1,222	825	504	381	287
Cap. Exp.	1,278	1,101	900	437	432	398	205	105	90.0	52.0
Cash Flow	913	734	543	428	301	196	132	91.0	65.0	32.0
Curr. Ratio	1.9	1.8	2.0	2.1	2.2	1.7	1.9	1.7	1.8	1.9
% LT Debt of Cap.	12.4	21.9	23.7	26.7	13.7	43.4	36.7	21.3	13.7	40.7
% Net Inc.of Revs.	4.7	4.8	5.0	5.1	4.9	4.3	4.1	3.8	3.7	2.4
% Ret. on Assets	11.1	11.5	10.5	11.0	11.2	11.7	12.2	12.4	11.0	5.8
% Ret. on Equity	17.4	19.2	17.8	17.8	19.9	27.0	24.8	21.7	21.2	18.1

Data as orig. reptd.; bef. results of disc. opers. and/or spec. items. Per share data adj. for stk. divs. as of ex-div. date. E-Estimated. NA-Not Available. NM-Not Meaningful. NR-Not Ranked.

Office—2727 Paces Ferry Rd., Atlanta, GA 30339. **Tel**—(404) 433-8211. **Chrmn, CEO & Secy**—B. Marcus. **Pres**—A. M. Blank. **EVP & CAO**—R. M. Brill.**CFO**—M. L. Day. **Investor Contact**—L. Fogel. **Dirs**—A. M. Blank, F. Borman, R. M. Brill, J. L. Clendenin, B. R. Cox, M. A. Hart III, J. W. Inglis, D. R. Keough, K. G. Langone, B. Marcus, M. F. Wilson. **Transfer Agent & Registrar**—First National Bank of Boston. **Incorporated**—in Delaware in 1978. **Empl**— 67,000. **S&P Analyst:** Karen J. Sack, CFA

Other services specialize in providing periodic summaries of publicly traded firm's operating performance and/or ratings of their debt and equity issues. Although these services generally cater to investors seeking information about companies in which they might invest, the information they provide can also be useful to underwriters or claim adjusters trying to develop standard ratios to assist in completing otherwise incomplete financial records or to provide benchmarks against which the performance and financial condition of an insured risk can be evaluated. Two sources of summary financial information for publicly traded noninsurance companies are the *Moody's Industrial Manual*, published by Moody's Investors Service, and *Standard & Poor's NYSE Stock Reports*, published by Standard & Poor's.

Exhibit 12-6 contains an S&P stock report for The Home Depot, Inc. As can be seen in the exhibit, the report not only provides a three-and-one-half year summary of the firm's weekly stock using the high-low-close reporting format, but it also provides a ten-year summary of key financial data from financial statements and summary financial ratios.

Financial Ratio Benchmarks

When an underwriter or claim adjuster needs only to find a set of standard financial ratio results for a particular industry segment or underwriting classification, a reference guide on industrial ratios should be consulted. Such sources provide key financial ratios for companies grouped by size (based on total assets) within standard industry classifications typically developed from SIC classification codes. Many of these references also report key ratios across ten years to allow analysts to identify trends in particular variables. Exhibit 12-7 provides examples of key financial ratios for four industry classifications for firms having between $100,000 and $250,000 in total assets. Reported in the exhibit are key financial ratios that could be used for benchmarking companies of a similar size in one of the following industry segments:

- Other special trade contractors
- Business services except advertising
- Building materials dealers
- Apparel and accessory stores

Although the size category for building materials dealers is much smaller than that which would be appropriate to benchmark Home Depot, the ratio results shown in Exhibit 12-7 can be used for illustration purposes as a basis for comparing ratios computed by using financial data for Home Depot reported in various exhibits of this text.

Exhibit 12-7
Benchmarks for Selected Industry Segments

Item Description for Accounting Period 7/92 Through 6/93	Other Special Trade Contractors	Business Services Except Advertising	Building Materials Dealers	Apparel and Accessory Stores
Number of Enterprises	14,384	20,808	2,485	6,395
Operating Costs/Operating Income (%)				
Cost of Operations	57.2	31.9	62.2	62.3
Rent	1.5	3.4	1.9	8.1
Taxes Paid	3.1	3.7	3.2	2.2
Interest Paid	0.6	0.7	0.6	0.4
Depreciation, Depletion, Amortization	2.8	2.3	1.1	0.7
Pensions and Other Benefits	1.4	1.9	1.0	0.5
Other	23.2	38.6	20.6	17.3
Officers Compensation	6.4	12.5	4.4	2.9
Operating Margin	3.8	5.0	5.0	5.7
Oper. Margin Before Officers' Compensation	10.2	17.5	9.4	8.5
Selected Financial Ratios (Times to 1)				
Current Ratio	1.6	2.0	2.3	2.9
Quick Ratio	1.4	1.7	1.2	1.1
Net Sales to Working Capital	24.9	15.4	12.0	5.9
Coverage Ratio	8.6	10.4	11.5	•
Total Asset Turnover	4.4	4.0	4.7	3.2
Inventory turnover	•	•	8.6	4.1
Total Liabilities to Net Worth	1.2	1.8	1.8	1.0
Selected Financial Factors (%)				
Debt Ratio	54.9	63.8	63.8	49.3
Return on Assets	23.8	30.7	32.3	20.3
Return on Equity	•	•	•	32.5
Return Before Interest on Equity	•	•	•	•
Profit Margin, Before Income Tax	4.8	6.9	6.3	6.0
Profit Margin, After Income Tax	4.6	6.6	6.1	5.1

Adapted from Leo Troy, *Almanac of Business and Industrial Financial Ratios*, 1996 Edition (Englewood Cliffs, NJ: Prentice Hall, 1996), pp. 30, 236, 254, and 320.

Summary

Explanatory notes to the financial statements are an integral part of the statements. These notes, sometimes called *the financial review*, result from the application of the full disclosure concept discussed in Chapter 2. The notes disclose details of amounts summarized for financial statement presentation, explain which permissible alternative accounting practices the entity has used, and provide detailed disclosure of information needed to have a full understanding of the financial statements.

Accounting policies disclosed include the depreciation method, inventory cost-flow assumption, and basis of consolidation. Accounting for the entity's income taxes, employee benefits, and amortization of intangible assets is described. Details of the calculation of earnings per share of common stock are sometimes provided. Employee stock option and stock purchase plans are discussed. Each of these disclosures is made to the extent material.

If the accounting for a material item has changed, the consistency concept requires disclosure of the effect of the change on the financial statements. Sometimes accounting or reporting changes are required by new FASB standards.

Any business combinations in which the entity has been involved are discussed.

Significant contingencies and commitments, such as litigation or loan guarantees, and significant events that have occurred since the balance sheet date are described. This is a specific application of the full disclosure concept.

The effect of inflation on the historical costs used in the financial statements may be reported, although this information is not currently required to be shown.

Segment information summarizes some financial information for the principal activity areas of the firm. The intent of this disclosure is to permit judgment about the significance to the entity's overall results of its activities in certain business segments and geographic areas.

The financial statements are the responsibility of management, not the auditors, and management's statement of responsibility acknowledges this. This acknowledgment usually includes a reference to the system of internal control.

Management's discussion and analysis of the firm's financial condition and results of operations provide an important and useful summary of the firm's activities.

Although not usually a part of the explanatory notes to the financial statements, most annual reports do include a summary of key financial data for several years. This summary permits financial statement users to evaluate trends easily.

The independent auditors' report includes their opinion about the fair presentation of the financial statements in accordance with generally accepted accounting principles and calls attention to special situations. Auditors do not guarantee that the company will be profitable, nor do they assure that the financial statements are absolutely accurate.

The Securities and Exchange Commission is responsible for administering federal securities laws. One of its principal concerns is that investors have full disclosure about securities and the companies that issue them. The reporting requirements of the SEC have led to many of the disclosures contained in corporate annual reports.

Refer to the financial review in the Armstrong World Industries, Inc., annual report in the Appendix to this text's companion course workbook and study guide and to the comparable part of other annual reports that you have. Observe the organization of this part of the financial statements and the comprehensive explanation of the material discussed. Read management's discussion and analysis of the firm's financial condition and results of operations. Find the summary of key financial data for several years, and evaluate the trends disclosed for sales, profits, total owners' equity, and other items reported in the summary. Chapter 14 will describe and illustrate some of the ways of analyzing financial statement data to support the informed judgments and decisions made by users of financial statements.

Key Words and Phrases

accounting change (p. 378) A change in the application of an accounting principle.

benchmark (p. 389) A predetermined standard used in financial analysis against which some measure of an entity's operations or financial condition is compared to determine its relative performance.

business combination (p. 379) A merger between two or more firms, or the purchase of one firm by another.

business segment (p. 382) A group of the firm's similar business activities; most large firms have several segments.

commitment (p. 381) A transaction that has been contractually agreed to but that has not yet occurred and is not reflected in the financial statements.

contingency (p. 381) An event that has an uncertain but potentially significant effect on the financial statements.

explanatory notes to the financial statements (p. 371) An integral part of the financial statements that contains explanations of accounting policies and descriptions of financial statement details.

financial review (p. 372) Another name for the footnotes to the financial statements.

five-year summary (p. 385) A summary of key financial data included in an organization's annual report; it is not a financial statement included in the scope of the independent auditor's report.

management's discussion and analysis (p. 374) A narrative description of the firm's activities for the year, including comments about its financial condition and results of operations.

management's statement of responsibility (p. 383) A discussion included in the explanatory notes to the financial statements describing management's responsibility for the financial statements.

pooling of interests accounting (p. 379) A method of accounting for the acquisition of another company that results in the book values of the acquired company's assets and liabilities being recorded by the acquiring company.

prospectus (p. 380) A summary of the characteristics of a security being offered for sale, including a description of the business and financial position of the firm selling the security.

proxy (p. 380) An authorization given by a stockholder to another person to vote the shares owned by the stockholder.

purchase accounting (p. 379) A method of accounting for the purchase of another company that records as the cost of the investment the fair market value of the cash and/or securities paid, less the liabilities assumed in the transaction.

significant accounting policies (p. 374) A brief summary or description of the specific accounting practices followed by the entity.

stock option plan (p. 377) A plan for compensating key employees by providing an option to purchase a company's stock at a future date at the market price of the stock when the option is issued (granted).

Chapter Notes

1. American Institute of Certified Public Accountants, *Accounting Trends and Techniques*, 48th ed. (New York, NY: American Institute of Certified Public Accountants, Inc., 1994), Table 1-8.

2. American Institute of Certified Public Accountants, Table 1-10.

3. Joseph F. Mangan and Connor M. Harrison, *Underwriting Principles* (Malvern, PA: Insurance Institute of America, 1995), p. 112.

4. Mangan and Harrison, p. 113.

Chapter 13

Capital Budgeting

Deciding in which projects to invest a firm's resources is perhaps the most perplexing task facing financial managers. Survival in today's competitive business environment requires that the firm use its resources productively—particularly its capital resources.

Although most insurance professionals rarely have the responsibility for deciding how to invest a firm's capital resources, they do need to understand the process by which alternative investments can be analyzed. As part of the underwriting process, producers and underwriters need to assess the effectiveness of the management of the firms that they insure. An entity that invests in projects that fail to produce adequate returns and that reduce its cash flows might present greater risk of loss or fraudulent claims when it tries to generate needed cash to continue operations. Claim managers need to be familiar with the financial techniques used in analyzing alternative investment projects because those same techniques are fundamental to developing structured settlements for disability or survivorship benefits. Examples of capital budgeting techniques every insurance professional should know include evaluating investment alternatives related to office equipment (such as buying a new computer) and which of several lease proposals provides the greatest long-term benefit.

Capital budgeting is the process of analyzing proposed capital expenditures—investments in plant, equipment, new products, and so on—to determine whether the proposed investment will generate, over time, a large enough

405

return on investment (ROI) to contribute to the organization's overall ROI objectives.

Capital budgeting differs from operational budgeting in the time frame being considered. Whereas operational budgeting involves planning for a period that is usually not longer than one year, capital budgeting concerns investments and returns that are spread over several years. (Even in multiyear operational budgeting, there is an opportunity to rebudget for periods beyond the current year.) Thus, the operating budget reflects the firm's strategic plans to achieve current period profitability, and the capital budget provides a blueprint to help the firm meet its long-term growth objectives.

Capital budgeting involves most of the functional areas of the organization. The managerial accountant might make the mathematical calculations, but the departments affected by the proposed capital expenditure will normally have significant input in the capital budgeting process.

Educational Objectives

After studying this chapter, you should be able to:

1. Describe the attributes of capital budgeting that make it significantly different from operational budgeting.

2. Explain why present value analysis is appropriate in capital budgeting.

3. Explain why not all management decisions are made strictly on the basis of quantitative analysis techniques.

4. Explain the concept of cost of capital and why it is used in capital budgeting.

5. Explain how the net present value technique is used to evaluate capital expenditure projects.

6. Explain how the present value ratio is used to assign a profitability ranking to alternative capital expenditure projects.

7. Explain how the internal rate of return technique differs from the net present value approach of evaluating capital expenditure projects.

8. Explain how the following affect the capital budgeting process:

   a. The need to estimate future cash flows

   b. Cash flows in the distant future

   c. Timing of cash flows within the year

   d. Making investments over a period of time

e. Taxes

f. Depreciation

g. Increases in working capital

9. Explain how the payback period of a capital expenditure project is calculated.

10. Explain why the accounting rate of return of a project is calculated and how it can be used most appropriately.

11. Explain why it is important to include the financing decision in the capital budgeting process.

12. Evaluate the estimated cash flows of capital expenditure projects using each of the techniques described in this chapter to determine which alternative projects should be included in an entity's capital budget.

13. Evaluate the alternatives available for financing capital budgeting projects including the following:

a. Operating lease

b. Capital lease

c. Debt financing

d. Equity financing

14. Define or describe each of the Key Words and Phrases introduced in this chapter.

Investment Analysis

Business entities regularly invest cash and other resources in the materials, plant, and equipment needed for their operations. Investment alternatives that require a long-term commitment of capital resources should be carefully analyzed to ensure that the return on investment is consistent with the firm's overall capital objectives. This section discusses the investment decision process, the cost of capital, and capital budgeting techniques.

Investment Decision Special Considerations

Investment decisions involve committing financial resources now in anticipation of a return that will be realized over an extended period of time. This extended time frame, which can be many years, adds complexity to the analysis of whether to make the investment because of compound interest and present value considerations. The time value of money can be ignored for most operating expenditure decisions because the benefit of an expenditure will be received soon after the expenditure is made, and a simple benefit/cost relationship can be determined. This is not the case for capital expenditures because the benefits of the expenditure will be received over several years, and $100 of benefit to be received five years from now is not the same as $100 of benefit to be received one year from now.

The concept of present value was explained in Business Procedure Capsule 13 in Chapter 7. Review that explanation now unless you fully understand present value techniques.

Most business firms and other organizations have more investment opportunities than resources available for investment. Capital budgeting procedures, especially those applying present value analysis techniques, are useful in helping management identify the alternatives that will contribute most to the future profitability of the firm. However, as is the case with most quantitative techniques, the quantitative "answer" will not necessarily dictate management's decision. The quantitative result will be considered along with qualitative factors in the decision-making process. Examples of qualitative factors include the willingness to assume competitive risks associated with expanding (or not expanding) into a new market area, the implications for keeping control of a board of directors if more stock must be sold to raise funds for the expansion, and, of course, top management's goals for the organization. Because capital budgeting involves projections into the future, top management attitudes about the risk of forecasting errors influence investment decisions.

Most firms involve the board of directors in capital budgeting by having the board approve all capital expenditures above a minimum amount. Depending on the company and its financial circumstances, this amount may range from $5,000 to $1 million. High-level approval is required because the capital expenditure represents a major commitment of company resources, and it involves many years.

Cost of Capital

The principal financial objective of a firm organized for profit is to earn a return on the assets invested that will permit payment of all borrowing costs (interest) and provide the owners a return on their investment (return on equity—ROE) that compensates them fairly for the financial risks being taken. To meet the requirements of these resource providers, whose claims are shown on the right-hand side of the balance sheet, attention must be focused on the assets that are reported on the left-hand side of the balance sheet. Thus, return on assets (return on investment—ROI) becomes a primary concern of financial managers who evaluate proposed capital expenditures.

The **cost of capital** is the rate of return on assets that must be earned to permit the firm to meet its interest obligations and provide the expected return to owners. Determining the cost of capital of a company is a complex process that is beyond the scope of this text. Cost of capital is a composite of borrowing costs and stockholder dividend and earnings' growth rate expectations. The cost of capital is most useful as a "worry point" guide to management (that is, an indication of an approximate *minimum* ROI that creditors and owners are expecting). Most firms set a cost of capital rate for investment analysis purposes that is greater than the true economic cost of acquiring funds. This allows for estimation errors in the calculation and provides a cushion for estimation errors in the data used in the investment analysis itself. The cost of capital used for analyzing proposed capital expenditures is also influenced by the perceived riskiness of the proposal being evaluated. More risky proposals (for example, new product development or expansion into a new activity) will be required to earn a higher rate of return than less risky proposals (for example, equipment replacement or expansion of an existing activity). This risk difference is related to the uncertainties with operating in a different environment than that in which the firm is experienced.

The cost of capital is the *discount rate* (that is, the interest rate at which future period **cash flows** are discounted) used to determine the present value of the investment proposal being analyzed. For most firms, the cost of capital is probably in the range of 10 to 20 percent. In the capital budgeting illustrations presented in this chapter, the cost of capital will be a given. However, in practice, the development of the cost of capital rate is both complex and time-consuming.

Capital Budgeting Techniques

Of the four generally recognized capital budgeting techniques, two use present value analysis, and two do not. Because money has value over time, the two methods that recognize this fact are clearly superior to those that ignore the time value of money. The four methods are as follows:

> Methods that use present value analysis:
>> Net present value (NPV) method
>> Internal rate of return (IRR) method
> Methods that do not use present value analysis:
>> Payback method
>> Accounting rate of return method

Each of these methods uses the amount to be invested in the capital project. The **net present value method, internal rate of return method,** and **payback**

method use the amount of *cash* generated by the investment each year. The **accounting rate of return method** uses accrual accounting net income resulting from the investment. For most investment projects, the difference between the cash generated each year and accrual accounting net income is depreciation expense—a noncash item that reduces accrual accounting net income. Again, because of their recognition of the time value of money and focus on cash flows, the NPV and IRR methods are much more appropriate than either the payback method or the accounting rate of return method.

Net Present Value

The net present value method involves calculating the present value of the expected cash flows from the project using the cost of capital as the discount rate and comparing the total present value of the cash flows to the amount of investment required. If the present value of the cash flows is greater than the investment, the net present value is positive, and it can be concluded that the rate of return of the project is greater than the cost of capital. If the present value of the cash flows is less than the investment, the net present value is negative, and it can be concluded that the rate of return of the project is less than the cost of capital. If the present value of the cash flows equals the investment, then the net present value is zero, and the rate of return of the project is equal to the cost of capital. Accordingly, the discount rate used in net present value analysis is sometimes referred to as the *hurdle rate* because it represents the minimum rate of return required for an investment to yield a positive NPV. Exhibit 13-1 illustrates the net present value method.

When alternative projects involving different investment amounts are being considered, the NPV approach must be carried one step further. Projects should not be assigned a profitability ranking for acceptance on the basis of the dollar amount of the net present value because of disparities in the investment amounts. The ratio of the present value of the cash flows to the investment, referred to as the **present value ratio** (or **profitability index**), provides a more appropriate ranking mechanism. For example, assume the following data for the projects indicated:

Project	Present Value of Cash Flows	Investment	Net Present Value	Present Value Ratio
A	$ 22,800	$ 20,000	$2,800	1.14
B	104,000	100,000	4,000	1.04

Even though project B has a greater net present value, project A has a higher rate of return and is thus a more desirable investment. When the NPV approach to investment analysis is used, the present value ratio should be calculated, especially when a selection must be made from several positive NPV projects.

Exhibit 13-1

Net Present Value (NPV) Analysis of a Proposed Investment

I. Assumptions:

A. A new packaging machine costing $100,000 installed has an estimated useful life of five years and an estimated salvage value of $6,000 after five years. The new machine will be purchased at the end of 1996.

B. Installation and use of the machine in the firm's operations will result in labor savings during each of the next five years as follows:

1997	$26,000
1998	27,000
1999	31,000
2000	35,000
2001	38,000

C. The firm's cost of capital is 16%.

II. Time-Line Presentation of Cash Flows From the Investment:

	12/31/96	1997	1998	1999	2000	2001
Cash flows from investment:						
Savings		26,000	27,000	31,000	35,000	38,000
Salvage						6,000
Total		26,000	27,000	31,000	35,000	44,000

III. Net Present Value Calculation:

		1997	1998	1999	2000	2001
Present value factors (Table 7-2, 16%)		0.8621	0.7432	0.6407	0.5523	0.4761
Present value of cash flows from investment		22,415	20,066	19,862	19,331	20,948

Total present value of cash flows from investment	$ 102,622
Investment	–100,000
Net present value at 16%	$ 2,622

IV. Conclusion From Analysis:

The net present value is positive; therefore, the projected rate of return on this investment is greater than the 16% cost of capital. Based on this quantitative analysis, the investment should be made.

Internal Rate of Return

The difference between the NPV and IRR methods is that the discount (interest) rate—the cost of capital—is a given in the NPV approach, whereas the IRR approach solves for the actual rate of return that will be earned by the proposed investment. This is the discount rate at which the present value of cash flows from the project will equal the investment (that is, the discount rate at which the NPV equals zero). Thus, the IRR method might require several calculations using different discount rates. Once the project's internal rate of return is known, the suitability of the investment is determined by comparing the IRR to the cost of capital. If the IRR is greater than the cost of capital, the investment will be recommended. If the IRR is less than the cost of capital, the investment will not be recommended.

With respect to the investment proposal illustrated in Exhibit 13-1, the IRR must be greater than 16 percent because the NPV is positive. Determination of the actual IRR requires another set of present value calculations using a higher discount rate (18 percent is the next higher rate in the Chapter 7 tables) and then interpolation to determine the actual discount rate at which the present value of cash flows would equal the investment. Exhibit 13-2 illustrates the IRR method.

The NPV approach to evaluating proposed capital expenditures has some theoretical advantages, but many managers use both approaches because they are more comfortable knowing the actual rate of return. Computer programs make the calculations easy; estimating the amount and timing of future cash flows associated with a proposal is the most challenging part of the process.

Some Analytical Considerations

Some important considerations should be kept in mind when performing a present value analysis. They relate to the accuracy of the cash flow estimates, the timing of cash flows, the tax effect of cash flows, and the context within which the analysis is performed.

Estimates

The validity of present value calculations will be a function of the accuracy with which future cash flows can be estimated. A great deal of effort should be expended in making estimates, recognizing that only *incremental* or *differential* cash flows that can be attributed to the proposed capital expenditure should be included in the analysis. This means that the analysis should consider *only* cash flows that change *because of the added project or investment* should be considered. When identifying cash flows, the analyst should not only look for those that are directly related to the capital investment project, but also for

Exhibit 13-2
Internal Rate of Return (IRR) Analysis of a Proposed Investment

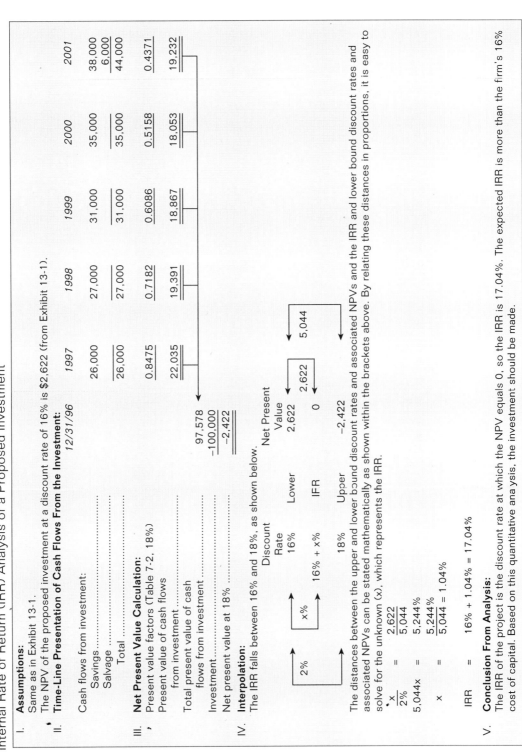

I. Assumptions:
Same as in Exhibit 13-1.
The NPV of the proposed investment at a discount rate of 16% is $2,622 (from Exhibit 13-1).

II. Time-Line Presentation of Cash Flows From the Investment:

	12/31/96	1997	1998	1999	2000	2001
Cash flows from investment:						
Savings		26,000	27,000	31,000	35,000	38,000
Salvage						6,000
Total		26,000	27,000	31,000	35,000	44,000

III. Net Present Value Calculation:

Present value factors (Table 7-2, 18%)		0.8475	0.7182	0.6086	0.5158	0.4371
Present value of cash flows from investment		22,035	19,391	18,867	18,053	19,232

Total present value of cash flows from investment 97,578
Investment .... –100,000
Net present value at 18% .... –2,422

IV. Interpolation:
The IRR falls between 16% and 18%, as shown below.

Discount Rate		Net Present Value
16%	Lower	2,622
16% + x%	IFR	0
18%	Upper	–2,422

$$2\% \quad x\%$$
$$5,044 \quad 2,622$$

The distances between the upper and lower bound discount rates and associated NPVs can be stated mathematically as shown within the brackets above. By relating these distances in proportions, it is easy to solve for the unknown (x), which represents the IRR.

$$\frac{x}{2\%} = \frac{2,622}{5,044}$$
$$5,044x = 5,244\%$$
$$x = \frac{5,244\%}{5,044} = 1.04\%$$

$$\text{IRR} = 16\% + 1.04\% = 17.04\%$$

V. Conclusion From Analysis:
The IRR of the project is the discount rate at which the NPV equals 0, so the IRR is 17.04%. The expected IRR is more than the firm's 16% cost of capital. Based on this quantitative ana ysis, the investment should be made.

those that are indirectly related. For example, increased warehouse space might be gained by investing in a robotic stock-picking system that requires less aisle space and allows added vertical storage. Direct cash flows are associated with the purchase, installation, and maintenance of the stock-picking system. Indirect cash flows might also be associated with the project if the firm can now store on-site raw materials that were previously stored at a site across town.

When the project involves a replacement machine, the estimates of future cash flows (inflows from expense savings and outflows for preventative and periodic maintenance) can be made relatively easily. When the project involves an investment in a new product or a major capacity expansion, the cash flows most important and most difficult to estimate are the revenues. Most firms will require a **post-audit** of the project to determine whether the anticipated benefits are actually being realized. Although it may be too late to affect a project already completed, knowledge about past estimating errors should permit analysts to improve future estimates. An understanding of the significance of various estimates on the results of the calculations can be obtained by changing the estimates. This process is a form of sensitivity analysis that helps identify the most significant estimates.

Cash Flows Far in the Future

Given the challenges of estimating, many capital budgeting analysts do not consider probable cash flows that are expected to occur more than ten years in the future. In essence, their position is that if the project will not have a satisfactory return considering the cash flows in the first ten years, then the project is too risky to accept even if later cash flows will give it a satisfactory rate of return. The present value of $100 to be received in eleven years, at a discount rate of 20 percent, is $13.46, so far-distant cash flows will not add significantly to the total present value of cash flows.

Timing of Cash Flows Within the Year

The present value factors in Tables 7-2 and 7-3 assume that all of the cash flow each year is received at the end of the year. The cash flows will probably be received fairly evenly throughout the year, and although present value can be calculated using that assumption, the end-of-the-year assumption is commonly used because it results in a slightly lower, more conservative present value amount.

Investment Made Over a Period of Time

Capital expenditure projects involving new products, new plants, and capacity expansion usually require expenditures made over time. For example, payments are usually made to a building contractor every month during construction, and for a major project, construction may extend over several years. When an extended period is involved, the investment amount used in the present value analysis should be determined as of the point at which the project is expected to be put into service. This means that interest on cash disbursements made during the construction, or preoperating period, should be considered so that the investment amount will include the time value of money invested during that period.

Income Tax Effect of Cash Flows From the Project

The cash flows identified with a proposed capital expenditure should include all of the associated inflows and outflows, including income taxes. The model for making this calculation is essentially the same as that used in the statement of cash flows to determine cash generated from operations. For example, assume that a capital expenditure proposal for a new product reflects the following makeup of operating income, income taxes, and net income for the first year the product is sold:

Revenues	$240,000
Variable expenses	100,000
Contribution margin	$140,000
Direct fixed expenses:	
Requiring cash disbursements	85,000
Depreciation of equipment	20,000
Operating income	$ 35,000
Income taxes @ 40%	14,000
Net income	$ 21,000

To calculate the amount of cash flow from this product, add back the depreciation expense to net income. *Remember that depreciation is a deduction for income tax purposes but is not a cash expenditure.* Therefore, the cash flow during the first year for this new product would be as follows:

Net income	$21,000
Add: Depreciation expense	20,000
Cash flow from the product	$41,000

In addition, any other differences between accrual basis earnings and cash flows would be recognized when using the NPV and IRR methods.

Working Capital Investment

Capital expenditure proposals that involve new products or capacity expansion usually require a working capital increase because accounts receivable and inventories will increase. The working capital increase required is treated as an additional investment (that is, it is a cash outflow at the beginning of the project, or later). If the new product or capacity expansion has a definite life, the investment in working capital will be recovered after the product is discontinued or the expansion is reversed. The expected recovery of the working capital investment should be treated as a cash inflow.

Least Cost Projects

Not all capital expenditures are made to reduce costs or increase revenues. Some expenditures required by law—environmental controls, for example—increase operating costs. (The "benefit" may be the avoidance of a fine.) Alternative expenditures in this category should also be evaluated using present value analysis; however, instead of seeking a positive NPV or IRR, the objective is to have the lowest negative result. Even though the present value ratio will be less than 1.0, the most desirable alternative is still the one with the highest present value ratio.

Payback

The payback method to evaluate proposed capital expenditures answers the question, How many years will it take to recover the amount of the investment? The answer to this question is determined by adding up the cash flows (beginning with the first year) until the total cash flows equal the investment, and then counting the number of years of cash flow required. For example, using the data from Exhibit 13-1, for a machine costing $100,000, the projected annual and cumulative cash flows were as follows:

Year	Cash Flow	Cumulative Cash Flow
1997 (1st year)	$26,000	$ 26,000
1998 (2nd year)	27,000	53,000
1999 (3rd year)	31,000	84,000
2000 (4th year)	35,000	119,000
2001 (5th year)	44,000	163,000

The investment will be recovered during the fourth year, after $16,000 of that year's $35,000 has been realized. Expressed as a decimal, 16/35 is 0.46, so the project's payback period would be expressed as 3.46 years.

The obvious advantage of the payback method is its simplicity. Present value analysis can be confusing, but payback period is fairly easily understood. There are two major disadvantages to the payback method. First, it does not consider the time value of money, and this is a significant flaw. Second, as traditionally used, the payback method does not consider cash flows that continue after the investment has been recovered. Thus, a project having a payback period of three years and no subsequent cash flows would appear to be more desirable than a project that has a payback period of four years and cash flows that continue for five more years.

Despite its flaws, many firms use the payback method, especially in connection with equipment replacement decisions. Business owners often have little confidence in estimates of cash flows far into the future. The widespread use of the payback method results from the clarity of its meaning and the fact that in a rapidly changing technological environment, the speed with which an investment is recovered is crucial. Many firms require early and significant cash flows from an investment in new plant and equipment because they do not have the financial capacity to finance their activities while waiting for the payoff from an investment to begin. Some analysts report the payback period along with NPV (or present value ratio) and IRR just to answer the question, "How long until the investment is recovered?"

Accounting Rate of Return

The accounting rate of return method focuses on the effect of the investment project on the financial statements. Accounting operating income (or net income) is related to the effect of the investment on the balance sheet. This is done on a year-by-year basis. Exhibit 13-3 illustrates the calculation for 1997, using data from Exhibit 13-1.

The flaw of the accounting rate of return approach is that the time value of money is not considered. Some financial managers make the accounting rate of return calculation not for investment evaluation purposes, but to anticipate the effect that the investment will have on the financial statements. Large start-up costs for a new product line or new production facility may adversely affect reported results for a year or two. Management should be aware of this and should put stockholders on notice in advance to minimize the effect of the start-up costs on the market price of the firm's common stock.

The Investment Decision

As is the case with virtually every management decision, both quantitative and qualitative factors are considered. After the results of the quantitative models just illustrated have been obtained, the project with the highest NPV or IRR may not be selected. Overriding qualitative factors could include the following:

- Commitment to a segment of the business that requires capital investment to achieve or regain competitiveness even though that segment does not have as great an ROI as others.
- Regulations that mandate investment to meet safety, environmental, or access requirements. Fines and other enforcement incentives aside,

Exhibit 13-3
Accounting Rate of Return Analysis of a Proposed Investment

I. **Assumptions:**
Same as in Exhibit 13-1.

II. **Calculation:**

$$\text{Accounting rate of return} = \frac{\text{Operating income attributable to investment}}{\text{Average investment}}$$

$$= \frac{\text{Savings} - \text{Depreciation expense}}{\text{Average investment}}$$

For 1997:

$$= \frac{26{,}000 - 18{,}800^*}{\dfrac{(100{,}000 + 81{,}200^{**})}{2}}$$

$$= \frac{7{,}200}{90{,}600}$$

$$= 7.9\%$$

* Straight-line depreciation expense:
(Cost – Salvage value) / Estimated life
(100,000 – 6,000) / 5 years = 18,800

**Net book value at end of 1997:
Cost – Accumulated depreciation
100,000 – 18,800 = 81,200

management's citizenship goals for the organization may result in a high priority for these investments.

- Technological developments within the industry may require new facilities to maintain customers or market share at the cost of lower ROI for a period of time.
- The organization may have limited resources to invest in capital projects, and, as a result of the capital-rationing process, less ambitious, lower ROI projects may be approved instead of large-scale, higher ROI projects for which resources cannot be obtained.

In addition to considering issues such as these, management's judgments about the accuracy of the estimates used in the capital budgeting model may result in the selection of projects for which the estimates are believed to be more accurate.

The important point is that although the use of appropriate quantitative models can significantly improve the management decision-making process, most decisions are significantly influenced by top management's values and experiences—qualitative factors. Whether the decision involves the use of time value of money calculations, cost behavior pattern information, analysis of variances, or other applications, all important managerial decisions involve uncertainty and require the use of judgment.

Integration of Capital Budget With Operating Budgets

Several aspects of the capital budget interact with the development of the operating budget. Contribution margin increases and cost savings from anticipated capital expenditure projects must be built into the expenditure and income statement budgets. Cash disbursements for capital projects must be included in the cash budget. The effect of capital expenditures on the balance sheet forecast must also be considered. Most importantly, capital budgeting expenditures affect the level at which the firm will be able to operate in future years. Investments in equipment, new plant facilities, and other long-term operational assets are necessary to support the firm's growth objectives. Thus, the development of the capital budget is an integral part of the overall budgeting and strategic planning process.

Other Uses of Capital Budgeting Techniques

The techniques used to evaluate capital budgeting expenditures can be applied to nearly any finance problem involving periodic cash flows. Not only are capital budgeting techniques useful in determining which investment alternatives will generate acceptable returns on investment for the firm (the traditional investing decision of capital budgeting), but they can also be used to determine how best to finance many of these investments. Capital budgeting techniques can be used to evaluate the options in lease versus purchase decision or whether to purchase an asset using debt or equity financing.

Many insurance professionals routinely face another type of finance problem—evaluating alternative options provided under a structured claim settlement. Claims that involve serious bodily injury, death, or disability are often settled on a *structured* basis using an annuity that provides the claimant a series of smaller periodic payments instead of one larger lump-sum payment. The structured settlement offers greater flexibility to the claimant while generally being more cost-effective to all parties involved. The following sections explain how capital budgeting techniques can be used to evaluate lease versus purchase alternatives and payment options under structured claim settlements.

Lease Versus Purchase Decisions

The evaluation process involved in making capital budgeting decisions is not complete until the best method for financing an acceptable project or activity is also determined. Many finance managers argue that the investing and financing decisions should be completely separated. Certainly, it would be absurd to suggest that simply because a firm has access to a low-cost line of credit or leasing option that the firm needs to add new equipment to its production line. Whether the new production equipment is needed should be determined based on ROI considerations and the value added to the firm. However, because costs are associated with leasing or financing by debt or equity, the financing decision should not be removed from the capital budgeting process. For example, an otherwise acceptable (desirable) asset acquisition that is rejected because the NPV is negative if purchased might be accepted if it is leased and the NPV is positive.

Chapter 7 introduced the operating lease and the capital lease (or financing lease). Recall that an operating lease is used to acquire the use of an asset, generally on a short-term basis, without acquiring any of the attributes of ownership. The rent expense associated with leasing the asset is reported in the income statement as an operating expense, but the asset is not shown on the lessee's balance sheet.

A lease that is used to acquire assets on a long-term basis, when virtually all of the benefits and risks of ownership of the leased asset are assumed by the lessee, is called a capital lease (or financing lease). Although the lessor retains actual ownership of the leased asset, the accounting treatment for assets acquired by capital lease is the same as if the asset were acquired by purchase and financed by signing a note. The following transactions reflect the accounting treatment given capital leases as described in Chapter 7:

1. Date of acquisition.
    Dr.   Equipment xx
        Cr.   Capital lease liability xx
2. Annual depreciation expense.
    Dr.   Depreciation expense xx
        Cr.   Accumulated depreciation xx
3. Annual lease payments.
    Dr.   Interest expense xx
    Dr.   Capital lease liability xx
        Cr.   Cash xx

The effects of these capital lease transactions on the financial statements using the horizontal model are as shown below:

Balance sheet	Income statement
Assets = Liabilities + Owners' equity ⟵	Net income = Revenues − Expenses

1. Date of acquisition:
   +Equipment +Capital
   　　　　　lease liability

2. Annual depreciation expense:
   −Accumulated　　　　　　　　　　　　　−Depreciation
   　depreciation　　　　　　　　　　　　　 expense

3. Annual lease payment:
   − Cash　　−Capital　　　　　　　　　　−Interest
   　　　　　lease liability　　　　　　　　 expense

Recall that at the date of acquisition, a capital lease liability is recorded at the present value of the future lease payments, based on the *interest rate used by the lessor* in determining the payment amount. Thus, the present value of the lease payments is not necessarily based on a discount rate equal to the firm's cost of capital or cost of debt financing.

If the firm were to purchase the asset and finance it by signing a note, then *notes payable* (instead of *capital lease liability*) would be credited in transaction 1 and debited in transaction 3. Because there are no differences in the accounting treatment for an asset acquired by capital lease or financed purchase, the economic effect to the firm should be the same. Then why do some entities lease their capital assets and others purchase them?

To compare the different financing options and understand how important a role the financing decision plays in capital budgeting analysis, consider the financing options available to the Dodson Insurance Agency for acquiring a computer network system. Dodson has determined that a new computer network would allow it to speed data access and improve customer service at the agency and that it is an acceptable capital resource expenditure based on NPV analysis. The network costs $100,000, and Dodson can acquire the asset by one of the following options:

a. Signing an operating lease agreement requiring six annual payments of $20,000 based on an effective interest rate of 10 percent
b. Signing a note to purchase the asset requiring six annual payments of $22,961 at an interest rate of 10 percent
c. Signing a capital lease agreement requiring six annual payments of $20,000 based on an effective interest rate of 10 percent
d. Using some of the retained earnings (equity) accumulated over the firm's years of operation

For the reasons explained in Chapter 7, Dodson will be required to treat this lease as either an operating lease or a capital lease. Dodson's decision will be explained later in the chapter.

Under either lease agreement, Dodson has the option to purchase the network for the estimated salvage amount of $5,000. For this analysis, however, assume the agency does not exercise that option because advancing technology would probably make retention of the system an undesirable alternative compared to replacing it with a newer state-of-the-art system. Also, under the debt and equity financing options, assume that Dodson sells the network system for the salvage value, incurring a taxable gain.

Evaluating an Operating Lease

Dodson assumes that the computer will have a salvage value of $5,000 at the end of six years. The agency's marginal tax rate is 34 percent, and its after-tax cost of capital is 10 percent. Contributing to the overall cost of capital, Dodson's cost of debt is 10 percent, and its cost of equity is 20 percent.

Assume for the time being that the lease can be recorded as an operating lease and that the full amount of the lease payment is an allowable deduction by Internal Revenue Service (IRS). Exhibit 13-4 summarizes the cost assumptions and provides an analysis of the cash outlays associated with leasing the computer under an operating lease.

Cash outlays are shown by period on a horizontal time line, totaled, and discounted to period zero (today) using present value factors obtained from Table 7-2 for the after-tax cost of capital of 10 percent. Because lease agreements generally require that the first payment be made at the beginning of the lease, a payment of $20,000 is recorded for period zero. Any cash outflows are recorded as negative (–), to identify them as a cost, and cash inflows are recorded as positive.

Because the full amount of the lease payment is an allowable deduction by the IRS as a business expense (to the extent the asset is used in business), the lease payment creates an effective *tax shield* by reducing the firm's income tax liability. The reduction in tax liability, however, is equal to the tax rate applied to the deduction, not the full deduction. Allowing the full amount to reduce the tax liability would be called a *tax credit* instead of an *allowable deduction*. Therefore, multiply the lease payment amount by the marginal tax rate ($20,000 × 34%) to get the effective lease payment tax shield of $6,800 for each of the six periods. Adding the cash outlays shows that the net cash outlay for each period is –$13,200. The net cash outlay is then multiplied by an appropriate discount factor (usually based on the firm's after-tax cost of capital) to determine the cash flow's present value. The result of summing the discounted cash outlays for individual periods is the net cost of leasing under

Exhibit 13-4
Analyzing the Cost of an Operating Lease

Option (a): Finance acquisition by signing an operating lease agreement requiring six annual payments of $20,000 based on an effective interest rate of 10 percent.

Assumptions:

Lease interest rate =	10.00%
Cost of debt =	10.00%
Cost of equity =	20.00%
Estimated useful life =	6 years

Marginal tax rate =	34.00%
After-tax cost of capital =	10.00%
Cost of computer network =	$100,000
Estimated salvage value =	$5,000

Lease the computer network (operating lease):

				Year		
	0	1	2	3	4	5
Lease payment	−20,000	−20,000	−20,000	−20,000	−20,000	−20,000
Lease pymt. tax shield[a]	6,800	6,800	6,800	6,800	6,800	6,800
Net cash outlay	−13,200	−13,200	−13,200	−13,200	−13,200	−13,200
PV factor for 10% (from Table 7-2)	1.0000	0.9091	0.8264	0.7513	0.6830	0.6209
Discounted outlays						
Year 0	−13,200					
Year 1	−12,000					
Year 2	−10,909					
Year 3	−9,917					
Year 4	−9,016					
Year 5	−8,196					
NPV operating lease	−63,238					

Note: [a] Lease payment tax shield = Lease payment × Marginal tax rate

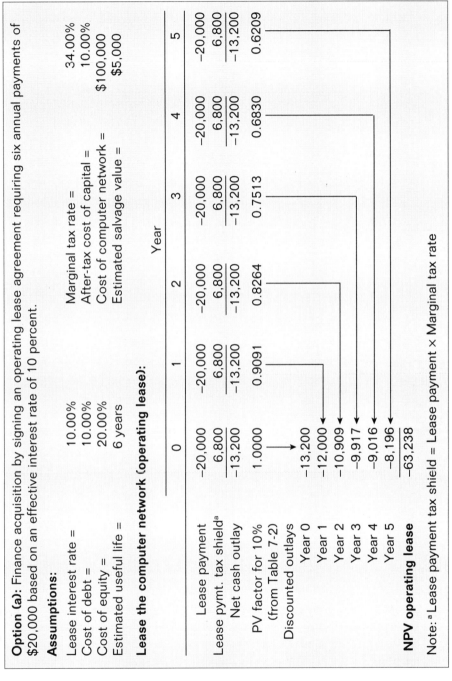

an operating lease. For Dodson's computer network, the cost of an operating lease would be $63,238.

Evaluating Debt Financing

A popular method used by firms to finance the acquisition of assets is debt financing. Although the discussion in this text is limited to debt financing obtained by a note (or loan), the same analysis could be applied to debt financing obtained by a bond issue (although bond financing would not be plausible in the Dodson example).

Continuing with the lease versus purchase analysis, the second alternative available to Dodson is to sign a 10 percent note requiring six annual payments of $22,961. At first glance, debt payments of $22,961 compared to lease payments of only $20,000 would indicate that leasing is obviously the better choice because it is less expensive, but not necessarily. Such cursory analysis might be (and probably is) deceiving because it fails to recognize the time value of money—an essential element in capital budgeting analysis. Exhibit 13-5 presents an analysis of the debt financing option using the cost of capital and interest assumptions that were presented in Exhibit 13-4.

Again, cash outlays are evaluated by period to determine the net cash outlay for each period. This debt financing example, however, has outlays for period zero. This is because the payment on a note is generally made at the end of the period. Thus, payments are made at the end of each period. Because Dodson is purchasing the asset and will acquire immediate ownership interest in the asset, the agency is allowed a deduction for depreciation by the IRS. Also, the interest paid on the note is an allowable business expense. Each of these expenses provides Dodson with an effective tax shield. As with the lease payment tax shield in the previous case, the marginal tax rate is multiplied by the expense to determine the amount by which the tax liability is reduced.

As described in Business Procedure Capsule 12, the IRS prescribes allowable depreciation amounts in schedules developed for the Modified Accelerated Cost Recovery System (MACRS). The allowable depreciation schedule for computer equipment (six-year class property) is provided in the table at the bottom of Exhibit 13-5. The depreciation and interest tax shields for a period are matched to the corresponding cash outlay (loan payment) for the period. Since full rights of ownership accrue to the Dodson Insurance Agency when the asset is purchased, sale of the asset for salvage value must be recognized as an after-tax crash inflow for period six. As in the operating lease analysis, each of the net cash outlays is discounted at the 10 percent cost of capital to period zero and totaled to determine the net present value of debt financing. For Dodson, the net cost of the debt financing option for acquiring the computer network is $61,883.

Exhibit 13-5
Analyzing the Cost of Debt Financing

Option (b): Finance acquisition by signing a note to purchase the asset requiring six annual payments of $22,961 at an interest rate of 10 percent using the same assumptions as in Exhibit 13-4.

				Year			
	0	1	2	3	4	5	6
Loan payment:		−22,961	−22,961	−22,961	−22,961	−22,961	−22,961
Depreciation tax shield[a]:		6,800	10,880	6,528	3,917	3,917	1,958
Interest tax shield[b]:		3,400	2,959	2,475	1,941	1,355	710
After-tax salvage value[c]:							3,300
Net cash outlay:		−12,761	−9,121	−13,958	−17,103	−17,689	−16,993
PV factor for 10%:		0.9091	0.8264	0.7513	0.6830	0.6209	0.5645
(from Table 7-2)							

Discounted outlays:
Year 1: −11,601
Year 2: −7,538
Year 3: −10,487
Year 4: −11,681
Year 5: −10,983
Year 6: −9,593

NPV of debt financing: −61,883

Notes: [a] Depreciation tax shield = Period depreciation × Marginal tax rate
[b] Interest tax shield = Period interest expense × Marginal tax rate
[c] After-tax salvage value (assuming sale of asset) = (1 − Marginal tax rate) × Estimated salvage

				Year			
	0	1	2	3	4	5	6
MACRS depreciation rate:		20.00%	32.00%	19.20%	11.52%	11.52%	5.76%
Depreciation amount:		20,000	32,000	19,200	11,520	11,520	5,760
Beginning loan balance:	100,000	87,039	72,782	57,100	39,849	20,873	
Interest component:	10,000	8,704	7,278	5,710	3,985	2,087	
Principal component:	12,961	14,257	15,682	17,251	18,976	20,873	
Ending loan balance:	87,039	72,782	57,100	39,849	20,873	0	

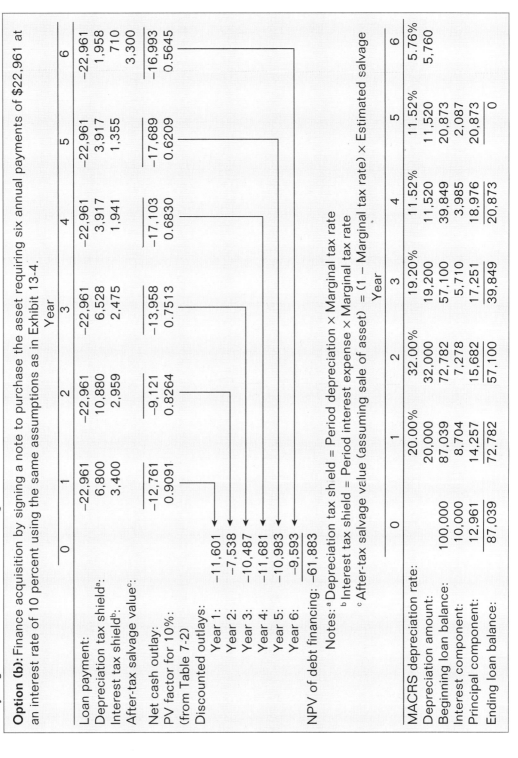

Evaluating a Capital Lease

It is unreasonable for Dodson to even consider an operating lease because by the rules identified in Chapter 7, this computer network would clearly necessitate reporting as a capital lease. If any of the following four characteristics describe the lease under consideration, it must be treated as a capital lease:

1. It transfers ownership of the asset to the lessee.
2. It permits the lessee to purchase the asset for a nominal sum at the end of the lease period.
3. The lease term is at least 75 percent of the economic life of the asset.
4. The present value of the lease payments is at least 90 percent of the fair value of the asset.

In the Dodson Agency case, the ownership of the asset is retained by the lessor, and although Dodson can purchase the network for $5,000 at the end of the lease, that residual amount is considered to be greater than a nominal fee. Thus, items 1 and 2 do not apply in this case. Item 4 states that if the present value of the lease payments is at least 90 percent of the fair value of the asset, the lease must be recorded as a capital lease. Because the first lease payment is due at the inception of the lease (period zero), the present value of the lease payments is computed as the sum of the first payment plus the product of the present value annuity factor for the remaining five years at 10 percent (see Table 7-3) times the lease payment amount. This is equivalent to (1 + the present value annuity factor) times the payment amount:

$$\text{PV of lease} = \$20,000 \times (1 + 3.7908)$$
$$= \$95,816$$

Because the present value of the lease payments exceeds 90 percent of the fair value of the asset ($95,816 > $90,000), and because the lease term exceeds 75 percent of the expected economic life of the asset (it is actually equal to the estimated six-year life for the computer network), the lease must be classified as a capital lease and presented accordingly in the financial statements.

Classifying the lease as a capital lease requires that it be evaluated differently than was the operating lease in Exhibit 13-4. The lease must be capitalized as the present value of the lease payments, $95,816, and amortized over the remaining term of the lease. The effective interest expense (at the assumed lease rate) and the allowable depreciation expense, as for a debt financed purchase, provide a tax shield for the lessee. Exhibit 13-6 illustrates the appropriate analysis for a capital lease.

Exhibit 13-6

Analyzing the Cost of a Capital Lease

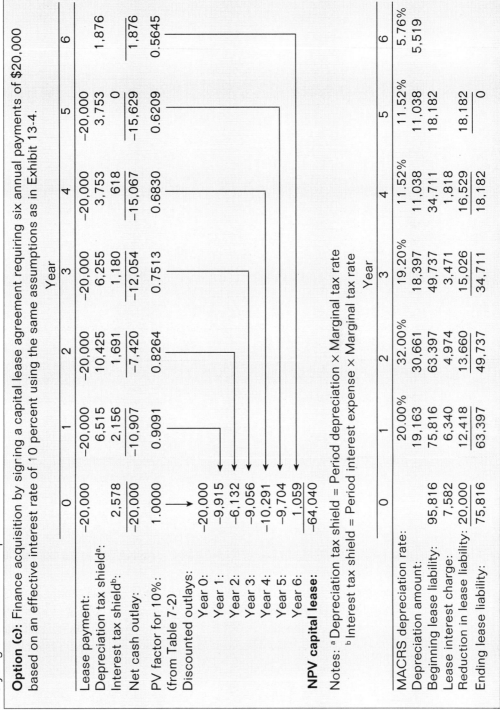

Option (c): Finance acquisition by signing a capital lease agreement requiring six annual payments of $20,000 based on an effective interest rate of 10 percent using the same assumptions as in Exhibit 13-4.

				Year			
	0	1	2	3	4	5	6
Lease payment:	-20,000	-20,000	-20,000	-20,000	-20,000	-20,000	
Depreciation tax shield[a]:		6,515	10,425	6,255	3,753	3,753	1,876
Interest tax shield[b]:	2,578	2,156	1,691	1,180	618	0	
Net cash outlay:	-20,000	-10,907	-7,420	-12,054	-15,067	-15,629	1,876
PV factor for 10%: (from Table 7-2)	1.0000	0.9091	0.8264	0.7513	0.6830	0.6209	0.5645
Discounted outlays:							
Year 0:	-20,000						
Year 1:	-9,915						
Year 2:	-6,132						
Year 3:	-9,056						
Year 4:	-10,291						
Year 5:	-9,704						
Year 6:	1,059						
NPV capital lease:	**-64,040**						

Notes: [a] Depreciation tax shield = Period depreciation × Marginal tax rate
[b] Interest tax shield = Period interest expense × Marginal tax rate

				Year			
	0	1	2	3	4	5	6
MACRS depreciation rate:		20.00%	32.00%	19.20%	11.52%	11.52%	5.76%
Depreciation amount:		19,163	30,661	18,397	11,038	11,038	5,519
Beginning lease liability:	95,816	75,816	63,397	49,737	34,711	18,182	
Lease interest charge:	7,582	6,340	4,974	3,471	1,818		
Reduction in lease liability:	20,000	12,418	13,660	15,026	16,529	18,182	
Ending lease liability:	75,816	63,397	49,737	34,711	18,182	0	

The timing of cash outlays for a capital lease is similar to the timing for both an operating lease and a debt-financed purchase. As for the operating lease, payments begin at the inception of the lease. As for the debt-financed purchase, the depreciation and interest tax shields are recognized at the end of the period. As with previous analyses, net cash outlays for each period are discounted at the firm's cost of capital to determine the NPV of the financing alternative. For Dodson's computer network, the cost of the capital lease option is $64,040.

Evaluating Equity Financing

One final financing alternative is available to the Dodson Insurance Agency for acquisition of its new computer network. But why should Dodson consider financing (or leasing) at all? If Dodson has adequate capital, could not the firm simply pay cash for the asset? That way the firm would not incur any additional cost. Equity, however, is not a free resource.

For every dollar of equity funds spent on an asset or other investment, one dollar of available capital resources is removed from funds that could be used for other investments. If the resources to fund other investments are not available, those investment opportunities and their associated returns on investment are lost. For Dodson, the before-tax rate of return on equity is equal to 20 percent. If the computer network does not provide at least that rate of return, it should not be considered as a prospect for equity financing. Some questions that should be considered when evaluating an equity financing decision are as follows:

1. Does the use of equity funds restrict capital resources for current operations or possible emergencies?
2. Do other projects afford a higher rate of return with less risk than the investment alternative being considered?
3. Will the commitment of equity resources to this capital expenditure adversely affect the availability or cost of debt financing?

In the evaluation of capital budgeting expenditures, each investment or project is evaluated on a discounted cash flow basis using the firm's cost of capital. That cost of capital, or hurdle rate, is composed of a combination of the individual costs of debt and equity determined by the mix of those sources in the firm's capital structure. Any use of equity resources can have an adverse effect on the firm's financial position if that use constrains current operations, limits future investment opportunities in projects offering greater returns on investment, or impairs the firm's margin of capital needed to withstand emergencies or catastrophes. Exhibit 13-7 provides an analysis of the purchase of the computer network with equity financing.

Exhibit 13-7
Analyzing the Cost of Equity Financing

Option (d): Finance acquisition using some of the retained earnings (equity) accumulated over the firm's years of operation using the same assumptions as in Exhibit 13-4.

				Year			
	0	1	2	3	4	5	6
Lease or loan payment:	0	0	0	0	0	0	0
Depreciation tax shield[a]:		6,800	10,880	6,528	3,917	3,917	1,958
Interest tax shield[b]:		0	0	0	0	0	0
Lost return on equity:		−20,000	−20,000	−20,000	−20,000	−20,000	−20,000
After-tax salvage value[c]:							3,300
Net period cash flow:	0	−13,200	−9,120	−13,472	−16,083	−16,083	−14,742
PV factor for 10%: (from Table 7-2)		0.9091	0.8264	0.7513	0.6830	0.6209	0.5645

Discounted outlays:

Year 1:	−12,000
Year 2:	−7,537
Year 3:	−10,122
Year 4:	−10,985
Year 5:	−9,986
Year 6:	−8,321

NPV equity financing: −58,952

Notes: [a] Depreciation tax shield = Period depreciation × Marginal tax rate
[b] Interest tax shield = Period interest expense × Marginal tax rate
[c] After-tax salvage value (assuming sale of asset) = (1 − Marginal tax rate) × Estimated salvage

				Year			
	0	1	2	3	4	5	6
Depreciation rate:		20.00%	32.00%	19.20%	11.52%	11.52%	5.76%
Depreciation amount:		20,000	32,000	19,200	11,520	11,520	5,760

To ensure that the earnings potential of Dodson's equity resources is adequately recognized, assuming that equity resources are available and in sufficient amount, an effective cash outlay for each period equal to the cost of equity funds or ROE times the purchase amount for the computer network system will be included. This amount, $20,000 for each period, represents the *lost opportunity cost* of using equity resources. Although Dodson cannot recognize an interest tax shield (because debt financing is not used), the firm can realize a depreciation tax shield based on the MACRS depreciation rate allowed and the present value of the estimated after tax gain if the network system were sold for the salvage value at the end of six years. As for other analyses, the net period cash flows are discounted to period zero using the firm's after-tax cost of capital. The cost of equity financing for Dodson's computer network is $58,952.

Comparing the Options

The following table summarizes the cost of financing the computer network acquisition under each of the options analyzed:

Method of Financing	Cost of Financing
Operating lease	$63,238
Purchase using debt	61,883
Capital lease	64,040
Purchase using equity	58,952

The analyses performed in Exhibits 13-4 through 13-7 are only one part of the capital budgeting process—the *financing decision*. Before considering how to finance a capital expenditure, management first must determine whether the expenditure is justified in terms of its ROI or value contributed to the organization—the *investing decision*.

When even the most critical analysis does not identify one financing option to be better than another or when the unique financial position of a firm limits the financing options available to it, considering other advantages of leasing might be worthwhile. Several *sensible* reasons for leasing are provided by one popular finance text:[1]

- Short-term leases are convenient.
- Cancellation options are valuable.
- Maintenance may be provided.
- Standardization leads to low administrative and transaction costs.
- Tax shields can be used.

The lessee can often realize advantages from the first four reasons cited because property ownership remains with the lessor. This is particularly true for operating leases. (Under a capital lease, however, virtually all risk and benefit of property ownership is transferred to the lessee.) Operating leases, including short-term car rental agreements, are generally very convenient because the terms are often negotiable (for example, the lease term) and typically include a provision for cancellation. Generally, the responsibility for maintenance and repair of the leased property remains with the lessor. The estimated cost for this responsibility can sometimes be used as a negotiating factor in setting the lease terms. If efficiencies can be gained by the lessee maintaining the item because it owns (or leases) a large number of similar units, the lessor may be willing to shift maintenance responsibility to the lessee with a commensurate reduction in lease payments.

Standardization of any transaction typically provides a cost savings to those involved. Lease companies that specialize in a particular class of property (such as heavy construction equipment, long-haul vehicles, and automobiles) can often provide lease terms that are hard to beat. One cannot assume that simply because it is a specialized lease company that it offers the best deal— one still needs to perform the cost analysis.

The analyses have already demonstrated the benefit of lease payment tax shields (for operating leases) and depreciation and interest tax shields (for capital leases). Because of the effect of tax shields and the *accelerated* benefit of depreciation provided by MACRS schedules, the firm needs to consider the *timing* of the tax shields. Although the difference in the costs between leasing and purchasing may be negligible, the timing of benefits realized from tax shields or the payment schedule for one or the other may provide greater benefit to a firm that has an unusually large tax liability.

Structured Claim Settlements

The structured settlement is a method for settling claims involving bodily injury or death. Until the early 1970s, such claims were usually settled using a lump-sum payment. The tremendous increase over the past three decades in the proportion of claims settled using a structured payment approach is believed to result from the increasing incidence of medical malpractice and the associated high verdicts, often exceeding $100,000.[2] With several verdicts today exceeding many times that amount, professional claims personnel must find ways that claims can be settled less expensively, yet still providing an equitable amount to the injured party.

A **structured settlement** is "the settlement of a claim or a lawsuit through cash payments that are made on an installment or periodic basis."[3] The ability to use a periodic or deferred payment structure offers greater flexibility for claims professionals to match settlement dollars to the actual needs of the claimant over time. For example, an industrial worker who is totally and permanently disabled on the job has greater need of wage replacement over the remaining years that he could have worked than he does a large lump-sum settlement amount. Claims requiring a regular and periodic income stream can often be structured to include an annuity as part of the claim structure. This is perhaps the most frequently used design component of a structured settlement. The key variables that need to be determined are the periodic payment amount, the length of the annuity period, and the appropriate discount rate to use in determining the present value of the annuity.

Another component that often appears in structured settlements is a deferred payment (payment does not commence until some future date), either in the form of a fixed sum or an annuity, that is intended to satisfy some specific future need. For example, suppose that the disabled worker must return to the rehabilitation center in three years for the reengineering of a custom prosthetic device. This need could be addressed by a deferred payment made possible by a structured claim settlement. Other common needs for which an annuity form of deferred payment might be appropriate are funding of college education (for example, providing benefit to a dependent child in a wrongful death case) and funding supplemental retirement needs for an individual forced to accept premature retirement as the result of an accident-related permanent partial disability.

Summary

Capital budgeting has a much longer-term time-frame perspective than operational budgeting. Capital expenditure analysis, which leads to the capital budget, tries to determine the effect of a proposed capital expenditure on the organization's ROI.

Capital budgeting procedures should involve the use of present value analysis because an investment is made today in expectation of returns far into the future. The time value of money must be recognized if appropriate capital expenditure decisions are to be made.

In addition to evaluating the results of numerical analyses, decision makers consider qualitative factors related to the proposed investment. Most qualitative factors relate to the risks associated with the investment or with the numbers used to support the investment decision.

Cost of capital is the minimum ROI that should be earned on the proposed investment. The risk associated with the proposal will affect the cost of capital, or desired ROI, used to evaluate the investment.

Net present value and internal rate of return are two investment analysis methods that recognize the time value of money. The net present value approach uses the cost of capital as the discount rate to calculate a difference between the present value of future cash flows from the investment and the amount invested. If the net present value is zero or positive, the proposed investment's ROI is equal to or greater than the cost of capital, and the investment is an appropriate one to make. The present value ratio, or profitability index, provides a means to rank alternative proposals. The internal rate of return approach solves for the proposal's ROI, which is then compared to cost of capital. The investment is an appropriate one to make if the ROI of the proposed investment equals or exceeds the cost of capital.

Some analytical considerations related to capital budgeting include estimating accuracy, timing of cash flows within a year, and investments made over a period of time. Many firms require a post-audit of a capital project to evaluate the estimates made in the initial analysis. Some projects require an increase in working capital, which is considered part of the investment.

Payback and accounting rate of return are two investment analysis methods that do not recognize the time value of money and are thus not appropriate analytical techniques. Nevertheless, many analysts and managers use the results of these methods along with the results of the NPV and IRR methods.

In addition to considering the results of the various quantitative models used to evaluate investment proposals, management also identifies and considers qualitative factors when deciding whether to proceed with an investment. These qualitative factors are frequently more significant than the quantitative model results.

The capital budget is integrated into the operating budget. The capital budget directly affects production capacity, depreciation expense, and cash outflows for purchases of new plant and equipment. A complete capital budgeting analysis must include both the investment decision and the financing decision. The most common situation in which the investment decision and the financing decision are intertwined is when evaluating the lease versus purchase decision.

Capital budgeting techniques can be applied to almost any finance problem involving periodic cash flows. One instance of particular interest to insurance professionals in which capital budgeting techniques are applicable is in evaluating the options available in a structured claim settlement.

Key Words and Phrases

accounting rate of return method (p. 410) A capital budgeting analytical technique that calculates the rate of return on the investment based on the financial statement effects of the investment.

capital budgeting (p. 405) The process of analyzing proposed investments in plant and equipment and other long-lived assets.

cash flows (p. 409) In capital budgeting, the cash receipts and disbursements associated with a capital expenditure over its life.

cost of capital (p. 409) The ROI that must be earned to permit the firm to meet its interest obligations and provide the owners their expected return; the discount rate used in the present value calculations of capital budgeting.

internal rate of return (IRR) method (p. 409) A capital budgeting analytical technique that solves for the time-adjusted rate of return on an investment over its life.

net present value (NPV) method (p. 409) A capital budgeting analytical technique that relates the present value of the returns from an investment to the present value of the investment, given a cost of capital.

payback method (p. 409) A capital budgeting analytical technique that calculates the length of time for the cash flows from an investment to equal the investment.

post-audit (p. 414) The process of comparing the assumptions used in a capital budgeting analysis with the actual results of the investment.

present value ratio (p. 410) The ratio of the present value of the cash flows from an investment to the investment. See *profitability index.*

profitability index (p. 410) The ratio of the present value of the cash flows from an investment to the investment; used for ranking proposed capital expenditures by profitability.

structured settlement (p. 431) The settlement of a claim or a lawsuit through cash payments that are made on an installment or periodic basis.

Chapter Notes

1. Richard A. Brealey and Stewart C. Myers, *Principles of Corporate Finance*, 4th ed. (New York, NY: McGraw-Hill, Inc., 1991), pp. 654-658.

2. Joseph W. Huver, *Structured Settlements: An Alternative Approach to the Settling of Claims* (Cincinnati, OH: The National Underwriter Co., 1992), p. 7.

3. Huver, p. 8.

Chapter 14

A Systematic Approach to Financial Statement Analysis

Financial statements are an important source of information for many business decisions. Banks, leasing companies, and suppliers of goods and services use financial statements as a source of information about a firm's credit risk. Labor unions use the information contained in a firm's financial statements as a basis for negotiating wage and benefit packages for their members. Government agencies also use financial statements as a means of monitoring business activity and as a basis for recommending public policy actions.

Previous chapters provided an in-depth discussion of accounting for assets, liabilities, owners' equity, revenues, and expenses, and of reporting the results of those transactions in a firm's financial statements. This chapter focuses on analyzing the relationships among financial statement items, both within a single accounting period and over time. It introduces financial statement analysis as a process for organizing, summarizing, and evaluating financial information to form sound business judgments and make rational business decisions. The discussion builds on the introduction to financial ratios provided in Chapter 5. This chapter also presents two additional techniques for analyzing financial statement relationships, vertical and horizontal analysis.

Educational Objectives

After studying this chapter, you should be able to:

1. Identify four steps in the financial analysis process.
2. Identify the five broad purposes of financial analysis.
3. Compare and contrast horizontal, vertical, and trend analysis.
4. Given a set of comparative financial statements:
    - Compute yearly percentage changes for a limited number of financial statement items.
    - Calculate and interpret the values of financial ratios.
    - Explain how alternative accounting methods can affect the values of financial ratios.
5. Define or describe each of the Key Words and Phrases introduced in this chapter.

Overview of the Analysis Process

Financial statement analysis is simply a systematic approach for extracting and evaluating accounting information needed for a specific business purpose. The tools and techniques used in a given analysis, as well as the level of detail required, depend for the most part on the particular business decision under consideration. Although every analysis is probably unique, the process used is likely to be similar. The process of financial statement analysis can be divided into four broad steps or phases, as follows:

- Establish the objective of the analysis
- Review the financial statements and other available information
- Select and apply the appropriate techniques
- Interpret the results

These four phases are general. In practice, almost every analysis has a different emphasis. Some are highly focused, considering only one or two dimensions of a firm's financial characteristics. Others are more general, considering several aspects of a firm's operations and financial condition.

Objectives of Financial Statement Analysis

Before undertaking a detailed analysis of a company's financial statements, it is important to establish the objective of the analysis. Knowing why the analysis is being done helps focus attention on information relevant to the decision at hand. Basically, financial statement analysis has five broad objectives. Exhibit 14-1 summarizes those objectives.

The first objective is **screening**. Financial analysis is often directed toward classifying (screening) the firm into one of two categories, such as "acceptable" or "not acceptable," based on whether the firm meets one or more pre-established criteria. For example, credit card issuers look for a minimum level of income before they will approve an applicant for a gold card. A bank may set minimum thresholds for certain financial ratios that must be met before it will approve a business loan. An insurance company may place a lower limit on the size of the companies from whom it will purchase reinsurance. In each of these cases, the objective is to perform some *pass-fail* analysis, focusing on specific financial data, applying pre-established criteria, and eliminating obviously unqualified candidates.

Exhibit 14-1
The Five Objectives of Financial Statement Analysis

	Objective	Purpose
1.	Screening	To classify the firm being analyzed—for example, acceptable or not acceptable, pass or fail
2.	Evaluation	To assess the firm's performance in one or all four of the standard operating dimensions: profitability, liquidity, solvency, or efficiency
3.	Diagnosis	To review acceptability of individual or related accounts, such as a supplier or customer
4.	Forecasting	To project a firm's future operating results or financial condition using historical information
5.	Reconstruction	To determine or estimate missing accounting information using a firm's prior period financial statements

The second objective is **evaluation**. An analysis for evaluation purposes is usually directed toward assessing one or more of a firm's financial characteristics. That is, the analysis might be focused on assessing the firm's profitability, liquidity, solvency, or efficiency. Or the analysis might be directed toward a more general evaluation, in which these characteristics are viewed together to form an overall financial picture of the firm. For example, a potential investor might choose to focus on a firm's relative profitability to help in selecting the investment with the greatest potential for capital appreciation. A bank considering extending a short-term loan might focus on a company's liquidity.

Creditors extending long-term loans would be expected to place great emphasis on the company's solvency. However, each of these parties is interested in the firm's ability to continue its operations into the future. Whether the company can continue as a going concern is a question that requires considering the firm's profitability. Consequently, even though the primary objective of the analysis might be relatively narrow, studying more than one aspect of a company's operating performance or financial condition might be required to draw meaningful conclusions.

The third objective is **diagnosis**. Financial analysis for the purpose of diagnosis is more focused than are analyses for other purposes, usually limiting the scope of the analysis to a set of related accounts. For example, a supplier might note that a customer is beginning to delay payments for its purchases made on account. An analysis of the firm's sales, inventory, and related accounts might show that the customer is experiencing cash-flow shortages because of difficulty in collecting its own accounts receivable. Or the analysis may show a downturn in the customer's profitability because of shrinking sales margins. Depending on whether the problem appears to be temporary or part of a long-term trend, the supplier may wish to re-evaluate the customer's line of credit. Similarly, an insurance regulator might note that an insurer has suddenly increased its written premium volume. An analysis of the insurer's liquidity could provide insight into whether this increase is a result of a deliberate attempt to grow or a means of generating needed cash in the face of impending financial difficulties.

The fourth objective is **forecasting**. Financial analysis for the purpose of forecasting may be directed toward generating data for further analysis. Historical information, including summary information provided by ratios, may be combined with current information and used as a basis for projecting future operating results or financial condition. Forecasting can involve techniques that are relatively simple, such as calculating averages or ranges of values. Or it can involve the application of very complex statistical tools. Forecasting can be particularly useful to management in planning long-term strategies and to others with a long-term interest in the firm. A detailed discussion of forecasting techniques and their application is beyond the scope of this text.

The fifth objective is **reconstruction**. Financial analysis for the purpose of reconstruction is focused on identifying and quantifying relationships among prior period financial statement items that can be used to reconstruct all or part of a firm's financial statements from a set of incomplete records. For example, suppose a business suffered a loss that destroyed not only property, but also important business records and papers. To determine the amount of loss, financial statement relationships drawn from prior years' records can be used to estimate the missing data. An example of how such relationships can be used to fill in missing financial statement data was provided in Exhibit 10-3.

Review the Financial Statements and Other Information

To draw meaningful conclusions from a financial analysis, some familiarity with the company being examined is essential. A firm's financial statements, including the supplemental information provided by management in the annual report's management's discussion and analysis (MD&A), can provide a wealth of information about what the firm does, how it competes in the marketplace, and what its plans for the future are. A brief review of the financial statements as a whole is an efficient way to gather this important background information. In addition, it might also call attention to specific areas that should be analyzed more carefully.

This phase generally involves three steps. When audited financial statements are available, the first step is to examine the auditor's report. The most favorable report contains an *unqualified opinion* (often referred to as a "clean" opinion), which states that, in the auditor's opinion, the financial statements are fairly presented in accordance with GAAP. Far less frequently, the audit opinion is *qualified*, with the reasons for the qualification given within the audit report. In very unusual circumstances, the auditor might conclude that the financial statements are not fairly presented and render an *adverse opinion*.

An auditor may issue an unqualified opinion, even though significant uncertainties could affect amounts reported in the financial statements or the application of accounting principles has changed from prior periods. In those cases, the auditor's report will be modified to draw attention to these items. These items are important to note because they can indicate areas where particular attention is required—in calculating ratios, identifying trends, or comparing results across years. A sudden change in profitability, for example, might be the result of a change in the company's accounting policies and not a fundamental change in its operations.

The second step involves looking at the accounting policies the firm uses in preparing its financial statements. The footnotes to the financial statements provide a description of the methods used to value inventories, to calculate depreciation, and to articulate other significant accounting policies. This step is particularly important if comparisons are going to be made among companies. Consider, for example, an analysis of two very similar companies. While reviewing the financial statements, an analyst finds that these two companies use different inventory valuation methods. This is an important discovery, because any ratios that use total assets, total current assets, or cost of goods sold in their computation will be affected. To make meaningful comparisons, the amounts reported in the financial statements would need to be adjusted.

The third step involves an overall examination of the financial statements and gathering background information from trade publications and other outside sources. The purpose is to better understand the firm's results of operations, its financial condition, its cash flows, and the environment in which the firm operates. Much of the data needed to draw the relevant financial statement relationships can be collected during this examination. In addition, unusual items encountered at this point often serve as warnings that a closer examination of the notes and schedules provided with the financial statements is needed before any computations are performed.

Select and Apply the Appropriate Techniques

Identifying the purpose of the analysis is equivalent to asking the right question. Knowing the right question to ask helps focus attention on the tools and techniques most appropriate to generating the information needed to provide a clear, concise answer. For example, if the goal is to evaluate a firm's profitability, more emphasis will be placed on the income statement. Attention will be drawn to profitability ratios such as return on sales, return on equity, and return on investment. If, however, the goal is to provide information on a firm's ability to meet its debt obligations, the focus of attention will be on the balance sheet. Debt-related ratios, including the current ratio, acid-test (or quick) ratio (discussed in Chapter 3), and debt-to-equity ratio (discussed later in this chapter), will be of greatest importance. The nature of the firm's business will also help determine the specific ratios to be used. This text, when examining an insurance company, for example, will emphasize industry-specific ratios focused on underwriting and investment performance rather than more general GAAP-based ratios.

Although ratios are an efficient means of communicating summary information about specific aspects of a firm, they are not the only tools available. Another useful technique is to convert income statement and balance sheet amounts to percentages. This process, often referred to as **vertical analysis**, highlights basic relationships among items within a single set of financial statements. Financial statements prepared in this percentage format, also called **common size financial statements**, are particularly useful when the analysis requires evaluating the relative performance or financial condition of two or more firms, particularly when those firms differ greatly in size.

Similarly, calculating the year-to-year percentage changes in financial statement accounts can highlight changes in basic relationships over time. Focusing on yearly percentage changes is often referred to as **horizontal analysis**. This technique is particularly useful for identifying trends and changes in trends for important financial statement items such as sales or net income.

Applying the appropriate techniques is largely a mechanical step. Preparing common size financial statements for vertical analysis and computing year-to-year percentage changes for horizontal analysis can be accomplished with a simple hand-held calculator. In some cases, this mechanical step can be avoided since many companies provide this information as part of their annual report to stockholders. Similarly, once the relevant financial information has been gathered, the task of actually calculating needed ratio values is straightforward. Again, many companies include commonly used financial ratios for both the current and prior periods in their annual report to stockholders. However, a word of caution is in order. There may be more than one method of calculating a given ratio. Recall, for example, that the combined ratio can be calculated on a trade basis or financial basis. Before relying on any published financial ratios, look for a description of how those ratios were calculated and perform several test calculations to assure that all elements of the analysis are based on the same definitions.

Interpret the Results

No analysis is complete until the results are reviewed and interpreted. By themselves, the numerical results obtained during the application phase are not very informative. To be meaningful, they must be put into context and brought together to form a complete picture of a firm's financial performance or condition. Interpretation, in turn, requires that comparisons be made—to some predetermined criteria, to the results obtained for other companies, to other time periods, or to industry averages. To make these comparisons, a set of standards—sometimes called "benchmarks"—is needed. They can be determined in advance, as in a screening analysis. They might be developed as part of the analysis—for example, when the purpose is to evaluate and rank the *relative* performance or financial condition of several companies. Or they might be obtained from outside sources—for example, when the analysis involves comparing one company's result to that of an industry. Without some basis for making these comparisons, it would be difficult—if not impossible—to determine whether a single value for a given ratio or percentage should be interpreted as good, average, or inadequate.

Applying Vertical and Horizontal Analysis

With the raw numbers published in a firm's financial statements, even basic financial relationships may be difficult to see, much less evaluate. Often, financial analysis can be useful to begin with a vertical analysis. This technique expresses the dollar amounts reported in the financial statements as percentages relative to some base. Income statement items, for example, are expressed as a percentage of sales. Similarly, balance sheet items are expressed as a percentage of total assets. This technique is particularly useful when intercompany comparisons and trend analysis are required. The resulting financial statements are called common size since the process of converting to percentages removes firm size as a complicating factor in making comparisons across companies and removes the effects of inflation and growth from the reported dollar amounts when comparisons are made across time.

Vertical Analysis

To see how these common size financial statements are constructed, consider the income statements of The Home Depot, Inc., and Argonaut Insurance Group provided in Exhibit 14-2. That exhibit demonstrates how several of the common size percentages in the exhibit were calculated from the reported income statement amounts.

Exhibit 14-2
Vertical Analysis of The Home Depot, Inc.'s, 1995 Income Statement

The Home Depot, Inc.

Net sales	$15,470.4	$\dfrac{\$15,470.4}{\$15,470.4} \times 100$	100.0%
Cost of goods sold	11,184.8	$\dfrac{\$11,184.8}{\$15,470.4} \times 100$	72.3
Gross profit	$ 4,285.6	$\dfrac{\$ 4,285.6}{\$15,470.4} \times 100$	27.7%
Net income	$ 731.5	$\dfrac{\$731.5}{\$15,470.4} \times 100$	4.7%

Argonaut Insurance Group

Premiums earned	$ 208.1	$\dfrac{\$\,208.1}{\$\,208.1} \times 100$	100.0%
Losses & LAE incurred	152.8	$\dfrac{\$\,152.8}{\$\,208.1} \times 100$	73.4
Other underwriting expenses	67.3	$\dfrac{\$\,67.3}{\$\,208.1} \times 100$	32.3
Net underwriting gain (loss)	$ (12.0)	$\dfrac{\$(\,12.0)}{\$\,208.1} \times 100$	–5.8%
Net income	$ 56.9	$\dfrac{\$\,56.9}{\$\,208.1} \times 100$	27.3%

Note the difference between the items reported in the income statements of these two companies. Obviously, the companies operate in different industries, and these differences are reflected in their respective financial statements. To repeat a point made earlier, familiarity with the company being examined and the industry in which it operates is essential before meaningful conclusions can be drawn from the analysis.

This type of analysis helps draw attention to items that have a significant effect on income. In the case of The Home Depot, Inc., for example, cost of goods sold is the single largest expense item reported by the company. This makes sense, of course, because the company is in the business of retailing products manufactured by others. Inventory management and product pricing are crucial to the company's ability to generate net income. However, other costs, such as wages and benefits, employee training, and advertising, can also be significant. These costs, which are summarized as "selling, general, and administrative expenses," consume about 20 percent of The Home Depot, Inc.'s, sales revenues. Clearly, this company's long-term profitability depends on its ability to control these costs as well.

In the case of Argonaut Insurance Group, incurred losses and loss adjustment expenses represent the largest single expense item on the company's income statement. Again, these expenses are consistent with the nature of the insurance business. Adequate pricing in the face of competition and control over losses and their associated costs—carried out through the underwriting and loss adjustment functions—are essential to an insurance company's ability to operate profitably.

A vertical analysis of the balance sheet begins by expressing all reported amounts as a percentage of total assets. Converting the reported balance sheet amounts to a percentage of total assets for a company focuses attention on the composition of assets and liabilities. When common size balance sheets of two or more companies are compared, the vertical analysis helps identify an unusual composition of assets or liabilities for the company.

Again, the importance of understanding the industry in which the company operates is extremely important. Argonaut Insurance Group and The Home Depot, Inc., have very different compositions of assets and liabilities. The Home Depot, Inc., for example, holds over 90 percent of its assets in inventories and property and equipment (see Exhibit 5-2). The investment in inventory reflects The Home Depot, Inc.'s, operation as a retail merchandiser. Its investment in property, plant, and equipment reflects the company's strategy of owning, rather than renting, its retail locations. In contrast, Argonaut holds about 72 percent of its total assets as investments in stocks and bonds (see Exhibit 5-2, GAAP-based balance sheet for Argonaut Insurance Group). It does not have a significant investment in fixed assets—land, buildings, or equipment—which reflects an emphasis on holding liquid assets.

Differences also exist on the liability side of the balance sheet. Home Depot's total liabilities amount to just over 32 percent of total assets (see Exhibit 5-2). Rather than relying on a mix of equity and debt to finance its operations, the company relies on internally generated funds (common stock and retained earnings) to meet its financing needs. Argonaut presents a very different picture, with total liabilities amounting to over 60 percent of total assets (see Exhibit 5-2). Although this ratio might be considered high for a retailer, it is typical of an insurer.

Information obtained from a vertical analysis can be useful in a variety of insurance contexts, particularly when several years' data are available. For example, insurance policies are available to cover the risks of business interruption caused by a number of perils. Having a clear picture of an applicant's operating history can assist an underwriter in assessing the applicant's risk to assure the proper premium is charged. Loss adjusters can also use this information, for example, to estimate the amount of inventory lost to a fire.

To illustrate how a loss adjuster might use this information, consider a business that holds all of its inventory in a rented warehouse away from its sales facility. On March 31, 1996, the warehouse and its contents are destroyed by fire. Business records verify that $450,000 of merchandise was on hand at December 31, 1995. Invoices support that an additional $150,000 of inventory had been purchased, and sales records show that $280,000 of sales were made during the first quarter of 1996. A common size analysis of the company's financial statements shows that the company has consistently maintained a 25 percent gross margin over the past several years. Using this information, the amount of inventory lost can be calculated as follows.

First, find the ratio of cost of goods sold to sales:

$$\frac{Sales}{Sales} - \frac{Cost\ of\ goods\ sold}{Sales} = \frac{Gross\ margin}{Sales}$$

$$1 - \frac{Cost\ of\ goods\ sold}{Sales} = .25$$

$$\frac{Cost\ of\ goods\ sold}{Sales} = 1 - .25 = .75$$

Next, estimate the amount of the cost of goods sold associated with the first quarter sales of $280,000:

$$Estimated\ cost\ of\ goods\ sold = Sales \times Cost\ of\ goods\ sold\ ratio$$
$$= \$280,000 \times .75$$
$$= \$210,000$$

With this estimate in hand, the amount of inventory lost to the fire can be calculated by using the method introduced in Chapter 10:

Inventory at 12/31/95	$450,000
Plus: Purchases 1/1/96 through 3/31/96	150,000
Goods on hand at 3/31/96	$600,000
Less: Estimated cost of goods sold 1/1/96 through 3/31/96	210,000
Estimated inventory on hand at 3/31/96	$390,000

Horizontal Analysis

Horizontal analysis involves comparisons across several years of data. Comparing the common size income statements of a firm over several years can provide a information about the firm's profitability. Comparing the common size balance sheets of a firm over several years can highlight changes in the composition of assets and liabilities that have occurred over time. To illustrate how a horizontal analysis can be used to examine profitability, consider the common size income statements of The Home Depot, Inc., provided in Exhibit 14-3. The financial data used to prepare these common size income statements are provided in the Appendix to this chapter.

Exhibit 14-3
Common Size Income Statements for The Home Depot, Inc.

Common Size Income Statements
The Home Depot, Inc., and Subsidiaries
Amounts as a Percentage of Net Sales

	Fiscal Year Ended				
	Jan. 28, 1996	Jan. 29, 1995	Jan. 30, 1994	Jan. 31, 1993	Feb. 2, 1992
Net sales	100.0%	100.0%	100.0%	100.0%	100.0%
Cost of merchandise sold	72.3%	72.1%	72.4%	72.5%	71.9%
Gross profit	27.7%	27.9%	27.6%	27.5%	28.1%
Selling, general, and administrative	19.7%	19.6%	19.6%	19.5%	20.3%
Pre-opening	0.3%	0.4%	0.4%	0.4%	0.3%
Total operating expenses	20.1%	20.0%	20.0%	19.9%	20.7%
Operating income	7.6%	7.9%	7.6%	7.7%	7.4%
Interest, net	0.1%	–0.1%	0.3%	0.4%	0.3%
Earnings before income taxes	7.7%	7.9%	8.0%	8.1%	7.7%
Income taxes (note 3)	3.0%	3.0%	3.0%	3.0%	2.9%
Net earnings	4.7%	4.8%	5.0%	5.1%	4.9%

See notes in full statement in Appendix.

A company's profitability is driven by its sales and gross margin, and also by its operating and interest expenses. As the percentages given in Exhibit 14-3 show, Home Depot has been successful in maintaining a better than 27 percent gross margin despite its rapid growth. At the same time, the company has been successful in controlling its operating expenses, keeping them to about 20 percent of sales. The company's overall success in maintaining profitability is demonstrated by its ability to maintain a consistent net margin (net income divided by sales) at about 5 percent of sales.

A similar analysis of The Home Depot, Inc.'s, balance sheet can be performed using these same techniques. The focus of attention is on whether the composition of the company's assets and liabilities has remained relatively stable or has changed over time. If there have been changes, an important consideration is whether the magnitude and direction of these changes are consistent with the company's business strategy. To illustrate, consider the common size balance sheets of The Home Depot, Inc., provided in Exhibit 14-4. The Appendix to this chapter contains the financial data used to prepare these common size balance sheets.

Exhibit 14-4
Common Size Balance Sheets for The Home Depot, Inc.

The Home Depot, Inc., and Subsidiaries
Common Size Balance Sheets
Amounts as a Percentage of Total Assets

| | Fiscal Year Ended | | | |
	Jan. 28, 1996	Jan. 29, 1995	Jan. 30, 1994	Jan. 31, 1993
Assets				
Current assets:				
Cash and cash equivalents	0.72%	0.02%	2.13%	3.10%
Short-term investments (note 1)	0.74	0.98	7.04	7.44
Receivables, net	4.42	4.71	4.22	4.51
Merchandise inventories	29.65	30.28	27.52	23.90
Other current assets	0.79	0.93	0.93	0.77
Total current assets	36.33%	36.91%	41.83%	39.73%
Property and equipment (note 2)	60.66	58.80	50.44	40.90
Long-term investments	0.35	1.70	5.99	17.66
Notes receivable	0.74	0.56	0.00	0.00
Goodwill	1.19	1.53	0.41	0.51
Other	0.73	0.50	1.32	1.21
Total assets	100.00%	100.00%	100.00%	100.00%
Liabilities				
Current liabilities:				
Accounts payable	11.22%	11.79%	11.09%	10.69%
Accrued salaries and expenses	2.70	3.33	3.56	3.23
Taxes payable	2.02	1.90	2.08	1.79
Other accrued expenses	3.30	3.61	3.92	3.45
Current portion of long-term debt	0.03	0.39	0.03	0.05
Total current liabilities	19.26%	21.01%	20.69%	19.20%
Long-term debt (note 3)	9.79	17.02	17.91	21.46
Other long-term liabilities	1.58	1.18	0.94	0.33
Deferred income taxes	0.51	0.33	0.59	0.41
Minority interest	1.04	0.88	0.00	0.00
Total liabilities	31.14%	39.54%	40.14%	41.40%

Continued on next page.

| | Fiscal Year Ended | | | |
Stockholders' Equity	Jan. 28, 1996	Jan. 29, 1995	Jan. 30, 1994	Jan. 31, 1993
Minority interest	1.04%	0.88%	0.00%	0.00%
Common stock, par value $0.05	0.32	0.39	0.48	0.56
Paid-in capital	32.74	26.42	30.55	34.08
Retained earnings	35.07	33.53	29.79	25.27
Cumulative translation adjustments	−0.08	−0.19		
Unrealized loss on investments	0.00	−0.03	—	—
	69.09%	61.01%	60.82%	59.91%
Less: other adjustments (note 5)	−0.23	−0.55	−0.95	−1.31
Total stockholders' equity	68.86%	60.46%	59.86%	58.60%
Total liab. and stockholders' equity	100.00%	100.00%	100.00%	100.00%

See notes in full statement in Appendix.

During the period covered by the financial statements, Home Depot has followed a strategy of growth. Consistent with this strategy, an analyst would expect to find that certain elements of the balance sheet have increased as a percentage of total assets, while expecting to find decreases in other elements of the balance sheet.

For example, a business experiencing rapid growth tends to show increasing investments in both accounts receivable and inventory. A company's investment in accounts receivable depends on the company's sales volume and the payment history of its customers. Similarly, a company's investment in inventory is influenced by the company's sales volume and its ability to keep its inventories of slow-moving or obsolete products to a minimum. Consequently, an analyst might view an increase in inventory without a corresponding increase in sales as a signal that the company is burdened with obsolete or slow-moving merchandise. This situation can present additional risk to an insurer if this obsolete inventory is not identified and its carrying value is not reduced to more current values.

In the case of Home Depot, merchandise inventories grew only moderately (less than 5 percent) as a percentage of total assets during the period covered by the financial statements. During this same period, net receivables held relatively constant at about 4 1/2 percent of total assets. This low percentage reflects that most of the company's sales are primarily for cash. Observing that the percentage of assets held as receivables has remained relatively stable, an analyst could conclude that the company has not sought to increase sales by offering credit terms to its customers.

The relative proportion of assets held in property and equipment will generally increase over time given a strategy of growth together with a policy favoring the ownership, as opposed to the rental, of the company's retail locations. For 1993 through 1996 The Home Depot, Inc.'s, investment in property and equipment increased from just under 41 percent of total assets to almost 61 percent of total assets. An important question for the analyst is how this growth in fixed assets was financed.

As mentioned earlier in this discussion, The Home Depot, Inc., follows a strategy of internally financing its growth, rather than relying on external debt. During these four years, The Home Depot, Inc.'s, current assets declined, as a percentage of total assets, from just under 40 percent at January 31, 1993, to just over 36 percent at January 28, 1996. This chapter has already noted that inventories increased modestly and receivables remained relatively constant. However, an analyst would also note that the company held relatively less of its assets as cash and cash equivalents at January 28, 1996 (.72 percent) than it did at January 31, 1993 (3.1 percent). Even more noticeable is the decline in the percentage of assets held as short-term investments, which dropped from over 7 percent at January 31, 1993, to under 1 percent at January 28, 1996.

Growth requires a source of funds to finance the necessary additional investments, and liquid current assets are one source of financing available to the company. Part of the decline in liquid current assets can be attributed to the need to finance the growth in merchandise inventories. For an expanding company, larger investments in inventory should be expected since additional product is needed to meet customer demand. However, if the company were following a no-growth strategy or were operating in a declining industry, these same changes would be cause for concern.

Considering the increase in The Home Depot, Inc.'s, inventories, the decline in current assets was sufficient to finance about 4 percent of the company's 20 percent increase in property and equipment. What provided the balance? A closer examination of Exhibit 14-4 provides the answer. Over this period, the proportion of Home Depot's total assets held as long-term investments declined by 17 percent. This is consistent with a strategy of internally financing the company's growth. This decline in long-term investments is consistent with a management decision that it was to the company's advantage to make investments in its own operations, as opposed to investing available funds in the securities of other companies. The opposite might be expected for a company following a no-growth strategy or one reducing the scope of its operations.

Additional evidence that the company is following a policy of internally financing growth can be found by examining the liability side of the balance sheet. If external financing is being used, then an analyst would expect to find additional long-term debt on the balance sheet. In this case, however, long-term debt has actually decreased as a percentage of total assets. An analyst can conclude, therefore, that financing the company's expansion is accomplished by reinvesting a significant portion of the company's earnings in its own operations, rather than distributing those earnings to stockholders in the form of dividends.

Horizontal analysis focuses on the composition of assets and liabilities and whether changes in the composition of assets and liabilities are consistent with the company's business strategy. It does not directly address the question of how much (in absolute or percentage terms) the company has grown or can grow. Those questions are best answered by extending the techniques of horizontal and vertical analysis to the analysis of trends.

Trend Analysis

Trend analysis is usually focused on quantifying the *changes* in a company's profitability over time. Interest is focused on the major components of the income statement: sales, cost of goods sold, gross margin, operating expenses, and net income. Although the same techniques can be applied to the balance sheet, this is not often done in practice.

Suppose that the analyst's objective is to quantify the growth rate of sales and net income over the most recent four-year period. This information might be used in combination with the results of a more comprehensive financial statement analysis, or it might provide a basis for projecting a company's performance for the coming year. Such an analysis begins with calculating the year-to-year percentage change for each income statement element of interest to the analyst. To illustrate the necessary computations, consider Exhibit 14-6, which provides Home Depot's net sales and net income reported for the fiscal years ended January 28, 1996, and January 29, 1995.

Calculating the percentage change in sales between any two periods can be done in three simple steps. First, calculate the dollar change in sales between the most recent year of interest and the prior year. Using the amounts reported for net sales in the financial statements dated January 1996 and January 1995, the dollar change in net sales is $2,993,661 ($15,470,358 – $12,476,697). Second, divide the change in sales by the base amount—in this case, 1995 sales ($2,993,661 / $12,476,697 = .2399). Third, multiplying by 100 to express the answer as a percentage gives the answer 24 percent (rounded).

Exhibit 14-5
Selected Historical Financial Information for The Home Depot, Inc.

The Home Depot, Inc., and Subsidiaries Amounts in thousands		
	Fiscal Year Ended	
	January 28, 1996	January 29, 1995
Net sales	$15,470,358	$12,476,697
Net earnings	$ 731,523	$ 604,501
Percentage change from fiscal '95 to '96		
Net sales	24.0%	
Net earnings	21.0%	

The same process can be used to determine the percentage change in net income. This can be an important consideration since a company that achieves growth at the expense of profits will be viewed very differently from a company that maintains profits despite experiencing growth. First, calculate the dollar change in net income reported in 1996 and 1995 ($731,523 – $604,501 = $127,022). Second, divide the change in net income by the base amount—in this case, 1995 reported net income ($127,022 / $604,501 = .2101). Last, express the result as a percentage by multiplying by 100, to give 21 percent (rounded).

Performing the same steps for each element of the income statement yields the percentage changes shown in Exhibit 14-6.

What conclusions could an analyst draw from these results? First, an analyst could conclude that the company has been successful in aggressively pursuing its growth strategy, maintaining sales growth above 20 percent per year. Although the growth in sales has declined from 30 percent in 1993 to 24 percent in 1996, the extent to which these annual percentage changes reflect changing economic and market conditions cannot be determined from the data alone. A substantial amount of outside information about the economy and the market for the company's products would be required to make that determination.

Second, the trend analysis provides further evidence of the company's ability to maintain its profitability. An analyst would note that the percentage changes in both cost of goods sold and gross margin closely parallel the percentage changes in sales, confirming that sales growth is not the result of the company's shifting to a competitive strategy emphasizing low price to the consumer. Third, there is additional evidence that the company has maintained control over its operating expenses during this period of growth. Again, the percentage changes associated with total operating expenses closely parallel the percentage changes in sales.

Exhibit 14-6
Annual Percentage Change Income Statement for The Home Depot, Inc.

The Home Depot, Inc., and Subsidiaries
Income Statements
Percentage Change from Prior Year

	1996-95	1995-94	1994-93	1993-92
Net sales	24.0%	35.0%	29.2%	39.2%
Cost of merchandise sold	24.4%	34.5%	29.1%	40.3%
Gross profit	23.0%	36.5%	29.7%	36.3%
Operating expenses:				
Selling, general, and administrative	24.8%	1.9%	1.6%	1.3%
Pre-opening	2.0%	39.4%	36.6%	52.6%
Total operating expenses	24.3%	35.3%	30.1%	33.6%
Operating income	19.5%	39.7%	28.6%	43.9%
Interest, net	-307.7%	-124.6%	13.7%	83.9%
Earnings before income taxes	22.0%	33.0%	27.9%	45.4%
Income taxes (note 3)	23.6%	34.3%	31.1%	45.0%
Net earnings	21.0%	32.2%	26.1%	45.6%

See notes in full statement in Appendix.

Fourth, the analyst could conclude that, overall, the company's net profits have not been sacrificed during this expansion, given how closely the yearly percentage changes in net income parallel the yearly percentage changes in net sales. This conclusion also implies that the company has maintained control over its operating cost and has not grown beyond its ability to manage its operations effectively.

As mentioned earlier, trend analysis generally focuses on the income statement. A vertical analysis of the balance sheet, like that illustrated earlier in the discussion, generally provides an analyst with most of the information needed to evaluate a company's financial condition. Occasionally, however, an analyst might find it necessary to apply trend analysis to the balance sheet. Because a trend analysis focused on the balance sheet involves the same mechanical steps illustrated above, it will not be discussed in detail here.

Applying Ratio Analysis

Both vertical and horizontal analysis are excellent tools for examining relationships among elements that appear within a single financial statement—for example, the income statement or the balance sheet. However, these techniques are not useful for examining relationships among items that appear on different financial statements. Ratios are particularly useful tools because they can highlight not only relationships among items that appear within a single financial statement, but also relationships among items that appear on different financial statements.

This discussion will focus on financial ratios that examine specific dimensions of a firm's operating performance or financial condition. The number of ratios considered is only a small subset of the possible ratios that could be used in a comprehensive analysis of a firm's financial statements. The intent is to emphasize these measures that are most commonly used to describe a firm's profitability, efficiency, liquidity, and leverage. This section will examine both commonly used GAAP-based ratios and their insurance-specific counterparts. In addition, it will introduce several ratios commonly used in the insurance industry.

Evaluating Profitability

A firm's ability to operate profitably is crucial to its survival as a going concern. Not surprisingly, then, evaluating a company's profitability is at the center of many financial statement analyses.

Appropriate Measures

Earlier chapters introduced several commonly used summary measures of profitability. Chapter 3 introduced two GAAP-based financial ratios, return on investment (ROI) and return on equity (ROE). Chapter 5 introduced a SAP-based ratio, return on net worth, as the insurance industry's equivalent of the more general return on equity ratio.

One additional ratio is introduced here—investment yield (the investment earnings ratio). This ratio relates net investment income for a period to an insurer's average admitted assets. It is roughly equivalent to the GAAP-based ROI measure. However, there are important differences. By definition, the net income component of ROI considers earnings from all sources during a period. The investment earnings ratio is more narrowly defined, considering only the earnings derived from invested assets. It does not consider profit or loss from the underwriting activities of the insurer. Exhibit 14-7 shows how these SAP-

based ratios for insurers differ from their more traditional GAAP-based counterparts.

Exhibit 14-7
Comparison of GAAP-Based and SAP-Based Profitability Measures

GAAP-Based Measure	SAP-Based Measure
$$\text{Return on equity} = \frac{\text{Net income}}{\text{Average owners' equity}}$$	$$\text{Return on net worth} = \frac{\text{Net income}}{\text{Average policyholders' surplus}}$$
$$\text{Return on investment} = \frac{\text{Net income}}{\text{Average owners' equity}}$$	$$\text{Investment yield} = \frac{\text{Net investment}}{\text{Average invested assets}}$$

Application

To put these ratios in context, consider a comparative analysis of profitability.
Since this is a comparative analysis, information from at least two companies
is required. For the purpose of illustration, data will be drawn from the
financial statements of Exemplar Insurance Company and Acme Insurance
Company, the hypothetical insurers introduced in Chapters 5 and Chapter 11,
respectively. Since both companies are insurers, the focus of attention will be
on SAP-based measures of profitability.

First, consider the return on net worth ratio. The income statement of Acme
Insurance Company reports net income of $21 million, and the balance sheet
reports policyholders' surplus of $218 million (common and preferred capital
stock, gross paid-in and contributed surplus, unassigned funds, and special
surplus funds) at the balance sheet date. Assuming that the prior year's balance
sheet showed policyholders' surplus of $210 million, the return on net worth
ratio would be calculated as follows:

$$\text{Return on net worth} = \frac{\text{Net income}}{\text{Average policyholders' surplus}}$$

$$= \frac{\$21 \text{ million}}{\dfrac{(\$210 \text{ million} + \$218 \text{ million})}{2}}$$

$$= .098, \text{ or } 9.8\%$$

Recall that in Chapter 5, a similar calculation was performed using the financial information presented for Exemplar Insurance Company. For convenience, that computation is reproduced below:

$$\text{Return on net worth} = \frac{\text{Net income}}{\text{Average policyholders' surplus}}$$

$$= \frac{\$36,000}{\dfrac{(\$298,000 + \$340,000)}{2}}$$

$$= .113, \text{ or } 11.3\%$$

Now, consider the investment yield ratio for these two companies. In its income statement, Acme Insurance Company reported earned investment income of $21 million. At the balance sheet date, cash and invested assets totaled $678 million. Assuming that cash and invested assets totaled $610 million at the beginning of the year, Acme's investment yield would be calculated as follows:

$$\text{Investment yield} = \frac{\text{Net investment income}}{\text{Average invested assets}}$$

$$= \frac{\$41 \text{ million}}{\dfrac{(\$610 \text{ million} + \$678 \text{ million})}{2}}$$

$$= .064, \text{ or } 6.4\%$$

In comparison, Exemplar Insurance Company reported investment income of $77,000 and a total of $1,295,000 of cash and invested assets at the balance sheet date. Assuming the company began the year with cash and invested assets of $1,210,000, Exemplar's investment yield would be calculated as follows:

$$\text{Investment yield} = \frac{\text{Net investment income}}{\text{Average invested assets}}$$

$$= \frac{\$77,000}{\dfrac{(\$1,210,000 + \$1,295,000)}{2}}$$

$$= .061, \text{ or } 6.1\%$$

The single most widely quoted measure of insurer profitability is the combined ratio. No analysis of insurer profitability would be complete without considering this important ratio. Recall that the combined ratio was introduced in Chapter 5, along with its two components—the loss ratio and the expense ratio. Recall that Exemplar's trade basis combined ratio was calculated in

Chapter 5 to be 96.9 percent. To complete this analysis, the trade basis combined ratio for Acme Insurance Company must be calculated.

Remember that the combined ratio is actually the sum of two other ratios—the net loss ratio and the trade basis expense ratio. Formally, the trade basis combined ratio is defined as follows:

$$\frac{\text{Combined ratio}}{\text{(trade basis)}} = \frac{\text{Net loss ratio}}{\$322 \text{ million}} + \frac{\text{Trade basis expense ratio}}{\$335 \text{ million}}$$

$$= \frac{\substack{\text{Losses} \\ \text{incurred}} + \substack{\text{Loss adjustment} \\ \text{expenses incurred}}}{\text{Premiums earned}} + \frac{\text{Underwriting expenses}}{\text{Premiums written}}$$

$$= \frac{\$177 \text{ million} + \$61 \text{ million}}{\$322 \text{ million}} + \frac{\$80 \text{ million}}{\$335 \text{ million}}$$

$$= .739 + .239$$

$$= .978, \text{ or } 97.8\%$$

With one exception, all of the amounts needed to compute this ratio can be taken directly from Acme's income statement. Only the premiums written amount does not appear on that statement. The amount of premiums written ($335 million) appeared as part of the computation needed to arrive at earned premiums in Chapter 11. In practice, this amount would normally be taken from the Underwriting and Expense Exhibit of the statutory Annual Statement. The Underwriting and Expense Exhibit and other key schedules from Argonaut Insurance Group's Annual Statement are reproduced in an Appendix of the course workbook and study guide. Refer to that statement and calculate the various financial ratios as they are discussed using Argonaut's reported financial data.

Interpreting the Results

No analysis is complete until the results have been reviewed and interpreted. The individual ratio values calculated above are, by themselves, not very informative. To properly interpret those values, they must be brought together so that meaningful comparisons can be made—in this case, comparisons between Acme Insurance Company and Exemplar Insurance Company. Only then can the *relative* performance of these two companies be properly judged. To facilitate the process, Exhibit 14-8 summarizes the ratio values for each of the two companies.

The results presented in Exhibit 14-8 show very similar performance for these two companies. There is only a small difference (.3 percent) in investment yield and only .9 percent difference in the combined ratios. The largest difference between the two companies is found in the return on net worth, where Exemplar Insurance Company outperformed Acme Insurance Company by 1.5 percent.

Exhibit 14-8
Summary of Profitability Ratios for Acme Insurance Company and Exemplar Insurance Company

Profitability Ratio	Acme Insurance Co.	Exemplar Insurance Co.
Return on net worth	9.8%	11.3%
Investment yield	6.4%	6.1%
Combined ratio (trade basis)	97.8%	96.9%

Although the lack of a clear "winner" or "loser" in the comparison may be a unsatisfactory to the analyst, at least at first, this type of result is really rather common. If the comparison is between two well-managed companies, neither of which exhibits any outward signs of financial distress, then roughly similar results should be expected. Consequently, there is no clear answer to the question of which company is better in terms of profitability. If a choice was to be made between the two companies, some additional information would be required. This additional information could take the form of a qualitative analysis of the respective companies' management, business strategy, or both. Or it could take the form of further financial statement analysis, focusing on another dimension of the firm's financial characteristics.

Evaluating Efficiency

Efficiency ratios are intended to provide summary measures of how well a business enterprise manages and uses its assets. Chapter 3 introduced this concept. Recall that the DuPont Model states that return on investment is equal to margin times turnover. In this discussion, efficiency focuses on turnover as an appropriate summary measure.

Appropriate Measures

Two turnover ratios are almost universally used in a GAAP-based analysis of nonfinancial company financial statements: the accounts receivable turnover ratio and the inventory turnover ratio. The **accounts receivable turnover ratio** relates net sales for a period to the average balance in accounts receivable. It provides a measure of how quickly a business collects the amounts owed by its customers. This ratio is important since every dollar of uncollected receivables requires an additional dollar of investment, and the longer those amounts are outstanding, the greater the risk that they will not be realized.

The **inventory turnover ratio** relates the amount of cost of goods sold for a given period to the average amount of inventory held during the period. It is similar to the accounts receivable turnover ratio in that it measures how quickly inventory is sold, generating either cash (from cash sales) or accounts receivable (from credit sales).

Because insurers generally receive premiums in advance and have no inventories, there are no comparable measures of efficiency used in an analysis of insurer financial statements. Consequently, only a GAAP-based application is included in this discussion.

Application

To illustrate how these ratios are computed, the financial statements of The Home Depot, Inc., will be used to provide the necessary amounts. Both the accounts receivable turnover ratio and the inventory turnover ratio draw information from both the income statement and the balance sheet. To calculate the accounts receivable turnover ratio, the amount of net sales for the current year is taken from the income statement. To arrive at the average balance of accounts receivable during the year, both the ending balance of accounts receivable—taken from the current year's balance sheet—and the beginning balance of accounts receivable—taken from the balance sheet of the prior year—are needed. Once those amounts are in hand, computing the ratio value is straightforward:

$$\text{Accounts receivable turnover ratio} = \frac{\text{Net sales}}{\text{Average receivables}}$$

$$= \frac{\$15,470,358}{\dfrac{(\$272,225 + \$325,384)}{2}}$$

$$= 51.8 \text{ times}$$

To calculate the inventory turnover ratio, the amount of cost of goods sold for the current year is taken from the income statement. To arrive at the average inventory balance during the year, both the ending inventory balance—taken from the current year's balance sheet—and the beginning inventory balance—taken from the balance sheet of the prior year—are needed. Computing the ratio turnover ratio would proceed as follows:

$$\text{Inventory turnover ratio} = \frac{\text{Cost of goods sold}}{\text{Average inventory}}$$

$$= \frac{\$11,184,772}{\dfrac{(\$1,749,312 + \$2,180,318)}{2}}$$

$$= 5.7 \text{ times}$$

Interpreting the Results

Home Depot's accounts receivable turnover ratio of 51.8 times is exceptionally high. It implies that the company collects its receivables 51.8 times per year, or once each week. Normally, an analyst would expect to find a ratio value of twelve or under. A ratio value of twelve would indicate that the company collects its outstanding receivables once each month, a result more consistent with offering credit terms that require payment within thirty days of billing. The exceptionally high ratio value for Home Depot is attributable to the fact that most of the company's sales are made on a cash basis. Theoretically, the numerator of the ratio should include only sales made on credit. Putting the net sales for the period—whether sold for cash or credit—into the numerator of the ratio inflates its value. However, there is little choice in this case because credit sales are not separately disclosed.

The inventory turnover ratio of 5.7 times indicates that the company converts its inventory into sales about every two months. A ratio value in this range indicates that the company is exposed to relatively little risk that it will be unable to convert its inventory to cash (through sales) in a reasonable amount of time. If the company were burdened with slow-moving or obsolete products, the average inventory level used in the denominator would tend to be higher, making the ratio value smaller. A decline in the value of this ratio over time would serve as a warning that the company may be experiencing inventory management problems.

Evaluating Liquidity

Liquidity refers to a firm's ability to convert assets to cash in order to satisfy its obligations. The ability to meet current obligations on time is important to all businesses. Liquidity has special importance in insurance, however, given the regulatory emphasis on maintaining solvency.

Appropriate Measures

For a noninsurance enterprise, information about current debt-paying ability is obtained from two ratios that were covered earlier in the text—the current ratio and the acid test (quick) ratio. The acid test ratio is a more conservative measure of liquidity because it excludes some assets from the numerator of the ratio while holding the denominator constant. Although these two ratios are widely used to assess the liquidity of noninsurance enterprises, they are of little use in an analysis of insurer financial statements. The reason lies in the difference in the composition of assets held by insurers and noninsurers, and the nature of their respective liabilities.

A retailing or manufacturing firm would generally be expected to hold a significant proportion of total assets in receivables and inventory. For an insurer, receivables are a relatively minor component of assets since premiums are generally paid in advance and inventories are nonexistent. Similarly, the current liabilities of noninsurers are generally composed of accounts payable, other short-term debt, and accrued expenses. For an insurer, the unearned premium reserve (representing premiums collected but not yet earned) and loss reserves are the primary liabilities.

Since neither the current ratio nor the acid test ratio is an appropriate measure of insurer liquidity, an equivalent measure has been constructed. It is referred to simply as the liquidity ratio, and is defined as follows:

$$\text{Liquidity ratio} = \frac{\text{Cash + Invested assets (at market value)}}{\text{Unearned premium + Reserve for losses and}}$$
$$\text{reserve} \qquad \text{loss adjustment expense}$$

The numerator of this ratio focuses on assets that are highly liquid, so it is more closely associated with the acid-test ratio than with the current ratio. Provided that the market value of invested assets is equal to (or at least nearly equal to) the carrying value of the investments reported in the insurer's balance sheet, computing the value of the ratio is straightforward. When the market value and carrying value of invested assets differ significantly, adjustments must be made that require reference to other schedules contained in the statutory financial statements.

Assuming that the carrying value of invested assets shown in the balance sheets of Acme Insurance Company and Exemplar Insurance Company are equal to their respective market values, the liquidity ratio can be calculated as follows:

Acme Insurance Company

$$\text{Liquidity ratio} = \frac{\text{Cash + Invested assets (at market value)}}{\text{Unearned premium} + \text{Reserve for losses and}}$$
$$\text{reserve} \qquad \text{loss adjustment expenses}$$

$$= \frac{\$678 \text{ million}}{\$118 \text{ million} + (\$340 \text{ million} + \$67 \text{ million})}$$

$$= 1.29$$

Exemplar Insurance Company

$$\text{Liquidity ratio} = \frac{\text{Cash + Invested assets (at market value)}}{\text{Unearned premium} + \text{Reserve for losses and}}$$
$$\text{reserve} \qquad \text{loss adjustment expenses}$$

$$= \frac{\$1,250,000}{\$251,000 + (\$530,000 + \$180,000)}$$

$$= 1.30$$

Interpreting the Results

Interpretation of the liquidity ratio is straightforward. A value greater than one is considered favorable because it indicates the insurer has more than $1 of assets, measured at current market values, for each $1 of obligations to policyholders. Conversely, a ratio value less than one is considered unfavorable. In that case, the cash available after liquidating investments at their market values would be insufficient to satisfy policyholders' claims, and the insurer would be forced to convert other, less liquid assets to cash—possibly at values less than that shown on the balance sheet.

The results obtained for these two companies are very close. Both exceed the rule-of-thumb benchmark of 1:1, indicating they are both sufficiently liquid. The difference in the computed values for these two companies is, again, relatively small and provides no convincing evidence that one company should be preferred to the other.

In an analysis of noninsurers, the companies being examined must use comparable GAAP accounting. Specifically, different inventory valuation methods will produce different carrying values for inventory on the balance sheet, affecting the numerator of the current ratio. Remember also that this picture of liquidity is simply a snapshot taken at a particular point in time. A firm's liquidity can be drastically affected by transactions entered into after the balance sheet date, such as taking on additional short-term debt.

When insurer liquidity is at issue, remember that the loss reserves appearing in the denominator of the liquidity ratio are subject to estimation error. If an insurer is too aggressive (optimistic) in valuing its reserves for losses and loss adjustment expenses, its actual liquidity may be very different from that indicated by the ratio's value. Particularly when the liquidity ratio value is close to what the analyst considers to be a minimum acceptable value, further examination into the adequacy of loss reserves is warranted.

Similarly, the value of the liquidity ratio depends on the market prices of the securities held in the investment portfolio. The market value of a common stock portfolio depends not only on the financial performance of the companies represented in the portfolio, but also on general market conditions. Investments in debt securities are subject to price changes as interest rates rise and fall in response to changing economic conditions. Consequently, an understanding of the types (equity or debt) and quality of the securities held by an insurer is necessary if an analyst is to draw meaningful conclusions about an insurer's liquidity.

Evaluating Leverage

Chapter 8 introduced the concept of leverage. The extent to which a firm employs financial leverage depends on the firm's capital structure. In the context of a financial statement analysis, leverage is a measure of the extent to which assets were acquired with borrowed funds (as opposed to purchasing assets with funds supplied by owners). A firm with no debt employs no leverage. Conversely, a firm that has relied on borrowed funds to acquire a large proportion of its assets would be said to be highly leveraged. Leverage can have favorable effects on a firm's return on equity, but it also exposes the firm to risk that operating profits will not be sufficient to cover the costs associated with the debt. If operating profits are insufficient to cover debt-related costs, depletion of equity will occur.

Appropriate Measures

Perhaps the most commonly used measure of leverage in noninsurer financial statement analyses is the **debt-to-equity ratio**. This ratio simply relates total liabilities to stockholders' equity. The Home Depot, Inc., had total liabilities of $2,289,704 and stockholders' equity of $4,987,766 at January 28, 1996. With these numbers, the value of the ratio can be calculated as follows:

$$\text{Debt-to-equity ratio} - \frac{\text{Total liabilities}}{\text{Stockholders' equity}}$$

$$= \frac{\$2,289,704}{\$4,987,766}$$

$$= .459, \text{ or } 45.9\%$$

A ratio value of 1:1, or 100 percent, would indicate that a company has acquired its assets with an equal proportion of debt and equity. That is, for each $100 of assets, the company would report liabilities of $50 and equity of $50. An analyst would normally expect a nonfinancial company to have a debt-to-equity ratio below 1:1. To get a different view of how The Home Depot, Inc., financed its assets, look at the company's **debt-to-total-assets ratio** (sometimes referred to simply as the debt ratio):

$$\text{Debt-to-total assets ratio} = \frac{\text{Total liabilities}}{\text{Total assets}}$$

$$= \frac{\$2,289,704}{\$7,354,033}$$

$$= .311, \text{ or } 31.1\%$$

One advantage of this ratio is that it shows how the assets of the company are financed. The Home Depot, Inc.'s, debt ratio of 31.1 percent indicates that each $100 of assets was financed with $31.10 of debt and $68.90 ($100 − $31.10) of equity.

The values of both the debt-to-equity ratio and the debt-to-total assets ratio can be affected by a company's depreciation policies. Depreciable assets shown in the balance sheet are net of accumulated depreciation. Consequently, two otherwise identical companies can have different debt-to-equity and debt-to-total-assets ratio values simply because one company uses straight-line depreciation and the other company uses an accelerated depreciation method.

Although the risks associated with leverage are of concern to all business enterprises, the solvency orientation of insurance regulators makes it a particularly important concern in the evaluation of insurance companies. Several measures of insurer leverage have been developed to account for the unique aspects of the insurance business. Of these, the **premiums-to-surplus ratio** and the **reserves-to-surplus ratio** are among those most commonly used.

Theoretically, if the insurance product is properly priced, then the premiums collected by the insurer will be sufficient to cover all insured losses. However, losses are not known with certainty when the insurance policies are sold and therefore must be estimated. This means that an insurer also does not know with certainty what the proper premium should be when the policy is underwritten. The premium-to-surplus ratio provides some indication of the insurer's ability to sustain adverse developments (when losses exceed originally estimated amounts, depleting policyholders' surplus). Clearly, if relatively small pricing errors would deplete an insurer's surplus, policyholders are at greater risk that the insurer will be unable to meet its obligations.

The reserves-to-surplus ratio takes another view of leverage, relating the unearned premium reserve plus reserves for losses and loss adjustment expenses to policyholders' surplus. This ratio provides some indication of an insurer's ability to withstand errors in the estimation of its liabilities. This ratio is also said to measure **insurance leverage**—an indication of the extent to which policyholders' surplus can support a given level of reserves. Insurance leverage is related to financial leverage, as measured by the debt-to-equity ratio. An insurer that could withstand relatively large errors in its reserve estimates without depleting its policyholders' surplus poses much less risk to the public than an insurer whose surplus would be depleted by relatively small errors in its loss reserve estimates. For Acme Insurance Company and Exemplar Insurance Company, the values for these ratios would be computed as follows:

Acme Insurance Company

$$\text{Premium-to-surplus ratio} = \frac{\text{Net premiums written}}{\text{Policyholders' surplus}}$$

$$= \frac{\$335 \text{ million}}{\$218 \text{ million}}$$

$$= 1.54$$

Exemplar Insurance Company

$$\text{Premium-to-surplus ratio} = \frac{\text{Net premiums written}}{\text{Policyholders' surplus}}$$

$$= \frac{\$515,000}{\$340,000}$$

$$= 1.51$$

Acme Insurance Company

$$\text{Reserves-to-surplus ratio} = \frac{\text{Unearned premium reserve} + \text{Loss reserve} + \text{Loss adjustment expense reserve}}{\text{Policyholders' surplus}}$$

$$= \frac{\$118 + \$340 \text{ million} + \$67 \text{ million}}{\$218 \text{ million}}$$

$$= 2.41$$

Exemplar Insurance Company

$$\text{Reserves-to-surplus ratio} = \frac{\text{Unearned premium reserve} + \text{Loss reserve} + \text{Loss adjustment expense reserve}}{\text{Policyholders' surplus}}$$

$$= \frac{\$251,000 + \$530,000 + \$180,000}{\$340,000}$$

$$= 2.83$$

Interpreting the Results

A rule of thumb against which the premium to surplus ratio can be evaluated states that premiums should not exceed surplus by more than two to one. Some readers may recognize this as the "Kenney casualty ratio" that has been part of the insurance lexicon for many years. There is, however, no theoretical justification for setting the maximum acceptable ratio at two to one. Consequently, be cautious about using that benchmark too strictly.

The Kenney casualty ratio is generally referred to as a **capacity ratio**—a ratio that summarizes an insurer's ability to underwrite additional risks. At other times, the premiums-to-surplus ratio is referred to as a measure of **insurance exposure**—a measure of the extent to which a given level of policyholders' surplus can support a given level of premiums.

Given the results of the above computations, there is little difference between Acme's and Exemplar's leverage (or insurance exposure) as measured by the premium-to-surplus ratio. Although neither firm appears to be exposed to excessive risk, further investigation into the lines of business written by each company can provide additional insights. If, for example, Acme tended to write the majority of its business in lines that were more stable and less subject to adverse development, then even a ratio as high as 2.5:1 might easily be viewed as being well within the bounds of acceptable risk. Conversely, if Exemplar tended to write the majority of its business in lines where losses tended to be paid over a short period of time but were highly variable, its ratio of 1.51:1 might be viewed as near the acceptable limit.

With regard to the reserves-to-surplus ratio, Exemplar's surplus appears to have more exposure to errors in reserve estimates than does Acme's. Unfortunately, there is no well-established benchmark for an acceptable value for this ratio, although greater leverage is usually associated with long-tail liability lines of insurance. Assessing the ratio is therefore left to professional judgment. With Acme's reserves-to-surplus ratio at 2.4:1 and Exemplar's reserves-to-surplus ratio at 2.8:1, both companies appear to be able to withstand relatively large upward revisions in reserve estimates before policyholders' surplus would be depleted. Before any conclusions can be drawn, however, further insights could be gained by investigating the companies' reserving history. If they have been reasonably accurate in establishing their reserves in the past, an analyst could be more confident that the companies are operating within reasonable bounds for leverage. On the other hand, if these companies have had a history of revising reserve estimates upward by substantial amounts, then the analyst might conclude that both are operating at or near the maximum acceptable levels of leverage.

Summary

Financial statement analysis can provide a remarkable amount of insight into a company's profitability and financial condition. A key element to conducting a financial statement analysis is understanding its purpose so that the information needed for a given business decision can be identified. Once the purpose is known, an analyst must become familiar with both the company being examined and the industry in which it operates. This familiarity then guides the analyst to selecting appropriate tools and techniques to accomplish the purpose of the analysis. Once those tools and techniques have been identified, attention turns to computing the ratio values, percentages, or percentage changes required by the techniques selected. The results of those computations must then be interpreted—an activity that requires an understanding of the measures being used, their strengths and weaknesses, and a good deal of professional judgment.

The discussion in this chapter was general. Every analysis involves a different business decision and has its own unique requirements. Whatever the purpose, however, the process of financial statement analysis generally proceeds through the four broad steps: establish the objective of the analysis; review the financial statements and other available information; select and apply the appropriate technique; and interpret the results. Focusing on those four organized steps can help make the process less intimidating and more efficient.

Key Words and Phrases

accounts receivable turnover ratio (p. 457) A ratio relating net credit sales for a period to the average balance in accounts receivable for that period. The ratio provides a measure of how quickly a business collects the amounts owed by its customers.

capacity ratio (p. 464) A ratio relating premiums written to policyholders' surplus that is used to identify how much risk, as measured by premium, an insurer safely should be able to underwrite given its surplus position. (See also *insurance exposure* and *premiums-to-surplus ratio*.)

common size financial statements (p. 440) Balance sheets or income statements on which each item is expressed as a percentage of total assets (balance sheet) or total sales (income statement). This format is particularly useful when comparing financial statements for multiple periods or one company's statements to another company's or to an industry benchmark.

debt-to-equity ratio (p. 462) A ratio relating total liabilities to stockholders' (owners') equity. Used to measure the extent to which an entity uses financial leverage.

debt-to-total-assets ratio (p. 462) Sometimes referred to as the debt ratio, provides a measure of how the entity finances its assets—by debt or by equity.

diagnosis (p. 438) An objective of financial statement analysis; attention is focused on evaluating selected accounts that may have become problematic because of payment patterns or other factors.

evaluation (p. 437) An objective of financial statement analysis; focuses on assessing one or more of a firm's financial characteristics, for example, profitability, liquidity, solvency, or efficiency.

forecasting (p. 438) An objective of financial statement analysis related to using data from past financial statements to estimate the entity's future financial position. Often used to develop pro forma income statements that estimate the firm's future sales activity.

horizontal analysis (p. 441) A form of financial statement analysis focusing on yearly percentage changes that is useful for identifying trends and changes in trends for key financial statement items such as sales or net income.

insurance exposure (p. 464) A ratio of premiums written to policyholders' surplus indicating to what extent an insurer's surplus is exposed to underwriting risk. Also referred to as a capacity measure. (See also *capacity* and *premiums-to-surplus ratio.*)

insurance leverage (p. 463) A ratio relating total reserves (not total liabilities) to policyholders' surplus that identifies to what extent an insurer can withstand errors in the estimation of its policy-related liabilities. The ratio is similar to conventional debt-to-equity ratios used to analyze measure financial leverage of a noninsurance entity.

inventory turnover ratio (p. 458) A ratio relating the amount of cost of goods sold for a given period to the average amount of inventory held during the period. Provides a measure of how quickly inventory is sold, or the number of times inventory is "turned over" given the cost of goods sold.

premiums-to-surplus ratio (p. 463) A ratio that relates premiums written to policyholders' surplus. The ratio is usually calculated using *net* premiums written but can also be calculated using *gross* premiums written (direct written premiums plus assumed reinsurance premiums). The net ratio provides a measure of the insurer's *retained* underwriting exposure related to its surplus. The gross ratio provides a measure of the insurer's total underwriting exposure if the insurer were unable to recover loss amounts paid through reinsurance agreements.

reconstruction (p. 438) An objective of financial statement analysis focused on identifying and quantifying relationships among prior period financial statement items that can be sued to reconstruct all or part of a firm's financial statements from a set of incomplete records.

reserves-to-surplus ratio (p. 463) A ratio relating all policy-related reserves (losses, loss adjustment expenses, unearned premium, and excess of statutory over statement reserves) to policyholders' surplus. (See also *insurance leverage.*)

screening (p. 437) An objective of financial statement analysis usually directed toward classifying the firm into one of two categories—acceptable or not acceptable—in terms of performance or financial condition when compared to a prescribed standard or benchmark.

vertical analysis (p. 440) Uses common size financial statements to identify problematic conditions that might be indicated by unusually large or small percentages when an item is related to total assets (balance sheet) or total sales (income statement). (See also *common size financial statements.*)

Appendix—Financial Statements For The Home Depot, Inc.

Consolidated Balance Sheets
The Home Depot, Inc., and Subsidiaries
Amounts in thousands, except per share data

	January 28, 1996	January 29, 1995	January 30, 1994	January 31, 1993
Assets				
Current assets:				
Cash and cash equivalents	$ 53,269	$ 1,154	$ 99,997	$ 121,744
Short-term investments (note 1)	54,756	56,712	330,976	292,451
Receivables, net	325,384	272,225	198,431	177,502
Merchandise inventories	2,180,318	1,749,312	1,293,477	939,824
Other current assets	58,242	53,560	43,720	30,452
Total current assets	$2,671,969	$2,132,963	$1,966,601	$1,561,973
Property and equipment (note 2)	4,461,024	3,397,237	2,370,904	1,607,984
Long-term investments	25,436	98,022	281,623	694,276
Notes receivable	54,715	32,528	—	—
Goodwill	87,238	88,513	19,503	20,136
Other	53,651	28,778	62,258	47,421
Total assets	$7,354,033	$5,778,041	$4,700,889	$3,931,790
Liabilities and Stockholders' Equity				
Current liabilities:				
Accounts payable	$ 824,808	$ 681,291	$ 521,246	$ 420,318
Accrued salaries and expenses	198,208	192,151	167,489	127,133
Taxes payable	148,280	109,728	97,893	70,188
Other accrued expenses	242,859	208,377	184,462	135,478
Current portion of long-term debt	2,327	22,692	1,548	1,828
Total current liabilities	$1,416,482	$1,214,239	$ 972,638	$ 754,945

Liabilities—continued	January 28, 1996	January 29, 1995	January 30, 1994	January 31, 1993
Long-term debt (note 3)	$ 720,080	$ 983,369	$ 841,992	$ 843,672
Other long-term liabilities	115,917	67,953	44,332	12,968
Deferred income taxes	37,225	19,258	27,827	16,124
Total liabilities	$2,289,704	$2,284,819	$1,886,789	$1,627,709
Stockholders' equity:				
Minority interest	76,563	50,999	—	—
Common stock, par value $0.05	23,855	22,668	22,468	22,179
Paid-in capital	2,407,815	1,526,463	1,436,029	1,339,821
Retained earnings	2,579,059	1,937,284	1,400,575	993,517
Cumulative translation adjustments (note 4)	(6,131)	(10,887)	(121)	—
Unrealized loss on investments	(47)	(1,495)	—	—
	$5,081,114	$3,525,032	$2,858,951	$2,355,517
Less: other adjustments (note 5)	(16,785)	(31,810)	(44,851)	(51,436)
Total stockholders' equity	$5,064,329	$3,493,222	$2,814,100	$2,304,081
Total liabilities and stockholders' equity	$7,354,033	$5,778,041	$4,700,889	$3,931,790

Note 1: This amount includes the current installments of long-term debt.

Note 2: Property and equipment is shown net of accumulated depreciation.

Note 3: Amount shown is net of the current installments included in current liabilities.

Note 4: The company owns a Canada-based subsidiary. Cumulative translation adjustments is a reconciling entry to account for changes in the value of the foreign currency.

Note 5: Other adjustments to stockholders' equity are related to the company's employee stock ownership plan (ESOP).

Consolidated Statements of Earnings
The Home Depot, Inc., and Subsidiaries
Amounts in thousands

	January 28, 1996	January 29, 1995	Fiscal Year Ended January 30, 1994	January 31, 1993	February 2, 1992
Net sales	$15,470,358	$12,476,697	$9,238,763	$7,148,436	$5,136,674
Cost of merchandise sold	11,184,772	8,991,204	6,685,384	5,179,368	3,692,337
Gross profit	$ 4,285,586	$ 3,485,493	$2,553,379	$1,969,068	$1,444,337
Selling, general, and administrative	3,053,390	2,446,996	1,809,874	1,392,688	1,044,991
Pre-opening	52,342	51,307	36,816	26,959	17,668
Total Operating expenses	$ 3,105,732	$ 2,498,303	$1,846,690	$1,419,647	$1,062,659
Operating income	$ 1,179,854	$ 987,190	$ 706,689	$ 549,421	$ 381,678
Interest, net	15,449	(7,439)	30,182	26,552	14,442
Earnings before Income taxes	$ 1,195,303	$ 979,751	$ 736,871	$ 575,973	$ 396,120
Income taxes (note 3)	463,780	375,250	279,470	213,110	146,970
Net earnings	$ 731,523	$ 604,501	$ 457,401	$ 362,863	$ 249,150

Note 3: The company adopted SFAS 109 as of February 1, 1993. The cumulative effect of this change in accounting for income taxes, which resulted in a tax benefit of $2,130,000, was determined as of February 1, 1993, and has been reflected in the consolidated statement of earnings for the fiscal year ended January 30, 1994.

Chapter 15

Fundamentals of Insurance Company Finance and Investments

Previous chapters provided an in-depth discussion of the accounting for assets, liabilities, owners' equity, revenues, and expenses, and reporting the results of those transactions in a firm's financial statements. The importance of understanding the financial statement effects of those transactions was emphasized in the discussion of financial statement analysis presented in Chapter 14. An important conclusion that can be drawn from the material presented thus far is that virtually every business decision has financial implications for the firm. Consequently, a basic understanding of financial management can help every business professional to understand why certain management decisions have been made, and to anticipate the financial implications of decisions made within their own specialized areas.

This chapter introduces some of the basic finance concepts most useful for making financial management decisions. A central issue in this discussion involves risk. Although previous chapters introduced risk as an important variable in business decisions, that discussion was limited to describing risk in qualitative terms. Many business decisions, however, require more than just a qualitative description of risk. A decision maker faced with choosing which projects should be included in the capital budget, which stocks and bonds should be added (or removed) from an investment portfolio, or which lines of insurance should receive greater underwriting (or greater marketing) emphasis needs a set of financial management tools to evaluate each of the available alternatives. These financial management tools must consider not only the rewards of a given investment, but also some quantitative measure of the risks associated with those rewards.

This chapter begins by examining management objectives as they relate to the financial decisions of the firm and identifying the types of risk of concern to financial decision makers. Then two quantitative measures of risk, standard deviation and coefficient of variation, are introduced. Following this foundation material, the chapter provides a more detailed discussion of issues relevant to managing a firm's investment and liability portfolios. Additional emphasis is given to issues unique to the financial management of an insurer's underwriting portfolio.

Educational Objectives

After studying this chapter, you should be able to:

1. Explain the primary objectives of a business firm.

2. Distinguish among general business risk, investment-related risk, and risks unique to insurers.

3. Explain the risk-return trade-off.

4. Calculate each of the following given information about the rates of return for an investment security:

   - Expected value

   - Standard deviation

   - Coefficient of variation

5. Explain how the coefficient of variation is useful when comparing the investment returns of different securities.

6. Explain how including more than one stock in an investment portfolio can be advantageous to an investor.

7. Explain what is measured by a stock's *beta* and why investors find that measure useful.

8. Describe the Capital Asset Pricing Model (CAPM) and explain how it helps in analyzing the trade-off between risk and return.

9. Explain why fixed maturity dates and fixed interest payment schedules make bonds an attractive investment for insurers.

10. Explain the relationship between a firm's need for cash and interest rate risk.

11. Define or describe each of the Key Words and Phrases introduced in this chapter.

Overall Management Objectives

At the most fundamental level, business entities engage in activities intended to create value for the firm's owners. From an accounting perspective, value is created when a firm's activities result in a net inflow of assets, that is, when the firm sells its products or services at a price greater than the cost to produce those products or services. In other words, value is created for the firm's owners when the firm earns net income.

Economists generally agree that the overall objective of the firm should be **profit maximization**. Although this goal is consistent with the accounting perspective, economic profit is not the same as accounting net income. Only the interest expense associated with acquiring financial resources from creditors affects accounting net income. Economists argue that all costs should be included when calculating economic profit—including costs associated with acquiring financial resources from the firm's owners. One example of such a cost is providing investors with a return on their investment in the form of dividends, a transaction excluded from the computation of accounting net income.

Another perspective comes from the study of finance. That view argues that the overall objective of the firm should be to **maximize shareholder wealth** as measured by the market value of the firm's stock. Proponents of wealth maximization as the appropriate objective for firms argue that it accounts for important factors that are not considered in profit maximization. Among the most important of these factors are the amount and timing of the cash flows associated with a firm's future earnings, the risk associated with the firm's future earnings, and the firm's capital structure (the firm's mix of debt and equity).

Although the differences between profit maximization and wealth maximization are interesting at a theoretical level, proponents of these two competing views would probably agree on at least one point. That is, a firm should seek to earn the highest possible return consistent with its ability to bear the associated risks.

Identifying and Measuring Risk

Every business is exposed to risk. Generally, risk is defined as the possibility that some unfavorable event will occur. Unfavorable events most important to financial management are those measurable in dollars, either as a loss in value or as a failure to earn as much as expected. Sound financial decisions require an understanding of the types of risks involved and a quantitative measure that can be incorporated into the decision-making process.

Types of Risk

A business can be exposed to many sources of risk. Which sources of risk a given company is exposed to depends on the nature of its business and the types of transactions in which it engages. Some sources of risk are related to a company's assets. Other sources of risk are related to a company's liabilities. This section identifies several of the most common sources of risk, including risks unique to insurers.

General Business Risks

Business risk refers to uncertainty about a company's future earnings. Every company faces some degree of business risk because future prices, the demand for its products or services, and the costs to produce those products or services are all subject to changes that cannot be forecast with complete accuracy. When measures of business risk are calculated, earnings are measured as earnings before interest and taxes (EBIT) without recognizing the effects of interest costs associated with debt financing. The logical argument is that business risk reflects uncertainties arising from a firm's operating activities, and interest costs result from the firm's decision to use debt, rather than equity, as a source of financing. The decision to take on debt, however, exposes a firm to an additional source of risk called financial risk.

Financial risk refers to uncertainty about a firm's ability to meet the principal and interest payments on its debt. Interest and principal payments are fixed contractual obligations of the firm. A firm is obligated to meet these commitments regardless of the level of its earnings. Consequently, the level of financial risk increases as a firm takes on additional debt. When viewed from the perspective of a creditor, uncertainty about the debtor's ability to meet interest and principal payments is often referred to as *credit risk, repayment risk,* or *default risk.*

Investment-Related Risk

Holding securities in an investment portfolio exposes a firm to several additional sources of risk. Of these, market risk, interest rate risk, and liquidity risk are among the most important.

Market risk refers to uncertainty about a securities price resulting from changes in the market as a whole. The prices of individual stocks tend to follow (that is, are correlated with) broad market swings. These price movements are independent of an individual company's performance. Consequently, even if a company's future performance could be predicted with certainty, uncertainty about the effect of future market movements would still remain as an element of risk.

Interest rate risk refers to uncertainty about an asset's value associated with changes in market-determined interest rates. Interest rate risk is most directly related to investments in debt securities. The market value of a debt security is determined, in large measure, by the present value of the security's cash flows (payment of interest and principal). As interest rates rise, the market value of debt securities declines; as interest rates decline, the market value of debt securities rises. Because of the effects of compound interest, the market value of long-term debt securities is more sensitive to interest rate changes than are short-term debt securities. Consequently, long-term debt securities expose the holder to a greater degree of interest rate risk than do short-term securities.

Liquidity risk refers to uncertainty about the price at which an asset can be sold on short notice. Assets for which an active market exists, such as common stocks, generally have little liquidity risk because the asset can almost certainly be sold at its market value. Other assets that are not as actively traded, such as land, have higher liquidity risk. To quickly convert an illiquid asset to cash, the seller may have to accept a price that is far below its market value.

Risk Unique to Insurance

Insurers are exposed to certain risks that are unique to the business of insurance. This section describes three of these unique risks: price inadequacy risk, reserve estimation risk, and underwriting risk.

Price Inadequacy Risk

Virtually all businesses are exposed to uncertainty about the price at which their products or services can be sold. For an insurer, **price inadequacy risk** refers to the uncertainty that the premiums charged will be sufficient to cover the costs associated with insurance coverage sold.

The true cost of an insurance policy may not be known for some time after the policy has expired. Consequently, the price of the insurance product must be based on estimates of what the ultimate costs associated with that product will be. The risk of price inadequacy can increase if insurers must delay implementing premium increases to meet state regulations requiring approval of any price adjustments. A highly competitive environment can also increase an insurer's price inadequacy risk. Competitive forces can drive prices below actual cost as insurers engage in price competition to gain market share.

Reserve Estimation Risk

Insurers establish a liability for losses and loss adjustment expenses (L&LAE)—representing the ultimate costs to settle policyholder claims—when insurance policies are issued. Since the actual costs may not be known for many years after the policy has expired, establishing the value of the L&LAE reserve requires that the ultimate costs be estimated. **Reserve estimation risk** refers to the uncertainty about the actual amount that will be paid to settle policyholder claims. There are several sources of reserve estimation risk. Unforeseen changes in the economic, social, and legal environments can increase the costs to settle claims. The actuarial techniques applied may not fully estimate the insurer's ultimate loss experience (actuaries refer to this as parameter risk). Even if the actuarial techniques are fully descriptive, an insurer's loss experience will probably differ from the actuary's best estimate simply because the future is always uncertain (actuaries refer to this as process risk). An insurer can never completely remove reserve estimation risk. It can, however, take steps to minimize it by assuring that all available information is incorporated into its estimates and that the most appropriate actuarial methods are used to estimate its reserves.

Underwriting Risk

Underwriting risk refers to the uncertainty about the exposures underwritten by an insurer, including the possibility that a single event (or set of events) will simultaneously affect multiple exposures. Uncertainty about the exposures underwritten by an insurer can arise because policyholders have failed to disclose all relevant information to the insurer when the policies were issued, or because of an unusual event—such as a natural or man-made catastrophe—that simultaneously affects multiple exposures.

The Risk-Return Trade-Off

Given a choice between investing in a government security that guarantees 9 percent interest or a risky common stock that is also expected to return 9 percent, most investors would choose to invest in the government security. The reason may seem obvious—investors can gain nothing by assuming the added risk associated with the investment in the common stock. Investors who prefer relative certainty to uncertainty are said to be **risk averse**. Conversely, investors who ignore uncertainty and base decisions solely on the potential rewards are said to be **risk neutral**.

Much of economic and financial theory depends on the assumption that investors and managers act as though they are risk averse. That is, from a set of investments that have the same potential rewards, a risk-averse decision maker will choose the investment with the least risk. Alternatively, from a set of investments that have the same level of risk, a risk-averse decision maker will choose the investment with the highest potential rewards.

Quantitative Measures of Risk

Risk is fundamentally related to uncertainty. If the future consequences of all decisions were known with certainty, no risk would be associated with making those decisions. The characteristic of uncertainty most important to financial management is the variability of future outcomes. That is, a decision maker expects to achieve a particular result, perhaps a given level of net income, as a result of investing in a new project. However, the decision maker realizes that the actual result may be higher or lower than what was expected. In simple terms, variability relates to how much higher or lower the actual outcome may be from what the decision maker expected. A project that is expected to yield an additional $1 million in income, plus or minus 10 percent, would be viewed as being less variable—and less risky—than a project expected to yield $1 million in income, plus or minus 40 percent.

The purpose of the following discussion is to develop quantitative measures of risk that can be incorporated into the investment management decision process.

Expected Value

Most decisions involve an evaluation of the probable consequences. A marketing executive might judge a new advertising campaign based on the expected increase in sales. A factory manager might consider a new automated process in terms of the expected increase in production or decrease in the cost of production. An investor would probably evaluate the purchase of a security based on the expected income and increase in stock price.

The intuitive concept of an expected result can be formalized into a definition for expected value. **Expected value** is simply the *weighted average* of possible uncertain outcomes. The weighting, in this definition, is determined by the *probability* associated with the occurrence of each outcome (less formally, the chance that a given result will occur). Expected values can be found for any uncertain outcome (for example, sales, production output, or production costs), but investment decisions generally focus on the expected returns of securities. In that context, the expected value of a security's return is referred to simply as the **expected return**.

- **BUSINESS PROCEDURE CAPSULE 22**
  Determining the Expected Value of a Random Variable

Those involved in making business decisions must often determine the expected value for a random variable. Expected value is a concept founded in a branch of mathematics called *statistics* and is equivalent to the arithmetic mean of a probability distribution. The mathematical expression for the expected value of a random variable, x, is given as follows:

$$E(x) = \sum_{i=1}^{n} (p_i\, x_i)$$

The expression is read as "the expected value of x is equal to the sum for all possible outcomes of x, from i=1 to n, of the value of the outcome, x, times the probability of its occurrence, p." In the above expression, E( ) is used to denote an expected value function for the variable identified within the parentheses. The capital Greek letter sigma, Σ, is used to indicate the process of summation, or addition of two or more numbers.

At first glance, this mathematical expression might not look like the procedure for calculating the arithmetic average with which you are probably familiar—adding all of the observed values for the variable and dividing by the number of values added. In this expression, the number of values is represented in each of the probabilities, p_i, multiplied by the individual values, x_i. For example, if four different values (1, 2, 3, and 4) were observed for a particular variable, x, each would have an equal chance or probability of occurring. The probability for each value would be 1/4, or a chance of one in four. For this example, four equals the number of observations, which is used as the divisor to determine the average. If each of the values is multiplied by its associated probability ($1 \times 1/4$; $2 \times 1/4$; $3 \times 1/4$; and $4 \times 1/4$) and are added, the result is 2.5. If the numbers 1, 2, 3, and 4 were simply added and then divided by the number of values, 4, the result would also be 2.5. This example is a special case because of the assumption that all of the outcomes have an equal chance of occurrence. Using the expected value formula is necessary when the probabilities associated with each of the possible outcomes are not all equal.

To illustrate how the concept of expected value can be applied to an investment decision, consider a decision that requires choosing between the securities of National Company and Regional Company. The returns on each of the securities depend on whether the stock market rises, remains flat, or declines. Suppose that the probability of the market rising is .5, the probability of a flat market is .3, and the probability of the market declining is .2.[1] Exhibit 15-1 provides a summary of the securities' returns under these three market conditions.

Exhibit 15-1
Security Returns and Probabilities for Three Market Conditions

	Rising Market (p = .5)	Flat Market (p = .3)	Declining Market (p = .2)
Return on investment in National Company	50.0%	2.5%	–35.0%
Return on investment in Regional Company	70.0%	0.0%	–40.0%

All that is needed to calculate the expected return for each of these two securities are the definition of expected value and the information given in Exhibit 15-1. Exhibit 15-2 summarizes the calculations.

Exhibit 15-2
Calculating the Expected Returns for Two Securities

Expected Return on Investment in National Company

Market condition	Return	Probability	Probability-weighted return
Rising	50.0%	.50	25.00%
Flat	2.5%	.30	0.75%
Declining	–35.0%	.20	–7.00%
Expected return (Sum of the probability-weighted returns)			18.75%

Expected Return on Investment in Regional Company

Market condition	Return	Probability	Probability-weighted return
Rising	70.0%	0.50	35.00%
Flat	0.0%	0.30	0.00%
Declining	–40.0%	0.20	–8.00%
Expected return (Sum of the probability-weighted returns)			27.00%

Basing the decision on expected returns leads to an obvious choice. Since the expected return on the investment in Regional Company is 8.25 percent higher than the expected return on the investment in National Company, an investor would clearly prefer to invest in the stock of Regional Company.

Expected returns provide a convenient measure by which a decision maker can rank potential investments. However, only a risk-neutral investor would focus on expected returns and ignore the risk associated with investment alternatives. The next section examines standard deviation as a quantitative measure of risk that investors can incorporate into the decision making process.

Before leaving this section, however, note that this simple example considers only three of the possible outcomes given three possible market conditions. In reality, both the market and the securities' returns can take on many values. If someone could list each possible outcome along with its probability of occurring, the format provided in Exhibit 15-2 could be used to calculate the needed expected returns. In such cumbersome cases, other methods are available for making the necessary computations. However, a discussion of those methods is beyond the scope of this text.[2]

Standard Deviation

Individuals often make personal judgments about risks. For most day-to-day decisions (such as choosing a place to eat lunch quickly), informally considering personal judgments about risks is sufficient (for example, the risk that the service will be slow and you will be late returning to work).

In contrast, investment decisions require a more objective way to incorporate risk into the decision process. Earlier, this chapter noted that the characteristic of uncertainty (risk) most important to financial management is the variability of future outcomes. To be most useful, a measure of risk should assign a definite (quantitative) value to the variability of outcomes in a given set of circumstances. One measure of risk that has gained wide acceptance is the standard deviation. The **standard deviation** is a statistic that describes how widely the actual outcomes are dispersed above and below the expected value.

The information provided in Exhibit 15-1 and Exhibit 15-2 can now be used to find the standard deviation of the returns for the securities of National Company and Regional Company. Calculating the standard deviation is accomplished in the four steps described below:

Step 1:   Calculate the expected return (the expected value of the possible outcomes). The expected return provides a reference point for determining how widely dispersed the possible outcomes are. Recall from Exhibit 15-2 that the expected return for an investment in National Company is 18.75 percent and that the expected return for an investment in Regional Company is 27 percent.

Step 2: For each possible outcome, subtract the expected return from the actual return (the difference is referred to as the deviation). Next, square each deviation.

National Company

Market condition	Possible Return	Expected Return	Deviation	Squared Deviation
Rising	50.0%	18.75%	31.25%	976.6
Flat	2.5%	18.75%	−16.25%	264.1
Declining	−35.0%	18.75%	−53.75%	2,889.1

Regional Company

Market condition	Possible Return	Expected Return	Deviation	Squared Deviation
Rising	70.0%	27.0%	43.0%	1,849.0
Flat	0.0%	27.0%	−27.0%	729.0
Declining	−40.0%	27.0%	−67.0%	4,489.0

Squaring the deviations eliminates the minus signs for the possible occurrences that fall below the expected value. This is necessary because *all* deviations contribute to risk. If positive differences were allowed to be offset by negative differences, the resulting measure would understate risk.

Step 3: Multiply each squared deviation by the probability associated with the possible outcome, and sum the results. In statistical terms, the resulting sum is called the *variance*.

National Company

Market condition	Squared Deviation	Probability	Probability-Weighted Squared Deviation
Rising	976.6	0.50	488.3
Flat	264.1	0.30	79.2
Declining	2,889.1	0.20	577.8
Sum (*variance*)			1,145.3

Regional Company

Market condition	Squared Deviation	Probability	Probability-Weighted Squared Deviation
Rising	1,849.0	0.50	924.5
Flat	729.0	0.30	218.7
Declining	4,489.0	0.20	897.8
Sum (*variance*)			2,041.0

Step 4: Take the square root of the variance to find the standard deviation.

Standard deviation of returns for National Company = $\sqrt{1,145.3}$ = 33.84%

Standard deviation of returns for Regional Company = $\sqrt{2,041.0}$ = 45.18%

In mathematical notation, the variance and standard deviation are defined as follows:

$$\text{Variance} = \sigma^2 = E\,(\text{Possible return} - \text{Expected return})^2$$

$$\text{Standard deviation} = \sigma \;= \sqrt{\sigma^2}$$

Larger values of the standard deviation indicate greater variability and greater risk. In the example shown above, Regional Company is riskier (in terms of the variability in its returns) than is National Company. Although you may have been able to foresee this conclusion, assigning a numerical value to your qualitative assessment would not have been easy.

Before concluding this section, a few additional points concerning the standard deviation should be mentioned. If the purpose is to rank securities by their degree of riskiness, then the computations could just as easily have stopped with the variance. The standard deviation is simply the square root of the variance, so the riskier security in terms of variance will always be the riskier security in terms of standard deviation.

The numerical value of the standard deviation depends on the units used in the calculations (that is, how the raw data are measured). In the example above, the securities' returns (and expected returns) were measured as percentages. In another analysis, there may be a choice of measurement units, for example, feet instead of yards, or dollars instead of thousands of dollars. Simply using a smaller measurement unit will result in a larger standard deviation. Before comparing the values of two or more standard deviations, the user must verify that the same units were used in each of the calculations.

The standard deviation provides important information about the variability of possible outcomes. Once the standard deviations of two or more investments is known, identifying the investment with the most or least variability in outcomes is a simple task. However, the standard deviation has one important limitation: it does not provide information about the *relative* risk of investment alternatives that have different expected returns.

Coefficient of Variation

The **coefficient of variation (CV)** is a *relative measure of risk* defined as the standard deviation divided by the expected value. It provides information about *the risk per unit of return*, for example, the variation or uncertainty of a security's possible returns relative to that security's expected return. The coefficient of variation is particularly useful in comparing the relative risk of two or more securities that have different expected returns. The mathematical expression for the coefficient of variation is as follows:

$$CV = \frac{\text{Standard deviation}}{\text{Expected value}} = \frac{\sigma}{E(x)}$$

Continuing with the illustration, the coefficient of variation of National Company and Regional Company can be found by dividing each security's standard deviation by its expected return. Doing so yields the following results:

$$\text{CV (National Company)} = \frac{\text{Standard deviation (National Company)}}{\text{Expected return (National Company)}}$$

$$= \frac{33.84\%}{18.75\%}$$

$$= 1.805$$

$$\text{CV (Regional Company)} = \frac{\text{Standard deviation (Regional Company)}}{\text{Expected return (Regional Company)}}$$

$$= \frac{45.18\%}{27.00\%}$$

$$= 1.673$$

The coefficient of variation shows that Regional Company has relatively less risk than does National Company. This result is probably unexpected, since it stands in sharp contrast to the conclusions drawn by using the standard deviation to measure risk. By that measure, National Company was found to have less variation in returns and was judged to be less risky than Regional Company. However, investors are generally interested in striking some balance between risk and return. A measure like the coefficient of variation is useful because it quantifies the average amount of risk associated with each unit of return. It provides an objective measure that can be used by a risk-averse investor to evaluate the trade-off between risk and return that must be made in choosing one of several alternative investments.

Managing Investment Portfolios

Every decision has the potential to affect a firm's exposure to risk. Some decisions can increase risk, and others can have the effect of reducing risk. At the level of the firm, attention focuses on the combined effect of decisions on the company's overall risk. Consequently, when a company is considering a new investment, focusing only on the risk and return associated with the new investment is no longer sufficient. This section examines how modern portfolio theory applies to insurer investment decisions.

Combining Investments To Reduce Risk

When two or more securities are combined to form an investment portfolio, the expected return of the portfolio is equal to the weighted-average returns of the individual securities in the portfolio. However, the same is not necessarily true of the portfolio's standard deviation. Generally, the standard deviation of a portfolio will be *less* than the weighted average of the standard deviations of the individual securities. This will be true only if the returns of the securities held in the portfolio do not move in unison.

In statistics, the degree to which any two variables tend to move together is measured by their *correlation coefficient*. This statistical measure ranges from +1 to –1. If, for example, the price changes of two securities are perfectly synchronized (at every instant varying together), they are referred to as being perfectly *correlated*. The two securities would have a correlation coefficient of +1 (*perfectly positively correlated*) if their price changes always moved in the same direction, and –1 (*perfectly negatively correlated*) if their price changes always moved in the opposite directions. If their price movements are totally unrelated, they would be referred to as *uncorrelated*, and the correlation coefficient would be zero.

Suppose that a company is considering investing $1 million in common stocks. It has identified two possible candidates, the Pacific Corporation and the Atlantic Company. The company has collected data on the returns of these two stocks over a four-year period and has prepared the summary presented in Exhibit 15-3.

Exhibit 15-3
Returns for the Pacific Company, Atlantic Corporation, and a
Portfolio Combining Equal Investment Amounts in Each

Year	Actual Returns		
	Pacific	Atlantic	Portfolio
1993	20.0%	–5.0%	7.5%
1994	–10.0%	50.0%	20.0%
1995	35.0%	–30.0%	2.5%
1996	–5.0%	25.0%	10.0%
Expected Return	10.0%	10.0%	10.0%
Standard Deviation	21.2%	34.9%	7.4%

The company could invest all of the $1 million in either security and expect to earn 10 percent. If company management is risk neutral, they would be indifferent as to which security is chosen. If, on the other hand, management is risk averse, the company would probably choose Pacific Company because its standard deviation and its coefficient of variation are less than those of Atlantic Corporation. Regardless of which security is chosen, however, the actual return on the investment could have been much higher or lower.

Suppose, instead, that the company chooses to invest $500,000 in each of these securities. The expected return would still be 10 percent—one-half of the return from Pacific Company plus one-half of the return from Atlantic Corporation. However, the risk of the portfolio, as measured by the standard deviation, is substantially less than the risk associated with either of the individual stocks.

The returns of Pacific Company and Atlantic Corporation over this four-year period show that the returns of these securities did not move in unison. In fact, their returns tended to move in opposite directions (they are negatively correlated), allowing the negative returns in one security to be counterbalanced by positive returns in the other security. However, negative correlation is not a necessary condition to reduce risk by combining securities. The only requirement is that the returns of the new security not be perfectly positively correlated with the returns of the existing portfolio. So the portfolio's risk can be reduced even further by adding a third security, even if its returns *tend* to move in the same direction as Pacific Company. Exhibit 15-4 shows the effect of adding a third security to the portfolio, Mountain, Inc. Again, the portfolio returns assume an equal investment in each of the three securities.

Exhibit 15-4
Returns for the Pacific Company, Atlantic Corporation, Mountain, Inc., and Portfolio Combining Equal Investment Amounts in Each

Year	Pacific Company	Atlantic Corp.	Mountain, Inc.	Portfolio
1993	20.0%	−5.0%	30.0%	15.0%
1994	−10.0%	50.0%	−5.0%	11.7%
1995	35.0%	−30.0%	25.0%	10.0%
1996	−5.0%	25.0%	−10.0%	3.3%
Expected Return	10.0%	10.0%	10.0%	10.0%
Standard Deviation	21.2%	34.9%	20.4%	4.9%

Adding Mountain, Inc., to the portfolio does further reduce risk even though its returns are highly correlated with those of Pacific Company. There is, however, a limit to how much risk can be reduced by continuing to add securities to the portfolio.

When a portfolio consists of the stock of a single company, the risk and return of the portfolio are equal to the risk and return of that security. Whether that investment proves profitable (earns a positive return) depends not only on that company's ability to manage its business and financial risk, but also on the occurrence (or nonoccurrence) of other events—such as strikes and lawsuits—that are beyond the control of company management. In a single stock portfolio, then, the investor is exposed to a high degree of **company-specific risk**. Adding stocks to the portfolio is a strategy to reduce the investor's exposure to unfavorable events that affect only a single company.

Diversification is the process of adding securities to an investment portfolio to reduce company-specific risk. An investor can continue to add securities to the portfolio, reducing specific risk with each addition, until this source of risk has been effectively eliminated. However, even if the investor continued to add securities to the portfolio until it contains some of every available security traded in the market, some risk will still remain. This remaining risk is called market risk, which is defined as the uncertainty in securities prices (or returns) associated with changes in the level of the market that diversification cannot eliminate.

Since diversification can eliminate company-specific risk, it is also referred to as **diversifiable risk** or **unsystematic risk**. Similarly, because diversification cannot eliminate market risk, it is also referred to as **nondiversifiable risk** or **systematic risk**.

Managing Equity Portfolio Risk

Eliminating unsystematic risk through diversification does not require an investor to hold a representative amount of every security traded in the market. In fact, statistical techniques can be used to show that unsystematic risk can be effectively eliminated with as few as twenty to thirty securities.

Theoretically, all possible portfolios could be examined to determine their expected returns and risk. Given that information, it would then be possible to identify the **efficient frontier**—portfolios that present an optimal combination of expected return and risk. An optimal combination of expected return and risk is any combination that represents the highest expected return for a given level of risk or the lowest risk for a given expected return. Investors should never prefer combinations that offer lower expected return for a given level of risk or higher risk for a given expected return. Rational, risk-averse investors would choose to invest only in portfolios that lie along this efficient frontier.

These concepts form the basis of modern portfolio theory, and were first advanced in Harry Markowitz's 1952 article titled "Portfolio Selection."[3] Despite its common-sense appeal, however, there are practical limitations in trying to determine the efficient frontier. With thousands of securities traded on U.S. stock exchanges and securities available on foreign exchanges, an investor could choose to hold many possible diversified portfolios. Evaluating each of these possible portfolios would be impossible. For example, in a market with just 3,000 available securities, there are over 13×10^{50} (13 followed by 50 zeros) possible portfolios of 20 stocks. Making the necessary calculations would be a time-consuming process for even the fastest computers. If the option of investing unequal amounts in each of the twenty stocks is allowed, the number of possible portfolios approaches infinity. Fortunately, extensions of Markowitz's theory have greatly simplified the problem of portfolio selection by showing that the only relevant risk is how a given security's return varies in response to changes in the market.

Beta as a Measure of Risk

Each security has two sources of risk: company-specific risk and market risk. Since company-specific risk can be eliminated through diversification, the only relevant risk to a diversified investor is the security's market risk. Recall that market risk is the uncertainty in securities prices (or returns) associated with changes in the level of the market. Although most security returns tend to rise and fall with changes in the market, the amount by which security returns change in response to a change in the market varies greatly among individual securities. Consequently, an investor can construct a diversified portfolio that has more, less, or the same variability as the market.

Some measure of a security's systematic (market) risk is now required. Financial managers, investors, and professional portfolio managers measure the tendency of a stock's returns to move in response to changes in the market in terms of the *stock's beta coefficient*, or simply its beta.[4] **Beta** is more formally defined as a measure of a stock's variability relative to that of the market.

Using beta as a measure of risk has some important advantages. First, interpreting its value is straightforward. A stock with a beta of 1 is considered to be an "average" stock, that is, one that has the same risk as the market as a whole. A beta less than 1 indicates that it is less risky than the "average" stock, and a beta greater than 1 indicates that it is more risky than the "average" stock.

Second, the beta of a portfolio is equal to the weighted average of the betas of the individual securities held in the portfolio. Consequently, the effect of adding a particular security to an existing portfolio is easy to determine. In practice, the majority of individual stock betas fall between 0.5 and 1.5. Portfolios with betas greater than 2 can be constructed selecting from among high-risk securities. Similarly, an investment portfolio with a beta less than 0.5 can be constructed by placing a portion of the firm's available funds in risk-free government obligations such as Treasury bills.

Selecting the appropriate beta for a portfolio involves striking a balance between the level of risk and the potential rewards. Investments that promise higher returns generally involve greater risk. To induce an investor to accept risk, the investment must provide additional compensation in the form of higher expected returns. By using beta as the relevant measure of risk, the relationship between risk and return can be formalized, either for an individual security or a portfolio. The Capital Asset Pricing Model enables investors to identify efficient portfolios for risk equal to a given beta.

The Capital Asset Pricing Model

Investors can invest some (or all) of their available funds in risk-free securities. Individuals can deposit their available funds into federally insured savings accounts or purchase federally insured certificates of deposit (CDs). Larger investors can purchase Treasury bills or other government obligations. As a result, the return on a risk-free investment establishes a baseline against which the returns of all other securities can be judged. To induce an investor to accept additional risk, the investment must promise a higher return as compensation. This additional compensation is referred to as the **market risk premium**, which is defined as the difference between the expected return on an "average" stock or the market portfolio (r_m) and the risk-free rate of return (r_f), or the quantity ($r_m - r_f$).

If the investor holds something other than the market portfolio or an "average" stock, the market risk premium must be adjusted to reflect the relevant risk of the investment as measured by its beta. Using beta as the appropriate scaling factor, the **portfolio risk premium** is defined as the market risk premium ($r_m - r_f$) multiplied by the portfolio's beta (β_p), or $\beta_p(r_m - r_f)$. This formula can also be used to find the risk premium for an individual security. In that case, the "portfolio" consists of only a single stock, and the portfolio beta is equal to the beta of the individual security. Given an appropriate risk-free rate of return and the portfolio risk premium, the rate of return required to induce risk-averse investors to hold a risky stock or portfolio can be determined. The **required rate of return on a risky portfolio** (R_p) is defined simply as the risk-free rate of return (r_f) plus the portfolio risk premium $\beta_p(r_m - r_f)$. This mathematical result has been formalized as the equation for the **security market line (SML)**, which shows the relationship between a security's (or portfolio's) risk and required rate of return. Finance texts usually present the SML in its expanded form, $R_p = r_f + \beta_p(r_m - r_f)$. The following table summarizes the relationship among the different terms in the equation for the SML:

Expected rate of return on the market portfolio	r_m
Risk-free rate of return	r_f
Market risk premium	$(r_m - r_f)$
Portfolio's beta	β_p
Portfolio risk premium	$\beta_p(r_m - r_f)$
Required rate of return on a risky portfolio, or the security market line (SML)	$r_f + \beta_p(r_m - r_f)$

A portfolio with risk of β_p must provide a return of $r_f + \beta_p (r_m - r_f)$, or it is not efficient. Not very long ago, only large institutional investors with access to mainframe computers and difficult-to-obtain data could calculate betas for portfolios and individual stocks. Now, desktop computers can handle the calculations, and the necessary data can be purchased from a variety of sources at relatively low cost. For those still disinclined to calculate betas on their own, publications from Value Line, Merrill Lynch, and other sources report betas for a large number of individual securities.

The **Capital Asset Pricing Model (CAPM)** provides a logical framework for analyzing the trade-off between risk and return. It does, however, have limitations. Market returns and betas must be estimated from past data, but investors are concerned with future returns and betas, and they price securities accordingly. Since the model relies on an assumption that past performance will indicate future performance, it is subject to considerable error when applied in practice. Still, most financial professionals agree that it provides valuable insights into how markets adjust for risk.

Investment Strategy

Insurance premiums provide immediate cash inflows to an insurer. In return for the payment of those premiums, an insurer provides a financial guarantee to pay covered losses when they occur. The delay between the receipt of the premiums and the payment of losses gives insurers the opportunity to invest those cash inflows and earn a positive return. A sound investment strategy seeks to earn the highest possible return for a given level of risk or, alternatively, to minimize the risk associated with earning a given expected return. However, this objective cannot be pursued in isolation. Rather, the investment strategy must support the needs of other functional areas of the firm, and it must explicitly recognize constraints imposed by shareholders, regulators, or other government authorities.

Integrating investment strategy with other functional areas is particularly important for insurers. Invested assets are a primary source of funds available to insurers to pay losses. Therefore, the investment portfolio must be structured to provide sufficient funds to pay losses as they come due. In general, property losses tend to be settled quickly, with most loss payments being made within two years. In contrast, some liability losses may be outstanding for ten or more years before they are fully settled. Consequently, an insurer's investment strategy must recognize the relationship between investment and underwriting decisions.

Issues in Managing Bond and Underwriting Portfolios

Bond portfolio management is particularly important for property-liability insurance companies. Generally, investments in bonds account for over 60 percent of insurers' admitted assets. Unlike equity investments in common or preferred stocks, bonds have a definite maturity date—a point in time when the issuer must repay the principal (face) amount of the bond. Although the payment of cash dividends on stocks is at the discretion of the company's board of directors, interest payments on debt are a contractual obligation that must be met according to a predetermined schedule. These two characteristics of debt securities, a fixed maturity date and a fixed interest payment schedule, are particularly valuable to insurers that must assure that adequate funds are available when needed to pay losses.

An important objective of portfolio management in general and bond portfolio management in particular is to structure the portfolio so that the amount and timing of investment cash inflows correspond to the firm's expected cash outflows. For property-liability insurers, the amount and timing of expected cash outflows are largely determined by the composition of the underwriting portfolio. Property losses tend to be settled quickly, with most loss payments being made within two years. Consequently, relatively short-term investments are needed to assure that adequate funds are available to pay losses when due. In contrast, some liability losses may be outstanding many years before they are fully settled. This extended payment period suggests that at least a portion of the insurer's assets be invested in longer-term investments.

Investing in bonds exposes investors to some additional sources of risk. One source of risk is credit risk (also called repayment risk or default risk). **Credit risk** refers to uncertainty about a debtor's (issuer's) ability to make the required principal and interest payments as they come due. Obligations backed by the United States government are considered to have no default risk and are commonly referred to as "risk free." All debt issued by corporations has an element of default risk, though it may be small for well-established companies. Investors do, however, require a risk premium in the form of higher interest rates to hold these securities; the higher the risk of default, the higher the risk premium. Since this risk is specific to an individual debtor, it can be minimized by diversifying the bond portfolio over a large number of issuers.

A second and very important source of risk is interest rate risk. Interest rate risk refers to uncertainty about an asset's value associated with changes in market determined interest rates. The market value of a debt security is determined by the present value of the security's cash flows (interest and principal payments). As interest rates rise, the market value of a debt security declines; as interest rates fall, the market value of a debt security rises. Because of the effects of compound interest, the change in price (present value of the future cash flows) caused by a change in interest rates will be greater for long-term debt securities than short-term debt securities. Consequently, long-term debt securities expose the holder to a greater degree of interest rate risk than do short-term securities. Interest rate risk cannot be eliminated through diversification since changes in the level of interest rates affect the prices of *all* debt securities.

Cash Matching and Interest Rate Risk

To see the effects of interest rate risk, suppose that an insurer specializes in writing property insurance. Based on an analysis of its underwriting portfolio, the insurer expects to make a single $1 million loss payment at the end of the year. A conservative approach would be to "cash-match" the investment and underwriting portfolios by purchasing a bond with a face amount of $1 million that will mature at the end of the year. For simplicity, assume that the bond pays no interest during the year (a security that only pays the face amount at maturity is called a "zero-coupon bond"). If the current market rate of interest is 8 percent, the insurer will pay $925,900 (rounded) to purchase the bond (the face amount of the bond × the present value of $1 due in 1 year at 8 percent = $1 million × .9259). When the bond matures, the insurer will receive the $1 million face amount from the issuer and can fully settle its claims.

The effect of interest rate risk can be seen by looking at the possibility of funding the same $1 million a year from now with a ten-year bond. A $2 million face amount zero-coupon bond could be bought for approximately $926,400 today (the present value of $2 million discounted at 8 percent for ten years). If interest rates do not change in the next year, the same bond in one year would be worth approximately $1 million (the present value of $2 million discounted at 8 percent for nine years is $1,000,500). However, what happens if interest rates go up? If interest rates increase to 10 percent, a zero-coupon bond with nine years to maturity is worth only $848,200. Not only would the rise in interest rates not make available the necessary $1 million, but the value of the investment has also gone down.

Cash matching, which is the process of precisely matching the maturity value of an investment with the amount of expected loss payment, is a good way to eliminate interest rate risk. An insurer only needs to hold the investment until it matures. Changes in interest rates will not matter because the insurer will not want to sell the investment in the market before it matures. However, this strategy has some limitations. First, it is "perfect" only when the insurer can purchase zero-coupon bonds whose maturity dates and maturity values precisely match the expected cash outflows from the underwriting portfolio. Second, even if they are available, the insurer must be able to purchase enough of each type of security to match its expected claims. In practice, nether condition can be expected to hold, especially for insurers with very large underwriting portfolios.

Matching Investment and Liability Duration

In the real world, most bonds pay interest on a predetermined schedule (usually every six months), losses are paid out over several years, and loss payments are spread throughout the year. These circumstances seriously complicate the problems associated with managing the investment and underwriting portfolios.

When an investor purchases bonds that pay interest, the investor must also consider what to do with those interest payments as they are received (assuming they will not be used to pay losses). If interest payments are going to be reinvested, the investor is now exposed to a second type of interest-related risk called reinvestment risk. **Reinvestment risk** refers to uncertainty about the rate at which periodic interest payments can be reinvested over the life of the investment. To illustrate, consider an investor who purchases a $1,000 ten-year bond that pays 10 percent interest at the end of each year. If those interest payments can be invested to earn 10 percent (in a savings account, for example), the balance in the savings account would be about $1,594 when the bond matures. If, however, interest rates fell to 8 percent just after the bond were purchased, then the savings account would grow to just $1,448. When periodic interest payments will be reinvested, the investor must not only worry about the interest rates available at the time the original investment is made, but also about the prevailing interest rates when each interest payment is received.

Techniques have been developed to help portfolio managers control interest rate risk. Although the maturity date of an investment gives some indication of its sensitivity to changes in interest rates, duration is generally accepted as a better measure. Basically, **duration** is a measure of the average life of a security. When applied to a bond, duration measures the time it takes for the present value of the bond's cash inflows to equal the price of the bond. Two important characteristics of duration should be noted. First, the duration of a zero-coupon bond is always equal to its time to maturity (when the face amount becomes due). Second, the duration of a bond that pays interest over its life will always be less than its time to maturity.

Knowing the duration of the underwriting portfolio allows a bond portfolio manager either to invest in one or more securities that have the same duration as the underwriting portfolio or to combine several securities with different durations into a portfolio that has, in the aggregate, the same duration as the underwriting portfolio. When the durations of the underwriting and investment portfolio are matched, the portfolio is said to be *immunized* against changes in interest rates.

Portfolio immunization, which is the process of matching investment and liability duration, works because it balances the change in a bond's price (the price effect) against the change in earnings obtained from reinvesting interest payments (the reinvestment effect). When interest rates decline, interest payments must be reinvested at a lower-than-expected rate, but the drop in interest rates also causes the market value of the bond to increase. If the duration of the investment and the liability are the same, then the insurer will have enough cash available to settle its obligations regardless of any change in interest rates. If the duration of the investment portfolio is longer than the duration of the liability, the price effect will outweigh the effect of reinvesting the interest payments at a rate higher or lower than expected. Conversely, if the duration of the investment portfolio is shorter than the duration of the liability, the reinvestment effect will outweigh the price effect that results from a change in interest rates.

Unfortunately, matching the duration of the bond portfolio and the underwriting portfolio is not a one-time problem. On the investment side, a change in interest rates affects the duration of the portfolio. Theoretically, the composition of the bond portfolio should be changed every time interest rates change in order to keep the duration of the bond and underwriting portfolios properly matched. On the liability side, changes in the insurer's mix of business also indicate a need to rebalance the bond portfolio. For example, an increased emphasis on underwriting liability lines will increase the duration of the underwriting portfolio. However, investments cannot be bought and sold without cost. The transactions costs associated with rebalancing a portfolio must be weighed against the risks of holding an imperfectly matched portfolio. This is especially true for insurers because the future cash outflows associated with the underwriting portfolio are not known with certainty and must be estimated. Both underwriting risk and reserve estimation risk, defined earlier in this chapter, make the process of managing the bond portfolio even more complex because they create uncertainty as to what the target duration of the bond portfolio should be.

Summary

Every enterprise is exposed to risk. At the firm level, risk can be segmented into business risk and financial risk. Insurance companies are exposed to three additional sources of risk: price inadequacy risk, reserve estimation risk, and underwriting risk. These sources of risk are unique to the business of insurance. Managing risks is important to accomplishing the overall objective of the firm, which is to maximize shareholder wealth.

Portfolio management is concerned with the relationship between investment risk and return. Each security has two sources of risk: market risk and company-specific risk. The risk of an individual security can be measured by its standard deviation or its coefficient of variation. Diversification can be used to eliminate company-specific (unsystematic) risk by combining several stocks to form a portfolio. The risk that remains in a fully diversified portfolio is systematic risk. This risk is measured in terms of the portfolio's beta.

Bond portfolio managers must also control interest rate risk and reinvestment rate risk. A portfolio can be immunized against interest rate changes by either cash matching the investment and underwriting portfolios or by structuring the bond portfolio so that its duration is equal to the duration of the underwriting portfolio. The duration of a bond portfolio depends not only on the investments held, but also on the level of interest rates. Consequently, changes in prevailing market interest rates will affect the duration of the bond portfolio. Similarly, changes in the composition of the underwriting portfolio will affect its duration. To keep the portfolio immunized, portfolio managers must monitor interest rates closely, be aware of changes in the underwriting portfolio, and be prepared to rebalance the portfolio to bring the duration of the bond portfolio and the underwriting portfolio back to equality.

Key Words and Phrases

beta (p. 487) A measure of the tendency of a stock's returns to move in response to changes in the market or, more formally, a measure of a stock's variability relative to that of the market or, alternatively, to that of an "average" stock.

business risk (p. 474) Refers to uncertainty about a company's future earnings.

Capital Asset Pricing Model (CAPM) (p. 489) A security market line based model used by investors to analyze the trade-off between risk and return.

cash matching (p. 492) For insurers, the process of precisely matching the maturity value of an investment with the amount of expected loss payment.

coefficient of variation (CV) (p. 482) A relative measure of risk defined as the standard deviation divided by the expected value. The measure provides information about the risk per unit of return.

company-specific risk (p. 486) Refers to the uncertainty about events that are unique to a particular company, such as strikes and lawsuits.

credit risk (p. 490) Refers to the uncertainty about a debtor's (issuer's) ability to make the required principal and interest payments as they come due.

diversifiable risk (p. 486) Risk that can be reduced or eliminated by diversification. Diversifiable risk is also referred to as *unsystematic risk* because it is company-specific (unique to the firm) and is not systematic (does not vary with the market).

diversification (p. 486) The process of adding securities to an investment portfolio to reduce company-specific risk.

duration (p. 493) A measure of the average life of a security (or portfolio).

efficient frontier (p. 486) Portfolios that present an optimal combination of expected return and risk.

expected return (p. 478) The expected value of a security's return.

expected value (p. 477) The weighted average of possible uncertain outcomes.

financial risk (p. 474) Refers to uncertainty about a firm's ability to meet the principal and interest payments on its debt.

interest rate risk (p. 475) Refers to uncertainty about an asset's value associated with changes in market-determined interest rates.

liquidity risk (p. 475) Refers to uncertainty about the price at which an asset can be sold on short notice.

market risk (p. 475) The uncertainty in securities prices (or returns) associated with changes in the level of the market. Market risk cannot be eliminated by diversification.

market risk premium (p. 488) The added amount of return required by investors to induce them to invest in securities that have greater risk than those offered by the federal government (generally considered risk free). Mathematically, the market risk premium is the difference between the risk-free rate of return and the expected return on an "average" stock or the market portfolio $(r_m - r_f)$.

maximize shareholder wealth (p. 473) Generally argued in finance as the overall objective of the firm, in contrast with the view that *profit maximization* should be the overall objective advanced by economists.

nondiversifiable risk (p. 486) Risk that is systematic or that varies with the market.

portfolio immunization (p. 493) The process of matching investment and liability duration.

portfolio risk premium (p. 488) The market risk premium $(r_m - r_f)$ multiplied by the portfolio's beta (β_p).

price inadequacy risk (p. 475) For an insurer, refers to the uncertainty that the premiums charged will not be sufficient to cover the costs associated with insurance coverage sold.

profit maximization (p. 473) Argued by economists as the overall objective of the firm, in contrast to the objective that *maximizing shareholder wealth* should be the firm's objective, as advanced in the field of finance.

reinvestment risk (p. 492) Refers to uncertainty about the rate at which periodic interest payments can be reinvested over the life of the investment.

required rate of return on a risky portfolio (p. 488) Defined as the risk-free rate of return (r_f) plus the portfolio risk premium $\beta_p(r_m - r_f)$.

reserve estimation risk (p. 476) Refers to the uncertainty about the true amount that will be paid to settle insured claims.

risk averse (p. 476) Profile of individuals who prefer relative certainty to uncertainty.

risk neutral (p. 477) Profile of individuals who ignore uncertainty and base decisions solely on the potential rewards.

security market line (SML) (p. 489) The straight line describing the relationship between a security's (or portfolio's) risk and required rate of return defined by the equation $R_p = r_f + \beta_p(r_m - r_f)$

standard deviation (p. 480) A statistic that describes how widely the actual outcomes are dispersed above and below the expected value.

systematic risk (p. 486) Risk that is related to uncertainty in securities prices (or returns) associated with changes in the level of the market.

underwriting risk (p. 476) Refers to the uncertainty about the exposures underwritten by an insurer, including the possibility that a single event (or set of events) will simultaneously affect multiple exposures.

unsystematic risk (p. 486) Risk that does not vary with the market and is company-specific.

Chapter Notes

1. In more general terms, the type of market would be referred to as a "state of nature" in statistics and economic texts.

2. Those methods require a knowledge of continuous probability distributions. Further information on this topic can be found in most probability and statistics textbooks.

3. Harry M. Markowitz, "Portfolio Selection," *Journal of Finance*, March 1952, pp. 77-91.

4. Mathematically, least-squares regression can be used to find a stock's beta. Beta is equal to the regression coefficient between the asset's returns and the market's returns. The formal mathematical definition is β (beta) $= Cov(r_i, r_i) / \sigma_m^2$. That is, beta is equal to the covariance between the returns of the security (r_i) with the returns the market (r_i), divided by the variance of market returns (σ_m^2). By definition, the market has a beta of one (it is perfectly correlated with itself). An "average" stock exactly mirrors the market and also has a beta of one.

Index

E